T0366780

LOEB CLASSICAL LIBRARY

FOUNDED BY JAMES LOEB 1911

EDITED BY

JEFFREY HENDERSON

BEDE

I

LCL 246

BEDE

HISTORICAL WORKS

ECCLESIASTICAL HISTORY OF THE
ENGLISH NATION
BOOKS I–III

WITH AN ENGLISH TRANSLATION BY

J. E. KING

HARVARD UNIVERSITY PRESS
CAMBRIDGE, MASSACHUSETTS
LONDON, ENGLAND

First published 1930

LOEB CLASSICAL LIBRARY® is a registered trademark
of the President and Fellows of Harvard College

ISBN 978-0-674-99271-9

*Printed on acid-free paper and bound by
The Maple-Vail Book Manufacturing Group*

CONTENTS

BAEDAE HISTORIA ECCLESIASTICA GENTIS ANGLORUM

HISTORIAE ECCLESIASTICAE ELENCHUS CAPITUM

ELENCHUS CAPITUM

ELENCHUS CAPITUM

ix

ELENCHUS CAPITUM

ELENCHUS CAPITUM

ELENCHUS CAPITUM

LIBER III

xii

ELENCHUS CAPITUM

ELENCHUS CAPITUM

INTRODUCTION

BETWEEN the years 635 and 804 a succession of three great scholars, whose fame extended far beyond their native land, adorned the Church in England, Aldhelm, Bede and Alcuin. Aldhelm belonged to Wessex, Bede and Alcuin to Northumbria. Aldhelm was abbot of Malmesbury and bishop of Sherborne, Alcuin was master of the school of York, and later passed into the service of Charlemagne.

Bede, says Fuller,[1] was "the profoundest scholar of his age for Latin, Greek, philosophy, history, divinity, mathematicks, musick and what not"? The simple facts of his life, as well as a list of his various writings, are given in his own words at the end of the *Ecclesiastical History*.[2] He was born in 672 or 673 upon lands which shortly afterwards were granted to Benedict Biscop[3] for the foundation of Wearmouth Abbey. At the age of seven he was "given by the care of his kinsfolk to abbot Benedict to be brought up," and the rest of his life was spent in the monastery, first at Wearmouth and then, a year after he had been received, at Jarrow, where he had been taken by Ceolfrid, its first abbot. He was no doubt educated in the monastery school, but of the brethren who taught him he only names

---

[1] Thomas Fuller, *Church-history*, cent. viii. §§ 15–18.
[2] V. 24.   [3] IV. 18.

Trumbert.[1] " He was no gadder about " : we have traces of visits to Lindisfarne and York, but in all probability he rarely went outside the bounds of the monastery. As he says, " I wholly applied myself to the study of Scripture, and amid the observance of monastic discipline, and the daily care of singing in the church, I always took delight in learning, teaching and writing," and so he might be spared the labours of the plough, the winnowing fan, the bakehouse, garden, kitchen and other work which fell to the lot of his less scholarly brethren,[2] according to the Benedictine rule. The monastery of Wearmouth was founded in the year 674, and that of Jarrow in 681 or 682, but, though at some distance apart, the two formed a single monastery. Of the abbots who ruled the two divisions of the monastery, jointly or separately, in Bede's lifetime, he has given an account in his *Lives of the Abbots*, and from this work we gain a picture of monastic life according to Bede's own ideal.

In his own monastery Bede had the advantage of a good library : he speaks with enthusiasm of the books which Benedict Biscop brought back from his visits to Rome, and this collection was doubled by the care of abbot Ceolfrid.[3] Books could also be borrowed by one monastery from another. Bede knew Latin, Greek and probably some Hebrew. The learning of Western Europe in his day was summed up in his various works, and so made available for his countrymen. The bulk of his writings are theological, taking the form mainly of commentaries which are largely based upon the

[1] IV. 3.   [2] *Hist. Abbat.*, 8.   [3] *Hist. Abbat.*, 6, 9, 15.

INTRODUCTION

writings of the four great Latin fathers, Augustine,
Jerome, Ambrose and Gregory, though these by no
means cover the full extent of his reading. Of the
ancient classical authors we find echoes of Vergil and
less frequently of Ovid and Horace, but these he
may have found quoted in other works, for Bede
would not have thought time profitably spent in
a prolonged study of pagan writers.[1] Besides his
theological writings, Bede wrote upon orthography,
metre and figures of speech for the benefit of his
scholars. He also wrote upon natural phenomena, a
work which summarized the natural philosophy of
the Roman Empire, and chronological treatises on
Times and the counting of Times. His historical
works comprise the *Ecclesiastical History*, the *History
of the Abbots* and the *Letter to Bishop Egbert*, as well
as lives of St. Cuthbert in verse and prose.

In these volumes we are concerned with Bede's
historical writings. Critics are agreed in praising
his learning and industry, his love of simplicity and
truth. In all that he relates he is careful to give
his authority. " I would not that my children
should read a lie," was one of his last utterances.
He quotes documents, if they are available, and
whether for ordinary or extraordinary events he
gives, where he can, first-hand evidence, and if that
is not forthcoming, or if he has nothing to rely upon
save common report, he frankly says so. It is
noticeable that of the many marvels which Bede
records he does not give one on his own knowledge,
and his lives of the first five abbots of his own
monastery contain no notice of a single miracle.

[1] Maitland, *Dark Ages*, No. XI.

INTRODUCTION

He also took great pains to get his chronology correct. His value for the century of which he wrote can best be estimated by comparing his work with that of his predecessor Gildas,[1] upon whom Bede had to depend for much of the earlier history of Britain, and in whose vague rhetoric it is difficult to find any solid basis of fact. Historians would have been grateful if a scholar of Bede's character had recorded with the same clearness and honesty the secular transactions of the inhabitants of Britain, and described their social and political life and institutions. But Bede is only concerned with wars and statecraft and Witenagemots, so far as they belong to the story of the introduction of Christianity into Britain and the progress of the Church throughout the land. He tells us but little of the beliefs and cults which Christianity supplanted. Their hold upon the people does not appear to have been very strong, and judging by the words and conduct of Coifi,[2] the priests were neither of great importance nor devoted to the older worship. Though the Christian missionaries were sometimes driven out, they seem to have suffered no actual persecution, and there is no record that any of them were put to death. Even the grim Penda did not persecute. He would not become a Christian, but despised those who accepted Christianity without showing the works of the faith.[3] The attitude of the kings to the new teaching was of great importance, for their people followed their lead, sometimes under compulsion.[4] They presided at conferences held to determine ecclesiastical questions, as Oswy did at Whitby.[5] They were

[1] P. 56, Oman p. 186.   [2] II. 13.
[3] III. 21.   [4] III. 8.   [5] III. 25.

xviii

consulted, if they did not actually decide the appointment of bishops,[1] who at first were their chaplains, and the stormy career of Wilfrid shows how powerful was the enmity of the kings in spite of the support which Wilfrid received from Rome.[2]   As regards the wars which so frequently took place, Bede tells us of those battles, like the victory of Oswald over Cadwallon,[3] and of Oswy over Penda,[4] which had a decisive result upon the fortunes of the Church.

Bede is no dull chronicler.   His history is full of stories rendered vivid by his sympathy and dramatic power: his characters are lifelike and distinct: they are made real to us by some revealing incident or saying, as in the story of Edwin's exile and his dealings with Paulinus,[5] or of the meeting of Oswin and Aidan in the king's hall after the day's hunting.[6] Most of Bede's work is occupied with the history of missionary enterprise and Church organisation, with the austerities of the anchorites, the life of the monasteries, the visions of monks and nuns, the marvellous preservation of the bodies of saints and the cures wrought by their relics, as well as (overmuch we sometimes feel), with the fluctuations of controversies like that dealing with the right time for celebrating Easter; but incidentally there occur sketches of the ordinary life of men in the outer world, such as the feasts in the houses of thanes,[7] the young nobles racing their horses to the grief of their venerable guide,[8] the adventures of the thane who had escaped the slaughter of a battle,[9] or, in humbler life, of the beer parties at which Caedmon

<table>
<tr><td>[1] III. 7, 28.</td><td>[2] Bright, 417.</td><td>[3] III. 2.</td></tr>
<tr><td>[4] III. 24.</td><td>[5] III. 12.</td><td>[6] III. 14.</td></tr>
<tr><td>[7] V. 4.</td><td>[8] V. 6.</td><td>[9] IV. 22.</td></tr>
</table>

was unable to sing,[1] of the belated traveller coming to the village festivity,[2] of the peasants flocking round the missionary preacher to listen to his words.[3]

Bede does not shrink from passing judgment upon public events which come within the plan of his work. He sympathizes with the Mercians when they threw off the Northumbrian yoke of Oswy.[4] He makes plain his disapproval of the unhappy enterprises of Egfrid against Ireland and against the Picts, the last of which proved fatal to the fortunes of Northumbria.[5] He condemned abuses in the Church, both in diocesan matters and in the monasteries. He was devoted to monastic life, and in such an age it is hard to see how a man of his character could have found scope for his gifts outside the cloister. His whole narrative shows the increasing hold of monasticism upon the life of the country. He sympathizes with those who, like Sigbert, king of the East Angles, renounce their earthly dignities and receive the tonsure,[6] or, like queen Ethelthryth, quit home and husband to take the veil.[7] To take vows or go on pilgrimage was to despise the world and follow the light. But all the same, at the end of his days, he sees the evil results of the passing of all available land into the possession of monastic institutions. No room could be found, after their time of service, for the fighting men who were needed to defend the country against the invasion of barbarians. Posterity would feel the consequences,[8] when so many, as well noblemen as

[1] IV. 24.   [2] III. 10.   [3] III. 26.
[4] III. 24.   [5] IV. 26.   [6] III. 18.
[7] St. Etheldred or Audrey, IV. 19.
[8] In 793 the Viking raids began and Lindisfarne was sacked.

INTRODUCTION

poor, laid aside their armour because they and their children became religious men.[1] And he was sensible, as his letter to Egbert shows, how the monastic ideal itself was spoilt by the intrusion of such numbers of those who had no true vocation.

Irish monasticism still bore traces of its Eastern origin in its extreme asceticism and its devotion to the eremetical life. Its discipline in the community, to judge from Colman's experience at Inisboffin, was defective.[2] The rule of St. Benedict,[3] which came to prevail in Saxon England, as in Europe generally, was strict, but did not impose austerities: it established corporate life and provided a rule of solitude, labour, silence and prayer incumbent upon all members of the community for life. Monks as such were not necessarily clergy. *Alia monachorum est causa: alia clericorum*, says St. Jerome. The clergy were often chosen from among the monks, and in Bede's day the leading ecclesiastics were monks. But in the convents there were not necessarily more ordained priests than were required for the needs of the community. Such priests being under the rule (*regula*) were called " regular." The clergy who were not under a monastic rule and lived in the world (*saeculum*) were distinguished as " secular." In Bede's time more clergy were needed and the parochial system was in its infancy, though a beginning had been made by Cedd and Wilfrid and Theodore.[4] In the *Prologue* of Chaucer, who lived centuries after Bede, we find the familiar figures of the developed medieval Church, the Clerk of Oxenford and the " povre Persoun of a toun,"

[1] V. 23. [2] IV. 4.
[3] c. 480–544. [4] Bright, p. 485.

who were seculars, and distinct from these the Monk, the Frere, and the Prioresse with her Nonne and Presstes three.

Bede was a Saxon. He was, says Fuller, wanting in charity to the Britons, and at any rate it may be admitted that his sympathy with them was imperfect. He has little pity for the slaughter of the British monks at Chester,[1] and in noting the unfriendliness of the British clergy towards the Roman mission he makes no allowance for the good reason which the Britons had to hate their Saxon conquerors. This lack of sympathy does not apply to the British Church before the days of the Saxon invasion, while to the missionary zeal of the Irish Church and the learning of its schools, to the example of Iona and Lindisfarne and the devoted labours of men like Columba and Aidan, in spite of ecclesiastical differences, he does the fullest justice.[2]

Bede's most important work, at any rate for later generations, is his *Ecclesiastical History*, which was only completed in the last years of his life. The first book begins with a summary of the early history of the country and of the Church in Britain down to the coming of Augustine, and ends with the death of Gregory, who had sent the Roman missionaries to Britain. The second book begins with a tribute to the memory of the great pope, narrates the failure of the overtures for union made to the British and Irish Churches, and ends with the death of Edwin, king of Northumbria, in whose reign Paulinus introduced Christianity into that country. The third book gives the history of Oswald and Oswy and the Scotic mission under Aidan, and ends with the despatch of Wighard to be consecrated archbishop of Canter-

[1] II. 2.   [2] III. 26.

bury at Rome. The fourth book relates the consecration of Theodore and the steps he took to organize the Church, and is carried down to the death of Cuthbert. The fifth book gives the story of the Frisian mission and the career of Wilfrid, and ends with a general survey of the condition of the Church in the year 731.

The lack of political unity, the constant changes of boundaries, due to the varying fortunes of Kent, Northumbria, Mercia and the smaller states, the differences between the British, Irish and Saxon Churches interrupt the continuity of the narrative. Hence the history tends to be a collection of isolated stories in which the interest shifts from one part of Britain to another. But for the division into books Bede chooses important events which mark distinct stages in the progress of the English Church, the main theme round which the different digressions are grouped. His style is clear and natural, and a spirit of even-minded fairness animates the whole work. It is his aim to ascertain the actual facts, to give a plain account of the common tradition according to the " true law of history." [1]

As early as the ninth century Bede was distinguished by the name of " Venerable." According to Fuller, " some say a dunce-monk, being to make his epitaph, was *non-pluss'd* to make that dactyle. which is onely of the *quorum* in the hexameter, and therefore at night left the verse gaping,

> *hic sunt in fossa Bedae . . . ossa,*

till he had consulted with his pillow, to fill up the *hiatus*; but returning in the morning, an angel (we have often heard of their singing, see now

[1] P. 11.

of their poetry) had filled up the *chasma* with
venerabilis." But the title was in those days a
common designation of priests, as the *Ecclesiastical
History* often shows, and has been permanently
attached to Bede.

Bede has told us but little of himself. One story
of his youth comes from another source. When the
plague of 686 had swept away at Jarrow all those
who could recite the antiphons and responses, except
the abbot and one little lad, it was decided that
the services should be conducted in their regular
course by means of these two alone, and the boy can
hardly have been any other than Bede himself.
Of his last days we have an account in a letter
written by Cuthbert (afterwards abbot of Wearmouth) to his friend Cuthwin.[1]

Bede's body was buried at Jarrow, but in the
eleventh century his bones were taken away by a
priest of Durham and put in St. Cuthbert's coffin,
where they were found at the translation of St.
Cuthbert in 1104 and placed in a casket of gold and
silver in the galilee of Durham cathedral. In 1541
the casket was rifled and the remains of Bede
dispersed. A cross was erected to his memory at
Roker Point near Jarrow and unveiled in 1904.

Fuller concludes his account in these words: "nor
have I ought else to observe of *Bede*, save onely this;
a foreign embassador, some two hundred yeares
since, coming to *Durham*, addressed himself first to
the high and sumptuous shrine of *St. Cuthbert*, If
thou beest a saint, pray for me: then coming to the
plain, low and little tombe of *Bede*, *Because* (said he)
thou art a saint, good Bede, *pray for me* "—a conclusion
which is finer than many more laboured eulogies.

[1] See p. xxvii.

INTRODUCTION

Bede's *Ecclesiastical History* was translated into Old English by Alfred the Great. The first rendering into modern English was that which has been adapted for the present edition, the work of Thomas Stapleton, who was born in 1535 and died in 1598. Stapleton was a scholar of Winchester, a fellow of New College and became prebendary of Chichester. Shortly after Elizabeth's accession, as he was one of those who adhered to the unreformed Church, he withdrew to Louvain, and in 1563 lost his prebend. But he and his friends did not give up the hope of winning the queen to their side, and his object in making his translation of Bede, which was published at Antwerp in 1565, is clearly stated in his dedication. " In this history it shall appear in what faith your noble Realm was Christened, and hath almost these thousand years continued, to the Glory of God, the enriching of the Crown, and great wealth and quiet of this realm. In this history your highness shall see in how many and weighty points the pretended reformers of the Church have departed from that sound and catholick faith planted first among Englishmen by holy St. Augustine, our apostle, and his virtuous company, described truly and sincerely by Venerable Bede, so called in all Christendom for his passing virtues and rare learning, the author of this history." But the " cockle boat of schismatical noisomeness," in which Elizabeth was embarked, was steered farther and farther away from " the steadfast ark of Noah," and Stapleton and his friends were doomed to disappointment. He became professor at Louvain and at Douay, was highly esteemed as an able controversialist, and is described by Wood, the Oxford antiquary, as the most learned Roman Catholic of all his time.

INTRODUCTION

The first critical edition of the text was that of Smith, 1722. Stapleton used the Basle edition of Bede's collected works, 1563, and this accounts for some errors in his translation. But apart from this it must be admitted that he treats the Latin of his author rather cavalierly. He paraphrases and amplifies and omits, and it is not too much to say that there is scarcely a sentence in which some alteration is not required, if the English version is to be a close rendering of Bede's Latin. But, notwithstanding such drawbacks, Stapleton belonged to the age of the Book of Common Prayer and the Authorised Version of the Bible. The structure of his clauses is nearer akin to the Latin than the more choppy sentences of modern English: he has a dignity and nobility of style and a constant happiness of phrase, which have deservedly kept his translation alive. And, apart from the intrinsic merits of his work, it is probably better to read an author dealing with an age like Bede's, so different from our own in its thoughts and ways, through the medium of a translation which does not belong to our own day. It gives an atmosphere in which we breathe more naturally: we see, as it were, the ancient building in a mellower and less garish light.

Editio princeps of the *Historia Ecclesiastica,* Eggestyn, Strasbourg, 1475 (about).

Collected edition of Bede's works, Basle, 1563.

First critical edition, Smith, Cambridge, 1722.

Latest critical edition, C. Plummer, Oxford, 1896.

Besides the notes of Plummer's edition, help may be obtained from Mayor and Lumby's edition of Bks. III, IV, Cambridge, 1879; W. Bright's *Chapters on Early Church History*, Oman's *England before the*

Norman Conquest, and Bishop Browne's *The Venerable Bede*, S.P.C.K. Maitland's *Dark Ages* describes the state of religion and literature in the centuries succeeding Bede's time. The early authorities for the period of Bede's History will be found in *Monumenta Historica Britannica*, 1848.

The Latin text of the present edition is that of Moberly, Oxford, 1881, which is practically Smith's text. Alterations taken from Plummer's edition, as well as notes which have been borrowed have been acknowledged with the letters *Pl.* Dr. Bright's lectures are referred to as *Bright*, and Oman's History as *Oman*. Matter that is common to different editors has not been specially acknowledged. The present editor has had the advantage, for which he must express his gratitude, of being allowed to use Dr. H. F. Stewart's notes for the introduction as well as his corrections of Stapleton's translation. He has had too the advantage of using Dr. Stewart's version of the *Lives of the Abbots*, and the *Letter to Egbert*. Further, for the translation of Cuthbert's letter on Bede's last days he had Plummer's translation before him, and in the identification of place names and other points he has had valuable help from Professor Mawer and Mr. Welldon Finn. The spelling of Saxon names in the translation is mainly that of Plummer.

These acknowledgments are so many that it may well be asked what is left for the present editor to claim as his own. He can only hope that he has not spoilt what he has ventured to touch, and can only plead that, in adapting the work of others to his own view of what might best secure uniformity of style, he has probably spent as much time as if he had attempted to give a version entirely his own.

CUTHBERTI EPISTOLA AD CUTHINUM

" Dilectissimo in Christo collectori Cuthuino Cuthbertus condiscipulus, in Deo aeternam salutem.[1]

" Munusculum quod misisti multum libenter suscepi; multumque gratanter literas tuae devotae eruditionis legi, in quibus, quod maxime desiderabam, missas videlicet et orationes sacrosanctas pro Deo dilecto patre ac nostro magistro Beda a vobis diligenter celebrari reperi. Unde delectat magis pro eius caritate, quantum fruor ingenio, paucis sermonibus dicere quo ordine migravit e seculo, cum etiam hoc te desiderasse et poposcisse intellexi.

" Gravatus quidem est infirmitate et maxime creberrimi anhelitus, pene sine aliquo dolore tamen, ante diem Resurrectionis Dominicae, id est, fere duabus hebdomadibus; et sic postea laetus et gaudens gratiasque agens Omnipotenti Deo, omni die et nocte, imo horis omnibus, usque ad diem Ascensionis Dominicae, id est, septimo Kalendas Iunii vitam ducebat, et nobis suis discipulis quotidie lectiones dabat, et quidquid reliquum erat diei in Psalmorum cantu, prout potuit, se occupabat; totam vero noctem in laetitia et gratiarum actione ducere studebat, nisi quantum modicus somnus impediret. Itemque autem evigilans statim consueta Scripturarum modulamina ruminabat extensisque mani-

---

[1] The text of this letter varies considerably in different versions. The text here used is that given in Moberly's edition with some alterations taken from Mayor and Lumby.

[1] The date in 735.

xxviii

CUTHBERT'S LETTER TO CUTHWIN

"To Cuthwin, his dearly beloved fellow-reader in Christ, Cuthbert, his fellow-disciple, eternal safety in God.

"The little gift which thou didst send I have received very gladly; and with much pleasure have I read your devout and learned letter, wherein, according to my earnest desire, I have found that masses and holy prayers are diligently celebrated of you for our master Bede, the father beloved of God. Wherefore I take delight the more out of the love I bear him to report in few words, so far as my skill permitteth, the manner of his departing from this world, seeing I understand that you also have desired the same and required it of me.

"He was afflicted before the day of the Lord's Resurrection, that is to say, for about two weeks, with weakness, and especially with very sorely quickened breathing, yet almost without any pain; and so he continued alive after, until the day of the Lord's Ascension, that is the 26th day of May,[1] being cheerful and rejoicing and giving thanks to Almighty God, every day and night, yea every hour, and he daily gave lessons to us his disciples, and all that was left of the day he occupied himself so far as he could in chanting the Psalms; moreover, he endeavoured to spend the whole night in joyful giving of thanks, save in so far as a light slumber might hinder him. Likewise upon waking he would, as was his wont, go over the melodies of Scripture, and stretching out his hands forgat not to give

bus Deo gratias agere non est oblitus. O vere beatus vir! Canebat autem sententiam Beati Pauli
Apostoli: 'Horrendum est incidere in manus Dei
viventis,' et multa alia de Sancta Scriptura, in
quibus nos a somno animae exsurgere praecogitando
ultimam horam admonebat, et in nostra quoque
lingua, ut erat doctus in nostris carminibus, dicens
de terribili exitu animarum e corpore :—

> ' Fore the neid faerae
> Naenig uuiurthit
> Thonc snotturra
> Than him tharf sie
> To ymb hycgannae
> Aer his hin-iongae
> Huaet his gastae
> Godaes aeththa yflaes
> Aefter deoth-daege
> Doemid uuieorthae.'

"Quod ita Latine sonat; 'Ante necessarium
exitum prudentior quam opus fuerit nemo exsistit,
ad cogitandum videlicet antequam hinc proficiscatur
anima, quid boni vel mali egerit, qualiter post
exitum iudicanda fuerit.'

"Cantabat etiam antiphonas ob nostram con-
solationem et suam, quarum una est : ' O rex gloriae,
Domine virtutum, qui triumphator hodie super
omnes caelos ascendisti, ne derelinquas nos orphanos,
sed mitte promissum Patris in nos Spiritum veritatis ;
Alleluiah!' Et cum venisset ad illud verbum,
' Ne derelinquas nos orphanos,' prorupit in lacrimas,
et multum flebat. Et post horam coepit repetere

---

[1] Hebr. x. 31.

thanks to God. O truly blessed man! Moreover, he would recite the saying of the blessed Apostle Paul.[1] 'It is a fearful thing to fall into the hands of the living God,' and many other things out of Holy Scripture, wherein he warned us to rise up from the sleep of the soul with thinking beforehand of our last hour, and in our own tongue beside (seeing he was skilled in our native songs), speaking of the dreadful departing of souls from the body,

> 'Ere he must journey
> None can be wiser
> Than shall his need be,
> If he but ponder
> Ere his departing,
> What for his ghost may,
> Evil or blessing,
> After his death day,
> Judgment be bringing.'

"The which according to the Latin rendering meaneth: 'Before the passing that is appointed there is none more wise than there shall be need, that is to say, to consider, before his soul departeth hence, after what manner it shall be judged, according to the good or evil he hath done.'

"He chanted also antiphons for our comfort and his own, whereof one is: 'O King of glory, Lord of might, Who didst this day ascend above all heavens in triumph, leave us not comfortless, but send unto us, according to the promise of the Father, the Spirit of truth; Hallelujah.' And when he was come to that word, 'Leave us not comfortless,' he burst into tears and began to weep much. And after a space he began to repeat what he had begun;

quae inchoaverat: et nos haec audientes luximus cum illo. Altera vice legimus, altera ploravimus, imo semper cum fletu legimus. In tali laetitia quinquagesimales dies usque ad diem praefatum deduximus, et ille multum gaudebat Deoque gratias agebat quia sic meruisset infirmari. Et saepe dicebat: 'Flagellat Deus omnem filium quem recipit,' et multa alia de Sancta Scriptura, sententiam quoque Ambrosii: 'Non sic vixi, ut me pudeat inter vos vivere; sed nec mori timeo, quia bonum Deum habemus.'

"In istis autem diebus duo opuscula multum memoria digna, exceptis lectionibus quas accepimus ab eo et cantu Psalmorum, facere studebat, Evangelium scilicet Sancti Iohannis in nostram linguam ad utilitatem ecclesiae convertit, et de libris Isidori episcopi excerptiones quasdam, dicens: 'Nolo ut pueri mei mendacium legant, et in hoc post obitum meum sine fructu laborent.' Cum venisset autem tertia feria ante Ascensionem Domini coepit vehementius aegrotare in anhelitu, et modicus tumor in pedibus apparuit. Totum tamen illum diem docebat, et hilariter dictabat, et nonnunquam inter alia dixit: 'Discite cum festinatione; quia nescio quamdiu subsistam, et si post modicum tollet me Factor meus.' Nobis autem videbatur quod suum exitum bene sciret, et sic noctem in gratiarum actione pervigil duxit.

"Et mane illucescente, id est quarta feria, praecepit diligenter scribi quae coeperamus; et hoc fecimus

---

[1] Between Easter and Pentecost.
[2] Hebr. xii. 6.
[3] Paulinus, *Vita Ambrosii*, c. 45, Pl.

and we hearing this lamented with him. One while we read, at another we mourned, yea, ever as we read we wept. With such fervent mind did we pass the 50 days [1] until the aforesaid day, and he greatly rejoiced and gave thanks to God that he was counted worthy to be thus weakened with sickness. And oft-times he would say: 'God scourgeth every son whom He receiveth,' [2] and also the saying of Ambrose: 'I have not so lived that I should be ashamed to live among you; yet do I not either fear to die, for we have a God Who is good.' [3]

"In those days, moreover, beside the lessons which we received from him and the chanting of the Psalms, there were two works very worthy of mention which he endeavoured to accomplish, to wit the Gospel of St. John, which he translated into our tongue for the profit of the Church, and certain extracts from the books of bishop Isidore, saying, 'I will not that my children should read a lie and herein labour without fruit after my death.' But when the third day before the Lord's Ascension was come, he began to be more sorely distressed in his breathing, and a slight swelling appeared in his feet. Yet all that day he continued to teach and dictate cheerfully, and sometimes he said among other things: 'Learn speedily, for I know not how long I have to live, and whether my Maker will shortly take me away.' To us, however, it seemed that he well knew the time of his departure, and so keeping awake he passed the night in giving of thanks.

"And about the dawning of the day, that is on the fourth day of the week, he commanded us to write diligently what we had begun; and this we did up to

usque ad tertiam horam. A tertia autem hora ambulavimus cum reliquiis sanctorum, ut consuetudo illius diei poscebat. Unus vero erat ex nobis cum illo qui dixit illi: 'Adhuc, magister dilectissime, capitulum unum deest; et videtur mihi difficile tibi esse plus te interrogare.' At ille: 'Facile est,' inquit; 'accipe tuum calamum, et tempera, et festinanter scribe'; quod ille fecit. Ad nonam autem horam dixit mihi: 'Quaedam preciosa in mea capsella habeo, id est, piperem, oraria, et incensa; sed curre velociter, et presbyteros nostri monasterii adduc ad me, ut et ego munuscula qualia mihi Deus donavit illis distribuam. Divites autem in hoc saeculo aurum, argentum, et alia quaeque preciosa dare student: ego autem cum multa caritate et gaudio fratribus meis dabo quod Deus dederat'; et hoc cum tremore feci. Et allocutus est unumquemque monens et obsecrans pro eo missas et orationes facere: quod illi libenter spoponderunt.

"Lugebant autem et flebant omnes, maxime quod dixerat quia faciem eius amplius non multo in hoc saeculo essent visuri; gaurebant autem quia dixit: 'Tempus est, ut revertar ad Eum, qui me fecit, qui me creavit, qui me ex nihilo formavit. Multum tempus vixi, beneque mihi pius Iudex vitam meam praevidit. Tempus resolutionis meae instat, et enim anima desiderat Regem meum Christum in decore suo videre': sic et multa alia locutus, in laetitia diem usque ad vesperam duxit. Et praefatus puer dixit: 'Adhuc una sententia, magister dilecte, non est descripta.' At ille, 'Scribe,' inquit, 'cito.'

---

[1] Acts xx. 38.

the third hour. But from the third hour we walked in procession with the relics of the saints, as the custom of that day required. But one of us which remained with him, said: ' There is still one chapter wanting, my beloved master; and to me it seemeth hard for thee that I question thee further.' Whereupon he said: ' It is easy; take thy pen, and make ready, and write quickly '; and so he did. But at the ninth hour he said to me: ' I have certain things of value in my casket, that is some pepper, napkins and incense; but run quickly and bring the priests of our monastery unto me hither, that I also may distribute to them the little gifts such as God hath granted me; nay, the rich in this world are fain to give gold, silver and all other costly things: but I with much love and delight will give to my brethren the gift I had from God '; and thus I did trembling. And he spake unto each of them severally, warning and beseeching them to offer masses and prayers for him: and this they gladly promised.

" Now they all lamented and wept, sorrowing most of all for the words which he spake, that they should not see his face much longer in this world,[1] but rejoicing because he said: ' It is time for me to return to Him Who made me, Who created me, Who fashioned me out of nothing. I have lived long and the merciful Judge hath well ordered my life. The time of my release is at hand, for my soul longeth to see Christ my King in his beauty ': and having spoken thus and many other things beside he passed the day in gladness until the evening. And the aforenamed boy said: ' There is still one sentence, beloved master, not yet written down.' Whereupon he said: ' Write it quickly.' After a little

Post modicum dixit puer: ' Modo descripta est.'
At ille, ' Bene,' inquit, ' veritatem dixisti; con-
summatum est. Accipe meum caput in manus tuas,
quia multum me delectat sedere ex adverso loco
sancto meo, in quo orare solebam, ut et ego sedens
Patrem meum possim invocare.' Et sic in pavimento
suae casulae, decantans ' Gloria Patri et Filio et
Spiritui Sancto,' cum Spiritum Sanctum nominasset,
spiritum e corpore exhalavit ultimum; et sic regna
migravit ad caelestia.

"Omnes autem qui audiere vel videre beati patris
obitum nunquam se vidisse ullum alium in tam
magna devotione atque tranquillitate vitam finisse
dicebant: quia, sicut audisti, quousque anima eius
in corpore fuit, ' Gloria Patri' et alia spiritualia
quaedam cecinit, et expansis manibus Deo vivo et
vero gratias agere non cessabat. Scito autem,
frater carissime, quod multa narrare possim de eo,
sed brevitatem sermonis ineruditio linguae facit."

space the boy said: 'Now it is written.' Whereupon he said: 'Well hast thou spoken truth; it is finished. Take my head in thy hands, for it delighteth me much to sit opposite my holy place, wherein I was wont to pray, that so too as I sit I may call upon my Father.' And thus upon the floor of his cell, singing 'Glory be to the Father, and to the Son and to the Holy Spirit,' when he had named the Holy Spirit, he drew his last breath; and so he passed to the heavenly realms.

"Now all they which heard and saw the death of the blessed father avowed that they had never seen any other end his life in so great devoutness and peace: for, as thou hast heard, so long as his soul was in the body, he sang 'Glory be to the Father' and sundry other spiritual songs, and with outstretched hands ceased not to give thanks to the living and true God. Moreover, you must know, my dear brother, that I could report many things about him, yet my unlearned tongue causeth my words to be brief."

THE VENERABLE BEDE

THE FIRST BOOK OF THE
ECCLESIASTICAL HISTORY OF THE
ENGLISH NATION

DE VENERABILIS BAEDAE

HISTORIA ECCLESIASTICA
GENTIS ANGLORUM

PRAEFATIO

GLORIOSISSIMO REGI CEOLUULFO BAEDA FAMULUS CHRISTI, ET PRESBYTER

HISTORIAM Gentis Anglorum Ecclesiasticam quam nuper edideram, libentissime tibi desideranti, rex, et prius ad legendum ac probandum transmisi, et nunc ad transscribendum ac plenius ex tempore meditandum retransmitto: satisque studium tuae sinceritatis amplector, quo non solum audiendis Scripturae sanctae verbis aurem sedulus accommodas, verum etiam noscendis priorum gestis sive dictis et maxime nostrae gentis virorum illustrium, curam vigilanter impendis. Sive enim historia de bonis bona referat, ad imitandum bonum auditor sollicitus instigatur; seu mala commemoret de pravis, nihilominus religiosus ac pius auditor sive lector devitando quod noxium est ac perversum, ipse sollertius ad exsequenda ea quae bona ac Deo digna esse cogno-

---

[1] For Ceolwulf cf. V. 23.
[2] *Angli* used not of the tribe but more generally.

2

OF THE VENERABLE BEDE'S

ECCLESIASTICAL HISTORY OF THE ENGLISH NATION

PREFACE

TO THE MOST GLORIOUS KING CEOL-WULF,[1] BEDE THE SERVANT OF CHRIST AND PRIEST

THE history of things done in the Church of the English [2] nation, which of late I had set forth, I did both first on your desire very gladly send your Grace to have a sight and proof thereof, and now do send it to you again, to the intent you may copy it out and more fully at your leisure consider it: and I cannot but highly commend this your unfeigned zeal, not only to give diligent ear to the words of Holy Scripture, but also exercise a watchful care to know of things done or spoken by worthy men before your time, and specially of our own country. For whether an history shall contain good things concerning good men, the careful hearer is thereby stirred up and provoked to follow after well-doing; or whether it shall report evil things concerning froward men, the devout and well-disposed hearer or reader none the less, by flying that is evil and noisome to his soul, is himself moved thereby more earnestly to follow after the things he knoweth

3

verit, accenditur. Quod ipsum tu quoque vigilantissime deprehendens, historiam memoratam in notitiam tibi simulque eis quibus te regendis divina praefecit auctoritas, ob generalis curam salutis latius propalari desideras.

Ut autem in his quae scripsi, vel tibi, vel ceteris auditoribus sive lectoribus huius Historiae occasionem dubitandi subtraham, quibus haec maxime auctoribus didicerim breviter intimare curabo. Auctor ante omnes atque adiutor opusculi huius Albinus abba reverentissimus vir per omnia doctissimus extitit; qui in ecclesia Cantuariorum a beatae memoriae Theodoro archiepiscopo et Hadriano abbate viris venerabilibus atque eruditissimis institutus, diligenter omnia quae in ipsa Cantuariorum provincia vel etiam in contiguis eidem regionibus a discipulis beati papae Gregorii gesta fuere, vel monimentis literarum vel seniorum traditione cognoverat: et ea mihi de his quae memoria digna videbantur, per religiosum Lundoniensis ecclesiae presbyterum Nothelmum, sive literis mandata sive ipsius Nothelmi viva voce referenda, transmisit. Qui videlicet Nothelmus postea Romam veniens, nonnullas ibi beati Gregorii papae simul et aliorum pontificum epistolas, perscrutato eiusdem sanctae ecclesiae Romanae scrinio permissu eius qui nunc ipsi ecclesiae praeest Gregorii pontificis,

---

[1] Succeeded Hadrian as abbot of the monastery of SS. Peter and Paul at Canterbury in 709 or 710.
[2] Consecrated 668.
[3] Archbishop of Canterbury 735.
[4] Gregory II, once librarian to the Church of Rome.
[5] Gregory I, the Great.

to be good and acceptable to God. Which very
thing you too, most warily pondering, (out of the
respect you have to the common good), desire to
have the said history more widely published, both
to the instruction of yourself and also to the edifying
of such other whom the authority of God hath committed unto your governance.

And to the intent I may put both you and all
other that shall hear or read the said History out
of all doubt of the verity in those things I have
written, I will be careful briefly to show you what
authors I have chiefly followed in the making thereof. The chiefest author and aider I had in compiling
this small work was the most reverend abbot
Albinus,[1] a man instructed in all manner of knowledge; which being brought up in the church of
Canterbury under archbishop Theodore,[2] of blessed
memory, and abbot Hadrian, men of great worship
and learning, hath diligently procured and sent unto
me all such things as were done by the disciples of
the blessed pope Gregory in the province of Canterbury itself, either also in other places adjoining and
bordering upon the same: which things the said
abbot had learned partly by writings, partly also
by tradition of elders; and such of these things as
seemed deserving of record he hath sent unto me
by the hands of Nothelm,[3] a devout priest of the
church of London, to be received either in writing,
either by mouth and relation of the said Nothelm.
Which same Nothelm going after unto Rome was
permitted by Gregory [4] the bishop which is now head
of the selfsame Church of pope Gregory [5] to search
the closets of the said holy Church of Rome, where
he found out certain epistles of the blessed pope

invenit, reversusque nobis nostrae Historiae in-
serendas, cum consilio praefati Albini reverentissimi
patris adtulit. A principio itaque voluminis huius
usque ad tempus quo gens Anglorum fidem Christi
percepit, ex priorum maxime scriptis hinc inde
collectis ea quae promeremus didicimus. Exinde
autem usque ad tempora praesentia, quae in ecclesia
Cantuariorum per discipulos beati papae Gregorii[1]
sive successores eorum, vel sub quibus regibus gesta
sint, memorati abbatis Albini industria Nothelmo,
ut diximus, perferente cognovimus. Qui etiam
provinciae Orientalium simul et Occidentalium
Saxonum nec non et Orientalium Anglorum atque
Nordanhymbrorum, a quibus praesulibus vel quorum
tempore regum gratiam evangelii perceperint, nonnulla mihi ex parte prodiderunt. Denique hortatu
praecipue ipsius Albini ut hoc opus adgredi auderem
provocatus sum. Sed et Danihel reverentissimus
Occidentalium Saxonum episcopus qui nunc usque
superest, nonnulla mihi de historia ecclesiastica
provinciae ipsius simul et proxima illi Australium
Saxonum nec non et Vectae insulae, literis mandata
declaravit. Qualiter vero per ministerium Ceddi
et Ceadda religiosorum Christi sacerdotum, vel
provincia Merciorum ad fidem Christi quam non
noverat, pervenerit, vel provincia Orientalium
Saxonum fidem quam olim exsufflaverat, recupera-

---

[1] Gregory I, the Great.   [2] Cf. V. 18.
[3] Cf. III. 21, 23.

6

PREFACE

Gregory [1] as well as of other bishops there, and at his return hath delivered unto us the said epistles to be put into our History with the counsel and advice of the most reverend father Albinus above mentioned. So that from the beginning of this book unto the time that the English nation received the faith of Christ we learned such things as to publish, the same being gathered from divers quarters out of the works chiefly of such as had wrote thereof before our time. And from thence unto this present, such things as hath been done in the church of Canterbury by the disciples of the blessed pope Gregory or their successors, or under what kings they have been done, we have known by the industry of the said abbot Albinus by the hand, as we have said, of Nothelm. Who also have brought me in some part of knowledge of such things as were done in the provinces of the East and West Saxons, and also of the East English and of the Northumbrians; that is, to wit, by what bishop's preaching and under what king each of the said provinces received the grace of the Gospel. And, to be short, by the exhortation of the said Albinus I was chiefly provoked and emboldened to set upon this enterprise. Moreover, Daniel [2] also the most reverend bishop of the West Saxons (which is yet alive), hath instructed me by writing in certain points of the ecclesiastical history of his province, and at the same time of the next adjoining province of the South Saxons and also of the Isle of Wight. Now in what sort either the province of Mercia attained to the faith which they knew not before, or the province of the East Saxons recovered the faith which they had rejected before (both by the ministry of Cedd and Chad,[3] devout priests of Christ),

7

verit, qualis etiam ipsorum patrum vita vel obitus
extiterit, diligenter a fratribus monasterii quod ab
ipsis conditum Laestingaeu cognominatur, agnovimus.
Porro in provincia Orientalium Anglorum quae
fuerint gesta ecclesiastica, partim ex scriptis vel
traditione priorum, partim reverentissimi abbatis
Esi relatione comperimus. At vero in provincia
Lindissi quae sint gesta erga fidem Christi quaeve
successio sacerdotalis extiterit, vel literis reverentissimi antistitis Cynibercti vel aliorum fidelium
virorum viva voce didicimus. Quae autem in Nordanhymbrorum provincia ex quo tempore fidem Christi
perceperunt usque ad praesens per diversas regiones
in ecclesia sint acta, non uno quolibet auctore, sed
fideli innumerorum testium qui haec scire vel
meminisse poterant adsertione cognovi, exceptis
his quae per meipsum nosse poteram. Inter quae
notandum, quod ea quae de sanctissimo patre et
antistite Cudbercto vel in hoc volumine vel in libello
Gestorum ipsius conscripsi, partim ex eis quae de
illo prius a fratribus ecclesiae Lindisfarnensis
scripta reperi, adsumpsi simpliciter fidem historiae
quam legebam accommodans, partim vero ea quae
certissima fidelium virorum adtestatione per me
ipse cognoscere potui sollerter adiicere curavi.
Lectoremque suppliciter obsecro, ut si qua in his
quae scripsimus aliter quam se veritas habet posita
repererit, non hoc nobis imputet qui, quod vera lex

---

¹ In Yorkshire.
² Nothing but this notice is known of him.
³ Belonged sometimes to Northumbria, sometimes to
Mercia.
⁴ Cf. IV. 12.　　　⁵ Cf. II. 16.　　　⁶ Cf. IV. 25.

and how the two said fathers both lived and died,
we have diligently learned of the brothers of the
monastery named Lastingham[1] by the said two
erected. Furthermore, the things done in the Church
throughout the province of the East English we
have learned partly from the writings or traditions of men of former time, partly by the relation
of the most reverend abbot Esi.[2] But as for such
things as were done in the territory of Lindsey[3]
touching the furtherance of the faith of Christ, or
what bishops there succeeded from time to time, we
have learned either by the writings of the most
reverend bishop Cynibert,[4] either by the lively
voice of other men of good credit.[5] Moreover, the
ecclesiastical history of the province of the Northumbrians, throughout the divers divisions thereof,
from the time they received the faith of Christ
unto this present, I have gotten, not by any one
author, but by relation of innumerable faithful
witnesses which might know and remember the same,
besides all that by my own experience I might know.
Among which you shall note that such things as I
have wrote of the most holy father and bishop
Cuthbert[6] either in this book, either in the treatise
that I have made of his life and acts, I have taken
partly out of those things which I found before
written of him by the brothers of the church of
Lindisfarne, following simply the faith of the history
which I read; but partly also have been careful to
add skilfully thereunto such things as I could learn
myself by the sure testimony of men of good credit.
And I humbly beseech the reader, that if he shall
find anything set down otherwise than truth in this
that I have written, he will not impute it unto us,

historiae est, simpliciter ea quae fama vulgante
collegimus ad instructionem posteritatis literis
mandare studuimus.

Praeterea omnes [1] ad quos haec eadem Historia
pervenire poterit nostrae nationis legentes sive
audientes suppliciter precor, ut pro meis infirmita-
tibus et mentis et corporis apud supernam Clementiam saepius intervenire meminerint; et in suis
quique provinciis hanc mihi suae remunerationis
vicem rependant, ut qui de singulis provinciis, sive
locis sublimioribus, quae memoratu digna atque
incolis grata credideram diligenter adnotare curavi,
apud omnes fructum piae intercessionis inveniam.

CAP. I

De situ Brittaniae vel Hiberniae, et priscis earum incolis.

BRITTANIA [2] oceani insula, cui quondam Albion
nomen fuit, inter septentrionem et occidentem locata
est, Germaniae, Galliae, Hispaniae, maximis Europae
partibus multo intervallo adversa. Quae per milia
passuum octingenta in boream longa, latitudinis
habet milia ducenta, exceptis dumtaxat prolixioribus

---

[1] *Praeterea . . . inveniam*] This last paragraph is placed
at the end of the History by most MSS.
[2] The first paragraph to *insulas habet* is pieced together
from Pliny, *N.H.*, iv. 30; Gildas, § 3, and Orosius, i. 2.

---

[1] The first twenty-two chapters dealing with the history of
Britain before the coming of Augustine are based upon the

as the which have endeavoured with all sincerity to put in writing to the instruction of our after comers such things as we have gathered by common report, which is the true law of history.

Furthermore, I earnestly pray all men unto whom this same History of our nation shall come, that, whether they read it or hear it, they will not cease to offer up intercessions before the heavenly Mercy for my infirmities both of mind and body; and that all men in their several provinces may render me the recompense of their reward, to the intent that, having diligently endeavoured to set forth concerning those provinces or yet more exalted places, such things as I thought worthy to be recorded and well-pleasing to the inhabitants thereof, I may have of all men the fruit of their pious supplications.

CHAPTER I

Of the situation of Britain and Ireland, and of the people who inhabited these of old time.

BRITAIN,[1] an island of the Ocean, which of old time was called Albion, doth stand betwixt the north and the west, right over against Germany, Gaul and Spain,[2] three of the greatest countries of Europe, albeit divided from them by a far gap. Which island being 800 miles of length northward is but 200 miles broad, except only you reckon the capes or

history of Orosius, a contemporary of St. Augustine *c.* 400, and Gildas, the earliest British historian, *c.* 516–570, as well as Constantius' life of St. Germanus.

[2] The ancients made Spain project too far to the west, *e.g.* Tac., *Agric.* 10: *Britannia . . . in occidentem Hispaniae obtenditur.*

diversorum promontoriorum tractibus, quibus efficitur ut circuitus eius quadragies octies septuaginta quinque milia compleat. Habet a meridie Galliam Belgicam, cuius proximum litus transmeantibus aperit civitas quae dicitur Rutubi portus, a gente Anglorum nunc corrupte Reptacaestir vocata, interposito mari a Gessoriaco Morinorum gentis litore proximo, traiectu milium quinquaginta, sive, ut quidam scripsere, stadiorum quadringentorum quinquaginta. A tergo autem, unde oceano infinito patet, Orcadas insulas habet.

Opima frugibus atque arboribus insula, et alendis apta pecoribus ac iumentis; vineas etiam quibusdam in locis germinans: sed et avium ferax terra marique generis diversi. Fluviis quoque multum piscosis, ac fontibus praeclara copiosis, et quidem praecipue issicio abundat et anguilla. Capiuntur autem saepissime et vituli marini, et delphines, necnon et ballenae: exceptis variorum generibus conchyliorum; in quibus sunt et musculae, quibus inclusam saepe margaritam, omnis quidem coloris optimam inveniunt, id est, et rubicundi, et purpurei, et iacintini et prasini, sed maxime candidi. Sunt et cochleae satis superque abundantes, quibus tinctura coccinei coloris conficitur, cuius rubor pulcherrimus nullo unquam solis ardore, nulla valet pluviarum iniuria pallescere; sed quo vetustior est, eo solet esse venustior. Habet fontes salinarum, habet et fontes calidos, et ex eis fluvios balnearum calidarum, omni aetati et sexui per distincta loca, iuxta suum cuique modum accommodos. Aqua enim (ut sanctus

---

[1] Richborough, usually *Rutupae* or *Rutupiae*.
[2] Boulogne, *Bononia*.

points of divers mountains which runneth out a long
far into the sea, whereby the island is in compass
full forty-eight times 75 miles. On the south side
it hath Belgic Gaul, to the nearest coast whereof
the town called the haven of Rutubus (which is cor-
ruptly called Reptacaestir [1] by the English nation)
giveth access for men passing over from Britain, by
a journey of 50 miles or, as some have written, of
450 furlongs across the sea dividing it from Gesso-
riacum,[2] the nearest coast of the nation of the Morini.
On the backside of it, where it lieth open unto the
main ocean, it hath the isles called Orkney.

It is an island very batful [3] of fruits of the earth
and trees, and fit for the rearing of cattle and beasts
of burden. In some places also it beareth vines;
it hath, moreover, plenty of fowls of divers sorts,
both by sea and land; it hath good fame too for
rivers full of fish and plentiful springs, and specially
both it abound in salmon [4] and eels. And there be
many times taken seals, dolphins, as well as whales,
beside many kinds of shell-fish; amongst others of
mussels in whom be found pearls [5] of all colours, as
red, purple, sapphire and green, but specially white:
there is also exceeding great store of cockles, whereof
is made the dye of crimson, whose fair rudde will
be appalled neither ever with heat of the sun neither
with wet of weather, but the older it is the more
bright and beautiful gloss it casteth. The island
hath springs fit to make salt, it hath too others of
hot waters where are builded places meet for all ages
according to their needs, as well for men as women
to bathe themselves severally. For water (as

[3] Battable, fertile.   [4] Or *pike*.
[5] *Subfusca ac liventia*, Tac., *Agr.* 12.

Basilius dicit) fervidam qualitatem recipit, cum per
certa quaedam metalla transcurrit, et fit non solum
calida, sed et ardens.   Quae etiam venis metallorum,
aeris, ferri, et plumbi et argenti fecunda, gignit et
lapidem gagatem plurimum optimumque : est autem
nigrogemmeus et ardens igni admotus, incensus
serpentes fugat, adtritu calefactus adplicita detinet
aeque ut succinum.   Erat et civitatibus quondam
viginti et octo nobilissimis insignita, praeter castella
innumera, quae et ipsa muris, turribus, portis, ac
seris erant instructa firmissimis.

Et quia prope sub ipso septentrionali vertice mundi
iacet, lucidas aestate noctes habet ; ita ut medio saepe
tempore noctis in quaestionem veniat intuentibus,
utrum crepusculum adhuc permaneat vespertinum,
an iam advenerit matutinum, utpote nocturno sole
non longe sub terris ad orientem boreales per
plagas redeunte : unde etiam plurimae longitudinis
habet dies aestate, sicut et noctes contra in bruma,
sole nimirum tunc Lybicas in partes secedente, id
est, horarum decem et octo : plurimae item brevitatis
noctes aestate et dies habet in bruma, hoc est, sex
solummodo aequinoctialium horarum : cum in
Armenia, Macedonia, Italia, ceterisque eiusdem
lineae regionibus longissima dies sive nox quindecim,
brevissima novem compleat horas.

---

[1] In the *Hexameron, Hom.* iv. 6, a treatise on the six days'
work of Creation.

[2] The Roman towns such as Eboracum, Camalodunum,
Deva, etc.   According to Caesar, *de Bell. Gall.* v. 21 : *Oppidum
Britanni vocant cum silvas impeditas vallo atque fossa munierunt.*

[3] Literally *bolts.*

[4] Equal hours, not the temporary hours of the sun-dial,
which vary.

Saint Basil writeth [1]), running through certain metals, receiveth thereof such virtue of heat, that it is not only made warm thereby but also scalding hot. This island also is stored with mines of sundry metals, as of copper, iron, lead and silver; it bringeth forth too, great plenty of the jet stone and that of the best, and this stone is glossy black and burneth being put to the fire, and then is of virtue good to chase away serpents. If you rub him till he be warm he holdeth fast such things as are laid unto him, even as amber doth. This island too had in it sometime 28 fair cities,[2] besides an innumerable sort of castles which same also were well and strongly fenced with walls, turrets, gates and bulwarks.[3]

And forasmuch as it is placed right in manner under the North Pole of the heavens, it hath light nights in the summer, so that at midnight many times men looking doubteth whether it be yet of the evening past or break of the day following, since the sun at night dwelleth not long beneath the earth but returneth shortly to the east through the northern regions: whereby too the days be of a great length there in summer, as contrary the nights in winter, that is to wit 18 hours, by reason for sure the sun then goeth away to the regions of Libya: and so in like manner the nights in summer are there very short, and the days in the winter, that is to wit six equinoctial [4] hours only: whereas in Armenia, Macedonia, Italy and the other countries subject to the same line,[5] the longest day or night passeth not 15, the shortest 9 hours in all.

[5] Parallel of latitude. Eratosthenes of Cyrene, b. 276 B.C., first drew lines parallel with the equator.

THE VENERABLE BEDE

Haec in praesenti, iuxta numerum librorum quibus Lex Divina scripta est, quinque gentium linguis, unam eandemque summae veritatis et verae sublimitatis scientiam scrutatur et confitetur, Anglorum videlicet, Brettonum, Scottorum, Pictorum et Latinorum, quae meditatione Scripturarum ceteris omnibus est facta communis.

In primis autem haec insula Brettones solum a quibus nomen accepit, incolas habuit, qui de tractu Armoricano, ut fertur, Brittaniam advecti, australes sibi partes illius vindicarunt. Et cum plurimam insulae partem, incipientes ab austro, possedissent, contigit gentem Pictorum de Scythia, ut perhibent, longis navibus non multis oceanum ingressam circumagente flatu ventorum, extra fines omnes Brittaniae Hiberniam pervenisse, eiusque septentrionales oras intrasse, atque inventa ibi gente Scottorum, sibi quoque in partibus illius sedes petisse, nec inpetrare potuisse. Est autem Hibernia insula omnium post Brittaniam maxima, ad occidentem quidem Brittaniae sita; sed sicut contra aquilonem ea brevior, ita in meridiem se trans illius fines plurimum protendens, usque contra Hispaniae septentrionalia, quamvis magno aequore interiacente, pervenit. Ad hanc ergo usque pervenientes navigio Picti, ut diximus,

---

[1] Latin is included as the language employed in the service of religion, not, it appears, as the language of any separate people of Britain.

[2] *Universae civitates quae Oceanum attingunt . . . Armoricae appellantur.* Caes., *de Bell. Gall.* vii. 57. Later the name was restricted to the north-west, *i.e.* modern Brittany.

[3] Scandinavia. The origin of the Picts is a much-debated question, see Rice Holmes, *Ancient Britons*, p. 409 ff. Stapleton calls them *Redshanks*.

THE PICTS

This island at this present, with five sundry languages equal to the number of the books in which the Divine Law hath been written, doth study and set forth one and the same knowledge of the highest truth and true majesty, that is, with the language of the English, the Britons, the Scots, the Redshanks and the Latin,[1] which last by study of the Scriptures is made common to all the rest.

And at the first this island was inhabited of none other nation but only of the Britons, of whom it received his name: which Britons sailing from the region of Armorica,[2] as it is thought, chose unto themselves the south part of this land. And after, when they moving from the south forward had in their possession the most part of the island, it chanced that certain people of the Redshanks from Scythia,[3] as it is said, travelling upon the seas with a few long ships (the wind driving them in compass about), and passing outside all the coasts of Britain, came aland on Ireland's side, on the north parts thereof, which they finding inhabited of the Scots[4] besought them to allow them also some part of the land, where they might plant themselves, but they cou d not obtain their desire. This Ireland next unto Britain is the greatest island of the ocean sea, and standeth westward of Britain; but as northward it is not so long as it, so southward it extendeth far beyond the boundaries of Britain and reacheth out to face the north parts of Spain, albeit with wide space of water running betwixt. The Redshanks then (as we have said) arriving as far as Ireland in their navy, required

---

[4] Applied by Bede apparently to all the inhabitants of Ireland, but properly the tribe in Antrim.

petierunt in ea sibi quoque sedes et habitationem
donari. Respondebant Scotti, quia non ambos eas
caperet insula: " sed possumus," inquiunt, " salubre
vobis dare consilium quid agere valeatis. Novimus
insulam aliam esse non procul a nostra, contra ortum
solis, quam saepe lucidioribus diebus de longe
aspicere solemus. Hanc adire si vultis, habitabilem
vobis facere valetis: vel si qui restiterit, nobis
auxiliariis utimini." Itaque petentes Brittaniam
Picti, habitare per septentrionales insulae partes
coeperunt, nam austrina Brettones occupaverant.
Cumque uxores Picti non habentes peterent a
Scottis, ea solum conditione dare consenserunt, ut
ubi res perveniret in dubium, magis de feminea
regum prosapia, quam de masculina regem sibi
eligerent; quod usque hodie apud Pictos constat
esse servatum.

Procedente autem tempore Brittania post Brettones
et Pictos, tertiam Scottorum nationem in Pictorum
parte recepit; qui duce Reuda de Hibernia progressi,
vel amicitia vel ferro sibimet inter eos sedes quas
hactenus habent, vindicarunt: a quo videlicet duce
usque hodie Dalreudini vocantur, nam lingua eorum
" daal " partem significat.

Hibernia autem et latitudine sui status, et salu-
britate, ac serenitate aerum multum Brittaniae
praestat, ita ut raro ibi nix plusquam triduana
remaneat: nemo propter hiemem aut foena secet

---

[1] For the law of Pictish succession we may compare what
Tacitus, *Germ.* 20, says of the Germans: *Sororum filiis
idem apud avunculum qui apud patrem honor.*

[2] West coast of modern Scotland.

[3] From the northern part of Antrim called *Dal Riada.*

[4] 300 M.p. broad: Pliny, *N.H.* iv. 102.

18

of the inhabitants that they too might be suffered there to rest and plant themselves. The Scots answered that the island was not big enough to hold them both: " but we can give you good counsel " (quoth they) " what we think best for you to do. We know well there is another island not far from ours, standing eastwards from hence, which we may often see from afar in a fair sunny day. If you will go thither, you are strong enough to inhabit there at will; or if there be any resistance made against you, rely on us to aid you! " Whereupon the Redshanks making for Britain began to plant themselves throughout the north parts of the island, for as for the south parts the Britons had taken them up before. And whereas the Redshanks having no wives did require of the Scots to marry their daughters, the Scots agreed to grant them their boon under condition only, that as often as the matter was in doubt, they should choose their king rather of the female than the male line of the royal house; which order it is well known the Redshanks keepeth to this day.[1]

Now in process of years, after the Britons and the Redshanks, the Scottish folk beside the other two were received into Britain in the portion held by the Redshanks; which coming out of Ireland under Reuda their captain, either by friendship or the sword, chose for themselves amongst the Redshanks the country which they inhabit even now:[2] and from their captain even unto this day they are called Dalreudings,[3] for in their language *daal* signifieth part.

Now Ireland both in extent of its breadth,[4] wholesomeness and fineness of air, far passeth Britain, so that there snow remaineth scant three days together: no man there for stress of winter either cutteth hay

aestate, aut stabula fabricet iumentis: nullum ibi
reptile videri soleat, nullus vivere serpens valeat:
nam saepe illo de Brittania adlati serpentes, mox ut
proximante terris navigio, odore aeris illius adtacti
fuerint, intereunt: quin potius omnia pene quae de
eadem insula sunt contra venenum valent. Denique
vidimus quibusdam a serpente percussis, rasa folia
codicum qui de Hibernia fuerant, et ipsam rasuram
aquae immissam ac potui datam, talibus protinus
totam vim veneni grassantis, totum inflati corporis
absumsisse ac sedasse tumorem. Dives lactis ac
mellis insula, nec vinearum expers, piscium volu-
crumque, sed et cervorum caprearumque venatu
insignis. Haec autem proprie patria Scottorum est:
ab hac egressi, ut diximus, tertiam in Brittania
Brettonibus et Pictis gentem addiderunt.

Est autem sinus maris permaximus, qui antiquitus
gentem Brettonum a Pictis secernebat, qui ab
occidente in terras longo spatio erumpit, ubi est
civitas Brettonum munitissima usque hodie quae
vocatur Alcluith: ad cuius videlicet sinus partem
septemtrionalem Scotti, quos diximus, advenientes,
sibi locum patriae fecerunt.

in the summer or buildeth stalls for his cattle: there is no noisome creeping beast to be seen there, no serpent that can live there: for many times serpents which hath been brought thither out of Britain, as soon as (the ship drawing near unto the land) they are touched with the smell of the air thereof, they dieth out of hand: yea, more than that, all things in manner that cometh from the said island is of sovereign virtue against poison. And this we saw with our own eyes, that when certain men that were stinged of venomous serpents had taken the scraped leaves of tree-stems [1] which had been of Ireland, and the scrapings of the same had been put in water and given to the stinged men for drink, forthwith all the force of the spreading venom was staunched and the swelling of the inflamed body utterly assuaged. This island is rich in milk and honey, nor void of vines, fish or fowl; moreover, too, it is famed for hunting of stags and wild-goats. And this is properly the country of the Scots,[2] out of which they issuing added a third nation to the Britons and Redshanks in Britain.

And there is a mighty creek of the sea [3] which severed of old times the nation of the Britons from the Redshanks, which from the west runneth far into the land, where unto this day there is a city of the Britons, very strong and well fenced, called Alclyde [4]: at the north side of the which creek the Scots, as we said, hath come and made their dwelling country.

---

[1] Might be leaves of a book, but Pliny, *N.H.* xxv. 6, speaks of a *herba Britannica salutaris contra serpentes*.
[2] In Bede's day *Scottia* meant Ireland.
[3] Firth of Clyde.
[4] Dumbarton; cf. chap. 12.

THE VENERABLE BEDE

CAP. II[1]

Ut Brittaniam primus Romanorum Gaius Julius adierit.

VERUM eadem Brittania Romanis usque ad Gaium Iulium Caesarem inaccessa atque incognita fuit: qui anno ab Urbe condita sexcentesimo nonagesimo tertio, ante vero incarnationis Dominicae tempus anno sexagesimo, functus gradu consulatus cum Lucio Bibulo, dum contra Germanorum Gallorumque gentes qui Rheno tantum flumine dirimebantur, bellum gereret, venit ad Morinos, unde in Brittaniam proximus et brevissimus transitus est, et navibus onerariis atque actuariis[2] circiter octoginta praeparatis, in Brittaniam transvehitur, ubi acerba primum pugna fatigatus, deinde adversa tempestate correptus, plurimam classis partem, et non parvum numerum militum, equitum vero pene omnem, disperdidit. Regressus in Galliam, legiones in hiberna dimisit, ac sexcentas naves utriusque commodi fieri imperavit: quibus iterum in Brittaniam primo vere transvectus, dum ipse in hostem cum exercitu pergit, naves in anchoris stantes, tempestate correptae, vel conlisae inter se, vel arenis inlisae ac dissolutae sunt: ex quibus quadraginta perierunt, ceterae cum magna difficultate reparatae sunt. Caesaris equitatus primo

---

[1] This chapter is taken from Orosius vi. 7 and 9, except the passage about the stakes at the ford.

---

[1] The right dates are 695 A.U.C. and 59 B.C. Caesar's invasions of Britain took place in 55 and 54 B.C.
[2] Ships of war and transport.

JULIUS CAESAR

CHAPTER II

*How that Gaius Julius was the first of the Romans that
came into Britain.*   55–54 B.C.

Now the Romans had never access unto the said
land of Britain nor knowledge thereof until Gaius
Julius Caesar came: who the 693rd year from the
building of Rome but the 60th before the time of the
incarnation of the Lord,[1] after filling the office of consul
with Lucius Bibulus, at the time that he had battle
against the nations of Germany and Gaul (which two
countries only the river Rhine doth sever) came in
the land of the Morini, whence is a very nigh and
short passage into Britain, and with about 80 ships
charged with warfare provision, and swift sailers,
passed over into Britain; where he being first tried
with a very sharp and hot bickering, and after
shaken by a contrary tempest, was fain to return
into Gaul with the loss of a great part of his navy,
and no small number of his soldiers, and of the most
part of all his horsemen.   And so for that season
he was forced to send his men into winter quarters,
and gave command for 600 ships of both services [2]
to be built: with the which he sailed over again into
Britain in the early spring [3]: where after he had
arrived and was now marching towards his enemy
with his main host, his ships riding at the anchor
were with a violent storm rent and cast either one
upon the other, either upon the quicksands, and
there broken in pieces: in such sort that 40 of them
were lost out of hand, and the rest with much ado
repaired.   Caesar's horsemen at the first encounter

[3] About the 6th July.   Holmes, *Ancient Britain,* p. 333.

congressu a Brittanis victus, ibique Labienus tribunus occisus est: secundo praelio cum magno suorum discrimine victos Brittanos in fugam vertit: inde ad flumen Tamensim profectus. In huius ulteriore ripa Cassobellauno duce immensa hostium multitudo consederat, ripamque fluminis ac pene totum sub aqua vadum acutissimis sudibus praestruxerat: quarum vestigia sudium ibidem usque hodie visuntur, et videtur inspectantibus quod singulae earum ad modum humani femoris grossae, et circumfusae plumbo immobiliter erant in profundum fluminis infixae: quod ubi a Romanis deprehensum ac vitatum est, barbari legionum impetum non ferentes, silvis sese obdidere; unde crebris eruptionibus [1] Romanos graviter ac saepe lacerabant. Interea Trinovantum firmissima civitas cum Androgio duce datis quadraginta obsidibus Caesari sese dedit: quod exemplum secutae urbes aliae complures in foedus Romanorum venerunt. Iisdem demonstrantibus, Caesar oppidum Cassobellauni inter duas paludes situm, obtentu insuper silvarum munitum, omnibusque rebus confertissimum, tandem gravi pugna cepit. Exin Caesar a Brittania reversus in Galliam, postquam legiones in hiberna misit, repentinis bellorum tumultibus undique circumventus et conflictatus est.

---

[1] For *irruptionibus*, Pl.

---

[1] Q. Laberius Durus, tribunus militum, *De Bell. Gall.* v. 15. Confounded by Orosius, Bede's authority, with the more famous Labienus, Caesar's *legatus* or General of Division.

were overthrown of the Britons, and Labienus,[1] one of his colonels, slain: at the second encounter, with great loss and danger of his army, he routed the Britons and put them to flight: from thence he set out to the river Thames. On the farther side thereof a vast host of the Britons warded the banks under Cassivellaunus their captain, which had sticked the bank of the river and well-nigh all the ford [2] thick of sharpened stakes, of which stakes certain remnants unto this day are to be seen on the same spot, and it is plain to view that each of them (of the bigness of a man's thigh and covered with lead) had been sticked fast in the bottom of the river: which when the Romans had espied and escaped, the barbarians not being able to stand the assault of the legions, hid themselves in the woods; out of which they often breaking out many times greatly endomaged the Romans. In the meantime the mighty state of the Trinovantes with their captain Androgius [3] yielded unto Caesar, delivering 40 hostages: which example other more cities following fell in league with the Romans. By advertisement of the same cities Caesar having intelligence of a stronghold that Cassivellaunus had builded between two marishes (well fenced beside with the cover of woods and farsed with plenty of all things) assailed it with great force and at length overcame it. After that returning from Britain into Gaul, having dismissed his army for the winter season, he was suddenly beset with great tumults of war raised against him on every side.[4]

---

[2] Halliford, or near Brentford where stakes have been discovered. Holmes, *Ancient Britain*, p. 697.
[3] Mandubracius, Caes. *De Bell. Gall.* v. 20.
[4] Rebellion of Ambiorix.

CAP. III[1]

*Ut eandem secundus Romanorum Claudius adiens,
Orcadas etiam insulas Romano adiecerit imperio.
Sed et Vespasianus ab eo missus Vectam quoque
insulam Romanis subdiderit.*

ANNO autem ab Urbe condita septingentesimo
nonagesimo octavo Claudius imperator, ab Augusto
quartus, cupiens se[2] utilem reipublicae ostentare
principem, bellum ubique, et victoriam undecumque
quaesivit.   Itaque expeditionem in Brittaniam movit,
quae excitata in tumultum propter non redhibitos
transfugas videbatur.   Transvectus in insulam est,
quam neque ante Iulium Caesarem, neque post eum
quisquam adire ausus fuerat, ibique sine ullo praelio
ac sanguine intra paucissimos dies plurimam insulae
partem in deditionem recepit.   Orcadas etiam insulas
ultra Brittaniam in oceano positas Romano adiecit
imperio, ac sexto quam profectus erat mense Romam
rediit, filioque suo Brittanici nomen imposuit.   Hoc
autem bellum quarto imperii sui anno complevit, qui
est annus ab incarnatione Domini quadragesimus
sextus : quo etiam anno fames gravissima per Syriam
facta est, quae in Actibus Apostolorum per prophetam
Agabum praedicta esse memoratur.

[1] This chapter is pieced together from Orosius vii. 6 and
Eutropius vii. 19.
[2] *cupiens se,* in Orosius.

[1] The right date is 796 A.U.C., A.D. 43.

CLAUDIUS

CHAPTER III

*How Claudius was the second of the Romans who came
to the same land, which did also add the Orkney Isles
unto the Roman empire. Moreover, how Vespasian
sent by him did subdue the Isle of Wight under the
Romans.* 43 A.D.

Now in the 798th year [1] from the building of Rome,
Claudius, the fourth emperor after Augustus, being
much desirous to show himself a prince profitable
unto the commonwealth, sought war on all sides and
victory whencesoever it might come. And so he
made a voyage unto Britain, which was all in a
mutiny, it seemed, for that such as were treacherously
fled from them were not restored. He passed over
into the island, whither, nor before Julius Caesar nor
after, any durst adventure, and there without battle
or bloodshed within very few days received by sub-
mission the greatest part of the island. Also he
brought into subjection to the Roman empire the
Orkney Isles [2] which lieth in the ocean above
Britain, which done he returned to Rome the sixth
month after that he departed thence, and caused
his son to be surnamed Britannicus. And this war
was brought to an end in the fourth year of his
empire; which was the 46th year of the incarnation
of our Lord: in the which year also there fell a
great famine throughout all Syria, which in the Acts
of the Apostles [3] is shewed to be fore-spoken by the
mouth of Agabus the prophet.

[2] Tac., *Agric.* 10. 5, says the Orkneys were first discovered
and subdued by Agricola.
[3] Acts xi. 28.

Ab eodem Claudio Vespasianus, qui post Neronem imperavit, in Brittaniam missus, etiam Vectam insulam Brittaniae proximam a meridie, Romanorum ditioni subiugavit; quae habet ab oriente in occasum triginta circiter milia passuum, ab austro in boream duodecim, in orientalibus suis partibus mari sex milium, in occidentalibus trium a meridiano Brittaniae litore distans. Succedens autem Claudio in imperium Nero, nihil omnino in re militari ausus est. Unde inter alia Romani regni detrimenta innumera Brittaniam pene amisit: nam duo sub eo nobilissima oppida illic capta atque subversa sunt.

CAP. IV

Ut Lucius Brittanorum rex missis ad Eleutherum papam literis Christianum se fieri petierit.

Anno ab incarnatione Domini centesimo quinquagesimo sexto Marcus Antoninus Verus, decimus quartus ab Augusto regnum cum Aurelio Commodo fratre suscepit : [1] quorum temporibus cum Eleutherus vir sanctus pontificatui Romanae ecclesiae praeesset, misit ad eum Lucius Brittaniarum rex epistolam, obsecrans ut per eius mandatum Christianus efficeretur: et mox effectum piae postulationis consecutus

[1] Orosius vii. 15.

---

[1] Three, viz. Camalodunum, Verulamium, Londinium. Tac. *Ann.* xiv. 31, 33.

[2] Commonly called Marcus Aurelius, who succeeded A.D. 161.

[3] Commonly called Lucius Aurelius Verus, who died A.D. 169. The earliest date for the accession of Eleutherus is

Vespasian, which after Nero was emperor, being sent of the same Claudius into Britain, subdued also unto the seigniory of the Romans the Isle of Wight, standing nigh Britain southward; which is of length from east to west about 30 miles, from south to north 12, being in the east part by 6 miles, in the west 3 miles off from the south shore of Britain. Nero, however, succeeding Claudius in the empire, never durst meddle at all with warlike matters. Whereby among other many hindrances which befell in his time unto the empire, one was that he had almost lost Britain: for under him two [1] most noble towns were there taken and overthrown.

CHAPTER IV

How that Lucius king of the Britons wrote to pope Eleutherus desiring to be christened.

THE 156th year of the incarnation of our Lord Marcus Antoninus Verus,[2] the 14th emperor after Augustus, governed the empire with his brother Aurelius Commodus [3]: in whose time Eleutherus, a holy man, being pope of the Church of Rome, Lucius [4] king of the Britains wrote unto him a letter, desiring that by his commandment he might be made Christian: which his pious request shortly was

A.D. 171. Bede probably confuses L. Verus with L. Aurelius Commodus, the son of Marcus Aurelius, who reigned jointly with his father A.D. 177–180.
[4] Bede is the earliest authority for the name of Lucius and the story of his conversion. The letter came probably from the Roman archives and was from Lucius king of Edessa in Mesopotamia, whose citadel was Birtha (Britium). Nothelm perhaps confused *Britium* with *Britannia*.

est, susceptamque fidem Brittani usque in tempora Diocletiani principis inviolatam integramque quieta in pace servabant.

CAP. V [1]

Ut Severus receptam Brittaniae partem vallo a cetera distinxerit.

Anno ab incarnatione Domini centesimo octogesimo nono, Severus genere Afer Tripolitanus, ab oppido Lepti, decimus septimus ab Augusto imperium adeptus, decem et septem annis tenuit. Hic natura saevus, multis semper bellis lacessitus, fortissime quidem rempublicam, sed laboriosissime rexit. Victor ergo civilium bellorum quae ei gravissima occurrerant, in Brittanias defectu pene omnium sociorum trahitur, ubi magnis gravibusque proeliis saepe gestis, receptam partem insulae a ceteris indomitis gentibus, non muro, ut quidam aestimant, sed vallo distinguendam putavit. Murus etenim de lapidibus, vallum vero quo ad repellendam vim hostium castra muniuntur fit de cespitibus, quibus circumcisis, e terra velut murus exstruitur altus supra terram, ita ut in ante sit fossa, de qua levati sunt cespites, supra quam sudes de lignis fortissimis praefiguntur. Itaque Severus magnam fossam firmis-

---

[1] From Orosius vii. 17, except for the passage about the *murus* and *vallum*.

---

[1] The right date is A.D. 193.
[2] Bede does not say where Severus built the *vallum*. It seems best to attribute the lines between the Clyde and the Forth to Antoninus Pius, and the wall from the Solway to the

granted him, whereby the Britons receiving then the faith kept it sound, and undefiled in rest and peace until Diocletian the emperor's time.

CHAPTER V

How Severus by a dyke drawn overthwart severed that part of Britain which he had recovered from the other. 193–211.

THE 189th[1] year of the incarnation of our Lord Severus, born in Africa at the town of Leptis in the district of Tripolis, the 17th emperor after Augustus, reigned 17 years. This man being rough of nature, at all times tried with much wars, governed the commonwealth very valiantly but with much travail. After then he had vanquished his civil enemies with which he was very sore assailed, he is drawn into the provinces of Britain by the falling away of nigh all the allies, where, after fighting many great and grievous battles, he thought fit to have a partition made betwixt the part of the island he had recovered and the other wild and savage people, not with building a wall of stone (as some suppose) but with a dyke or rampart.[2] For a wall is built with stones, but a rampart, whereby a camp is fenced to ward off the force of enemies, is made with turfs, wherewith, when they are cut about, as it were a wall is raised out of the earth high above the earth, so that in front there be the trench whence the turfs were lifted, and above it be sticked stakes of the stoutest timber. And in such manner Severus caused a

Tyne to Hadrian. What Severus did must be regarded as uncertain. There is an earthwork immediately behind the wall of Hadrian, but its origin and object are disputed.

simumque vallum crebris insuper turribus com-
munitum, a mari ad mare duxit: ibique apud
Eboracum oppidum morbo obiit. Reliquit duos
filios, Bassianum et Getam: quorum Geta hostis
publicus iudicatus interiit; Bassianus Antonini
cognomine adsumpto, regno potitus est.

CAP. VI [1]

De imperio Diocletiani, et ut Christianos persecutus sit.

Anno incarnationis Dominicae ducentesimo octogesimo sexto, Diocletianus tricesimus tertius ab Augusto
imperator ab exercitu electus, annis viginti fuit, Maxi-
mianumque cognomento Herculium socium creavit
imperii. Quorum tempore Carausius quidam, genere
quidem infimus, sed consilio et manu promptus,
cum ad observanda oceani litora quae tunc Franci et
Saxones infestabant, positus, plus in perniciem quam
in profectum[2] reipublicae ageret, ereptam praedonibus
praedam nulla ex parte restituendo dominis, sed sibi
soli vindicando; accendens suspicionem quia ipsos
quoque hostes ad incursandos fines artifici negligentia
permitteret. Quamobrem a Maximiano iussus occidi,
purpuram sumpsit ac Brittanias occupavit; quibus
sibi per septem annos fortissime vindicatis ac retentis,
tandem fraude Allecti socii sui interfectus est.

---

[1] From Orosius vii. 25.   [2] For *provectum*, Pl.

[1] Marcus Aurelius Antoninus, better known by his nick-
name of Caracalla.
[2] The right date is A.D. 284.

great trench and rampart thick fenced beside with
many turrets to be drawn from one sea to the other:
and in Britain at the town of York he fell sick and
died. He left behind him two sons, Bassianus and
Geta, of which Geta being condemned of treason
died: Bassianus taking upon him the surname of
Antoninus [1] became master of the empire.

CHAPTER VI

*Of the reign of Diocletian and of the persecution he
raised against the Christians.*

THE 286th [2] year of our Lord's incarnation,
Diocletian, the 33rd emperor after Augustus, being
chosen of the army, reigned 20 years, and he created
Maximian, named Herculius, his fellow in government
of the empire. In whose time one Carausius, a man
of low degree in birth but valiant in arms and politic
in counsel, was appointed to ward the sea-coast
against the Franks and the Saxons, which then with
continual robberies much wasted that country, but
he so behaved himself that he did more hurt than
advantage to the commonwealth; for such pillage
as he had wrested from the robbers he did not in
any part restore it to the right owners, but reserved
to himself alone; whereby he kindled suspicion that
by not paying heed to his charge he even suffered
the enemy to assail the boundaries at their pleasure.
Whereupon being commanded to be put to death of
Maximian, he took upon him the princely authority
and usurped the governance of the British provinces;
which, after he had taken and kept seven years right
valiantly, at length by treason of his fellow Allectus

Allectus postea ereptam Carausio insulam per
triennium tenuit, quem Asclepiodotus Praefectus
Praetorio oppressit, Brittaniamque post decem annos
recepit.

Interea Diocletianus in oriente, Maximianus
Herculius in occidente, vastari ecclesias, affligi
interficique Christianos decimo post Neronem loco
praeceperunt: quae persecutio omnibus fere ante
actis diuturnior atque inmanior fuit; nam per
decem annos, incendiis ecclesiarum, proscriptionibus
innocentum, caedibus martyrum incessabiliter acta
est. Denique etiam Brittaniam tum plurima con-
fessionis Deo devotae gloria sublimavit.

CAP. VII

Passio sancti Albani et sociorum eius, qui eodem tempore
pro Domino sanguinem fuderunt.

Siquidem in ea passus est sanctus Albanus, de quo
presbyter Fortunatus in Laude Virginum, cum
beatorum martyrum qui de toto orbe ad Dominum
venirent mentionem faceret, ait:

" Albanum egregium fecunda Britania profert."

Qui videlicet Albanus paganus adhuc, cum perfidorum

---

[1] Connecting with end of preceding chapter.

[2] Bede's account is probably taken from some earlier
unknown chronicler. In parts the narrative is not easy to
follow and has not the simplicity of Bede's style. The earliest
trace of the story of St. Alban is in the Life of Germanus,
cf. ch. xvii.

34

he was slain. Which Allectus after kept the possession of the island, which he had wrested from Carausius, three years; whom Asclepiodotus, commander of the emperor's guard, overcame and received Britain in his possession the tenth year after it was usurped.

In the meantime Diocletian in the East, Maximian Herculius in the West, raising the tenth persecution after Nero, commanded the churches to be spoiled, the Christians to be tormented and killed: which persecution was longer and also crueller than wellnigh all which had been before; for by the space of ten years it continued in burning the churches, in outlawry of innocents, in murdering the martyrs and never ceased. Briefly, among other places Britain also was then exalted with the exceeding great glory of the confession of faith offered to God.

CHAPTER VII

The passion of Saint Alban and his fellows, which at the same time did shed their blood for the Lord.

INASMUCH as [1] in that persecution there suffered Saint Alban [2] of whom Fortunatus,[3] priest, in the book he wrote in the Praise of Virgins, speaking of the blessed martyrs which from all coasts of the world came unto the Lord, saith:

The fruit abounding land of Brittany
Bringeth forth Alban a Martyr right worthy.

This Alban to wit being yet but a pagan, when the cruel commandments of the unbelieving princes were

[3] Bishop of Poictiers beginning of 7th century.

35

principum mandata adversum Christianos saevirent, clericum quendam persecutores fugientem hospitio recepit: quem dum orationibus continuis ac vigiliis die noctuque studere conspiceret, subito Divina gratia respectus exemplum fidei ac pietatis illius coepit aemulari, ac salutaribus eius exhortationibus paulatim edoctus, relictis idolatriae tenebris Christianus integro ex corde factus est. Cumque praefatus clericus aliquot diebus apud eum hospitaretur, pervenit ad aures nefandi principis confessorem Christi cui necdum fuerat locus martyrii deputatus, penes Albanum latere. Unde statim iussit milites eum diligentius inquirere. Qui cum ad tugurium martyris pervenissent, mox se sanctus Albanus pro hospite ac magistro suo, ipsius habitu, id est caracalla qua vestiebatur indutus, militibus exhibuit, atque ad iudicem vinctus perductus est.

Contigit autem iudicem ea hora qua ad eum Albanus adducebatur, aris adsistere ac daemonibus hostias offerre. Cumque vidisset Albanum, mox ira succensus nimia quod se ille ultro pro hospite quem susceperat militibus offerre ac discrimini dare praesumpsisset, ad simulacra daemonum quibus adsistebat eum iussit pertrahi: " Quia rebellem," inquiens, " ac sacrilegum celare quam militibus reddere maluisti, ut contemptor divum meritam blasphemiae suae poenam lueret, quaecumque illi

---

[1] *Vestis clericorum talaris*, Ducange. The name, Amphibalus (cloak), given to the fugitive in the Lives of St. Alban, may be due to the story of the change of garment.

now fierce against the Christians, received into his house one of the clergy which was flying from the persecutors: whom he perceiving both night and day to continue instant in prayer and watching, being suddenly touched with the grace of God began to follow the example of his faith and virtue, and by little and little instructed by his wholesome exhortations, forsaking his blind idolatry became Christian with his whole heart. And whereas the said person of the clergy tarried with him certain days, it came to the ears of the wicked prince that this holy confessor of Christ (for whom the place of martyrdom had not yet been appointed) lay hid in Alban's house. Whence he commanded his soldiers at once to search for him with all diligence. And when they were come to the cot of the martyr, Saint Alban in the stead of his guest and master, and apparelled in the garment, that is to say, the hooded cloak,[1] wherewith the said guest was clad, shortly offered himself to the soldiers and so was brought bound unto the judge.

Now it chanced that the judge, the same time Alban was brought unto him, was doing sacrifice unto the devils before the altars. And when he had seen Alban, forthwith being all chafed with anger, for that he feared not voluntarily to offer himself unto the soldiers and come in peril of his life for the guest whom he had harboured, he commanded him to be dragged before the idols of devils before whom he was stood: " And for so much," quoth he, " as thou hadst rather to conceal the rebel and traitor to our gods than deliver him up unto the soldiers, that he might sustain due punishment for his blasphemous despising of the gods; look, what pains

debebantur supplicia tu solvere habes, si a cultu
nostrae religionis discedere tentas." At sanctus
Albanus qui se ultro persecutoribus fidei Christianum
esse prodiderat, nequaquam minas principis metuit;
sed accinctus armis militiae spiritalis, palam se[1] iussis
illius parere nolle pronuntiabat. Tum iudex:
" Cuius," inquit, " familiae vel generis es ? " Albanus
respondit: " Quid ad te pertinet qua sim stirpe
genitus ? sed si veritatem religionis audire desideras,
Christianum iam me esse, Christianisque officiis
vacare cognosce." Ait iudex: " Nomen tuum
quaero, quod sine mora mihi insinua." Et ille:
" Albanus," inquit, " a parentibus vocor, et Deum
verum ac vivum qui universa creavit adoro semper
et colo." Tum iudex repletus iracundia dixit: " Si
vis perennis vitae felicitate perfrui, diis magnis
sacrificare ne differas." Albanus respondit " Sacrificia haec quae a vobis redduntur daemonibus, nec
auxiliari subiectis possunt, nec supplicantium sibi
desideria vel vota complere. Quinimmo quicumque
his sacrificia simulacris obtulerit, aeternas inferni
poenas pro mercede recipiet." His auditis iudex
nimio furore commotus, caedi sanctum Dei confessorem a tortoribus praecepit, autumans se verberibus,
quam verbis non poterat, cordis eius emollire con-
stantiam. Qui cum tormentis afficeretur acerrimis,
patienter haec pro Domino, immo gaudenter ferebat.
At ubi iudex tormentis illum superari vel a cultu

[1] *se* Pl.

he should have suffered, the same shalt thou suffer, if thou assay to forsake the rites of our religion." But Saint Alban, which voluntarily had before discovered himself to the persecutors of the faith to be a Christian, in no wise heeded the menaces of the prince; but being thoroughly fenced with the armour of spiritual warfare, told him plainly to his face that he would not obey his commandment. Then said the judge: " Of what house or descent art thou? " Alban answered: " What is that to thee of what stock I am come? But if thou be desirous to know of what religion I am, be it known unto thee that I am now a Christian, and that I employ myself to Christian manners and exercises ! " The judge saith: " I ask thy name, and tell me this without delay ! " " My parents," quoth he, " named me Alban, and I honour ever and worship the true and living God which made all things." Then the judge being very wroth said: " If thou wilt enjoy the happiness of long life, come off and do sacrifice unto the great gods ! " Alban answered: " These sacrifices which you offer up unto the devils, neither can help them that are subject unto them, nor obtain for their worshippers their desires or prayers. Nay, rather, whosoever shall do sacrifice to these idols shall receive for his reward eternal pains in hell fire." The judge hearing this, being stirred with rage and fury, commanded the holy confessor of God to be all beaten of the tormentors, thinking the constancy of his heart would relent at stripes, which refused to yield to words; but he shewed himself not only patient but rather joyful in the bearing of his sharp torments. But the judge, when he saw he could be neither turned with torments

Christianae religionis revocari non posse persensit, capite eum plecti iussit.

Cumque ad mortem duceretur, pervenit ad flumen quod muro et harena [1] ubi feriendus erat, meatu rapidissimo dividebatur: viditque ibi non parvam hominum multitudinem utriusque sexus, conditionis diversae et aetatis, quae sine dubio Divinitatis instinctu ad obsequium beatissimi confessoris ac martyris vocabatur, et ita fluminis ipsius occupabat pontem ut intra vesperam transire vix posset. Denique cunctis pene egressis, iudex sine obsequio in civitate substiterat. Igitur sanctus Albanus cui ardens inerat devotio mentis ad martyrium ocius pervenire, accessit ad torrentem, et dirigens ad caelum oculos, illico siccato alveo, vidit undam suis cessisse ac viam dedisse vestigiis. Quod cum inter alios etiam ipse carnifex qui eum percussurus erat, vidisset, festinavit ei ubi ad locum destinatum morti venerat occurrere, Divino nimirum admonitus instinctu, proiectoque ense quem strictum tenuerat, pedibus eius advolvitur, multum desiderans ut cum martyre vel pro martyre quem percutere iubebatur, ipse potius mereretur percuti. Dum ergo is ex persecutore factus esset collega veritatis et fidei, ac iacente ferro esset inter carnifices iusta cunctatio, montem cum turbis reverentissimus Dei confessor ascendit : qui opportune

[1] The reading of the MSS. gives no proper meaning. Plummer suggests *quo murus ab harena.*

---

[1] The river Coln.

nor won with words from the worship of Christ's religion, commanded that he should be beheaded.

And in the way, as he was led to death, he came to a flood [1] which with a very swift course ran betwixt the town wall and the open place where he should suffer: and he saw there a great company of all sexes, degrees and ages (moved thereto beyond doubt by inspiration of God), following along with the blessed confessor and martyr, and so great numbers had possession of the bridge over the said flood that it would be toward night ere they all could get over. To be short, whereas nigh all had gone forth, the judge was left alone in the town without any to attend upon him. Therefore Saint Alban, in whom there was a fervent longing of mind to haste to his martyrdom, coming to the river-side and lifting up his eyes unto heaven, saw forthwith the bottom to have been dried up and the water to have given place to make a path for his steps. Which when among other the executioner who was to behead him did also himself see, he made haste to meet the martyr, when he had come to the place appointed for his death; and there (doubtless not without the holy inspiration of God) he fell down flat before his feet, and casting from him the sword which he had held in his hand ready drawn, earnestly desired that he should himself rather be found worthy to be executed, either with the martyr or for the martyr upon whom he was ordered to do execution. When therefore it fell that this man was made a fellow of the truth and faith whereof before he was persecutor, and the executioners were right staggered over the sword lying on the ground before them, the most reverend confessor of God climbed a hill with

laetus, gratia decentissima, quingentis fere passibus
ab harena situs est, variis herbarum floribus depictus,
immo usquequaque vestitus, in quo nihil repente
arduum, nihil praeceps, nihil abruptum, quem
lateribus longe lateque deductum in modum aequoris
natura complanat, dignum videlicet eum, pro insita
sibi specie venustatis, iam olim reddens qui beati
martyris cruore dicaretur. In huius ergo vertice
sanctus Albanus dari sibi a Deo aquam rogavit,
statimque incluso meatu ante pedes eius fons
perennis exortus est, ut omnes agnoscerent etiam
torrentem martyri obsequium detulisse: neque enim
fieri poterat ut in arduo montis cacumine martyr
aquam quam in fluvio non reliquerat, peteret, si hoc
opportunum esse non videret. Qui videlicet fluvius
ministerio persoluto, devotione completa officii
testimonium relinquens, reversus est ad naturam.

Decollatus itaque martyr fortissimus ibidem
accepit coronam vitae quam repromisit Deus dili-
gentibus se. Sed ille qui piis cervicibus impias
intulit manus gaudere super mortuum non est
permissus: namque oculi eius in terram una cum
beati martyris capite deciderunt. Decollatus est
ibi tum etiam miles ille, qui antea superno nutu
correptus sanctum Dei confessorem ferire recusavit:
de quo nimirum constat, quia etsi fonte baptismatis
non est ablutus, sui tamen est sanguinis lavacro
mundatus ac regni caelestis dignus factus est ingressu.

---

[1] Difficulty has been made about this passage, but the
narrative is clearer if we understand that it means that the
river, stayed in its course for the saint's passage, ascended
afterwards through the hill at his request, and having performed its office returned to its former course.

the people there assembled: which hill, fitly gay and
comely with excellent beauty, was about half a
mile from the appointed place, and was garnished,
indeed clothed everywhere, with divers flowering
herbs; whereon was no sudden rise, nothing steep,
nothing sheer, but the sides lengthways and breadth-
ways were drawn by nature into the fashion of a smooth
slope, plainly rendering it worthy and meet from
of old (for its delectable natural grace) to be sanctified
with the blood of the blessed martyr. Unto the top
whereof when he was ascended, Saint Alban required
of God to give him water, and straightway there
arose a spring of fair flowing water narrowed in his
channel, whereby all might perceive that the river
too before had done obedience to the martyr: for
it might not have been that he which had left no
water in the stream would have required it on the
high top of the mountain, but that he saw that it
was expedient. For behold the stream, his service
accomplished, his offering fully made, leaving behind
the testimony of his obedience returned to his nature
again.[1]

In this place accordingly the most valiant martyr,
being beheaded, received the crown of life which
God hath promised to them that love him. But he
which set unholy hands upon godly necks was not
suffered to have joy over the dead: for his eyes fell
unto the ground along with the head of the blessed
martyr. There also was beheaded at that time the
soldier, which, suddenly touched before with the
sign from on high, refused to strike the holy confessor of God: of whom it is open and plain that
though he was not christened in the font of baptism,
yet he was cleansed in the laver of his blood and so

Tum iudex tanta miraculorum caelestium novitate
perculsus, cessari mox a persecutione praecepit,
honorem referre iucipiens caedi sanctorum, per quam
eos opinabatur prius a Christianae fidei posse devotione cessare. Passus est autem beatus Albanus
die decimo Kalendarum Iuliarum, iuxta civitatem
Verolamium, quae nunc a gente Anglorum 'Verlamacaestir sive Vaeclingacaestir appellatur, ubi postea
redeunte temporum Christianorum serenitate ecclesia
est mirandi operis atque eius martyrio condigna
exstructa. In quo videlicet loco usque ad hanc diem
curatio infirmorum et frequentium operatio virtutum
celebrari non desinit.

Passi sunt ea tempestate Aaron[1] et Iulius Legionum
Urbis cives, aliique utriusque sexus diversis in locis
perplures, qui diversis cruciatibus torti et inaudita
membrorum discerptione lacerati, animas ad supernae
civitatis gaudia perfecto agone miserunt.

CAP. VIII

*Ut hac cessante persecutione, ecclesia in Britaniis
aliquantulam usque ad tempora Arrianae vesaniae
pacem habuerit.*

At ubi turbo persecutionis quievit, progressi in
publicum fideles Christi qui se tempore discriminis

[1] To *lacerati* from Gildas, §§ 10, 11.

---

[1] St. Albans. Bede does not give the year.
[2] Probably Caerleon-on-Usk. Constantius, who governed

made worthy to enter into the heavenly kingdom.
Then the judge, amazed by the sight of such wondrous
strange and heavenly miracles, gave shortly commandment that the persecution should cease,
beginning to give due honour to the slaughter of the
saints, by the which he thought at first they could
be stayed from the devotion of the Christian faith.
Now the blessed Alban suffered the 22nd day of
June, nigh unto the city of Verulamium [1] (which
is now of the English called Verlamacaestir or
Vaeclingacaestir), where, after, when the settled
calm of Christian times returned, there was a church
builded of a marvellous rich work and worthy of such
a martyrdom. In the which place truly even unto this
day are sick persons cured, and the doing of manifold
mighty works ceaseth not to be openly wrought.

There suffered about that time Aaron and Julius,
town-dwellers of the City of Legions,[2] and many
others, both men and women, in sundry places,
which, after divers fell and cruel torments and their
bodies torn by unheard of rending of their limbs,
yielded their souls to the joys of the heavenly city
when their warfare was accomplished.

CHAPTER VIII

*How that when this persecution ceased, the Church in the
Britains was somewhat quiet until the time of the
Arian fury.*

But after the storms of this persecution were over-
blown, Christ's faithful, which in time of danger had
lain hid in the forests and deserts or secret dens,

Britain at the time, did not himself carry out the persecution
ordered by Diocletian, according to Euseb. *Hist. Eccl.* viii.
13, 12.

silvis [1] ac desertis abditisve speluncis occulerant,
renovant ecclesias ad solum usque destructas, basilicas
sanctorum martyrum fundant, construunt, perficiunt,
ac veluti victricia signa passim propalant, dies festos
celebrant, sacra mundo corde atque ore conficiunt:
mansitque haec in ecclesiis Christi quae erant in
Brittania pax usque ad tempora Arrianae vesaniae,
quae corrupto orbe toto, hanc etiam insulam extra
orbem tam longe remotam veneno sui infecit erroris:
et hac quasi via pestilentiae trans oceanum patefacta,
non mora, omnis se lues haereseos cuiusque, insulae
novi semper aliquid audire gaudenti et nihil certi
firmiter obtinenti infudit.

His temporibus Constantius qui vivente Diocletiano
Galliam Hispaniamque regebat, vir summae mansuetudinis et civilitatis in Brittania morte obiit. Hic
Constantinum filium ex concubina Helena creatum
imperatorem Galliarum reliquit.[2] Scribit autem
Eutropius,[3] quod Constantinus in Brittania creatus
imperator, patri in regnum successerit: cuius
temporibus Arriana haeresis exorta et in Nicaena
synodo detecta atque damnata, nihilominus exitiabile
perfidiae suae virus, ut diximus, non solum orbis totius
sed et insularum ecclesiis aspersit.

---

[1] To *conficiunt* quoted, to *infudit* adapted from Gildas,
§§ 11, 12.
[2] Orosius vii. 25.   [3] X. 2.

---

[1] A.D. 306.
[2] Legally married, as Diocletian insisted on her divorce.

cometh forth and sheweth themselves abroad, reneweth their churches which before were thrown flat to the ground, foundeth, buildeth and perfecteth new temples in honour of the holy martyrs, and everywhere as it were displayeth their ensigns in sign of conquest, celebrateth holy days, doth consecrate the holy mysteries with pure mouth and heart: and this peace continued in the churches of Christ in Britain until the times of the Arian fury, which, after infecting the whole world, corrupted also with his venemous errors this island, though situate so far out of the compass of the world : and when that thus the disease had once found as it were an open vent to pass over the ocean, shortly after all the pestilence of all manner of heresies flowed into this island, and they were there received of the inhabitants, as being men delighting ever to hear new things and steadfastly retaining nothing assured.

About this time [1] died Constantius in Britain, which in Diocletian's lifetime governed Gaul and Spain, a man very mild and of much courtesy. He left Constantine, his son by Helen his concubine,[2] created emperor of the Gauls. Eutropius writeth further that Constantine, being created emperor in Britain, succeeded his father in the kingdom : in whose time the heresy of the Arians, springing and being discovered and condemned in the council of Nicaea, did none the less infect not only all the other parts of the world but also the churches of these islands with the deathly venom of his infidelity.

THE VENERABLE BEDE

CAP. IX [1]

Ut regnante Gratiano Maximus in Brittania imperator creatus, cum magno exercitu Galliam redierit.

ANNO ab incarnatione Domini trecentesimo septuagesimo septimo Gratianus quadragesimus ab Augusto, post mortem Valentis sex annis imperium tenuit: quamvis iamdudum antea cum patruo Valente, et cum Valentiniano fratre regnaret: qui cum adflictum et pene collapsum reipublicae statum videret, Theodosium Hispanum virum, restituendae reipublicae necessitate apud Syrmium purpura induit, Orientisque et Thraciae simul praefecit imperio. Qua tempestate Maximus, vir quidem strenuus et probus, atque Augusto dignus nisi contra sacramenti fidem per tyrannidem emersisset, in Brittania invitus propemodum ab exercitu imperator creatus in Galliam transiit. Ibi Gratianum Augustum subita incursione perterritum atque in Italiam transire meditantem, dolis circumventum interfecit, fratremque eius Valentinianum Augustum Italia expulit. Valentinianus in Orientem refugiens, a Theodosio paterna pietate susceptus, mox etiam imperio restitutus est: clauso videlicet intra muros Aquileiae, capto atque occiso ab eis Maximo tyranno.

---

[1] This chapter is taken from Orosius vii. 34.

[1] The right date is A.D. 378.

CHAPTER IX

*How that in the reign of Gratian, Maximus being made
  emperor in Britain returned to Gaul with a great
  army.*

THE 377th[1] year of the incarnation of our Lord,
Gratian, the 40th emperor after Augustus, reigned
6 years after the death of Valens, though for long
before he reigned also with Valens his uncle and
Valentinian his brother: which, seeing the state
of the commonwealth miserably plagued and nigh
altogether decayed, was driven of necessity for the
better repairing of the commonwealth to bestow
the imperial purple upon Theodosius, a Spaniard
born, at Syrmium, and set him over the government
of the East and Thrace together. In which time
one Maximus passed over into Gaul, a valiant man
and a good, and worthy of the dignity of Augustus,
had it not been that contrary to his oath and
allegiance he had risen by usurpation, half in manner
against his will being created emperor by the army
in Britain. After slaying in Gaul Gratian Augustus
(which was circumvented by cunning wiles and
suddenly stolen upon, that he was affrighted and was
in mind to pass into Italy), Maximus chased Valentinian Augustus his brother out of Italy. Valentinian
fleeing for succour into the East, and there with all
fatherly piety being received of Theodosius, was also
shortly restored unto the empire; while Maximus
the tyrant, being shut up by siege within the walls
of Aquileia, was there taken and slain by them.

THE VENERABLE BEDE

CAP. X

Ut Arcadio regnante, Pelagius Bretto contra gratiam Dei superba bella susceperit.

ANNO ab incarnatione Domini trecentesimo nonagesimo quarto Arcadius filius Theodosii cum fratre Honorio, quadragesimus tertius ab Augusto regnum suscipiens, tenuit annos tredecim. Cuius temporibus Pelagius Bretto contra auxilium gratiae supernae venena suae perfidiae longe lateque dispersit, utens cooperatore Iuliano de Campania, quem dudum amissi episcopatus intemperans cupido exagitabat: quibus sanctus Augustinus sicut et ceteri patres orthodoxi multis sententiarum catholicarum millibus responderunt, nec eorum tamen dementiam corrigere valebant: sed, quod gravius est, correpta eorum vesania magis augescere contradicendo quam favendo veritati voluit emundari: quod pulcre versibus heroicis Prosper Rhetor insinuat, cum ait:

" Contra Augustinum narratur serpere quidam
    Scriptor, quem dudum livor adurit edax.
Quis caput obscuris contectum utcunque cavernis
    Tollere humo miserum propulit anguiculum?
Aut hunc fruge sua aequorei pavere Britanni,
    Aut hic Campano gramine corda tumet."

---

[1] As being of British origin. He denied the doctrine of universal original sin.

[2] Deposed by Pope Zosimus in 418.

PELAGIUS

CHAPTER X

*How that Arcadius being emperor, Pelagius Bretto made
arrogant warfare against the grace of God.*

THE 394th year of the Lord's incarnation, Arcadius,
son to Theodosius, with his brother Honorius, being
the 43rd Emperor after Augustus, reigned 13 years.
In whose time Pelagius Bretto [1] disparkled the
venom of his faithless doctrine against the aid of
heavenly grace very far abroad, using herein the
help of Julian of Campania, who was intemperately
stirred with desire to regain his lost bishopric [2]:
to whom Saint Augustine, just as also the other
orthodox fathers, hath answered with many thousand
Catholic sentences, nor yet availed to correct their
folly, but (which is the weightier matter) being
rebuked for their madness they rather would increase
it by defending and maintaining it than be purified
by joining themselves to the truth: which thing
Prosper the rhetoriker [3] declareth nobly in heroic [4]
verse, saying:

" Against Augustine crawled, 'tis told, to write
 One whom the tooth of envy gnawed with spite.
 Who spurred the paltry snake to leave its bed
 In cavern's shelter dim and rear its head?
 Their fruit the Britons gave on Ocean's side,
 Or else Campanian pastures swelled its pride."

[3] Prosper of Aquitaine died after 463.
[4] Elegiacs, called heroic also in V. 8.

THE VENERABLE BEDE

CAP. XI [1]

*Ut regnante Honorio Gratianus et Constantinus in
Brittania tyranni creati, et mox prior in Brittania,
secundus in Gallia sint interempti.*

ANNO ab incarnatione Domini quadringentesimo
septimo tenente imperium Honorio Augusto filio
Theodosii minore loco ab Augusto quadragesimo
quarto, ante biennium Romanae inruptionis quae per
Halaricum Regem Gothorum facta est, cum gentes
Halanorum, Suevorum, Vandalorum, multaeque cum
his aliae protritis Francis, transito Hreno, totas per
Gallias saevirent, apud Brittanias Gratianus municeps
tyrannus creatur et occiditur. Huius loco Constantinus ex infima militia, propter solam spem nominis
sine merito virtutis eligitur: qui continuo ut invasit
imperium in Gallias transiit; ibi saepe a barbaris
incertis foederibus inlusus detrimento magis reipublicae fuit: unde mox iubente Honorio Constantius
comes in Galliam cum exercitu profectus, apud
Arelatem civitatem eum clausit, cepit, occidit:
Constantemque filium eius quem ex monacho
Caesarem fecerat, Gerontius comes suus apud
Viennam interfecit.

Fracta est autem Roma a Gothis anno millesimo
centesimo [2] sexagesimo quarto suae conditionis, ex
quo tempore Romani in Brittania regnare cessarunt,
post annos ferme quadringentos septuaginta ex quo
Gaius Iulius Caesar eandem insulam adiit. Habita-

[1] This chapter to *interfecit* is pieced together from Orosius
vii. 36, 42.
[2] *centesimo* not in MSS.

---

[1] The right date is 410.

USURPERS

CHAPTER XI

How that Honorius being emperor, Gratian and Constantine were made tyrants in Britain, where the first shortly after was slain and the other in Gaul.

THE 407th[1] year of the Lord's incarnation, Honorius Augustus, younger son of Theodosius, being emperor in the 44th place after Augustus, two years before that Rome was invaded by Alaric king of the Goths (when the nations of the Alani, the Suevi and the Vandals, and many such other with them, having beaten down the Franks, passed the Rhine and raged throughout all the provinces of Gaul), about that time Gratian a burgher is created tyrant in the Britains and is slain. In his place Constantine, being but a common soldier, was chosen, only for the sake of the hope given by his name without any desert of merit: which, so soon as he had usurped the empire, passed over into the Gauls; where being oft deluded by the barbarous nations, as uncertainly making his league with them, very greatly endomaged the commonwealth: whereupon, Honorius sending count Constantius into Gaul with an army, Constantine was besieged at Arles and there taken and slain: and Constans his son, whom of a monk he had made Caesar, was slain at Vienne by Gerontius,[2] his own officer.

Rome was broken of the Goths the 1164th year after it was builded, after which time the Romans left to rule in Britain, being almost 470 years since Gaius Julius Caesar first entered the said island. Now they dwelt within the dyke which (as we have

---

[2] A Briton; cf. the name Geraint.

bant autem intra vallum quod Severum trans insulam
fecisse commemoravimus, ad plagam meridianam,
quod civitates, farus, pontes, et stratae ibidem factae
usque hodie testantur : ceterum ulteriores Brittaniae
partes, vel eas etiam quae ultra Brittaniam sunt
insulas iure dominandi possidebant.

CAP. XII

*Ut Brettones a Scottis vastati Pictisque, Romanorum
auxilia quaesierint qui secundo venientes, murum
trans insulam fecerint ; sed hoc confestim a praefatis
hostibus interrupto, maiore sint calamitate depressi.*

Exin [1] Brittania in parte Brettonum, omni armato
milite, militaribus copiis universis, tota floridae
iuventutis alacritate spoliata, quae tyrannorum
temeritate abducta nusquam ultra domum rediit,
praedae tantum patuit, utpote omnis bellici usus
prorsus ignara : denique subito duabus gentibus
transmarinis vehementer saevis, Scottorum a circio,
Pictorum ab aquilone, multos stupet gemitque per
annos. Transmarinas autem dicimus has gentes,
non quod extra Brittaniam essent positae ; sed quia a
parte Brettonum erant remotae, duobus sinibus
maris interiacentibus, quorum unus ab orientali
mari, alter ab occidentali, Brittaniae terras longe
lateque inrumpit, quamvis ad se invicem pertingere
non possint. Orientalis habet in medio sui urbem

[1] To *per annos* from Gildas, § 14.

---

[1] Originally *lighthouse*, Φάρος.
[2] In Gildas *transmarinus* is used of Scots from Ireland and
Picts from oversea.

54

said) Severus drew overthwart the island, at the south part, which thing may appear by the cities, towers,[1] bridges and paved streets made in the same: notwithstanding they had in possession and under their dominion the farther parts of Britain and also the islands which are above Britain.

CHAPTER XII

How the Britons being spoiled of the Scots and Redshanks sought aid of the Romans, which at the second time of their coming builded a wall across the island; but when this was shortly after broken by the aforesaid enemies they were oppressed with greater miseries than ever they were in before.

Henceforth Britain in the part held of the Britons, being robbed of all men at arms, the whole of their provision for war, and the full flower of their lusty youth (which led away by the rashness of the tyrants never returned home again), lay only for a prey to the spoiler, forasmuch as the people was altogether ignorant of the handling of weapons of war: in short upon a sudden for many years together they groaned helplessly under the oppression of two most cruel and outlandish nations, the Scots from the west and the Redshanks from the north. Now I call these nations outlandish,[2] not that they were out of the circuit of Britain, but that they were divided from the part held by the Britons by two arms of the sea[3] running betwixt them, of the which one from the east sea, the other from the west runneth in far and wide into the lands of Britain, though they may not reach to the other. In the middle of the east

[3] The Firths of Forth and Clyde.

THE VENERABLE BEDE

Giudi, occidentalis supra se, hoc est, ad dexteram sui
habet urbem Alcluith, quod lingua eorum significat
petram Cluith; est enim iuxta fluvium nominis illius.

Ob [1] harum ergo infestationem gentium, Brettones
legatos Romam cum epistolis mittentes, lacry-
mosis precibus auxilia flagitabant, subiectionemque
continuam dummodo hostis imminens longius arcere-
tur, promittebant. Quibus mox legio destinatur
armata, quae ubi in insulam advecta et congressa
est cum hostibus, magnam eorum multitudinem
sternens, ceteros sociorum finibus expulit: eosque
interim a dirissima depressione liberatos hortata
est instruere inter duo maria trans insulam murum
qui arcendis hostibus posset esse praesidio: sicque
domum cum triumpho magno reversa est. At
insulani murum quem iussi fuerant, non tam lapidibus
quam cespitibus construentes, utpote nullum tanti
operis artificem habentes, ad nihil utilem statuunt.
Fecerunt autem eum inter duo freta vel sinus de
quibus diximus maris, per millia passuum plurima:
ut ubi aquarum munitio deerat, ibi praesidio valli
fines suos ab hostium inruptione defenderent: cuius
operis ibidem facti, id est, valli latissimi et altissimi

<hr>

[1] To *reversa est* from Gildas, §§ 15, 16.

<hr>

[1] Perhaps Inchkeith.
[2] Dumbarton.
[3] Gildas, the West Briton, seems to be Bede's authority
here, and Gildas admits that there were no records for him
to follow, only oral traditions collected abroad.

creek there is a city builded called Giudi [1]; above
the west creek, that is to say, toward the right hand,
standeth a city called Alclyde,[2] which in their
language is as much as to say as the rock Clyde; for
it standeth by a flood of that name.

The Britons then being thus afflicted by the said
nations sent their ambassadors with letters unto
Rome with lamentable supplications,[3] requiring of
them aid and succour, promising them their continual fealty, so that the enemy which threatened
them were kept to a farther distance. Whereupon
shortly here was sent unto them a legion of armed
soldiers, which coming to the island and encountering
with the enemies overthrew a great number of them,
and drave the rest out of the frontiers of their allies:
and so, setting them meanwhile at liberty and free
from the misery with which they were before so
grievously overcharged, counselled them to build
a wall athwart the island between the two seas,
which might be of force to keep out their enemies:
and that done they returned home with great
triumph. But the islanders, building the wall which
they were bid to make, not of stone, as they were
willed, but of turf, as having none among them that
had skill for so great an undertaking, raised it to be
of use for no purpose. And this wall they made
between the two great arms or creeks of the sea
(whereof we have already spoken), many miles long:
in such sort that, whereas the fence of the water
lacked, there by the help of the dyke they might
keep their boundaries free from the breaking in of
their enemies: of which piece of work, that is, of the
very broad and high dyke, there remaineth even
unto this day most assured tokens to be seen on the

57

usque hodie certissima vestigia cernere licet. Incipit autem duorum ferme milium spatio a monasterio Aebbercurnig ad occidentem, in loco qui sermone Pictorum Peanfahel, lingua autem Anglorum Penneltun appellatur; et tendens contra occidentem terminatur iuxta urbem Alcluith.

Verum[1] priores inimici ut Romanum militem abisse conspexerant, mox advecti navibus inrumpunt terminos, cæduntque omnia, et quasi maturam segetem obvia quaeque metunt, calcant, transeunt: unde rursum mittuntur Romam legati, flebili voce auxilium implorantes, ne penitus misera patria deleretur, ne nomen Romanae provinciae quod apud eos tam diu claruerat, exterarum gentium improbitate obrutum vilesceret. Rursum mittitur legio, quae inopinata tempore autumni adveniens magnas hostium strages dedit, eosque qui evadere poterant omnes trans maria fugavit, qui prius anniversarias praedas trans maria nullo obsistente cogere solebant.

Tum Romani denuntiavere Brettonibus, non se ultra ob eorum defensionem tam laboriosis expeditionibus posse fatigari: ipsos potius monent arma corripere et certandi cum hostibus studium subire, qui non aliam ob causam quam si ipsi inertia solverentur eis possent esse fortiores. Quin etiam, quia[2] et hoc sociis quos derelinquere cogebantur aliquid commodi adlaturum putabant, murum a

---

[1] To end of chapter mainly Gildas, §§ 18, 19.
[2] For *quod*, Pl.

---

[1] Abercorn. The dyke was made by Antoninus Pius, p. 30.
[2] Bede seems to have taken literally a metaphor of Gildas comparing the slaughter of the enemy to the fall of autumn leaves.
[3] Built by Hadrian, A.D. 117–138, from Solway to Tyne.

same spot it was made. Now it beginneth about two miles off from the monastery of Aebbercurnig,[1] to the west, in a place which in the Pict's language is called Peanfahel, but in the English tongue called Penneltun; and running out westward is ended by the city of Alclyde.

But the former enemies when they had once perceived that the Roman soldiers were gone, forthwith being set on land by boats invadeth the borders and maketh havoc of all things, and as it were corn ready to be cut, they moweth, trampleth and passeth over all before them: whereupon ambassadors be sent again to Rome, with lamentable voice requiring their succour, beseeching them they would not suffer their miserable country to be utterly destroyed, lest the name of Roman province, which through them had so long flourished, should now thus despitefully be extinguished by the wicked cruelty of their foreign people. Again there is sent a legion, which in the autumn-time[2] coming upon the sudden made a great slaughter of the enemies, and them that could escape, they chased over the seas, which before were wont to gather booty yearly to take over the seas without resistance.

Then the Romans told the Britons plain that it was not for their ease to take any more such travailous journeys for their defence: and bid them rather to snatch up their weapons themselves, and undertake to learn to withstand their enemy, whom nothing else did make stronger than they but their own faint and cowardous hearts. Moreover also, for so much they thought that would be some help and strength unto their allies whom they were now forced to forsake, they built up a wall of hard stone[3] from

mari ad mare recto tramite inter urbes quae ibidem
ob metum hostium factae fuerant, ubi et Severus
quondam vallum fecerat, firmo de lapide conlocarunt:
quem videlicet murum hactenus famosum atque
conspicuum, sumptu publico privatoque, adiuncta
secum Brittanorum manu construebant, octo pedes
latum et duodecim altum, recta ab oriente in occasum
linea, ut usque hodie intuentibus clarum est: quo
mox condito dant fortia segni populo monita, praebent
instituendorum exemplaria armorum. Sed et in
litore oceani ad meridiem quo naves eorum habe-
bantur, quia et inde barbarorum inruptio timebatur,
turres per intervalla ad prospectum maris collocant,
et valedicunt sociis tanquam ultra non reversuri.
Quibus ad sua remeantibus, cognita Scotti Pictique
reditus denegatione, redeunt confestim ipsi, et
solito confidentiores facti, omnem aquilonalem
extremamque insulae partem pro indigenis ad
murum usque capessunt. Statuitur ad haec in edito
arcis acies segnis, ubi trementi corde stupida die
noctuque marcebat. At contra non cessant uncinata
hostium tela: ignavi propugnatores miserrime de
muris tracti solo adlidebantur. Quid plura? relictis
civitatibus ac muro, fugiunt, disperguntur. Insequitur hostis, adcelerantur strages cunctis crudeliores
prioribus. Sicut enim agni a feris, ita miseri cives

sea to sea with a straight course between the two
cities which were made for fear of the enemy, in
the same place where Severus before had cast the
trench: which wall indeed (which even to this day
remaineth famous and to be seen) they did build
with public and private charges, the Britons also
putting to their helping hands. It was eight foot
broad and twelve high, right as it were by a line
from east to west, as it doth to this day plainly
appear: which being soon made they gave the fearful
people straight warning, they furnish patterns for
fashioning weapons. Moreover, too, by the seaside
southward where their ships lay at anchor, because
on that side also there was fear of the invasion of the
barbarians, they maketh up towers to have view of
the sea, one somewhat distant from the other, and
this done biddeth their allies farewell as minded no
more to return. And when these were on the way
back to their home, the Scots and Redshanks, having
intelligence that they had made promise they would
come no more, returneth forthwith again to their
wonted business, and heartened yet more than they
were wont, taketh for their own all the north and end
part of the island right as far as the wall. To meet
this assault the fearful array of the Britons is set
on the height of the fortress where with faint hand
and trembling heart they wasted away day and night.
But over against them the grappling weapons of the
enemy cease not to be plied: the cowardous defenders
were miserably pulled from the walls and dashed
against the ground. Why say more? Leaving the
cities and the wall they fly, and they are scattered.
The enemy followeth upon them, hasteth to slay
more cruelly than ever he did before. For even as

61

discerpuntur ab hostibus: unde a mansionibus ac possessiunculis suis eiecti, imminens sibi famis periculum latrocinio ac rapacitate mutua temperabant, augentes externas domesticis motibus clades, donec omnis regio totius cibi sustentaculo, excepto venandi solatio, vacuaretur.

CAP. XIII[1]

Ut regnante Theodosio minore, cuius tempore Palladius ad Scottos in Christum credentes missus est, Brettones ab Aetio consule auxilium flagitantes non impetraverint.

Anno Dominicae incarnationis quadringentesimo vigesimo tertio, Theodosius iunior post Honorium quadragesimus quintus ab Augusto regnum suscipiens viginti et sex annos tenuit; cuius anno imperii octavo Palladius ad Scottos in Christum credentes a pontifice Romanae ecclesiae Caelestino primus mittitur episcopus. Anno autem regni eius vigesimo tertio, Aetius vir inlustris qui et patricius fuit, tertio cum Symmacho gessit consulatum. Ad hunc pauperculae Brettonum reliquiae mittunt epistolam, cuius hoc principium est: " Aetio ter consuli gemitus Brittanorum: " et in processu epistolae, ita suas calami-

[1] Mainly from Gildas, § 20.

---

[1] No mention is made of St. Patrick who according to other writers was sent by Pope Celestine to Ireland in 432.
[2] *i.e.* the Irish.

the lambs of the wild beasts, so were the wretched citizens mangled of their enemies : whereupon being driven out of their own homes and possessions they falleth a robbing and spoiling one the other of them, to stay the peril of hunger that threatened them, thus increasing the mischief of the foreign enemy with their civil commotions, until all the country was brought to that exigent, that they had none other sustenance of victual but that relief they got by hunting of wild beasts.

CHAPTER XIII

How in the reign of Theodosius the younger the Britons sought help of Aetius then consul, but could not obtain it : and how in his time Palladius was sent to the Scots which believed in Christ.

THE 423rd year of the incarnation of our Lord, Theodosius the younger, succeeding Honorius, came to the throne, which he held 26 years, being the 45th emperor after Augustus ; in the eighth year of whose empire Palladius [1] was sent of Celestine, bishop of the Roman Church, to the Scots [2] which believed in Christ, to be their first bishop. And the 23rd year of his reign, Aetius, a man of the degree of illustrious [3] (as the which was also a patrician), for the third time held the consulship with Symmachus. The wretched leaving of the Britons directed unto him a letter whereof this was the beginning : " to Aetius, thrice consul, the groan of the Britons " : and in the process of this epistle they thus setteth forth

[3] In the hierarchy of officials instituted by Constantine *Illustrious* was the title of honour bestowed upon patricians amongst other high dignitaries.

63

tates explicant: "Repellunt barbari ad mare,
repellit mare ad barbaros; inter haec oriuntur duo
genera funerum, aut iugulamur, aut mergimur."
Neque haec tamen agentes quicquam ab illo auxilii
impetrare quiverunt, utpote qui gravissimis eo
tempore bellis cum Blaedla et Attila regibus Hunorum
erat occupatus. Et quamvis anno ante hunc proximo
Blaedla Attilae fratris sui sit interemptus insidiis,
Attila tamen ipse adeo intolerabilis reipublicae
remansit hostis, ut totam pene Europam excisis
invasisque civitatibus atque castellis conroderet.
Quin et iisdem temporibus fames Constantinopolim
invasit: nec mora pestis secuta est; sed et plurimi
eiusdem urbis muri cum quinquaginta septem turribus
corruerunt; multis quoque civitatibus conlapsis
fames et aerum pestifer odor plura hominum milia
iumentorumque delevit.

CAP. XIV [1]

*Ut Brettones fame famosa coacti, barbaros suis e finibus
pepulerint ; nec mora, frugum copia, luxuria,
pestilentia, et exterminium gentis secutum sit.*

Interea Brettones fames sua praefata magis
magisque adficiens, ac famam suae malitiae posteris
diuturnam relinquens, multos eorum coegit victas
infestis praedonibus dare manus, alios vero nunquam,
quin potius confidentes in Divinum ubi humanum
cessabat auxilium, de ipsis montibus speluncis ac

[1] Mainly from Gildas, § 20.

[1] Through earthquake, 447.

their pitiful estate: "the barbarous enemy driveth us upon the sea, the sea again upon the enemy; between these twain riseth two manner of deaths, either we are killed or drowned." And yet for all their suit they could obtain no aid of him, as he which had then both his hands full of grievous wars with Blaedla and Attila, kings of the Huns. And though, the year before, Blaedla was murdered by the wily treason of his brother Attila, yet he alone remained so intolerable an enemy unto the commonwealth, that he wasted almost all Europe, assaulting and destroying both cities and castles. Moreover, too, about the same time a famine attacked Constantinople, and without pause followed the pestilence; further, too, a great part of the walls of the said city fell to the ground with 57 towers [1]; many cities too being overthrown with earthquake, hunger and the pestilential stench of the air destroyed yet more thousands of men and beasts.

CHAPTER XIV

How the Britons being forced by a notable famine drove the barbarous people out of their boundaries ; and without delay there ensued plenty of corn, riot, pestilence and destruction of the people.

In the mean season their aforesaid hunger more and more prevailing against the Britons (insomuch that many years after it left to later men remembrance of the hurt it did) drove many of them to yield themselves beaten into the hands of the robbers which assaulted them; but others would never so do, but, rather trusting in God where man's help failed them, from the caves in the mountains and

saltibus continue rebellabant : et tum primum
inimicis qui per multos annos praedas in terra agebant,
strages dare coeperunt. Revertuntur ergo impu-
dentes grassatores Hiberni domus, post non longum
tempus reversuri; Picti in extrema parte insulae tunc
primum et deinceps quieverunt, praedas tamen
nonnunquam exinde et contritiones de Brettonum
gente agere non cessarunt.

Cessante autem vastatione hostili, tantis frugum
copiis insula quantas nulla retro aetas meminit,
affluere coepit : cum quibus et luxuria crescere, et
hanc continuo omnium lues scelerum comitari
adceleravit, crudelitas praecipue, et odium veritatis
amorque mendacii, ita ut siquis eorum mitior, et
veritati aliquatenus propior videretur, in hunc quasi
Brittaniae subversorem, omnium odia telaque sine
respectu contorquerentur. Et non solum haec saecu-
lares viri, sed etiam ipse grex Domini eiusque
pastores egerunt; ebrietati, animositati, litigio, con-
tentioni, invidiae, ceterisque huiusmodi facinoribus
sua colla, abiecto levi iugo Christi, subdentes.
Interea subito corruptae mentis homines acerba
pestis corripuit, quae in brevi tantam eius multitudinem stravit ut ne sepeliendis quidem mortuis vivi
sufficerent : sed ne morte quidem suorum nec timore
mortis, hi qui supererant a morte animae qua peccando

brakes where they lurked, ceased not to make resistance; and by such means then first of all they began to make overthrow of the enemy which many years together had been plundering in the land. Therefore the shameless Irish robbers drew homeward, intending not long after to return; the Redshanks at that time and long time after kept themselves quiet in the farthest part of the island, save only that notwithstanding they ceased not now and then to come forth and plunder and afflict the nation of the Britons.

Now when the pilling of the enemy ceased, there came to be such plentiful store of grain as never was seen the like before in the island, as far as man could remember: whereof the people grew to loose and wanton living, and straight after there hasted to ensue this a plague of all manner of lewdness, specially cruelty, hate of truth and love of lying, insomuch that, if any were gentler and seemed somewhat more given to truth than other, against him all men would hurl the darts of their hate without regard, as one that sought to overthrow Britain. And this did not only the lay folk, but also the very flock of the Lord and the shepherds thereof; casting from them the light yoke of Christ and submitting their necks to drunkenness, highmindedness, variance, strife, envy and all other such wickedness. In the mean season of a sudden a bitter plague seized upon the men of debased mind, consuming in short time such a multitude of people that the quick were not sufficient even to bury the dead: but not even their friends' death, neither the fear of their own, could call the remnant back from the murrain of their soul, which brought

sternebantur, revocari poterant: unde non multo post acrior gentem peccatricem ultio diri sceleris secuta est. Initum namque est consilium quid agendum, ubi quaerendum esset praesidium ad evitandas vel repellendas tam feras tamque creberrimas gentium aquilonalium inruptiones : placuitque omnibus cum suo rege Vurtigerno ut Saxonum gentem de transmarinis partibus in auxilium vocarent: quod Domini nutu dispositum esse constat, ut veniret contra inprobos malum, sicut evidentius rerum exitus probavit.

CAP. XV

Ut invitata Brittaniam gens Anglorum, primo quidem adversarios longius eiecerit ; sed non multo post iuncto cum his foedere, in socios arma verterit.

ANNO ab incarnatione Domini quadringentesimo quadragesimo nono, Marcianus cum Valentiniano quadragesimus sextus ab Augusto regnum adeptus, septem annis tenuit. Tunc Anglorum sive Saxonum gens invitata a rege praefato, in Brittaniam tribus longis navibus advehitur, et in orientali parte insulae iubente eodem rege locum manendi, quasi pro patria pugnatura, re autem vera hanc expugnatura, suscipit. Inito ergo certamine cum hostibus qui ab aquilone ad aciem venerant, victoriam sumpsere Saxones. Quod ubi domi nuntiatum est, simul et

---

[1] King in South Wales it seems, but may have been head of a confederacy; see Oman, *England before the Norman Conquest,* chap. xi.
[2] The coast from Hampshire to the Wash was known in

THE SAXONS

them low through their sinful living: whereby, not
long after, a greater stroke of vengeance for their
abominable iniquity ensued upon the sinful nation.
For they devised with themselves what was best to
do, and where they might seek rescue to escape
or beat off the cruel and continual assaults of the
northern nations; and they agreed all with their
king Vurtigern [1] to call to their aid the nation of the
Saxons beyond the seas: which thing doubtless
was done by God's appointment, that the wicked
people might be thereby plagued, as by the end it
hath right manifestly been shewn.

CHAPTER XV

*How the nation of the English being sent for into Britain
did at first cast out the enemy to a farther distance,
but shortly after joining themselves in league with
them turned their weapons upon their allies.*

THE 449th year of the incarnation of our Lord,
Marcian having with Valentinian obtained the
kingdom, the 46th in succession from Augustus,
held it seven years. In whose time the nation of
the English or Saxons,[2] being sent for of the said
king into Britain, landed there in three long ships,
and by the same king's commandment is appointed
to abide in the east part of the island, as to defend
the country like friends, but indeed, as it proved
afterward, as minded to conquer it as enemies.
Encountering therefore with the enemy who had
come to battle from the north, the Saxons had the
better. Whereof they sending word home, as also

Roman times as the Saxon Shore, and there may well have
been Saxon settlements in Britain before 450.

insulae fertilitas, ac segnitia Brettonum, mittitur
confestim illo classis prolixior armatorum ferens
manum fortiorem, quae praemissae adiuncta cohorti
invincibilem fecit exercitum. Susceperunt ergo qui
advenerunt, donantibus Brittanis, locum habitationis
inter eos, ea conditione ut hi pro patriae pace et
salute contra adversarios militarent, illi militantibus
debita stipendia conferrent. Advenerant autem de
tribus Germaniae populis fortioribus, id est, Saxonibus,
Anglis, Iutis. De Iutarum origine sunt Cantuari et
Victuari, hoc est, ea gens quae Vectam tenet insulam,
et ea quae usque hodie in provincia Occidentalium
Saxonum Iutarum natio nominatur, posita contra
ipsam insulam Vectam. De Saxonibus, id est, ea
regione quae nunc Antiquorum Saxonum cognominatur, venere Orientales Saxones, Meridiani Saxones,
Occidui Saxones. Porro de Anglis, hoc est, de illa
patria quae Angulus dicitur et ab eo tempore usque
hodie manere desertus inter provincias Iutarum
et Saxonum perhibetur, Orientales Angli, Mediterranei Angli, Merci, tota Nordanhymbrorum
progenies, id est, illarum gentium quae ad Boream
Humbri fluminis inhabitant ceterique Anglorum
populi sunt orti. Duces fuisse perhibentur eorum
primi duo fratres Hengist et Horsa; e quibus Horsa
postea occisus in bello a Brettonibus, hactenus in
orientalibus Cantiae partibus monumentum habet
suo nomine insigne. Erant autem filii Victgilsi,

---

[1] Holstein.   [2] Sleswick.

of the batfulness of the island and the cowardice
of the Britons, the Saxons forthwith sent thither
a larger navy with a stronger band of men-at-arms,
which being now joined with the former company,
drew to a stronger army than the Britons were able
to overcome. They then who came were allowed
by the Britons a place to dwell among them, with
that condition that the one should war for the peace
and safety of the country against the enemy, the
other should pay them due wages for their warfare.
Now the strangers had come from three of the more
mighty nations in Germany, that is, the Saxons, the
Angles and the Jutes. Of the Jutes came the people
of Kent and the settlers in Wight, that is the folk
that hold the Isle of Wight, and they which in the
province of the West Saxons are called unto this
day the nation of the Jutes, right over against the
Isle of Wight. Of the Saxons, that is, of that region
which now is called of the Old Saxons,[1] descended
the East Saxons, the South Saxons and the West
Saxons. Further, of the Angles, that is, of that
country which is called Angeln [2] and from that time
to this is said to stand deserted between the provinces
of the Jutes and the Saxons, descendeth the East
Angles, the Uplandish Angles, the Mercians and all
the progeny of the Northumbrians, that is, of that
people that inhabiteth the north side of the flood
Humber, and the other nations of the Angles. The
first captains of the strangers are said to have been
two brothers, Hengist and Horsa; of the which,
Horsa being after slain in battle of the Britons
was buried in the east parts of Kent, where his
tomb bearing his name is yet to shew. And they
were sons of Wictgils, whose father was Witta, whose

cuius pater Vitta, cuius pater Vecta, cuius pater
Voden, de cuius stirpe multarum provinciarum
regium genus originem duxit. Non mora ergo con-
fluentibus certatim in insulam gentium memoratarum
catervis, grandescere populus coepit advenarum, ita
ut ipsi quoque qui eos advocaverant indigenis essent
terrori. Tum subito inito ad tempus foedere cum
Pictis quos longius iam bellando pepulerant, in
socios arma vertere incipiunt. Et primum [1] quidem
annonas sibi eos affluentius ministrare cogunt,
quaerentesque occasionem divortii, protestantur, nisi
profusior sibi alimentorum copia daretur, se cuncta
insulae loca rupto foedere vastaturos. Neque aliquanto
segnius minas effectibus prosequuntur: siquidem, ut
breviter dicam, accensus manibus paganorum ignis,
iustas de sceleribus populi Dei ultiones expetiit,
non illius impar qui quondam a Chaldaeis succensus
Hierosolymorum moenia immo aedificia cuncta con-
sumpsit. Sic enim et hic agente impio victore,
immo disponente iusto Iudice, proximas quasque
civitates agrosque depopulans, ab orientali mari
usque ad occidentale, nullo prohibente, suum con-
tinuavit incendium, totamque prope insulae pereuntis
superficiem obtexit. Ruebant aedificia publica simul
et privata, passim sacerdotes inter altaria trucida-
bantur, praesules cum populis sine ullo respectu honoris
ferro pariter et flammis absumebantur, nec erat qui
crudeliter interemptos sepulturae traderet. Itaque

[1] To end of chapter abridgment of Gildas, §§ 24, 25, except
the reference to the Chaldees.

father was Wecta, whose father was Woden, of
whose issue the royal house of many provinces had
their original. Now then great companies of the
said nations flocking emulously into the island, the
stranger folk began to wax so great that the natives of
the country who had called them in stood themselves
also in great fear of their puissance. Then suddenly
taking league for a season with the Redshanks,
whom they had by now driven farther off by fighting,
the strangers began to turn their force upon their
allies. And the first thing they did require of them
to furnish more plenty of victuals, and picking
matter of falling out with them threateneth them
that, except more abundant store of provision be
given them, they would break off with them and
spoil all parts of the island. And they were in no
manner more backward in carrying out their threats
in deed than in making them: insomuch as, to be
short, the fire once kindled in the hands of the
pagans took God's just revenge of the wickedness
of the people, not much unlike unto that fire which
sometime kindled of the Chaldees, consumed the
walls, nay rather all the buildings of Jerusalem. For
so also this fire (the wicked conqueror handling it,
or rather the righteous Judge disposing it), raging
first upon all the cities and country next unto it,
after (from the east sea unto the west, without any
resistance made to quench it), carried on the destruction and overwhelmed almost the whole face of the
perishing island. Both public and private houses
fell to the ground, the priests far and wide were
slain standing at the altar, the bishops with their
flock were cut off by sword as well as by fire without
respect of their dignity, nor was there any that

73

nonnulli de miserandis reliquiis in montibus compre-
hensi acervatim iugulabantur: alii fame confecti
procedentes manus hostibus dabant, pro accipiendis
alimentorum subsidiis aeternum subituri servitium,
si tamen non continuo trucidarentur: alii transmarinas regiones dolentes petebant: alii perstantes
in patria trepidi pauperem vitam in montibus, silvis,
vel rupibus arduis suspecta semper mente agebant.

CAP. XVI [1]

*Ut Brettones primam de gente Anglorum victoriam, duce
Ambrosio Romano homine, sumpserint.*

AT ubi hostilis exercitus, exterminatis dispersisque
insulae indigenis, domum reversus est, coeperunt et
illi paulatim vires animosque resumere, emergentes
de latibulis quibus abditi fuerant, et unanimo consensu auxilium caeleste precantes ne usque ad
internecionem usquequaque delerentur. Utebantur
eo tempore duce Ambrosio Aureliano viro modesto,
qui solus forte Romanae gentis praefatae tempestati
superfuerat, occisis in eadem parentibus regium
nomen et insigne ferentibus. Hoc ergo duce vires
capessunt Brettones, et victores provocantes ad
proelium, victoriam ipsi, Deo favente, suscipiunt.
Et ex eo tempore nunc cives, nunc hostes vincebant,
usque ad annum obsessionis Badonici montis, quando

---

[1] Abridgment of Gildas, § 25.

[1] To Thanet apparently.

would give burial to them that had been cruelly slain. And so some of the miserable leavings being taken in the hills were there killed in heaps: other being starved with hunger were fain to come forth and submit themselves to the enemy, as minded to buy the sustenance of victual with sale of their liberties for ever, if yet they were not killed out of hand: other in sorrow made for lands oversea: other tarrying still in their country in fear of death passed their life in want in the mountains, woods and high cliffs with minds ever in apprehension of evil.

CHAPTER XVI

How the Britons obtained the first victory of the nation of the English, with Ambrose a Roman for their captain.

But when the army of the enemy, having now driven out and disparkled the land-dwellers, were come back again,[1] the Britons also by little and little began to recover unto them strength and courage, coming out of the lurking-places in which they lay hid before, and with one uniform consent calling for heavenly help that they might not for ever utterly be destroyed. They had then for their captain Ambrosius Aurelianus, a gentle-natured man, which only of the Roman people chanced then to remain alive from the aforenamed calamity, his parents being slain in the same, which bore the name and token of kings. This man therefore being their captain, the Britons put on strength, and provoking the victors to the fight, through God's assistance themselves achieved the victory. And from that day forward, now the men of the country,

non minimas eisdem hostibus strages dabant, quadragesimo circiter et quarto anno adventus eorum in Brittaniam. Sed haec postmodum.

CAP. XVII[1]

Ut Germanus episcopus cum Lupo Brittaniam navigans, et primo maris, et postmodum Pelagianorum tempestatem divina virtute sedaverit.

ANTE paucos sane adventus eorum annos haeresis Pelagiana per Agricolam inlata, Severiani Episcopi Pelagiani filium, fidem Brittaniarum foeda peste commaculaverat. Verum Brittani cum neque suscipere dogma perversum gratiam Christi blasphemando ullatenus vellent, neque versutiam nefariae persuasionis refutare verbis certando sufficerent; inveniunt salubre consilium, ut a Gallicanis antistitibus auxilium belli spiritalis inquirant. Quam ob causam collecta magna synodo quaerebatur in commune, qui illic ad succurrendum fidei mitti deberent: atque omnium iudicio electi sunt apostolici sacerdotes Germanus Autissidorensis, et Lupus Trecasenae civitatis episcopi, qui ad confirmandam fidem gratiae caelestis Brittanias venirent. Qui cum prompta devotione preces et iussa sanctae ecclesiae suscepissent, intrant oceanum, et usque ad medium itineris quo a Gallico sinu Brittanias usque tenditur, secundis

---

[1] Chapters XVII–XXI are taken with few alterations from *Vita S. Germani* by Constantius, written towards the end of the fifth century.

---

[1] The date of the battle is matter of much controversy. It was fought in the West Country, but the place is not certain.

now the enemy had the victory, until the year that
Mount Badon[1] was besieged, where they gave the
same enemy a great overthrow, which was about the
four-and-fortieth year of their coming into Britain.
But of this we shall speak more hereafter.

CHAPTER XVII

*How Germanus the bishop, sailing with Lupus into
Britain, ceased both first the tempest of the sea and,
after, the tempest of the Pelagians by the power of
God.*

A few years[2] in deed before the coming of the
strangers, the Pelagian heresy being brought in by
Agricola, the son of Severian, a Pelagian bishop,
had stained the faith of the provinces of Britain
with that vile pestilence. But the Britons, being
nowise willing either to receive their lewd doctrine
by blaspheming the grace of Christ, neither able
by controversy to refute their wily and wicked
persuasions, they devised this wholesome counsel,
to seek for aid of the bishops of Gaul in their spiritual
warfare. And so these calling a great council
consulted together among themselves, whom of them
to send to Britain to help the faith: and by the assent
of them all there were chosen two apostolic priests,
Germanus bishop of Auxerre and Lupus bishop of
the town of Troyes, which should pass over into
Britain to confirm the faith of heavenly grace.
Which, with ready obedience accepting the commands in answer to the prayers of the holy Church,
set sail on the ocean, and until they were half-way
over the passage from the shore of Gaul to Britain

[2] About 429.

flatibus navis tuta volabat. Tum subito occurrit pergentibus inimica vis daemonum, qui tantos talesque viros ad recuperandam tendere populorum salutem inviderent: concitant procellas, caelum diemque nubium nocte subducunt; ventorum furores vela non sustinent; cedebant ministeria victa nautarum; ferebatur navigium oratione, non viribus: et casu dux ipse vel pontifex fractus corpore, lassitudine ac sopore resolutus est. Tum vero quasi repugnatore cessante, tempestas excitata convaluit, et iam navigium superfusis fluctibus mergebatur. Tum beatus Lupus omnesque turbati excitant seniorem elementis furentibus opponendum; qui periculi inmanitate constantior Christum invocat, et adsumpto in nomine sanctae Trinitatis levi aquae spargine fluctus saevientes opprimit, collegam commonet, hortatur universos, oratio uno ore et clamore profunditur: adest divinitas, fugantur inimici, tranquillitas serena subsequitur, venti e contrario ad itineris ministeria revertuntur, decursisque brevi spatiis pelagi, optati littoris quiete potiuntur. Ibi conveniens ex diversis partibus multitudo excepit sacerdotes, quos venturos etiam vaticinatio adversa praedixerat. Nuntiabant enim sinistri spiritus quod

the ship speeded safe before prosperous winds.
Then suddenly, as they were sailing, the might of
evil spirits cometh to withstand them, much envying
that men of such worth and power should go to
recover the salvation of the people: they raiseth
tempests, they take away the day from heaven with
a night of clouds; the sails are not able to bear the
boisterous fury of the winds; the mariners in despair
gave over their office; the ship was guided by
prayer rather than by power of men; and their
captain and bishop Germanus himself, his strength
being spent, had chanced to fall asleep through
weariness. Thereupon, as though none was left to
withstand it, the might of the storm grew greater,
and the ship was now like to sink beneath the waves
that poured over it. Then blessed Lupus and the
other in their trouble wakeneth and calleth upon
their elder that he might withstand the fury of the
elements; who, made more resolute by the fear-
fulness of the tempest, calleth upon Christ and,
taking in the name of the Holy Trinity a few sprinkles
of water, he breaketh the raging of the waves,
cheereth his fellow, encourageth all, and prayer is
poured forth with one mouth and voice: God
deferreth not His help, their foes are chased away, a
clear calm ensueth, the winds which were against
them returneth to forward their voyage, and running
over the face of the sea they shortly after are peace-
fully set aland in the coast where they desired.
There a great multitude coming together from
sundry parts received the bishops, of whose coming
too the enemies which resisted them gave warning
before they landed. For the evil spirits proclaimed
their fear, which afterward, when they were expelled,

timebant, qui imperio sacerdotum dum ab obsessis
corporibus detruduntur, et tempestatis ordinem et
pericula quae intulerant fatebantur, victosque se
eorum meritis et imperio non negabant.

Interea Brittaniarum insulam apostolici sacerdotes
raptim opinione, praedicatione, virtutibus impleve-
runt : divinusque per eos sermo quotidie non solum in
ecclesiis, verum etiam per trivia, per rura praedicabatur ; ita ut passim et fideles catholici firmarentur,
et depravati viam correctionis agnoscerent. Erat
illis apostolorum instar, et gloria et auctoritas per
conscientiam, doctrina per literas, virtutes ex
meritis. Itaque regionis universitas in eorum sententiam prompta transierat. Latebant abditi sinistrae
persuasionis auctores, et more maligni spiritus,
gemebant perire sibi populos evadentes, ad extremum
diuturna meditatione concepta praesumunt inire
conflictum. Procedunt conspicui divitiis, veste ful-
gentes, circumdati adsentatione multorum : dis-
crimenque certaminis subire maluerunt, quam in
populo quem subverterant pudorem taciturnitatis
incurrere, ne viderentur se ipsi silentio damnavisse.
Illic plane inmensa multitudo, etiam cum coniugibus
ac liberis excita convenerat, aderat populus expecta-

by commandment of the bishops, out of the bodies
of them that were possessed, declared both the
ordering of the tempest which they had raised, and
the danger which they had brought the bishops, and
did not deny that they were overcome by their
merits and commandment.

Meanwhile the apostolic priests in short time
after their arrival filled the island of the Britains
with their good name, their preaching and their
powers; and the word of God was through them
daily preached not only in the churches but through
the open streets and through the fields; in such
sort that in all places both the faithful Catholics were
confirmed, and they that before swerved out of the
right way were amended. Like the apostles they
had both honour and authority by reason of a good
conscience, learning given by letters, and powers the
fruit of good desert. And so in short time the whole
country had readily come over to their opinion.
The authors of the perverse teaching lay lurking in
hiding, and, like the evil spirit much spited that the
people making a way to escape were lost to them,
and at length after long advisement used they taketh
upon them to try the matter by open disputation.
They came forth richly appointed, gorgeously
apparelled, accompanied by a number of flattering
favourers, choosing rather to commit their cause to
the hazard of open contention, than fall into the
shame of speechlessness, for fear that in the eyes
of the people, whom they had subverted, they should
seem to have given sentence against themselves
by their own silence. Thither had assembled a
truly great concourse of men stirred up to come
with their wives and children as well; the people

tor, et futurus iudex, adstabant partes dispari
conditione dissimiles; hinc divina fides, inde humana
praesumptio; hinc pietas, inde superbia; inde Pelagius
auctor, hinc Christus. Primo in loco beatissimi
sacerdotes praebuerunt adversariis copiam disputandi,
quae sola nuditate verborum, diu inaniter et aures
occupavit et tempora: deinde antistites venerandi,
torrentes eloquii sui cum apostolicis et evangelicis
imbribus profuderunt: miscebatur sermo proprius
cum divino, et adsertiones molestissimas lectionum
testimonia sequebantur: convincitur vanitas, perfidia
confutatur; ita ut ad singulas verborum obiectiones
errare se, dum respondere nequiit, fateretur: populus
arbiter vix manus continet, iudicium tamen clamore
testatur.

CAP. XVIII

*Ut idem filiam tribuni caecam inluminaverit, ac deinde ad
sanctum Albanum perveniens, reliquias ibidem et
ipsius acceperit, et beatorum apostolorum, sive
aliorum martyrum posuerit.*

Tum subito quidam tribunitiae potestatis cum
coniuge procedit in medium, filiam decem annorum
caecam curandam sacerdotibus offerens, quam illi
adversariis offerri praeceperunt: sed hi conscientia

was there to see and to judge: the parties there
were far unlike of condition: on the one side was
divine faith, on the other man's presumption: on
the one side godliness, on the other pride: on the
one side Pelagius for authority, on the other Christ.
First of all the blessed bishops gave their adversaries
leave to speak, which for long time vainly occupied
both the time and ears of the people with nought
but naked words: after, the venerable bishops poured
out the streams of their own eloquence with speech
of apostles and evangelists like showers of rain:
they joined with their own words the words of God,
and after the grievous assault of their own declara-
tions they read the witness of others upon the same:
the vanity of heretics is convicted, unbelief is confuted; so that at every objection they were forced
to confess their error, not being able to answer them:
the people that was umpire had much to do to keep
their hands from them, yet shewed their judgment
by their shouting.

CHAPTER XVIII

*How the same Germanus restored the blind daughter of
the tribune to her sight, and after, coming to Saint
Alban's shrine, did in that same place both take
the relics of the saint himself and set there relics
of the blessed apostles and other martyrs.*

THIS done, suddenly a certain man of the dignity
of the tribunes cometh forth amongst them with his
wife, offering his daughter of ten years old, which
was blind, to be cured by the bishops. They bid
him have her to the adversaries; but these made
fearful by pricking of their conscience, joyneth their

83

puniente deterriti, iungunt cum parentibus preces, et
curationem parvulae a sacerdotibus deprecantur: qui
inclinatos animo adversarios intuentes, orationem
breviter fundunt: ac deinde Germanus plenus
Spiritu sancto, invocat Trinitatem; nec mora,
adhaerentem lateri suo capsulam cum sanctorum reliquiis collo avulsam manibus comprehendit, eamque
in conspectu omnium puellae oculis adplicavit, quos
statim evacuatos tenebris lumen veritatis implevit.
Exultant parentes, miraculum populus contremiscit:
post quam diem ita ex animis omnium suasio iniqua
deleta est, ut sacerdotum doctrinam sitientibus
desideriis sectarentur.

Compressa itaque perversitate damnabili, eiusque
auctoribus confutatis, atque animis omnium fidei
puritate compositis, sacerdotes beatum Albanum
martyrem, acturi Deo per ipsum gratias, petierunt,
ubi Germanus omnium apostolorum, diversorumque
martyrum secum reliquias habens, facta oratione
iussit revelli sepulcrum, pretiosa ibidem munera
conditurus; arbitrans opportunum, ut membra
sanctorum ex diversis regionibus collecta, quos pares
meritis receperat caelum, sepulcri quoque unius
teneret hospitium. Quibus depositis honorifice,
atque sociatis, de loco ipso, ubi beati martyris effusus
erat sanguis, massam pulveris secum portaturus
abstulit, in qua apparebat, cruore servato, rubuisse
martyrum aedem[1] persecutore pallente. Quibus

---

[1] For *caedem*, Pl.

---

[1] *i.e.* budget, a bag usually of leather.
[2] The dust of the martyr still keeps the red of life (for the
blood is the life, Lev. 17. 14) while the persecutor is pale in
death.

prayers together with the parents and desireth the bishops to do their cure upon the girl: which, seeing their adversaries to yield, in short while pour forth prayer; and after Germanus, full of the Holy Ghost, calleth upon the Trinity; and straight teareth from his neck a little bugget [1] which he had by his side full of the relics of saints, and seizing it in his hands in the sight of them all putteth it to the eyes of the maiden, which straight were emptied of darkness and filled with the light of truth. The parents much joy thereat, the people are all amazed at the sight of the miracle; and after that day the perverse doctrine was so pulled out of the minds of all that with thirsty longing they embraced the teaching of the bishops.

Thus the damnable heresy being suppressed and the authors thereof utterly confuted and all men's minds quieted with the purity of the faith, the bishops went unto the blessed martyr Alban's tomb, to give thanks to God by the saint, and there Germanus having with him relics of all the apostles and of divers martyrs, making his prayer ordered the tomb to be opened, intending to leave in that same place those precious treasures; thinking good that the members of the saints gotten in divers countries should have the shelter of one tomb, as, being like of merits, they had been all received into heaven. Which being left there with much honour and mingled together, he took a clot of dust from the very spot where the blessed martyr's blood had been shed, to carry away with him, wherein it was made clear by the abiding of the blood that the sanctuary of the martyrs had remained ruddy while the persecutor waxed pale.[2] Which things being

ita gestis, innumera hominum eodem die ad Dominum turba conversa est.

CAP. XIX

Ut idem causa infirmitatis ibidem detentus, et incendia domorum orando restinxerit ; et ipse per visionem a suo sit languore curatus.

UNDE dum redeunt, insidiator inimicus casualibus laqueis praeparatis, Germani pedem lapsus occasione contrivit, ignorans merita illius, sicut Job beatissimi, afflictione corporis propaganda: et dum aliquandiu uno in loco infirmitatis necessitate teneretur, in vicina qua manebat casula exarsit incendium: quod consumptis domibus quae illic palustri harundine tegebantur, ad eum habitaculum in quo idem iacebat, flabris stimulantibus ferebatur. Concursus omnium ad antistitem convolavit, ut elatus manibus periculum quod imminebat evaderet: quibus increpatis, moveri se fidei praesumptione non passus est. At multitudo omnis desperatione perterrita, obviam currit incendio. Sed ut Dei potentia manifestior appareret, quidquid custodire tentaverat turba, consumitur; quod vero iacens et infirmus defenderat, reserato hospitio sancti viri, expavescens flamma transilivit, ultra

thus disposed a very great multitude of people was that same day converted to the Lord.

CHAPTER XIX

How the same being driven by sickness to remain in that place, did both quench a great fire among the houses with his prayers, and was by a vision himself healed of his infirmity.

As they were coming back thence, the crafty enemy, by the procurement of snares that fell in the way, bruised the foot of Germanus by means of a fall he had. Little knew the devil that by the affliction of the body (as it was in blessed Job) the merits of the holy man should be thereby the more increased; and whiles for the time by the reason of his weakness he was forced to tarry still in one place, the next hut to that he lodged in was set on fire, so that, after it had consumed the houses about, that were there thatched with reed, it was now being carried through the blowing of the wind to that lodging wherein this good man was lying. All came running in great haste to the bishop, willing to carry him in their arms out of the danger that threatened: whom he rebuking, through confidence in his faith, would not be removed out of the place he was in. Yet the crowd all frighted with fear and despair came running to quench the fire. But that the power of God might appear the plainer, the fire still consumed whatsoever the people sought to save; but what the sick man lying in his bed did defend, that the fire skipped, as being afraid of the holy man's refuge that lay open to it; and both above and beneath fiercely burned without stay,

citraque desaeviens, et inter globos flammantis
incendii, incolume tabernaculum quod habitator
inclusus servabat, emicuit. Exultat turba miraculo,
et victam se divinis virtutibus gratulatur. Excu-
babat diebus ac noctibus ante tugurium pauperis
vulgus sine numero; hi animas curare cupientes, hi
corpora. Referri nequeunt quae Christus operabatur
in famulo, qui virtutes faciebat infirmus: et cum
debilitati suae nihil remedii pateretur adhiberi,
quadam nocte candentem niveis vestibus vidit sibi
adesse personam, quae manu extensa iacentem
videretur adtollere, eumque consistere firmis vestigiis imperabat: post quam horam ita fugatis doloribus
recepit pristinam sanitatem, ut die reddito itineris
laborem subiret intrepidus.

CAP. XX

*Ut iidem episcopi Brettonibus in pugna auxilium caeleste
tulerint, sicque domum reversi sint.*

Interea Saxones Pictique bellum adversum Brettones iunctis viribus susceperunt, quos eadem
necessitas in castra contraxerat: et cum trepidi
partes suas pene inpares judicarent, sanctorum
antistitum auxilium petierunt: qui promissum
maturantes adventum, tantum paventibus fiduciae
contulerunt, ut accessisse maximus crederetur exerci-
88

so that in the middle of the flakes and flames of the fire the lodging, that the imprisoned dweller kept, shone forth sound and untouched. The people much joyed at the miracle, and rejoiced in God to see His power to save that their labour could not. Before the cottage lay there watching day and night a multitude of people of the poorer sort without number, some to be cured of the maladies of their souls, some of their bodies. The works cannot be told which Christ wrought in His servant who did cures when he was sick: and in the mean, suffering no remedies to be applied unto his own infirmities, on a certain night he saw a person clad all in shining white apparel to stand by his bedside, which stretching out his hand seemed to lift him up as he lay in his bed and bid him stand upright upon his feet: after which time his pains being assuaged, he was so restored unto his former health, that as soon as it was day, he underwent the toil of travel without fear.

CHAPTER XX

How the said bishops by the power of God aided the Britons in battle, and so returned home.

In this meantime the Saxons and Redshanks waged war with united forces against the Britons, which had been assembled together in camp by the same need of making face against them; and through fear judging that they on their side should fall short of proving a match for them, they required the help of the holy bishops: which hastening their promised coming put their fearful hearts in such confidence, as though a great army had been come at that instant

tus. Itaque apostolicis ducibus Christus militabat in castris. Aderant etiam quadragesimae venerabiles dies, quos religiosiores reddebat praesentia sacerdotum, in tantum ut cotidianis praedicationibus instituti certatim populi ad gratiam baptismatis convolarent. Nam maxima exercitus multitudo undam lavacri salutaris expetiit, et ecclesia ad diem resurrectionis Dominicae frondibus contexta componitur, atque in expeditione campestri instar civitatis aptatur. Madidus baptismate procedit exercitus, fides fervet in populo, et conterrito armorum praesidio, divinitatis expectatur auxilium. Institutio vel forma castitatis hostibus nuntiatur, qui victoriam quasi de inermi exercitu presumentes, adsumpta alacritate festinant; quorum tamen adventus exploratione cognoscitur. Cumque emensa sollemnitate paschali, recens de lavacro pars major exercitus arma capere, et bellum parare tentaret, Germanus ducem se praelii profitetur, eligit expeditos, circumiecta percurrit, et e regione qua hostium sperabatur adventus, vallem circumdatam mediis [1] montibus intuetur. Quo in loco novum componit exercitum, ipse dux agminis. Et iam aderat ferox hostium multitudo, quam adpropinquare intuebantur in insidiis constituti. Tum

[1] In Constantius *editis*, which gives a better sense.

[1] Before he was bishop, Germanus had been duke of Aquitania, and a soldier.
[2] With reference to the baptism.

to aid them. And so, they being their apostolic captains, Christ warred with them in their camp. This also happened in the forty days of solemn season, which were the more devoutly observed through the presence of the bishops, insomuch that being instructed with daily preaching the people eagerly flocked to receive the grace of baptism. For the greatest part of the army required the water of the health-giving laver, and against the day of the Lord's resurrection they made the likeness of a church framed of leafy boughs, and so prepared it for an army in the field as it had been in a city. Moistened with the water of baptism the army marcheth forth, the people becometh fervent in faith and bold in the hope of God's help, which before were in despair of their own arms. The enemy had word of the manner and form of their pure living, whereupon they thinking easily to obtain the victory over them as over an army that were unarmed, maketh all the haste they could towards them; but yet by scouts their coming is known in good time. And now the holy days of Easter being past, the greater part of the host goeth fresh from baptism to their armour and to make ready for war. Among them Germanus,[1] declaring himself as captain in the battle, picketh a certain number of light soldiers, overrunneth the surrounding country and, on the side by which it was thought the enemy would pass, observeth a valley beset with hills on every side. In the which place he posteth the army now made new,[2] with himself as leader of the march. And shortly after cometh on the proud host of the enemy, which when they that were set in the ambush perceived to approach, Germanus

subito Germanus signifer universos admonet, et praedicat ut voci suae uno clamore respondeant; securisque hostibus qui se insperatos adesse confiderent, *Alleluiam* tertio repetitam sacerdotes exclamant. Sequitur una vox omnium, et elatum clamorem repercusso aere montium conclusa multiplicant: hostile agmen terrore prosternitur, ut super se non solum rupes circumdatas, sed etiam ipsam caeli machinam contremiscunt, trepidationique iniectae vix sufficere pedum pernicitas credebatur: passim fugiunt, arma proiiciunt, gaudentes vel nuda corpora eripuisse discrimini: plures etiam timore praecipites, flumen quod transierant devoravit. Ultionem suam innocens exercitus intuetur, et victoriae concessae otiosus spectator efficitur. Spolia colliguntur exposita, et caelestis palmae gaudia miles religiosus amplectitur. Triumphant pontifices hostibus fusis sine sanguine, triumphant victoria fide obtenta, non viribus.

Composita itaque insula securitate multiplici, superatisque hostibus vel invisibilibus vel carne conspicuis, reditum moliuntur pontifices. Quibus tranquillam navigationem, et merita propria et

---

1 Welsh tradition places the battle near Mold in Flintshire, but how should Picts and Saxons be so far west ?

bearing the standard suddenly giveth warning unto them all and proclaimeth that as they heard him begin, all they should cry and answer the same; and the enemy being heedless, as having assurance that their coming was unlooked for, the priests cried out thrice together "Alleluia." All the rest straight answereth the same, and the sound of their voices is caught up and often repeated by the echo rebounding from the mountains wherewith it was shut in: the host of the enemy is cast down with fear as they tremble, not only at the rocks that encompassed them, but also the very frame of the heaven above them, and believed that the speed of their feet could scarce avail them to escape the terror that was flung upon them: they fly in all directions, casting away their weapons and thinking it enough if they might with even their naked bodies snatch themselves from the danger: the more part also in the hurry of their fear were swallowed up in the river which lay between them and home.[1] The army that did them no hurt beholdeth the revenge of their enemies, and seeth themselves made to look upon a victory that had been granted to them without deed of theirs. The spoils are collected and set out to be seen, and the soldiers devoutly acknowlegeth with joy the glory that was due to heaven. The bishops triumpheth to see the enemy put to flight without bloodshed, and the victory to have been gotten by faith and not by might of man.

Thus the island being set in safety in manifold measure, the enemies whether invisible or visible in the flesh being overcome, the bishops set about their return homeward. To whom calm passage is granted, both for their own virtues' sake and also

intercessio beati martyris Albani paraverunt, quietosque eos suorum desideriis felix carina restituit.

CAP. XXI

Ut renascentibus virgultis Pelagianae pestis Germanus cum Severo Brittaniam reversus, prius claudo iuveni incessum, deinde et populo Dei, condemnatis sive emendatis haereticis, gressum recuperarit fidei.

Nec multo interposito tempore, nuntiatur ex eadem insula, Pelagianam perversitatem iterato paucis auctoribus dilatari : rursusque ad beatissimum virum preces sacerdotum omnium deferuntur, ut causam Dei, quam prius obtinuerat, tutaretur. Quorum petitioni festinus obtemperat. Namque adiuncto sibi Severo totius sanctitatis viro, qui erat discipulus beatissimi patris Lupi Trecasenorum episcopi, et tunc Treviris ordinatus episcopus gentibus primae Germaniae verbum praedicabat, mare conscendit, et consentientibus elementis tranquillo navigio Brittanias petiit.

Interea sinistri spiritus pervolantes totam insulam, Germanum venire invitis vaticinationibus nuntiabant ; in tantum ut Elafius quidam regionis illius primus,[1] in occursu sanctorum sine ulla manifesti nuntii relatione properaret, exhibens secum filium quem in

---

[1] *Ut* after *primus* omitted, Pl.

---

[1] *i.e. superioris*, west of the Rhine.

at the intercession of the blessed martyr Alban, and the happy vessel restored them in peace to their own people that longed after them.

CHAPTER XXI

How, the slips of the Pelagian pestilence shooting forth again, Germanus returning to Britain with Severus first restored to a lame young man the power of walking, then also, condemning or correcting the heretics, restored the steps of the faith to the people of God.

AND not long after, there was word brought out of the same island, that the Pelagian frowardness began of new to grow and multiply by means of certain few that were helpers thereof: and again are directed to the blessed man the prayers of all the clergy that he would maintain the cause of God which he had taken in hand before. Whose petition he quickly accepteth. For joyning to himself Severus, a man of all holiness (as the which was the disciple of the blessed father Lupus, bishop of Troyes, and at that time was ordained bishop of the Treveri and preached the word to the Upper[1] Germany), he took ship and with the help of the elements maketh for the coasts of Britain with prosperous voyage.

In this mean season, the evil spirits fleeing about the island did foreshew everywhere by constrained prophecies that Germanus was coming; insomuch that Elafius, one of the chief of that country, without the report of any manifest messenger, hastened to meet the holy men at their arrival, bringing with him his son, which in the very flower of his youth

95

ipso flore adolescentiae debilitas dolenda damnaverat.
Erat enim arescentibus nervis contracto poplite, cui
per siccitatem cruris usus vestigii negabatur. Hunc
Elafium provincia tota subsequitur: veniunt sacerdotes, occurrit inscia multitudo, confestim benedictio,
et sermonis divini doctrina profunditur. Recog-
noscunt populum in ea qua reliquerat credulitate
durantem: intelligunt culpam esse paucorum,
inquirunt auctores, inventosque condemnant. Cum
subito Elafius pedibus advolvitur sacerdotum, offerens
filium, cuius necessitatem ipsa debilitas etiam sine
precibus adlegabat: fit communis omnium dolor,
praecipue sacerdotum, qui conceptam misericordiam
ad divinam clementiam contulerunt: statimque
adolescentem beatus Germanus sedere compulit,
adtrectat poplitem debilitate curvatum, et per tota
infirmitatis spatia medicabilis dextera percurrit, salu-
bremque tactum sanitas festina subsequitur. Ariditas
succum, nervi officia receperunt, et in conspectu
omnium filio incolumitas, patri filius restituitur.
Implentur populi stupore miraculi, et in pectoribus
omnium fides catholica inculcata firmatur. Praedicatio deinde ad plebem de praevaricationis emendatione convertitur, omniumque sententia pravitatis
auctores, qui erant expulsi insula, sacerdotibus
96

was under judgment of grievous infirmity. **For**
through the dryth of his sinews the hollow of the
knee was so shrunk, that by the numbing of his
leg he could not set foot upon the ground. Close
after this Elafius cometh the whole province: the
bishops arrive, the ignorant folk meet them, forthwith blessing is given and the doctrine of godly
discourse poured out. They find the people as
touching their faith in the selfsame stay as they
left them: they learneth the fault to remain in a
few, after whom they seek and finding them out
they condemn them. This done, upon a sudden
Elafius falleth down at the feet of the bishops,
offering them his son, whose pitiful case of itself
alone needed no prayers to intreat for the relief
thereof: every man of himself pitied the young
man, especially the bishops, who altogether (according to the pity they felt) beseeched the clemency
of God; and forthwith blessed Germanus made the
young man sit down, he feeleth the knee bowed
inward by the infirmity, and with his curing right
hand runneth over all the affected place as far as
the grief went, and each part as soon as it felt his
healing touch quickly became sound. Dryth returned to moisture, the sinews to their natural
course, and in the sight of all health is restored to the
son, the son to his father. The people are filled
with astonishment at the sight of the miracle, and
in all their hearts is the catholic faith confirmed and
strengthened. After that he turneth to preach to
the people of the redress of the abandonment of
faith, and by the assent of them all the first authors
of corruption, who had been banished the land, are
delivered unto the bishops to be conveyed to parts

adducuntur ad mediterranea deferendi, ut et regio absolutione et illi emendatione fruerentur. Factumque est ut in illis locis multo ex eo tempore fides intemerata perduraret.

Itaque compositis omnibus beati sacerdotes ea qua venerant prosperitate redierunt. Porro Germanus post haec ad Ravennam pro pace Armoricanae gentis supplicaturus advenit, ibique a Valentiniano, et Placidia matre ipsius summa reverentia susceptus, migravit ad Christum. Cuius corpus honorifico agmine comitantibus virtutum operibus, suam defertur ad urbem. Nec multo post Valentinianus ab Aetii patricii quem occiderat satellitibus interimitur, anno imperii Marciani sexto, cum quo simul hesperium concidit regnum.

CAP. XXII

Ut Brettones quiescentibus ad tempus exteris, civilibus sese bellis contriverint simul et maioribus flagitiis submerserint.

INTEREA [1] Brittania cessatum quidem est parumper ab externis, sed non a civilibus bellis. Manebant exterminia civitatum ab hoste dirutarum ac desertarum, pugnabant contra invicem qui hostem evaserant cives. Attamen recente adhuc memoria calamitatis et cladis inflictae servabant utcumque reges, sacerdotes, privati, et optimates suum quique ordinem. At illis decedentibus, cum successisset aetas tem-

---

[1] To *appareret* from Gildas, § 26.

---

[1] Who had revolted.   [2] A.D. 455.

removed from the sea, that both the country might
be rid of them and they have the fruit of correction.
Whereby it came to pass that in those parts the
faith long after remained undefiled.

And all things thus ordered the blessed bishops
returned with like good speed as they came. Furthermore, Germanus went after this to Ravenna to treat
for peace for the people of the Armoricans,[1] and
there with great reverence being received of Valentinian and Placidia his mother he departed unto
Christ. Whose corpse with an honourable company was conveyed to his city, not without the
effectual working of his virtues by the way. And
not long after Valentinian is killed [2] of the soldiers
of Aetius the patrician whom he had slain, in the
sixth year of Marcian's reign, and with him the
West Empire decayed and came to ruin.

CHAPTER XXII

*How the Britons, being free for a time from all foreign
wars, wore themselves away with civil wars and
therewithal were plunged into greater mischiefs.*

IN the meantime there came for a season an end
of foreign wars in Britain, but not of war within
themselves. The ruins remained of the cities which
the enemy had destroyed and left wasted, and the
citizens which had escaped the hands of the enemies
were now fighting against their own fellows. But
yet having still as fresh in mind the late calamities
and slaughters they had sustained, their kings,
priests, peers and subjects in some sort observed
each of them his several rank. But after their
death the generation that followed, little knowing

pestatis illius nescia, et praesentis solum serenitatis statum experta, ita cuncta veritatis ac justitiae moderamina concussa ac subversa sunt, ut earum non dicam vestigium, sed ne memoria quidem, praeter in paucis, et valde paucis ulla appareret. Qui inter alia inenarrabilium scelerum facta, quae historicus eorum Gildus[1] flebili sermone describit, et hoc addebant, ut numquam genti Saxonum sive Anglorum secum Brittaniam incolenti, verbum fidei praedicando committerent. Sed non tamen divina pietas plebem suam, quam praescivit, deseruit, quin multo digniores genti memoratae praecones veritatis, per quos crederet, destinavit.

CAP. XXIII

Ut sanctus papa Gregorius Augustinum cum monachis ad praedicandum genti Anglorum mittens, epistola quoque illos exhortatoria ne a laborando cessarent, confortaverit.[2]

Siquidem anno ab incarnatione Domini quingentesimo octogesimo secundo, Mauricius ab Augusto quinquagesimus quartus imperium suscipiens, viginti et uno annis tenuit. Cuius anno regni decimo Gregorius, vir doctrina et actione praecipuus, pontificatum Romanae et apostolicae sedis sortitus rexit annos tredecim menses sex et dies decem; qui divino admonitus instinctu anno decimo quarto

---

[1] More commonly Gildas.
[2] With the coming of Augustine the introductory matter

the storms past in their fathers' days, and having only experience of that peaceful estate in the which they then lived, were so set to shake and overthrow all good orders of truth and justice that, I do not say no token, but not even any remembrance thereof remained, save only in few, and that in very few. Among other of their evil deeds not to be spoke of, which their historiographer Gildus [1] doth lamentably set forth in writing, this also is added, that they never took care to preach the word of faith to the folk of the Saxons or English which inhabited the land along with them. But yet the goodness of God did not so forsake His people which He foreknew to be saved, but provided for the said folk much more worthy heralds of the truth, by whom they might be brought unto His faith.

CHAPTER XXIII [2]

How the holy pope Gregory, sending Augustine with monks to preach to the folk of the English, also with a letter of exhortation encouraged them not to rest from their labour.

SEEING that [3] in the 582nd year of the Lord's incarnation, Maurice the 54th in succession after Augustus, became emperor and reigned 21 years. The 10th year of whose reign Gregory, being a man foremost in learning and business, was chosen bishop of the Roman and Apostolic See, which he governed 13 years, 6 months and 10 days; which the 14th year of the reign of the said emperor, but about the 150th

comes to an end and the proper subject of the work begins.
  [2] Connecting with chapter before.

eiusdem principis, adventus vero Anglorum in
Brittaniam anno circiter centesimo quinquagesimo,
misit servum Dei Augustinum, et alios plures cum
eo monachos timentes Dominum, praedicare verbum
Dei genti Anglorum. Qui cum iussis pontificalibus
obtemperantes, memoratum opus adgredi coepissent,
iamque aliquantulum itineris confecissent, perculsi
timore inerti, redire domum potius, quam barbaram,
feram, incredulamque gentem, cuius ne linguam
quidem nossent, adire cogitabant, et hoc esse tutius
communi consilio decernebant. Nec mora, Augustinum, quem eis episcopum ordinandum si ab Anglis
susciperentur disposuerat, domum remittunt, qui
a beato Gregorio humili supplicatu obtineret ne tam
periculosam, tam laboriosam, tam incertam pere-
grinationem adire deberent. Quibus ille exhortatorias mittens litteras, in opus eos verbi, divino
confisos auxilio, proficisci suadet. Quarum videlicet
litterarum ista est forma:

"Gregorius servus servorum Dei, servis Domini
nostri. Quia melius fuerat bona non incipere, quam
ab his quae coepta sunt, cogitatione retrorsum redire,
summo studio, dilectissimi filii, oportet ut opus
bonum, quod auxiliante Domino coepistis, impleatis.
Nec labor vos ergo itineris, nec maledicorum hominum
linguae deterreant: sed omni instantia, omnique fervore, quae inchoastis Deo auctore peragite: scientes
quod laborem magnum maior aeternae retributionis

---

[1] Provost of the monastery of St. Andrew, which Gregory
had built on the Cœlian hill at Rome.

[2] Somewhere in Provence.

year of the coming of the English into Britain, being
moved by inspiration of God thereunto, sent the
servant of God Augustine [1] and other more monks
fearing the Lord with him to preach the word of
God unto the nation of the English. Which obeying
the bishop's commandment, when they began to
take the said enterprise in hand and had already
travelled some small part of the way,[2] being stricken
with sluggish cowardice bethought themselves it
should be better for them to return home again than
to go unto that barbarous, savage and unbelieving
nation whose language even they knew not, and this
by common consent they determined to do, as being
the more sure way. Whereupon they sendeth
Augustine back again to the blessed Gregory (by
whom he had been appointed to be ordained bishop
there, if they were received of the English), humbly
to require him that they might not have to go forward
in that so perilous, so painful and uncertain journeying. Whom he yet exhorted by letter that, putting
their trust in God, they should proceed to the work
of the word. Of the which letter to wit this is the
copy:

"Gregory, the servant of the servants of God,
to the servants of our Lord. For so much as better
it were never to begin a good work, than after this is
once begun to go from it again in the inward thought,
you must needs, my beloved sons, now fulfil the
good work which by the help of God you have taken
in hand. Let therefore neither the travail of the
journey nor the talk of evil-tongued men dismay
you: but with all force and all fervour make up that
you have by the motion of God begun: assuring
yourselves that after your great labour the greater

gloria sequitur. Remeanti autem Augustino prae-
posito vestro, quem et abbatem vobis constituimus,
in omnibus humiliter obedite: scientes hoc vestris
animabus per omnia profuturum, quidquid a vobis
fuerit in eius admonitione completum. Omnipotens
Deus sua vos gratia protegat, et vestri laboris
fructum in aeterna me patria videre concedat; quatenus etsi vobiscum laborare nequeo, simul in gaudio
retributionis inveniar, quia laborare scilicet volo.
Deus vos incolumes custodiat, dilectissimi filii.

"Data die decima kalendarum Augustarum,
imperante domino nostro Mauricio Tiberio piissimo
Augusto anno decimo quarto, post consulatum
eiusdem domini nostri anno decimo tertio, indictione
decima quarta."

CAP. XXIV

*Ut Arelatensi episcopo epistolam pro eorum susceptione
miserit.*

MISIT etiam tunc isdem venerandus pontifex ad
Etherium Arelatensem archiepiscopum,[1] ut Augustinum Brittaniam pergentem benigne susciperet, litteras
quarum iste est textus:

"Reverentissimo et sanctissimo fratri Etherio
coepiscopo, Gregorius servus servorum Dei.

"Licet apud sacerdotes habentes Deo placitam

▲ For *episcopum*, Pl.

---

[1] Indictions are cycles of fifteen years. Gregory was the
first pope to reckon in this way.

glory of eternal reward shall follow. And be you in all points humbly obedient to Augustine your provost, that now returneth to you, whom also we have made to be your abbot: knowing that shall profit in all things your souls whatsoever you shall fulfil in obedience of his commandment. The Almighty God defend you with His grace, and grant me to see the fruit of your labours in the eternal country; that, though I cannot myself labour with you, I may be found to enjoy part of your reward along with you, for that surely I have a will to labour. God keep you in safety, my dear beloved children.

"Dated the 23rd of July, our lord Maurice Tiberius reigning, the most religious Augustus, in the 14th year of his reign, the 13th year after the consulship of the same our lord, in the 14th indiction." [1]

CHAPTER XXIV

How he sent to the bishop of Arles a letter to receive them.

THE same venerable pope sent also at that time a letter to Etherius, archbishop of Arles,[2] that he should favourably entertain Augustine going unto Britain, of the which letter this is the tenor:

"To the most reverend and most holy, his brother and fellow bishop Etherius, Gregory the servant of the servants of God.

"Though with such priests as haveth the love

___

[2] Etherius was bishop of Lyons, Vergilius archbishop of Arles. Almost identical letters were written to Marseilles, Vienne, Autun, etc.

caritatem religiosi viri nullius commendatione indigeant; quia tamen aptum scribendi se tempus ingessit, fraternitati vestrae nostra mittere scripta curavimus; insinuantes, latorem[1] praesentium Augustinum servum Dei, de cuius certi sumus studio, cum aliis servis Dei, illic nos pro utilitate animarum, auxiliante Domino, direxisse: quem necesse est ut sacerdotali studio sanctitas vestra adiuvare, et sua ei solatia praebere festinet. Cui etiam, ut promptiores ad suffragandum possitis existere, causam vobis iniunximus subtiliter indicare; scientes quod ea cognita, tota vos propter Deum devotione ad solaciandum, quia res exigit, commodetis. Candidum praeterea presbyterum, communem filium, quem ad gubernationem patrimonioli ecclesiae nostrae transmisimus, caritati vestrae in omnibus commendamus. Deus te incolumem custodiat, reverentissime frater.

" Data die decima kalendarum Augustarum, imperante domino nostro Mauricio Tiberio piissimo Augusto, anno decimo quarto, post consulatum eiusdem domini nostri anno decimo tertio, indictione decima quarta."

CAP. XXV

Ut veniens Brittaniam Augustinus, primo in insula Tanato regi Cantuariorum praedicarit ; et sic accepta ab eo licentia, Cantiam praedicaturus intraverit.

Roboratus ergo confirmatione beati patris Gregorii Augustinus cum famulis Christi qui erant cum eo,

---

[1] For *latores*, Pl.

well pleasing unto God religious men needeth no
man's commendation, yet because opportunity to
write did serve, we thought it good to direct our
letter to your brotherhood; advertising you that
we have sent on this way the bearer hereof, Augustine,
the servant of God, of whose zeal we are well assured,
with other servants of God for the health of souls
with the help of the Lord: whom it behoveth your
holiness to help with the zeal that the order of
priesthood requireth and be forward to furnish the
comfort due unto him. And to the intent also that
you may be the better willing to favour him, we have
willed him to discover unto you privily the cause
of his journey; not doubting but, that known, with
all devotion for God's sake you will set yourself
to comfort him, because the matter so requireth.
We commend also unto your charity in all things
our common son Candidus, priest, whom we have
sent to oversee a small patrimony of our church.
God keep you in safety, most reverend brother.

"Dated the 23rd of July, our lord Maurice
Tiberius reigning, the most religious Augustus, in
the 14th year of his reign, the 13th year of the
consulship of the same our lord, in the 14th
indiction."

CHAPTER XXV

*How that Augustine coming unto Britain first preached
unto the king of Kent in the Isle of Thanet ; and
so being licensed of him came after into Kent to
preach.*

Augustine therefore being much encouraged with
the comfort of the blessed father Gregory, returned

rediit in opus verbi, pervenitque Brittaniam. Erat eo
tempore rex Aedilberct in Cantia potentissimus, qui
ad confinium usque Humbrae fluminis maximi quo
meridiani et septentrionales Anglorum populi dirimuntur, fines imperii tetenderat. Est autem ad
orientalem Cantiae plagam Tanatos insula non modica,
id est, magnitudinis iuxta consuetudinem aestima-
tionis Anglorum, familiarum sexcentarum, quam a
continenti terra secernit fluvius Vantsumu, qui est
latitudinis circiter trium stadiorum, et duobus
tantum in locis est transmeabilis : utrumque enim
caput protendit in mare. In hac ergo adplicuit
servus Domini Augustinus, et socii eius, viri, ut
ferunt, ferme quadraginta. Acceperunt autem, prae-
cipiente beato papa Gregorio, de gente Francorum
interpretes, et mittens ad Aedilberctum, mandavit se
venisse de Roma, ac nuntium ferre optimum, qui sibi
obtemperantibus, aeterna in caelis gaudia, et regnum
sine fine cum Deo vivo et vero futurum, sine ulla
dubietate promitteret. Qui haec audiens, manere
illos in ea quam adierant insula, et eis necessaria
ministrari, donec videret quid eis faceret, iussit.
Nam et antea fama ad eum Christianae religionis pervenerat, utpote qui et uxorem habebat Christianam
de gente Francorum regia, vocabulo Bercta ; quam
ea conditione a parentibus acceperat, ut ritum fidei
ac religionis suae cum episcopo quem ei adiutorem

---

[1] As much land as would support a family, the extent of
which varied in different parts.

[2] Branch of the Stour.

[3] Daughter of Charibert king of Paris.

to the work of the word with the servants of Christ
which were with him, and came into Britain. Ethelbert at that time was king in Kent, a man of great
puissance, as the which had enlarged the frontiers
of his empire as far as the bound of the great flood
Humber by the which the south and north folk
of the English are divided. Now at the east end of
Kent there is Thanet, an isle of goodly size, that is
to say, containing 600 hides [1] according to the custom
of the estimation of the English, which island is
parted from the land by the flood Wantsum,[2] which
is of about three furlongs breadth and in two places
only passable: for both the heads of him runneth
to the sea. In this island then was Augustine the
servant of the Lord set on land, and his fellows to
the number, it is said, of almost 40 persons. And
they took with them certain Franks by command of
the blessed pope Gregory to be their interpreters,
and sending unto Ethelbert, Augustine informed
him that he came from Rome, and that he brought
him very good tidings, which promised that such as
did obey him, should have without any doubt everlasting joys in heaven and a kingdom without end
with the living and true God. And he, hearing this,
commanded that they should tarry in that island
whereunto they were come, and be furnished with
things needful until he should see what was his
pleasure about them. For the bruit of the Christian
religion had come also before unto him, as the
which had married a Christian woman of the royal
family of the Franks, named Bertha [3]; whom he
had married with these conditions taken from her
parents, that it should be lawful for her to keep
unbroken the rites of her faith and religion, with

fidei dederant, nomine Liudhardo, inviolatum servare
licentiam haberet.

Post dies ergo venit ad insulam rex, et residens
sub divo, iussit Augustinum cum sociis ad suum
ibidem advenire colloquium. Caverat enim ne in
aliquam domum ad se introirent, vetere usus augurio,
ne superventu suo, si quid maleficae artis habuissent,
eum superando deciperent. At illi non daemonica,
sed divina virtute praediti veniebant, crucem pro
vexillo ferentes argenteam, et imaginem Domini
Salvatoris in tabula depictam, laetaniasque canentes,
pro sua simul et eorum propter quos et ad quos
venerant salute aeterna, Domino supplicabant. Cumque ad iussionem regis residentes, verbum ei vitae,
una cum omnibus qui aderant eius comitibus praedi-
carent, respondit ille dicens: " Pulchra sunt quidem
verba et promissa quae adfertis; sed quia nova sunt,
et incerta, non his possum adsensum tribuere,
relictis eis quae tanto tempore cum omni Anglorum
gente servavi. Verum quia de longe huc peregrini
venistis, et ut ego mihi videor perspexisse, ea quae
vos vera et optima credebatis, nobis quoque com-
municare desiderastis, nolumus molesti esse vobis:
quin potius benigno vos hospitio recipere, et quae
victui sunt vestro necessaria, ministrare curamus:
nec prohibemus quin omnes quos potestis fidei
vestrae religionis praedicando societis." Dedit ergo
eis mansionem in civitate Doruvernensi, quae imperii

her bishop, Liudhard by name, whom they had appointed her to help her in matters of her faith.

Within therefore some days hereof the king came unto the island, and sitting in an open place he bid Augustine with his fellows to come to commune with him therein. For he would not, by reason of an old superstition, suffer him to come unto him in any house, lest, if they were skilful in sorcery, they might the rather by surprise deceive him and prevail against him. But they came not armed with the force of the devil but with the strength of God, carrying before them in place of a banner a cross of silver and the image of the Lord Saviour painted in a table, and singing the litanies, prayed the Lord both for their own eternal salvation and that of them as well to whom and for whose sake they had come thither. And when they sitting down, as the king did bid them, preached unto him the word of life and also to all his household there present, he answered them, saying: "The words and promises you give us are fair; but yet, for that they are strange and uncertain, I cannot rashly assent unto them, forsaking those things which this long time I have observed with all the people of the English. But for so much as you are come hither so far, and, as I seem to have discerned, have longing to impart to us also such knowledge as you took to be right good and true, we will not seek your trouble: nay rather with all courtesy will receive you, and be careful to minister you such things as are behoveful for your livelihood: neither do we let but that you may win unto the faith of your religion with your preaching as many as you may." He allowed them, therefore, a lodging in the city of Canterbury,

sui totius erat metropolis, eisque ut promiserat, cum administratione victus temporalis, licentiam quoque praedicandi non abstulit. Fertur autem quia adpropinquantes civitati, more suo cum cruce sancta, et imagine magni Regis Domini nostri Iesu Christi, hanc laetaniam consona voce modularentur: " Deprecamur te, Domine, in omni misericordia tua, ut auferatur furor tuus et ira tua a civitate ista, et de domo sancta tua, quoniam peccavimus. Alleluia."

CAP. XXVI

Ut idem in Cantia primitivae ecclesiae et doctrinam sit imitatus et vitam, atque in urbe regis sedem episcopatus acceperit.

AT ubi datam sibi mansionem intraverant, coeperunt apostolicam primitivae ecclesiae vitam imitari; orationibus videlicet assiduis, vigiliis, ac ieiuniis serviendo, verbum vitae quibus poterant praedicando, cuncta huius mundi velut aliena spernendo, ea tantum quae victui necessaria videbantur, ab eis quos docebant, accipiendo, secundum ea quae docebant ipsi per omnia vivendo, et paratum ad patiendum adversa quaeque, vel etiam ad moriendum pro ea quam praedicabant veritate, animum habendo. Quid mora? crediderunt nonnulli, et baptizabantur, mirantes simplicitatem innocentis vitae, ac dulcedinem doctrinae eorum caelestis. Erat autem prope ipsam civitatem ad orientem ecclesia in honorem sancti Martini antiquitus facta dum adhuc Romani Brit-

---

¹ Dan. 9. 16, an antiphon belonging to the Rogation Days of processional supplications in time of distress.

which was the head city of all his dominion, and,
as he promised, provided them of temporal neces-
saries and did not withhold the licence of preaching
as well.   Moreover, it is said that, as they approached
near the city, having the holy cross and image of the
mighty King our Lord Jesus Christ, as their manner
was, before them, they sung all in one tune this
litany following: "We beseech Thee, Lord, in all
Thy mercy, that Thy fury and anger may be taken
from this city and from Thy holy house, because we
have sinned.[1]   Alleluia."

CHAPTER XXVI

*How the said Augustine living in Kent did follow the
primitive Church both in teaching and living, and
received the seat of his bishopric in the king's city.*

But after they were now entered into their lodging,
they began to follow the apostolical life of the primitive Church; that is to wit by submitting to continual
prayer, watching and fasting, preaching the word
of life to as many as they could, despising all the
commodities of this world as things none of their
own, taking of them whom they instructed only
so much as might serve their necessities, living
themselves in all things according to what they taught
other, and having a spirit ready to suffer all adversities
or even death in defence of that truth they preached.
Why make delay? Some believed and were baptized,
marvelling much at the simplicity of their innocent
life and the sweetness of their heavenly doctrine.
Now there was right close to the city at the east end
a church built of ancient time in honour of Saint
Martin, made while the Romans were yet dwelling

taniam incolerent, in qua regina, quam Christianam
fuisse praediximus, orare consueverat. In hac ergo
et ipsi primo convenire, psallere, orare, missas facere,
praedicare et baptizare coeperunt; donec rege ad
fidem converso, maiorem praedicandi per omnia, et
ecclesias fabricandi vel restaurandi licentiam acciperent.

At ubi ipse etiam inter alios delectatus vita
mundissima sanctorum, et promissis eorum sua-
vissimis, quae vera esse miraculorum quoque multorum ostensione firmaverant, credens baptizatus est,
coepere plures ad audiendum verbum confluere, ac
relicto gentilitatis ritu, unitati se sanctae Christi
Ecclesiae credendo sociare. Quorum fidei et con-
versioni ita congratulatus esse rex perhibetur, ut
nullum tamen cogeret ad Christianismum; sed
tantummodo credentes arctiori dilectione, quasi
concives sibi regni caelestis, amplecteretur. Didicerat enim a doctoribus auctoribusque suae salutis,
servitium Christi voluntarium, non coactitium esse
debere. Nec distulit, quin etiam ipsis doctoribus
suis locum sedis eorum gradui congruum, in Doruverni
metropoli sua donaret, simul et necessarias in
diversis speciebus possessiones conferret.

---

[1] His own palace; Bright, p. 53.

in Britain, in the which the queen (which as we have said was a Christian woman) did use commonly to pray. They also themselves therefore began at first to assemble in the same church, to sing service, pray, say mass, preach and christen; until such time as, the king being converted to the faith, they received more ample licence of preaching where they would, and either to build of new or repair old churches.

But when the king himself too among other (being much delighted with the purity of the holy men's life as likewise with their sweet promises which to be true they had proved by the shewing also of many miracles) did believe and was baptized, there began more and more to resort together to hear the word, and renouncing the rites of their kinsfolk to join themselves by believing to the unity of the holy Church of Christ. Of whose faith and conversion though, it is said, the king much rejoiced, yet he would force none to become Christian, but only embrace the believers with a closer affection, as being fellow-citizens with him of the heavenly kingdom. For he had learned of the masters and authors of his salvation that the service of Christ must be voluntary and not forced. And without further delay he granted to his said teachers a place wherein to settle [1] seemly for their degree, in his head city of Canterbury, and at the same time bestowed on them possessions in divers kinds necessary for the maintenance thereof.

CAP. XXVII

Ut idem episcopus factus, Gregorio papae, quae sint Brittaniae gesta mandarit, et simul de necessariis eius responsa petens acceperit.

INTEREA vir Domini Augustinus venit Arelas, et ab archiepiscopo eiusdem civitatis Aetherio, iuxta quod iussa sancti patris Gregorii acceperant, archiepiscopus genti Anglorum ordinatus est, reversusque Brittaniam, misit continuo Romam Laurentium presbyterum, et Petrum monachum, qui beato pontifici Gregorio gentem Anglorum fidem Christi suscepisse, ac se episcopum factum esse referrent: simul et de eis quae necessariae videbantur quaestionibus, eius consulta flagitans. Nec mora, congrua quaesitui responsa recepit; quae etiam huic Historiae nostrae commodum duximus indere.

I. Interrogatio beati Augustini episcopi Cantuariorum ecclesiae. " De episcopis, qualiter cum suis clericis conversentur, vel de his quae fidelium oblationibus accedunt altario; quantae debeant fieri portiones, et qualiter episcopus agere in ecclesia debeat."

Respondit Gregorius papa urbis Romae. " Sacra Scriptura testatur, quam te bene nosse dubium non est, et specialiter beati Pauli ad Timotheum epistolae, in quibus eum erudire studuit qualiter in domo Dei

---

[1] Vergilius was the name of the archbishop of Arles, p. 105.
[2] June 22, 601.

CHAPTER XXVII

How the same being created bishop did advertise Gregory the pope of such things as he had done in Britain, and likewise requiring his answers upon matters necessary, received the same.

In the meantime the man of the Lord, Augustine, came to Arles, and was ordained archbishop of the nation of the English by Etherius, archbishop of the said city,[1] according to the commandments they had received from the holy father Gregory; and returning unto Britain he sent forthwith Laurence, a priest, and Peter, a monk, unto Rome, which should make relation to the blessed pope Gregory how that the nation of the English had received the faith of Christ, and he was made their bishop: at the same time too requiring his advice upon certain doubts necessary for him to be informed of. And without delay[2] he received fitting answer to his inquisition; which also we thought good to put into this our History.

1. *Question of the blessed Augustine, bishop of the Church of the men of Kent.* "Concerning bishops, how they should behave themselves among their clergy, or concerning the gifts made to the altar by the offerings of the faithful; what portions should be distributed and what is the bishop's office in the Church."

Gregory pope of the city of Rome answered. "The Holy Scripture testifieth, the which I am sure you know well, and specially the epistles of the blessed Paul unto Timothy, in the which he goeth about to instruct him after what sort he ought to be con-

conversari debuisset. Mos autem sedis apostolicae
est, ordinatis episcopis praecepta tradere, ut in omni
stipendio quod accedit, quatuor debeant fieri portiones; una videlicet episcopo et familiae propter
hospitalitatem, atque susceptionem; alia clero;
tertia pauperibus; quarta ecclesiis reparandis. Sed
quia tua fraternitas monasterii regulis erudita, seorsum fieri non debet a clericis suis, in ecclesia Anglorum, quae auctore Deo nuper adhuc ad fidem
adducta est, hanc debet conversationem instituere,
quae initio nascentis ecclesiae fuit patribus nostris;
in quibus nullus eorum ex his quae possidebant,
aliquid suum esse dicebat, sed erant eis omnia
communia.

"Si qui vero sunt clerici extra sacros ordines
constituti, qui se continere non possunt, sortiri uxores
debent, et stipendia sua exterius accipere. Quia
et de hisdem patribus de quibus praefati sumus,
novimus scriptum, quod dividebatur singulis prout
cuique opus erat. De eorum quoque stipendio
cogitandum atque providendum est, et sub ecclesiastica regula sunt tenendi, ut bonis moribus vivant
et canendis psalmis invigilent, et ab omnibus inlicitis
et cor et linguam et corpus Deo auctore conservent.
Communi autem vita viventibus iam de faciendis
portionibus, vel exhibenda hospitalitate, et adim-
plenda misericordia, nobis quid erit loquendum?

---

[1] Acts 4. 35.

versant in the house of God. Now the manner of the see apostolic is to give commandment unto such as be made bishops, that all manner of oblations that be given should be divided into four portions; to wit, the one thereof given unto the bishop and his household towards his hospitality and entertaining of guests; the second to the clergy; the third to the poor; the fourth to the reparation of the churches. But for so much as you, brother, being brought up under regular discipline, must not by the order of your rule live apart from your clergy, in the Church of the English (which is as yet but newly brought by the motion of God to the faith), you must follow that manner of living which was used in the beginning at the birth of the Church among our fathers; among whom there was none that said anything to be his of the things that they possessed, but all their things were common.

" If now there be any among the clergy out of holy orders, which cannot have continency, they shall take wives and have their stipend allowed them without. For too of the same fathers of which we have spoken before, we know it is written, that it was divided to every man according as he had need.[1] You must also think and provide for their stipend, and they are to be kept under the ecclesiastical rule, and seen unto that they live honestly, and ply their psalmody, and keep both heart and tongue and body from all unlawful things by the help of God. But as for them that liveth after the common sort what need I to speak now, either what portions they shall give, either what hospitality they shall keep, either what work of mercy they shall fulfil? Seeing that it is commanded that all which

Cum omne quod superest, in causis piis ac religiosis erogandum est; Domino omnium magistro docente: Quod superest, date eleemosynam, et ecce omnia munda sunt vobis."

II. Interrogatio Augustini. "Cum una sit fides, sunt ecclesiarum diversae consuetudines, et altera consuetudo missarum in sancta Romana ecclesia, atque altera in Galliarum tenetur?"

Respondit Gregorius papa. "Novit fraternitas tua Romanae ecclesiae consuetudinem, in qua se meminit nutritam. Sed mihi placet, sive in Romana, sive in Galliarum, seu in qualibet ecclesia, aliquid invenisti quod plus omnipotenti Deo possit placere, sollicite eligas, et in Anglorum ecclesia, quae adhuc ad fidem nova est, institutione praecipua, quae de multis ecclesiis colligere potuisti, infundas. Non enim pro locis res, sed pro bonis rebus loca amanda sunt. Ex singulis ergo quibusque ecclesiis, quae pia, quae religiosa, quae recta sunt elige, et haec quasi in fasciculum collecta, apud Anglorum mentes in consuetudinem depone."

III. Interrogatio Augustini. "Obsecro quid pati debeat, si quis aliquid de ecclesia furtu abstulerit?"

Respondit Gregorius. "Hoc tua fraternitas ex persona furis pensare potest, qualiter valeat corrigi. Sunt enim quidam qui habentes subsidia furtum perpetrant; et sunt alii qui hac in re ex inopia delinquunt: unde necesse est ut quidam damnis,

---

[1] Luke 11. 41.

is superfluous should be employed upon godly and devout uses; according as the Lord, the Master of all, doth teach us:[1] 'Of that which is left, give alms, and lo! all shall be clean unto you.'"

II. *Question of Augustine.* "Whereas there is but one faith, why be there sundry customs of Churches, and one custom of masses be observed in the holy Roman Church, another in the Church of France?"

Gregory, pope, answereth. "Your brotherhood knoweth the custom of the Church of Rome, in the which you remember that you were brought up. But it pleaseth me, if you have found anything (be it other in the Church of Rome, of France or any other, that may more please Almighty God), that you zealously choose and spread in the Church of the English (which as yet is but late come to the faith), by the best order you can choose, the things that you have been able to gather from many Churches. For the things are not to be loved for the place, but the place is to be loved for the good things that are in it. Choose then out of each Church that that is godly, that is religious, that is right in any of them, and these being gathered as it were in a bundle deliver unto them and inure the minds of the English thereunto."

III. *Question of Augustine.* "I pray you, how shall he be punished, which by theft taketh anything from the Church?"

Gregory answereth. "This your brotherhood may consider by the person of the thief in what sort it be good for him to be corrected. For there be some which having otherwise to live, yet stealeth; and some there be which in this matter are driven to err by need: whereby some must be merced with

quidam vero verberibus, et quidam districtius, quidam autem levius corrigantur. Et cum paulo districtius agitur, ex caritate agendum est, et non ex furore: quia ipsi hoc praestatur qui corrigitur, ne gehennae ignibus tradatur. Sic enim nos fidelibus tenere disciplinam debemus, sicut boni patres carnalibus filiis solent, quos et pro culpis verberibus feriunt, et tamen ipsos quos doloribus adfligunt habere heredes quaerunt; et quae possident ipsis servant quos irati insequi videntur. Haec ergo caritas in mente tenenda est, et ipsa modum correptionis dictat, ita ut mens extra rationis regulam omnino nihil faciat. Addes etiam, quomodo ea quae furtu de ecclesiis abstulerint reddere debeant. Sed absit ut ecclesia cum augmento recipiat quod de terrenis rebus videtur amittere, et lucra de vanis quaerere."

IV. Interrogatio Augustini. "Si debeant duo germani fratres singulas sorores accipere, quae sunt ab illis longa progenie generatae?"

Respondit Gregorius. "Hoc fieri modis omnibus licet: nequaquam enim in sacris eloquiis invenitur quod huic capitulo contradicere videatur."

V. Interrogatio Augustini. "Usque ad quotam generationem fideles debeant cum propinquis sibi coniugio copulari? et novercis et cognatis si liceat copulari coniugio?"

fines but some must be punished with stripes, and some more sharply but some more lightly. And when punishment a little more sharp is exercised, it must be done in charity and not in fury: for therefore is punishment dealt to the selfsame man that is corrected, that he might not be delivered to the fires of hell. For so ought we to exercise correction upon the faithful as the good fathers useth with their carnal children, whom though they punish with stripes for their faults, yet they seek to have for their heirs the very same whom they visiteth with pains; and their possessions they keepeth for the very same whom they seem to chasten in their anger. This charity therefore is to be kept in mind, and of itself enjoyneth that correction is to be so measured that the mind exceedeth in no way the rule of reason. Thou shalt also tell them in what way they must make restitution of such things as they have taken by theft from the churches. But God forbid that the Church should look to receive back with increase of gain such earthly things as it seemeth to lose, and to be greedy of lucre from that which is vanity."

IV. *Question of Augustine.* " Whether two german brothers may marry two sisters which be many degrees from them in kin? "

Gregory answereth. " That may be done lawfully by all means, for there is nothing found in the sacred utterances such as seemeth to be contrary to this head."

V. *Question of Augustine.* " Unto what generation should the faithful be joined together in wedlock with their kinsfolk? And is it lawful to be joined together in wedlock with a stepmother or a brother's wife? "

Respondit Gregorius. "Quaedam terrena lex in
Romana republica permittit, ut sive frater et soror,[1]
seu duorum fratrum germanorum vel duarum sororum filius et filia misceantur. Sed experimento
didicimus, ex tali coniugio sobolem non posse suc-
crescere: et sacra lex prohibet cognationis turpitudinem revelare. Unde necesse est ut iam tertia vel
quarta generatio fidelium licenter sibi iungi debeat:
nam secunda quam praediximus, a se omni modo
debet abstinere. Cum noverca autem miscere grave
est facinus, quia et in Lege scriptum est: 'Turpitudinem patris tui non revelabis.' Neque enim patris
turpitudinem filius revelare potest. Sed quia scriptum est: 'Erunt duo in carne una'; qui turpitudinem novercae quae una caro cum patre fuit revelare
praesumpserit, profecto patris turpitudinem revelavit.
Cum cognata quoque miscere prohibitum est, quia
per coniunctionem priorem caro fratris fuerat facta.
Pro qua re etiam Iohannes Baptista capite truncatus
est, et sancto martyrio consummatus, cui non est
dictum ut Christum negaret, et pro Christi confessione occisus est; sed quia isdem Dominus noster
Iesus Christus dixerat: 'Ego sum veritas'; quia
pro veritate Iohannes occisus est, videlicet et pro
Christo sanguinem fudit.

"Quia vero sunt multi in Anglorum gente, qui
dum adhuc in infidelitate essent, huic nefando, coniugio dicuntur admixit, ad fidem venientes admonendi sunt ut se abstineant, et grave hoc esse pecca-

---

[1] *fratris et sororis* are required, Pl.

[1] Arcadius and Honorius, A.D. 405.
[2] Gen. 9. 23.   [3] Lev. 18. 7.   [4] Gen. 2. 24.

QUESTIONS

Gregory answereth. " It is permitted by a secular law of the Roman commonwealth [1] that the son and daughter of a brother and sister [2] or of two brothers german or two sisters may be joined together. But experience sheweth that of such wedlock there can grow up no children: and the holy law forbiddeth that we should reveal the nakedness [3] of our kindred. Wherefore it is necessary that it be not until the third or fourth generation that believers should be permitted to marry: for the second (of which we have already spoken) must in any wise forbear one from the other. But to marry with a stepmother, it is a grievous offence, for it is written too in the Law: 'Thou shalt not reveal the nakedness of thy father.'[4] How? for the son cannot reveal the nakedness of his father. But because it is written: 'They too shall be one flesh'; he that presumeth to reveal the nakedness of his stepmother, which was one flesh with his father, he truly revealeth the nakedness of his father. It is also forbidden thee to marry withal thy brother's wife, for that by her former marriage she was one flesh with thy brother. For which cause also John Baptist was beheaded and suffered holy martyrdom, who though he was not told to deny Christ, yet was he killed for the confession of Christ; but in that the same our Lord Jesus Christ had said: 'I am the truth'; for that John was slain for the truth, surely also he shed his blood for Christ.

" But whereas there be many of the people of the English which, while they were yet infidels, are said to have been coupled in this infamous wedlock, when they cometh to the faith they are to be warned that they forbear, and take it to be a right grievous

tum cognoscant. Tremendum Dei iudicium timeant, ne pro carnali dilectione tormenta aeterni cruciatus incurrant. Non tamen pro hac re, sacri corporis ac sanguinis Domini communione privandi sunt, ne in eis illa ulcisci videantur, in quibus se per ignorantiam ante lavacrum baptismatis adstrinxerunt. In hoc enim tempore sancta ecclesia quaedam per fervorem corrigit, quaedam per mansuetudinem tolerat, quaedam per considerationem dissimulat, atque ita portat et dissimulat, ut saepe malum quod adversatur portando et dissimulando compescat. Omnes autem qui ad fidem veniunt, admonendi sunt, ne tale aliquid audeant perpetrare. Si qui autem perpetraverint, corporis et sanguinis Domini communione privandi sunt: quia sicut in his qui per ignorantiam fecerunt, culpa aliquatenus toleranda est, ita in his fortiter insequenda, qui non metuunt sciendo peccare."

VI. Interrogatio Augustini. " Si longinquitas itineris magna interiacet, ut episcopi non facile valeant convenire, an debeat sine aliorum episcoporum praesentia episcopus ordinari ? "

Respondit Gregorius. " Et quidem in Anglorum ecclesia, in qua adhuc solus tu episcopus inveniris, ordinare episcopum non aliter nisi sine episcopis potes. Nam quando de Gallis episcopi veniunt, qui in ordinatione episcopi testes adsistant ? Sed fraternitatem tuam ita volumus episcopos ordinare, ut ipsi sibi episcopi longo intervallo minime disiun-

offence. Teach them to fear the dreadful judgment of God, lest for the sake of carnal affection they run in danger of eternal torment. Yet for this thing are they not to be kept from the communion of the sacred body and blood of the Lord, lest you may seem to punish such things in them, wherein they have bound themselves through ignorance before coming to the laver of baptism. For at this present time the holy Church with a zeal doth punish some things, some other of a meekness it doth tolerate, at some other it winketh upon consideration, yea, it so beareth and winketh thereat that often the evil which it hateth, by bearing and winking at, it checketh. But all such as cometh to the faith are to be warned that they dare not to do any such thing. And if there be any that then do so, they are to be restrained from the communion of the Lord's body and blood : for as they are somewhat to be borne withal, which of ignorance hath offended, so they are sharply to be corrected, which wittingly fear not to sin."

VI. *Question of Augustine.* " If the bishops are so far apart from the other that they cannot conveniently assemble together, whether one may be ordained a bishop without the presence of other bishops."

Gregory answereth. " It is true that in the Church of the English in which thou only art as yet found to be bishop, thou canst ordain none but without other bishops. For when come there any bishops out of France that might be present as witnesses at the ordination of a bishop ? But we will your brotherhood to ordain bishops, yet so that the selfsame bishops be the least distance separated one

gantur; quatenus nulla sit necessitas, ut [1] in ordinatione episcopi, pastores quoque alii quorum praesentia
valde est utilis, facile debeant convenire. Cum
igitur auctore Deo ita fuerint episcopi in propinquis
sibi locis ordinati, per omnia episcoporum ordinatio
sine adgregatis tribus vel quatuor episcopis fieri non
debet. Nam in ipsis rebus spiritalibus ut sapienter
et mature disponantur, exemplum trahere a rebus
etiam carnalibus possumus. Certe enim dum con-
iugia in mundo celebrantur, coniugati quique con-
vocantur, ut qui in via iam coniugii praecesserunt,
in subsequentis quoque copulae gaudio misceantur.
Cur non ergo et in hac spiritali ordinatione, qua per
sacrum ministerium homo Deo coniungitur, tales
conveniant, qui vel in provectu ordinati episcopi
gaudeant, vel pro eius custodia omnipotenti Deo
preces pariter fundant."

VII. Interrogatio Augustini. "Qualiter debemus
cum Galliarum Britaniarumque episcopis agere?"

Respondit Gregorius. "In Galliarum episcopos
nullam tibi auctoritatem tribuimus: quia ab antiquis
praedecessorum meorum temporibus pallium Arela-
tensis episcopus accepit, quem nos privare auctoritate percepta minime debemus. Si igitur contingat
ut fraternitas tua ad Galliarum provinciam transeat,
cum eodem Arelatense episcopo debet agere, qualiter,
si qua sunt in episcopis vitia, corrigantur. Qui si

---

[1] The words *nulla sit necessitas ut* are not required and
spoil the sense, Pl.

---

[1] Originally the Greek cloak. It became a general mark
of honour and favour bestowed at first by the emperor, then
by the pope in the emperor's name on certain distinguished
prelates. Its form differed at different times.

from the other; in order that there be no lack but that there ought easily to come together at the ordination of a bishop other pastors also, whose presence is right useful. When then by the help of God the bishops shall be so ordained that they be not far asunder one from the other, there ought not to be made anywhere ordination of bishops without three or four bishops assemble together. For in spiritual matters themselves, how they may be wisely and providently disposed, we may take example even from carnal matters. For assuredly when marriages are solemnized in the world, all that are married are called thereunto, that such as have gone forward already in the way of wedlock should have their part in the joy of such as are married after. Why then may it not be like also in this spiritual ordinance (in the which by spiritual ministry a man is joined unto God), that such then should resort together, which either may rejoice in the promotion of him that is made bishop, or may pour forth prayers together unto Almighty God for his keeping of his charge?"

VII. *Question of Augustine.* "How ought we to deal with the bishops of the provinces of France and Britain?"

Gregory answereth. "We give thee none authority over the bishops of France: for that of ancient time of my predecessors the bishop of Arles received his pall,[1] whom we must not in the least degree deprive of the authority he hath obtained. If therefore it chance that your brotherhood go over to France, you shall treat with the said bishop of Arles how such defaults as are in the bishops may be redressed. Who if perchance he be lukewarm in the

forte in disciplinae vigore tepidus existat, tuae
fraternitatis zelo accendendus est. Cui etiam epistolas fecimus, ut cum tuae sanctitatis praesentia in
Galliis et ipse tota mente subveniat, et quae sunt
Creatoris nostri iussioni contraria, ab episcoporum
moribus compescat. Ipse autem extra auctoritatem
propriam episcopos Galliarum iudicare non poteris;
sed suadendo, blandiendo, bona quoque opera eorum
imitationi monstrando, pravorum mentes ad sanctitatis studia reforma: quia scriptum est in lege:
' Per alienam messem transiens, falcem mittere non
debet, sed manu spicas conterere et manducare.'
Falcem enim iudicii mittere non potes in ea segete,
quae alteri videtur esse commissa; sed per affectum
boni operis, frumenta dominica vitiorum suorum
paleis exspolia, et in ecclesiae corpore monendo et
persuadendo quasi mandendo converte. Quicquid
vero ex auctoritate agendum est, cum praedicto
Arelatense episcopo agatur, ne praetermitti possit
hoc, quod antiqua patrum institutio invenit. Brittaniarum vero omnes episcopos tuae fraternitati
committimus, ut indocti doceantur, infirmi persua-
sione roborentur, perversi auctoritate corrigantur."

VIII. Interrogatio Augustini. " Si praegnans
mulier debeat baptizari? aut postquam genuerit, post

---

[1] The British Celtic Churches.

execution of discipline, your brotherhood must move
him and prick him forward thereunto. To whom also
we have written that, joyning with your holiness
being there present, he will also himself with all
readiness of mind help to restrain from the manners
of the bishops all such ways as are contrary to the
command of our Creator. But you yourself outside your own authority shall not be able to give
judgment upon the bishops of France; but by
persuading, by courteously entreating, by giving
example also of good works for them to follow,
reform to the pursuits of holiness the minds of the
evil disposed: for why? it is written in the Law:
'He that passeth through another man's field shall
not thrust his sickle in the corn, but rub the ears
with his hand and so eat them.' For thou canst
not thrust the sickle of thy judgment into the corn
that seemeth to have been committed to the other
man's charge; but with the love of thy well-doing
rub off from the Lord's corn the chaff of the sins
found therein, and by treating and persuading with
them convert them in the body of the Church as a
man doth the meat he eateth in his own body.
But whatsoever there is to be done by authority,
let it be done along with the aforesaid bishop of
Arles, lest that order should be neglected which was
devised by the ancient institution of our forefathers.
But as for all the bishops of the Britains,[1] we commit them unto the charge of your brotherhood, that
the unlearned may be instructed, the weak by good
persuasions be strengthened, the froward be corrected
by authority."

VIII. *Question of Augustine.* " Whether a woman
that is great with child ought to be baptized? Or

quantum tempus possit ecclesiam intrare? aut etiam
ne morte praeoccupetur quod genuerit, post quot
dies hoc liceat sacri baptismatis sacramenta percipere? aut post quantum temporis huic vir suus
possit in carnis copulatione coniungi? aut si menstrua
consuetudine tenetur, an ecclesiam intrare ei liceat,
aut sacrae communionis sacramenta percipere? aut
vir suae coniugi permixtus, priusquam lavetur aqua,
si ecclesiam possit intrare? vel etiam ad mysterium
communionis sacrae accedere? Quae omnia rudi
Anglorum genti oportet haberi comperta."

Respondit Gregorius. "Hoc non ambigo fraternitatem tuam esse requisitam, cui iam et responsum
reddidisse me arbitror. Sed hoc quod ipse dicere
et sentire potuisti, credo quia mea apud te volueris
responsione firmari. Mulier etenim praegnans cur
non debeat baptizari, cum non sit ante omnipotentis
Dei oculos culpa aliqua fecunditas carnis? Nam
cum primi parentes nostri in paradiso deliquissent,
immortalitatem quam acceperant, recto Dei iudicio
perdiderunt. Quia itaque isdem omnipotens Deus
humanum genus pro culpa sua funditus exstinguere
noluit, et immortalitatem homini pro peccato suo
abstulit; et tamen pro benignitate suae pietatis,
fecunditatem ei sobolis reservavit. Quod ergo
naturae humanae ex omnipotentis Dei dono servatum est, qua ratione poterit a sacri baptismatis
gratia prohibere? In illo quippe mysterio, in quo

how long, after she is brought a-bed shall she tarry ere she can enter a church? Or also the child that is born, how many days shall it tarry before it may receive the sacrament of holy baptism, lest it be prevented by death? Or how long after she is brought a-bed shall her husband forbear her carnal company? Or if she be in her monthly custom, whether she may come to the church or receive the sacrament of holy communion? Or the man, after he hath carnally known his wife, whether he may enter the church before he be washed with water? or also may draw near to the mystery of holy communion? Of all the which the rude nation of the English hath need to be informed."

Gregory answereth. "I doubt not but your brotherhood hath been required counsel in these matters, and I think also I have made you already answer therein. Yet that which yourself could say and judge therein I think you would have it confirmed with my answer. For instance, the woman with child, why should she not be baptized, seeing to be teeming is no blame before the eyes of Almighty God? For our first parents, when they had sinned in Paradise, by the right judgment of God lost the immortality which they had received. For so much as accordingly Almighty God would not utterly destroy mankind for his sin, in punishment for his sin he also took from man the benefit of immortality; and yet of His mercy and goodness He reserved unto him the increase of issue. That then which of the gift of Almighty God is reserved unto the nature of man, by what reason can it be restrained from the grace of holy baptism? For in that mystery, in the which all blame is utterly taken away, it is great

133

omnis culpa funditus exstinguitur, valde stultum est, si donum gratiae contradicere posse videatur.

"Cum vero enixa fuerit mulier, post quot dies debeat ecclesiam intrare, Testamenti veteris praeceptione didicisti, ut pro masculo diebus triginta tribus, pro femina autem diebus sexaginta sex debeat abstinere. Quod tamen sciendum est quia in mysterio accipitur. Nam si hora eadem qua genuerit, actura gratias intrat ecclesiam, nullo peccati pondere gravatur: voluptas etenim carnis, non dolor in culpa est. In carnis autem commixtione voluptas est: nam in prolis prolatione gemitus. Unde et ipsi primae matri omnium, dicitur, ' In doloribus paries.' Si itaque enixam mulierem prohibemus ecclesiam intrare, ipsam ei poenam suam in culpam deputamus.

"Baptizare autem vel enixam mulierem, vel hoc quod genuerit, si mortis periculo urgetur, vel ipsam hora eadem qua gignit, vel hoc quod gignitur, eadem qua natum est, nullo modo prohibetur: quia sancti mysterii gratia sicut viventibus atque discernentibus cum magna discretione providenda est, ita his quibus mors inminet, sine ulla dilatione proferenda; ne dum adhuc tempus ad praebendum redemptionis mysterium quaeritur, interveniente paululum mora inveniri non valeat qui redimatur.

"Ad eius vero concubitum vir suus accedere non debet, quoadusque qui gignitur, ablactatur. Prava autem in coniugatorum moribus consuetudo sur-

---

[1] Lev. 12. 4, 5.   [2] Gen. 3. 16.

fully to think that the gift seem able to be contrary to the grace.

" Further, when the woman is delivered, how many days after she should enter the church, you have learnt by the commandment of the Old Testament,[1] that for a man child she should forbear 33 days, but for a female child, 66 days. Which yet is to be known that it is taken as said in a parable. For if the same hour that she is delivered she entereth the church to give thanks, she is burdened with the weight of no sin : for it is the pleasure of the flesh, not the pain that is to be blamed. But the pleasure is in the carnal begetting, for in the travail of bearing is the suffering. Whereupon it is said also to the first mother of all herself,[2] ' Thou shalt bring forth in sorrow.' If then we forbid the woman that is delivered to come to the church, we reckon her punishment itself for a blame to her.

" Moreover, by no ways is it forbidden to baptize either the woman that is delivered or the child whereof she is delivered, if it be beset with peril of death, or the woman herself the same hour that she beareth, either that which is brought forth in the same hour it be born : for the grace of the holy mystery, as it is to be given unto the living and such as are discerning with great discretion, so it is to be offered without any delay to them which draweth towards their death ; lest while time convenient to give the mystery of our redemption is yet sought for, by means of a small moment of delay the party that should be redeemed have not strength to be found.

" Moreover, the man shall not carnally accompany with his wife until the child that is born be weaned. But a corrupt custom hath risen up in the manners

rexit, ut mulieres, filios quos gignunt, nutrire con-
temnant, eosque aliis mulieribus ad nutriendum
tradant, quod videlicet ex sola causa incontinentiae
videtur inventum: quia dum se continere nolunt,
despiciunt lactare quos gignunt. Hae itaque quae
filios suos ex prava consuetudine aliis ad nutriendum
tradunt, nisi purgationis tempus transierit, viris
suis non debent admisceri: quippe quia et sine partus
causa, cum in suetis menstruis detinentur, viris suis
misceri prohibentur; ita ut morte Lex sacra feriat, si
quis vir ad menstruatam mulierem accedat. Quae
tamen mulier dum consuetudinem menstruam patitur, prohiberi ecclesiam intrare non debet; quia ei
naturae superfluitas in culpam non valet reputari:
et per hoc quod invita patitur, iustum non est ut
ingressu ecclesiae privetur. Novimus namque quod
mulier quae fluxum patiebatur sanguinis, post ter-
gum Domini humiliter veniens, vestimenti eius
fimbriam tetigit, atque ab ea statim sua infirmitas
recessit. Si ergo in fluxu sanguinis posita laudabiliter potuit Domini vestimentum tangere: cur quae
menstruam sanguinis patitur, ei non liceat Domini
ecclesiam intrare? Sed dicis: 'Illam infirmitas
compulit; has vero de quibus loquimur, consuetudo
constringit.' Perpende autem frater carissime, quia
omne quod in hac mortali carne patimur ex infirmitate naturae, est digno Dei iudicio post culpam

---

[1] Lev. 20. 18.

of them that are married, that the women think
scorn to nurse the sons born of their own body and
commit them to the charge of other women to
nurse, which thing surely seemeth to have been
found out only of incontinence: for therefore they
refuse to give suck to their own children, because
they will not forbear the company of their husbands.
Wherefore such as of an evil custom do put out
their children to nurse, shall not lie with their
husband until the day of their purification be fully
complete: seeing that also without excuse of child-
birth they are forbid to keep company with their
husbands in the time of their flowers; so that the
holy Law[1] doth punish with death them which
hath to do with a woman in that case. Which
woman yet is not to be forbidden to come to church
whilst she suffereth the monthly custom; because
the superfluity of nature cannot be imputed to her
for sin: and for that she suffereth that against her
will, it is no reason she should be restrained from
coming into the church. For we know that the
woman which was diseased with the bloody flux,
coming humbly behind our Lord touched the hem
of His garment, and thereby forthwith her malady
departed. If then the woman which had the bloody
flux might laudably touch the garment of the Lord,
why may not she enter into the church, that suffereth
her monthly flowers? But you say: 'As for her,
her malady forced her to seek remedy; but she
of whom we speak is taken of her customable weakness.' Consider, however, this with thyself, my
dear brother, that all that we suffer in this mortal
flesh by feebleness of nature, it was by the just
judgment of God ordained after fault committed;

ordinatum. Esurire namque, sitire, aestuare, algere,
lassescere, ex infirmitate naturae est. Et quid est
aliud, contra famem alimenta, contra sitim potum,
contra aestum auras, contra frigus vestem, contra
frigus vestem, contra lassitudinem requiem quaerere,
nisi medicamentum quidem contra aegritudines
explorare? Feminae itaque et menstruus sui sanguinis fluxus aegritudo est. Si igitur bene praesum-
sit quae vestimentum Domini in languore posita
tetigit, quod uni personae infirmanti conceditur, cur
non concedatur cunctis mulieribus, quae naturae
suae vitio infirmantur?

"Sanctae autem communionis mysterium in
eisdem diebus percipere non debet prohiberi. Si
autem ex veneratione magna percipere non praesu-
mit, laudanda est; sed si perceperit, non iudicanda.
Bonarum quippe mentium est, et ibi aliquo modo
culpas suas agnoscere, ubi culpa non est; quia saepe
sine culpa agitur quod venit ex culpa: unde etiam
cum esurimus, sine culpa comedimus, quibus ex
culpa primi hominis factum est ut esuriamus. Menstrua enim consuetudo mulieribus non aliqua culpa
est, videlicet quae naturaliter accedit. Sed tamen
quod natura ipsa ita vitiata est, ut etiam sine voluntatis studio videatur esse polluta, ex culpa venit
vitium, in quo se ipsa, qualis per iudicium facta sit,
humana natura cognoscat. Et homo qui culpam
sponte perpetravit, reatum culpae portet invitus.
Atque ideo feminae cum semet ipsis considerent, et

as hunger, thirst, heat, cold, weariness proceedeth of the infirmity of nature. And what other thing is it to seek food against hunger, drink against thirst, open air against heat, garment against cold, rest against weariness, but to search out a remedy in deed against distresses? And so unto the woman that monthly flow of her blood is a distress. If then she did well presume, which being sick touched the garment of the Lord, that which is granted to one woman having a malady, why should it not be granted to all women which have malady by the fault of their nature?

" Moreover, she ought not to be forbidden in the said days to receive the mystery of the holy communion. But if of a great reverence she hath thereunto, she doth not presume to receive she is to be praised; but if she shall receive it, she is not to be judged. For it is the point of well-disposed minds even there to acknowledge their fault in some way, where there is no fault ; for many times that is committed without fault which yet proceeded of a fault: whereupon too to eat when we are hungry is no fault, and yet hunger in us began and sprang first of the fault of the first man. As that monthly custom is not any fault to the woman, for that it cometh naturally. But yet because nature itself is so corrupted, that even without inclination of will it seemeth to be defiled, corruption cometh of fault, to the intent human nature might therein know of itself what it is become through the judgment of God. And that man which did commit fault with his will should bear the accusation of blame against his will. And further, therefore, let women consider with themselves herein, and if in the monthly

si in menstrua consuetudine ad sacramentum Dominici corporis et sanguinis accedere non praesumant,
de sua recta consideratione laudandae sunt; dum
vero percipiendo ex religiosae vitae consuetudine,
eiusdem mysterii amore rapiuntur, reprimendae,
sicut praediximus, non sunt.

"Sicut enim in Testamento veteri exteriora
opera observantur, ita in Testamento novo, non
tam quod exterius agitur, quam id quod interius
cogitatur, sollicita intentione adtenditur, ut subtili
sententia puniatur. Nam cum multa Lex velut
inmunda manducare prohibeat; in Evangelio tamen
Dominus dicit: 'Non quod intrat in os, coin-
quinat hominem; sed quae exeunt de ore, illa
sunt quae coinquinant hominem.' Atque paulo
post subiecit exponens: 'Ex corde exeunt cogitationes malae.' Ubi ubertim indicatum est,
quia illud ab omnipotente Deo pollutum esse in
opere ostenditur, quod ex pollutae cogitationis
radice generatur. Unde Paulus quoque apostolus
dicit: 'Omnia munda mundis, coinquinatis autem
et infidelibus nihil est mundum.' Atque mox eiusdem causam coinquinationis adnuntians subiungit:
'Coinquinata sunt enim et mens eorum et conscientia.' Si ergo ei cibus immundus non est cui
mens immunda non fuerit: cur quod munda mente
mulier ex natura patitur, et in immunditiam repu-
tetur?

"Vir autem cum propria coniuge dormiens, nisi
lotus aqua, intrare ecclesiam non debet; sed neque

---

[1] Being it may be nuns. [2] Matt. 15. 11.
[3] Matt. 15. 19. [4] Tit. 1. 15.

custom they should meekly refuse to come to the
sacrament of the Lord's body and blood, they are
to be commended of their good consideration;
whiles, however, of the custom of religious life [1]
they have a fervent love of the said mystery by
receiving the same, they are not to be forbidden,
as we have said before.

"For as in the Old Testament outward works
are observed, so in the New Testament that
is not regarded so straitly and carefully which
is outwardly done, as that which is inwardly
thought, so that it may be punished with discerning judgment. For whereas the Law forbiddeth
us to eat many things as unclean; yet in the
Gospel the Lord saith: [2] 'Not that which entereth
into the mouth defileth the man, but that which
cometh out of the mouth, this defileth the man.'
And shortly after He addeth, expounding the same:
'Out of the heart cometh evil thoughts.' [3] Where
it is abundantly declared, that that is shewn by the
Almighty God to be unclean in deed which springeth
out of the root of an unclean heart. Whereupon the
Apostle Paul also saith: [4] 'Unto the pure all things
are pure, but unto them that are defiled and unbelieving is nothing pure.' And soon after declaring
farther the cause of the said defilement, he addeth:
'For even their mind and conscience is defiled.' If
then the meat be not unclean unto him which hath
not an unclean mind, why is that which the woman,
having a clean mind, doth suffer of nature to be
reckoned unto her as impurity?

"Now as for the man which sleepeth with his
own wife, he shall not come into the church except
he be washed with water; but he shall not either,

lotus intrare statim debet. Lex autem veteri populo
praecepit, ut mixtus vir mulieri, et lavari aqua
debeat, et ante solis occasum ecclesiam non intrare :
quod tamen intelligi spiritaliter potest. Quia mulieri
vir miscetur, quando inlicitae concupiscentiae animus
in cogitatione per delectationem coniungitur ; quia
nisi prius ignis concupiscentiae a mente deferveat,
dignum se congregationi fratrum aestimare non
debet, qui se gravari per nequitiam pravae voluntatis videt. Quamvis de hac re diversae hominum
nationes diversa sentiant, atque alia custodire videantur ; Romanorum tamen semper ab antiquioribus
usus fuit, post admixtionem propriae coniugis, et
lavacri purificationem quaerere, et ab ingressu
ecclesiae paululum reverenter abstinere.

" Nec haec dicentes, culpam deputamus esse
coniugium ; sed quia ipsa licita admixtio coniugis sine
voluptate carnis fieri non potest, a sacri loci ingressu
abstinendum est ; quia voluptas ipsa esse sine culpa
nullatenus potest. Non enim de adulterio, sive fornicatione, sed de legitimo coniugio natus fuerat qui
dicebat : ' Ecce enim in iniquitatibus conceptus sum,
et in peccatis concepit me mater mea.' Qui enim
in iniquitatibus conceptum se noverat, a delicto se
natum gemebat : quia portat in ramo humorem vitii,
quem traxit ex radice. In quibus tamen verbis non
admixtionem coniugum iniquitatem nominat, sed
ipsam videlicet voluptatem admixtionis. Sunt etenim
multa quae licita probantur esse ac legitima, et

if he be washed, enter forthwith. Moreover, the
Law commanded the old people that the man which
hath had to do with a woman shall both wash himself with water and not enter the church before the
going down of the sun: which saying may yet be
spiritually construed; for then the man hath to do
with the woman when the mind doth delight himself
in being joined in thought to unlawful lust; for,
except the fire of lust be first quenched in the mind,
he shall not think himself worthy the company of
the brethren, which findeth himself under the
burden of the iniquity of unchaste desire. Though
of this thing divers countries are of divers minds,
and some keepeth one way, some another; yet the
manner of the Romans was ever of ancient time,
after the company of their own wives, both to
purify themselves in the bath and of reverence
awhile to forbear coming into the church.

"And we say not this for that we reckon marriage to
be blame; but, for that the very lawful company of
man and wife cannot be without pleasure of the flesh,
he should forbear from entering a holy place; for
that pleasure itself can in no way be without blame.
For he was not born of adultery or fornication but
of lawful wedlock, which said: 'Behold, I was
shapen in iniquity and in sin did my mother conceive me.' For he which knew himself to have
been shapen in iniquity mourned to remember his
sinful birth: seeing the tree doth bear in his branch
the corrupt humour which he drew of the root. In
the which words yet he doth not call the carnal
company of man and wife iniquity, but only assuredly
the pleasure therein. For there be many things
which are approved to be lawful and allowable, and

143

tamen in eorum actu aliquatenus foedamur; sicut
saepe irascendo culpas insequimur, et tranquilli-
tatem in nobis animi perturbamus: et cum rectum
sit quod agitur, non est tamen adprobabile quod in
eo animus perturbatur. Contra vitia quippe delin-
quentium iratus fuerat qui dicebat; ' Turbatus est
prae ira oculus meus.' Quia enim non valet nisi
tranquilla mens in contemplationis se lucem sus-
pendere, in ira suum oculum turbatum dolebat:
quia dum male acta deorsum insequitur, confundi
atque turbari a summorum contemplatione coge-
batur. Et laudabilis ergo est ira contra vitium, et
tamen molesta, qua turbatum se aliquem reatum
incurrisse aestimabat.

" Oportet itaque legitimam carnis copulam, ut
causa prolis sit, non voluptatis; et carnis com-
mixtio, creandorum liberorum sit gratia, non
satisfactio vitiorum. Si quis vero suam coniugem
non cupidine voluptatis raptus, sed solummodo
creandorum liberorum gratia utitur, iste profecto
sive de ingressu ecclesiae, seu de sumendo
Dominici corporis sanguinisque mysterio, suo est
iudicio relinquendus; quia a nobis prohiberi non
debet accipere, qui in igne positus nescit ardere.
Cum vero non amor ortandi sobolis, sed voluptas
dominatur in opere commixtionis: habent coniuges
etiam de sua commixtione quod defleant. Hoc
enim eis concedit sancta praedicatio; et tamen de
ipsa concessione metu animum concutit. Nam cum

---

[1] Ps. 6. 7.

yet in the doing of them we are somewhat defiled; as oftentimes being angry we punish other men's faults, whereby the calmness of our mind is troubled: and though it be well done that we do, yet it is not commendable that in doing it our mind is put out of quiet. For he was angry with the vice of the offenders which said:[1] 'Mine eye is troubled with anger.' For whereas the mind cannot lift himself up to the light of contemplation except it be still and quiet, therefore he sorrowed to see his eye distempered in his anger: for while he looked downward to punish the transgressions, he was forced to be withdrawn in his trouble from the contemplation of things which are above. And therefore it is a commendable thing to be angry against error, and yet it is a grief, by the trouble of which he judged that he fell under some accusation of guilt.

" Accordingly the right use of carnal union is to breed offspring, not pleasure; and the carnal company between man and wife is for the sake of the procreation of children, not the satisfaction of lusts. If however any man doth use his wife (not being carried away by desire of pleasure, but to the end of procreation only), this man truly is to be left unto his own discretion, whether for coming into the church, whether for the taking of the mystery of the Lord's body and blood; for he is not to be kept from receiving by us, which being in the fire cannot be burned. But when, not the love of begetting issue, but pleasure beareth the chiefest rule in the work of copulation, they have both cause also to bewail their coming together. For though holy declaration doth grant them so much, yet doth it not so grant it them that their mind be not shaken with

THE VENERABLE BEDE

Paulus Apostolus diceret: 'Qui se continere non
potest, habeat uxorem suam'; statim subiungere
curavit: 'Hoc autem dico secundum indulgentiam,
non secundum imperium.' Non enim indulgetur
quod licet, quia iustum est. Quod igitur indulgere
dixit, culpam esse demonstravit.

"Vigilanti vero mente pensandum est, quod in
Sina monte Dominus ad populum locuturus, prius
eundem populum abstinere a mulieribus praecepit.
Et si illic[1] ubi Dominus per creaturam subditam
hominibus loquebatur, tanta provisione est munditia
corporis requisita, ut qui verba Dei perciperent
mulieribus mixti non essent; quanto magis mulieres,
quae corpus Domini omnipotentis accipiunt, custodire in se munditiam carnis debent, ne ipsa inaestim-
abilis mysterii magnitudine graventur? Hinc etiam
ad David de pueris suis per sacerdotem dicitur, ut
si a mulieribus mundi essent, panes propositionis
acciperent, quos omnino non acciperent, nisi prius
mundos eos David a mulieribus fateretur? Tunc
autem vir qui post admixtionem coniugis lotus aqua
fuerit, etiam sacrae communionis mysterium valet
accipere, cum ei iuxta praefinitam sententiam etiam
ecclesiam licuerit intrare."

IX. Interrogatio Augustini. "Si post inlusionem
quae per somnium solet accidere, vel corpus Domini
quilibet accipere valeat; vel, si sacerdos sit, sacra
mysteria celebrare?"

[1] For *illuc*, Pl.

[1] Cor. 7. 2, 9.   [2] 1 Cor. 7. 6.   [3] 1 Sam. 21. 4.

146

fear. For when Paul the Apostle said: 'He that cannot contain, let him have his wife;'[1] he was careful straight to say farther: 'Now this I say by permission, not of commandment.'[2] For there is no permission of that which is lawful, seeing it is right. Wherefore in that he used this word *permission* he shewed it to be faulty.

"Moreover, it is to be pondered with good heed that the Lord intending to speak to the people in the mount of Sinai, first gave commandment that the same people should abstain from women. And if the purity of the body was there so earnestly required, where the Lord by means of a creature made subject to Him did speak unto men, that they which should hear the words of God should be free from women; how much more the women which receive the body of the Almighty Lord shall seek to preserve in themselves the cleanness of the flesh, lest they may take hurt by the very greatness of that inestimable mystery. Hereof also it is said by the priest[3] unto David as touching his servants, that, if they were clean from women, they should eat of the Shew Bread, which otherwise they should no way be suffered to take, except David would first say that they were clean from women. Then, moreover, the man who hath been washed with water after the carnal knowledge of his wife may also receive the mystery of the holy Communion, when according to the judgment before laid down he may come also to the church."

IX. *Question of Augustine.* "Whether after the illusion which is wont to befall unto a man in his dream, either anyone may receive the body of the Lord or, if he be priest, celebrate the holy mysteries?"

Respondit Gregorius. "Hunc quidem Testamentum veteris Legis, sicut in superiori capitulo iam diximus, pollutum dicit, et nisi lotum aqua, usque ad vesperam intrare ecclesiam non concedit. Quod tamen aliter populus spiritalis intelligens, sub eodem intellectu accipiet quo praefati sumus: quia quasi per somnium inluditur qui tentatur immunditia, veris imaginibus in cogitatione inquinatur; sed lavandus est aqua, ut culpas cogitationis lacrymis abluat: et nisi prius ignis tentationis reciderit,[1] reum se quasi usque ad vesperum cognoscat. Sed est in eadem inlusione valde necessaria discretio, quae subtiliter pensari debeat, ex qua re accidat menti dormientis: aliquando enim ex crapula, aliquando ex naturae superfluitate vel infirmitate, aliquando ex cogitatione contingit.

"Et quidem cum ex naturae superfluitate vel infirmitate evenerit, omnimodo haec inlusio non est timenda; quia hanc animum nescientem pertulisse magis dolendum est, quam fecisse. Cum vero ultra modum appetitus gulae in sumendis alimentis rapitur, atque idcirco humorum receptacula gravantur, habet exinde animus aliquem reatum, non tamen usque ad prohibitionem percipiendi sancti mysterii, vel missarum sollemnia celebrandi: cum fortasse aut festus dies exigit, aut exhiberi mysterium (pro eo quod sacerdos alius in loco deest), ipsa necessitas compellit. Nam si adsunt alii qui implere

---

[1] For *recesserit*, Pl.

QUESTIONS

Gregory answereth. " The Testament of the old Law indeed, as we have said already under a former head, saith him to be defiled, and suffereth him not to enter the church before evening, and not but first bathed. Which thing yet the spiritual people otherwise understanding, shall take it in like sense as we have above declared: for he is deluded as it were by dream, which being tempted with uncleanness is defiled with true imaginations in his thoughts; but he is to be washed with water that so he may cleanse with tears the faults of his thoughts: and except the fire of temptation go out, let him take himself guilty, as it were, unto the evening. But there is in this same manner of illusion a difference very much to be had, for a man must narrowly examine of what cause this thing cometh into his mind when he is asleep: for sometimes it cometh of surfeit, sometimes of superfluity or weakness of nature, sometimes of thought.

" It is true that when it cometh of superfluity or infirmity of nature, this illusion is nothing to be feared; for the mind is more to be pitied that it hath unwittingly suffered, than that it hath anything committed. When, however, the man is carried away through inordinate gluttonous desire in diet, whereby the vessels of the humours are overburdened, the mind thereby is not clear of fault, yet it is not guilty of so great fault that the man thereby is to be withholden either from receiving the holy mystery, either from celebrating the solemnity of mass: when it may happen that either holy-day requireth, either of necessity the party is forced to show the mystery, for that there is no other priest to be gotten in his place. For if there

149

ministerium valeant, inlusio pro crapula facta a
perceptione sacri mysterii prohibere non debet;
sed ab immolatione sacri mysterii abstinere, ut
arbitror, humiliter debet: si tamen dormientis mentem turpi imaginatione non concusserit. Nam sunt
quibus ita plerumque inlusio nascitur, ut eorum
animus, etiam in somno corporis positus, turpibus
imaginationibus non foedetur. Qua in re unum
ibi ostenditur, ipsa mens rea, non tamen vel suo
iudicio libera, cum se, etsi dormienti corpore, nihil
meminit vidisse, tamen in vigiliis corporis, meminit
in ingluviem cecidisse. Sin vero ex turpi cogitatione
vigilantis oritur inlusio dormientis, patet animo
reatus suus: videt enim a qua radice inquinatio illa
processerit, quia quod cogitavit sciens, hoc pertulit
nesciens.

"Sed pensandum est, ipsa cogitatio utrum suggestione, an delectatione, vel, quod maius est,
peccati consensu acciderit. Tribus enim modis
impletur omne peccatum; videlicet suggestione,
delectatione, consensu. Suggestio quippe fit per
diabolum, delectatio per carnem, consensus per
spiritum: quia et primam culpam serpens suggessit,
Eva velut caro delectata est, Adam vero velut
spiritus consensit: et necessaria est magna discretio,
ut inter suggestionem atque delectationem, inter
delectationem et consensum, iudex sui animus
praesideat. Cum enim malignus spiritus peccatum
suggerit in mente, si nulla peccati delectatio sequa-

be other at hand able to fulfil the ministry, yet the illusion coming only of surfeit is no sufficient cause to make a man forbear the receipt of the holy mystery; yet from the sacrifice of the holy mystery he ought (as I think) meekly forbear; though not from receiving, except the mind in sleep be troubled with foul phantasies. For there be some to whom the illusion cometh for the most part in such manner that their mind, even in his place in the sleeping body, is not defiled with foul phantasies. Wherein one thing is clearly there shewn, to wit, that the mind of itself is guilty, and (when the person, albeit with the body asleep, doth not remember that he hath seen anything, yet, with the body. awake, remembereth that he hath offended in gluttonous feeding) is not clear notwithstanding by his own judgment. But if indeed the illusion in sleep riseth of foul thoughts which he had waking, his offence is manifest to the mind: for he doth see out of what root that pollution did spring, for the evil that he wittingly thought upon, this unwittingly he suffered.

" But we must consider whether the selfsame thought befell of suggestion or delight or, which is weightier, by sinful consent. For in three ways all manner of sin is fulfilled, to wit, suggestion, delight, consent. For suggestion is by the devil, delight by the flesh, consent by the spirit: for that also the serpent was prompter to the first fault, Eve, as it were the flesh, took delight therein, but Adam, as it were the spirit, consented: and herein is requisite great discretion, that the mind as judge over himself should discern betwixt suggestion and delight, betwixt delight and consent. For when the evil spirit doth raise the motion unto sin in the

151

tur, peccatum omnimodo perpetratum non est : cum vero delectari caro coeperit, tunc peccatum incipit nasci : si autem etiam ex deliberatione consentit, tunc peccatum cognoscitur perfici.

" In suggestione igitur peccati initium est, in delectatione fit nutrimentum, in consensu perfectio. Et saepe contingit ut hoc quod malignus spiritus seminat in cogitatione, caro in delectationem trahat ; nec tamen anima eidem delectationi consentiat. Et cum caro delectare sine animo nequeat, ipse tamen animus carnis voluptatibus reluctans, in delectatione carnali aliquo modo ligatur invitus, ut ei ex ratione contradicat, ne consentiat ; et tamen delectatione ligatus sit, sed ligatum se vehementer ingemiscat. Unde et ille caelestis exercitus praecipuus miles gemebat dicens : ' Video aliam legem in membris meis repugnantem legi mentis meae, et captivum me ducentem in lege peccati, quae est in membris meis.' Si autem captivus erat, minime pugnabat ; sed et pugnabat : quapropter et captivus erat, et pugnabat igitur legi mentis, cui lex, quae in membris est, repugnabat. Si autem pugnabat, captivus non erat. Ecce itaque homo est, ut ita dixerim, captivus et liber ; liber ex iustitia quam diligit, captivus ex delectatione quam portat invitus."

---

[1] Rom. 7. 23.

mind, if there shall follow no delight in sin, there is no sin at all committed: but when the flesh beginneth to take delight therein, then sin beginneth to spring: if, moreover, advisedly he doth also agree thereunto, then sin is found to be perfected.

" So then in suggestion is the beginning, in delight comes the feeding, in consent the finishing of sin. And it oft chanceth that the evil that the wicked spirit soweth in the thought, the flesh draweth unto delight, and yet the soul doth not agree to the same delight. And though the flesh can feel no delight without the mind, yet the mind himself striving against the pleasures of the flesh is in a measure against his will bound in the pleasure of the flesh, in such sort that with reason he doth gainsay it, lest he should agree unto it; and yet is bound with delight, but so that he much lamenteth his band. Whereupon that principal champion of the heavenly army, Saint Paul, bewaileth himself, saying,[1] ' I see another law in my members, warring against the law of my mind, and bringing me into captivity to the law of sin which is in my members.' Now if he was in captivity, least of all did he fight; but yet too he did fight: wherefore he was both in captivity and therefore strove with the law of his mind, against the which law, which is in our members, did fight. But if he fought, he was not in captivity. Lo! then man, that I may so speak, is in captivity and free; free through righteousness which he loveth, in captivity through delight which he beareth against his will."

CAP. XXVIII

Ut papa Gregorius epistolam Arelatensi episcopo, pro adiuvando in opere Dei Augustino, miserit.

Hucusque responsiones beati papae Gregorii ad consulta reverentissimi antistitis Augustini. Epistolam vero quam se Arelatensi episcopo fecisse commemorat, ad Vergilium Aetherii successorem dederat: cuius haec forma est.

"Reverentissimo et sanctissimo fratri Vergilio coepiscopo, Gregorius servus servorum Dei.

"Quantus sit affectus venientibus sponte fratribus impendendus, ex eo quod plerumque solent caritatis causa invitari, cognoscitur. Et ideo si communem fratrem Augustinum episcopum ad vos venire contigerit, ita illum dilectio vestra, sicut decet, affectuose dulciterque suscipiat, ut et ipsum consolationis suae bono refoveat, et alios, qualiter fraterna caritas colenda sit, doceat. Et quoniam saepius evenit, ut hi qui longe sunt positi, prius ab aliis quae sunt emendanda, cognoscant: si quas fortasse fraternitati vestrae sacerdotum vel aliorum culpas intulerit, una cum eo residentes subtili cuncta investigatione perquirite, et ita vos in ea quae Deum offendunt, et ad iracundiam provocant, districtos ac solicitos exhibete, ut ad aliorum emendationem et vindicta culpabilem

LETTER TO ARLES

CHAPTER XXVIII

How the pope Gregory sent a letter unto the bishop of Arles, that he should aid Augustine in the work of God.

THUS far the answers of the blessed pope Gregory unto the demands of the most reverend prelate Augustine. The epistle of a truth which he saith he had addressed unto the bishop of Arles he had sent to Vergilius the successor of Etherius, and is of this fashion.

" Gregory, the servant of the servants of God, unto the most reverend and holy brother, Vergilius, his fellow bishop.

" With what affection our brothers coming of their own accord unto us are to be entertained, it may thereby well appear, for that many times we are wont to bid them unto our house for charity's sake. And therefore if it chanceth to your brother and mine, Augustine, bishop, to come unto you, I pray your love to receive him with such hearty and friendly entertainment, that both he himself may be refreshed to the good of his comfort, and other taught how brotherly charity is to be maintained. And for that it often times chanceth that they which be far off shall sooner learn by report of other, such things as are to be reformed: if it be so that your brotherhood hear by him of faults among your priests or other, sitting in examination along with him make all diligent search and scruting thereof, and in such things as offendeth God and provoketh His wrath, shew yourselves so careful and hard to be entreated that, both to the correction of other, the offender be stricken with punishment, and the

feriat, et innocentem falsa opinio non affligat. Deus te incolumem custodiat, reverentissime frater.

" Data die decima kalendarum Iuliarum, imperante domino nostro Mauricio Tiberio piissimo Augusto anno decimo nono, post consulatum eiusdem domini anno decimo octavo, indictione quarta."

CAP. XXIX

Ut idem Augustino pallium, et epistolam, et plures verbi ministros miserit.

PRAETEREA idem papa Gregorius Augustino episcopo, quia suggesserat ei multam quidem ibi esse messem, sed operarios paucos, misit cum praefatis legatariis suis plures cooperatores, ac verbi ministros: in quibus primi et praecipui erant Mellitus, Iustus, Paulinus, Rufinianus; et per eos generaliter universa, quae ad cultum erant ac ministerium ecclesiae necessaria, vasa videlicet sacra, et vestimenta altarium, ornamenta quoque ecclesiarum, et sacerdotalia vel clericalia indumenta, sanctorum etiam apostolorum ac martyrum reliquias, nec non et codices plurimos. Misit etiam litteras in quibus significat se ei pallium direxisse, simul et insinuat qualiter episcopos in Brittania constituere debuisset; quarum litterarum iste est textus.

" Reverentissimo et sanctissimo fratri Augustino coepiscopo Gregorius servus servorum Dei.

" Cum certum sit pro omnipotente Deo laborantibus ineffabilia aeterni regni praemia reservari; nobis

---

[1] Luke 10. 2.   [2] Laurence and Peter.

innocent through false surmise be not oppressed. God keep you in safety, most reverend brother!

" Given the 22nd of June, the 19th year of the reign of our lord Maurice Tiberius, the most religious Augustus, the 18th year after the consulship of the same lord, in the 4th indiction."

CHAPTER XXIX

How the same sent unto Augustine a pall with a letter and more ministers of the word.

FURTHERMORE the said pope (for so much that Augustine had advertised him that the harvest truly was great but the labourers were few [1]) sent unto the bishop with his aforenamed emissaries [2] more helpers and ministers of the word: among whom the first and chiefest were Mellitus, Justus, Paulinus, Rufinianus; and by them he sent in general all things that were necessary for the furniture and ministry of the Church, as holy vessels and altar-cloths, ornaments also for the churches and apparel for the priests or clergy, relics too of the holy apostles and martyrs as well as many books. He sent him also a letter, by the which he signifieth unto him that he hath sent him a pall, and at the same time maketh him to know what order he should keep in making of bishops in Britain; of which letter this is the tenor.

" To his most reverend and holy brother Augustine and fellow bishop, Gregory servant of the servants of God.

" Though it be assured that for such as labour in the work of Almighty God He doth reserve unspeak-

tamen eis necesse est honorum beneficia tribuere,
ut in spiritalis operis studio ex remuneratione valeant
multiplicius insudare. Et quia nova Anglorum
ecclesia ad omnipotentis Dei gratiam eodem Domino
largiente, et te laborante perducta est, usum tibi
pallii in ea ad sola missarum sollemnia agenda con-
cedimus, ita ut per loca singula duodecim episcopos
ordines, qui tuae subiaceant ditioni, quatenus Lundoniensis civitatis episcopus semper in posterum a
synodo propria debeat consecrari, atque honoris
pallium ab hac sancta et apostolica, cui Deo auctore
deservio, sede percipiat. Ad Eburacam vero civitatem te volumus episcopum mittere, quem ipse
iudicaveris ordinare; ita duntaxat, ut si eadem
civitas cum finitimis locis verbum Dei receperit, ipse
quoque duodecim episcopos ordinet, et metropolitani
honore perfruatur; quia ei quoque, si vita comes
fuerit, pallium tribuere Domino favente disponimus,
quem tamen tuae fraternitatis volumus dispositioni
subiacere : post obitum vero tuum ita episcopis quos
ordinaverit praesit, ut Lundoniensis episcopi nullo
modo ditioni subiaceat. Sit vero inter Lundoniae
et Eburacae civitatis episcopos in posterum honoris
ista distinctio, ut ipse prior habeatur qui prius fuerit
ordinatus: communi autem consilio et concordi
actione quaeque sunt pro Christi zelo agenda dis-
ponant unanimiter; recte sentiant, et ea quae

---

[1] Paulinus was not consecrated till A.D. 625.

LONDON AND YORK

able reward in the eternal kingdom, we nevertheless
stand bound to shew them honour and favour, that
they may by way of recompense be the more
earnestly bent to take more manifold pains in further-
ing their spiritual work. And for so much as by
the goodness of the Lord and your travail the new
Church of the English is brought unto the grace
of Almighty God, we grant unto you therein the
use of the pall (that to wear such times only as
you celebrate the solemnity of mass), to the intent
that you ordain 12 bishops, one to each place, to
be under your jurisdiction, but so that the bishop
of the town of London must be ever hereafter
consecrated of his own synod, and receive the pall
of honour of this holy and apostolic see wherein I
by the authority of God do now serve. Moreover,
we will that you send a bishop unto the city of
York,[1] whom you yourself shall think worthy to be
appointed; on such condition only that, if the said
town with the country about receive the word of
God, he himself be authorized to make 12 bishops
more and enjoy the honour to be their metropolitan;
for we purpose to give him also a pall by the favour
of the Lord, if life attend us, whom nevertheless we
will to be subject to the disposition of your brotherhood: but after your death so have the oversight
of the bishops whom he hath ordained, that he be
in no case subject unto the authority of the bishop
of London. But betwixt the bishops of the towns
of London and York let this be the difference hereafter, that he be held highest that is first ordained:
moreover, all things that is done for zeal of Christ
let them with one mind dispose to be done with
common counsel and mutual concord; let them think

159

senserint, non sibimet discrepando perficiant. Tua
vero fraternitas non solum eos episcopos quos ordinaverit, neque hos tantummodo qui per Eburacae
episcopum fuerint ordinati, sed etiam omnes Brittaniae sacerdotes habeat Deo Domino nostro Iesu
Christo auctore subiectos; quatenus ex lingua et
vita tuae sanctitatis, et recte credendi et bene
vivendi formam percipiant, atque officium suum fide
ac moribus exsequentes, ad caelestia cum Dominus
voluerit regna pertingant. Deus te incolumem
custodiat, reverentissime frater.

"Data die decima kalendarum Iuliarum, imperante domino nostro Mauricio Tiberio piissimo Augusto
anno decimo nono, post consulatum eiusdem domini
anno decimo octavo, indictione quarta."

CAP. XXX

*Exemplar epistolae quam Mellito abbati Brittaniam
pergenti misit.*

Abeuntibus autem praefatis legatariis, misit post
eos beatus pater Gregorius litteras memoratu dignas,
in quibus aperte quam studiose erga salvationem
nostrae gentis invigilaverit, ostendit, ita scribens:
"Dilectissimo filio Mellito abbati Gregorius servus
servorum Dei.
"Post discessum congregationis nostrae quae
tecum est, valde sumus suspensi redditi, quia nihil
de prosperitate vestri itineris audisse nos contigit.

---

[1] The word may imply that they were monks of the
monastery of St. Andrew.

rightly, and such things as they have rightly thought, accomplish without variance. We will farther that unto your brotherhood be subject not only the bishops which you shall make yourself, or such only as shall be made by the bishop of York, but also all the priests of Britain by the authority of God our Lord Jesus Christ; in order that from the conversation and life of your holiness they may receive a pattern both to believe aright and to lead a good life, and executing their offices in integrity of faith and conduct they may attain to the kingdom of heaven when the Lord shall so please. God keep you in safety, most reverend brother.

"Given the 22nd of June, the 19th year of the reign of our lord Maurice Tiberius the most religious Augustus, the 18th year of the consulship of the same lord, in the fourth indiction."

CHAPTER XXX

The copy of a letter which he sent to Mellitus the abbot going to Britain.

WHEN now the said emissaries were in their journey abroad, the blessed father Gregory sent a letter after them worthy of memory, in the which he openly declared how earnestly he watched over the salvation of our country, writing thus:

"Unto his dearly beloved son Mellitus, abbot, Gregory the servant of the servants of God.

"After the departure of you and the company [1] which is with you we were brought into much uncertainty of mind, for that we happened to hear nothing how you sped in your journey. When then

161

Cum ergo Deus omnipotens vos ad reverentissimum virum fratrem nostrum Augustinum episcopum perduxerit, dicite ei, quid diu mecum de causa Anglorum cogitans tractavi: videlicet quia fana idolorum destrui in eadem gente minime debeant; sed ipsa quae in eis sunt idola destruantur; aqua benedicta fiat, in eisdem fanis aspergatur, altaria construantur, reliquiae ponantur: quia si fana eadem bene constructa sunt, necesse est ut a cultu daemonum in obsequio veri Dei debeant commutari; ut dum gens ipsa eadem fana sua non videt destrui, de corde errorem deponat, et Deum verum cognoscens ac adorans, ad loca quae consuevit, familiarius concurrat. Et quia boves solent in sacrificio daemonum multos occidere, debet eis etiam hac de re aliqua sollemnitas immutari: ut die dedicationis, vel natalitii sanctorum martyrum quorum illic reliquiae ponuntur, tabernacula sibi circa easdem ecclesias quae ex fanis commutatae sunt, de ramis arborum faciant, et religiosis conviviis sollemnitatem celebrent; nec diabolo iam animalia immolent, et ad laudem Dei in esu suo animalia occidant, et donatori omnium de satietate sua gratias referant: ut dum eis aliqua exterius gaudia reservantur, ad interiora gaudia consentire facilius valeant. Nam duris mentibus simul omnia abscidere impossibile esse non dubium est, quia et is qui summum locum ascendere nititur, gradibus vel passibus non autem saltibus elevatur. Sic Israelitico populo in Ægypto

Almighty God shall bring you unto our most reverend brother Augustine, bishop, tell him what I have long time devised with myself of the cause of the English: that is, to wit, that the temples of the idols in the said country ought not to be broken; but the idols alone which be in them; that holy water be made and sprinkled about the same temples, altars builded, relics placed: for if the said temples be well built, it is needful that they be altered from the worshipping of devils into the service of the true God; that whiles the people doth not see these their said temples spoilt, they may forsake their error of heart and be moved with more readiness to haunt their wonted place to the knowledge and honour of the true God. And for that they are wont to kill many oxen in sacrifice to the devils, some solemnity shall be granted also by way of exchange in this matter: as that in the dedication days or birthdays of holy martyrs of whom the relics be there placed, they make them bowers of branches of trees about the said churches which have been changed from temples, and hold solemn feast together after a religious sort; and that they no more sacrifice animals to the devil but kill them to the refreshing of themselves to the praise of God, and render thanks to the Giver of all things for their abundance: that whiles some outward comforts are reserved unto them, they may be brought the more readily to agree to accept the inward comforts. For it is doubtless impossible to cut off all abuses at once from rough hearts, seeing that he too that laboureth to climb up into a high place, goeth upward by steps and paces but not by leaps. So unto the children of Israel, being in Egypt, the Lord did indeed make Himself

Dominus se quidem innotuit; sed tamen eis sacri-
ficiorum usus quae diabolo solebat exhibere, in cultu
proprio reservavit, ut eis in suo sacrificio animalia
immolare praeciperet; quatenus cor mutantes, aliud
de sacrificio amitterent, aliud retinerent: ut etsi
ipsa essent animalia quae offerre consueverant, vero
tamen Deo haec et non idolis immolantes, iam
sacrificia ipsa non essent. Haec igitur dilectionem
tuam praedicto fratri necesse est dicere, ut ipse in
praesenti illic positus perpendat, qualiter omnia
debeat dispensare. Deus te incolumem custodiat,
dilectissime fili.

" Data die decima quinta kalendarum [1] . . . . . , imperante domino nostro Mauricio Tiberio piissimo
Augusto anno decimo nono, post consulatum eiusdem
domini anno decimo octavo, indictione quarta."

CAP. XXXI

*Ut Augustinum per litteras, ne de virtutibus suis gloria-
retur, hortatus sit.*

Quo in tempore misit etiam Augustino epistolam
super miraculis quae per eum facta esse cognoverat,
in qua eum, ne per illorum copiam periculum elationis
incurreret, his verbis hortatur:

" Scio, frater carissime, quia omnipotens Deus
per dilectionem tuam in gentem, quam eligi voluit,
magna miracula ostendit: unde necesse est ut

---

[1] *Augustarum* must be supplied. The MSS. either omit
or have *Iuliarum*, Pl.

known; but yet he retained unto them the use of the sacrifices (which they were wont to offer to the devil) in His own worship, by requiring them to slay the animals in sacrifice to Him; in order that with change of heart they should lose one thing in the sacrifice but preserve another: that is, that the beasts they offered before they should now offer still, but yet in slaying them unto the true God and not unto idols they should not be the same sacrifices as they were before. These then be the things which I think it expedient for your love to declare unto our said brother, to the intent that he being there at this present may consider with himself how each thing is to be disposed. God keep you in safety, my dearly beloved son.

"Given the 18th day of July, the 19th year of the reign of our lord Maurice Tiberius, the most religious Augustus, the 18th year after the consulship of the same lord, in the fourth indiction."

CHAPTER XXXI

How he exhorted Augustine by a letter that he should not glory in himself of his miracles.

ABOUT this time he sent also to Augustine an epistle touching such miracles as he had known to be done by the said Augustine, in the which epistle he exhorteth him that he should not come into danger of pride of mind for the number of them, in these words:

"I know, my dear brother, that it pleaseth Almighty God to shew by thy love great miracles among the people whom He hath willed to be chosen: whereupon it is needful that of the same

de eodem dono caelesti et timendo gaudeas, et gaudendo pertimescas. Gaudeas videlicet, quia Anglorum animae per exteriora miracula ad interiorem gratiam pertrahuntur: pertimescas vero, ne inter signa quae fiunt, infirmus animus in sui praesumptione se elevet, et unde foras in honorem tollitur, inde per inanem gloriam intus cadat. Meminisse etenim debemus quia discipuli cum gaudio a praedicatione redeuntes, dum caelesti Magistro dicerent: ' Domine, in nomine tuo etiam daemonia nobis subiecta sunt '; protinus audierent: ' Nolite gaudere super hoc, sed potius gaudete quia nomina vestra scripta sunt in caelo.' In privata enim et temporali laetitia mentem posuerant qui de miraculis gaudebant; sed de privata ad communem, de temporali ad aeternam laetitiam revocantur quibus dicitur: ' In hoc gaudete quia nomina vestra scripta sunt in caelo.' Non enim omnes electi miracula faciunt; sed tamen eorum nomina omnium in caelo tenentur adscripta. Veritatis etenim discipulis esse gaudium non debet, nisi de eo bono quod commune cum omnibus habent, et in quo finem laetitiae non habent. Restat itaque, frater carissime, ut inter ea quae operante Domino exterius facis, semper te interius subtiliter iudices, ac subtiliter intelligas, et temetipsum quis sis, et quanta sit in eadem gente gratia, pro cuius conversione etiam faciendorum signorum dona percepisti. Et siquando te Creatori

---

[1] Luke 10. 17, 20.

heavenly gift both thou joyest with fear and fearest with joy. Thou hast to joy, namely, for that by means of outward miracles the souls of the English are won to inward grace: but thou hast to fear, lest, in the midst of the miracles which be done, thy weak heart be lifted up in exaltation of thyself, falling as far inwardly by vainglory as thou art outwardly raised to honour. For we must remember that the disciples returning with joy from their preaching, when they said unto their heavenly Master:[1] 'Lord, even the devils are subject unto us through thy name;' forthwith heard the words: 'In this rejoice not, but rather rejoice, because your names are written in heaven.' For they had fastened their mind upon a private and temporal joy, when they joyed of their miracles; but they are called back from private joy unto common, and from temporal to eternal, to whom it is said: 'In this rejoice, because your names are written in heaven.' For not all the chosen of God doth miracles; but yet all their names are recorded in heaven. For why? They which be the disciples of the truth ought to joy in nothing, but only in that good thing which they have in common with all, and whereof they have joy without end. This therefore remaineth, dear beloved brother, that of the things which by the power of God thou workest outwardly, thou exactly ever discuss with thyself inwardly, and accurately understand both thyself who thou art, and what plenty of grace there is in that same country for whose sake (to the intent it might be the rather converted) thou hast received the gift of working miracles. And if thou remember that thou hast at any time either by word or deed offended

nostro seu per linguam, sive per opera reminisceris deliquisse, semper haec ad memoriam revoces, ut surgentem cordis gloriam memoria reatus premat. Et quidquid de faciendis signis acceperis vel accepisti, haec non tibi sed illis deputes donata, pro quorum tibi salute collata sunt."

CAP. XXXII

Ut Aedilbercto regi litteras et dona miserit.

MISIT idem beatus papa Gregorius eodem tempore etiam regi Aedilbercto epistolam, simul et dona in diversis speciebus perplura: temporalibus quoque honoribus regem glorificare satagens, cui gloriae caelestis suo labore et industria notitiam provenisse gaudebat. Exemplar autem praefatae epistolae hoc est:

" Domino gloriosissimo atque praecellentissimo filio Aedilbercto regi Anglorum, Gregorius episcopus.

" Propter hoc omnipotens Deus bonos quosque ad populorum regimina perducit, ut per eos omnibus quibus praelati fuerint, dona suae pietatis impendat. Quod in Anglorum gente factum cognovimus: cui vestra gloria idcirco est praeposita, ut per bona quae vobis concessa sunt, etiam subiectae vobis genti superna beneficia praestarentur. Et ideo, gloriose fili, eam quam accepisti divinitus gratiam, solicita mente custodi, Christianam fidem in populis tibi

our Creator, call that ever back to thy remembrance, that the oft thinking upon thy guilt may press down the mounting pride of thy heart. And whatsoever grace thou either hast received or shalt receive to work miracles, think that they have been granted not unto thee but unto them for whose salvation they have been bestowed upon thee."

CHAPTER XXXII

How he sent a letter and presents to the king Ethelbert.

THE said blessed pope Gregory at the selfsame time also sent unto king Ethelbert a letter as well as a number of gifts withal of divers sorts: being much occupied also to glorify the king with temporal honours, which through his diligent travail he rejoiced was grown to knowledge of the glory of heaven. Now the copy of the said letter is this:

" Unto the right honourable and his most worthy son, Ethelbert, King of the English, Gregory bishop.

" God Almighty for this cause doth call all that are good to the governance of His people, that by their hands He may distribute the gifts of His goodness unto all such over whom they have the governance. Which thing we know to have been done among the nation of the English over whom your glory is therefore set to rule, that by the gifts employed upon you, the blessings from on high might be given to all such as are under your dominion. And therefore, O noble son, labour diligently to keep the grace which you have received from God, seek with speed to set forth the faith of Christ to

subditis extendere festina, zelum rectitudinis tuae
in eorum conversione multiplica, idolorum cultus
insequere, fanorum aedificia everte, subditorum
mores ex [1] magna vitae munditia, exhortando, ter-
rendo, blandiendo, corrigendo, et boni operis exempla
monstrando aedifica : ut illum retributorem invenias
in caelo, cuius nomen atque cognitionem dilataveris
in terra. Ipse enim vestrae quoque gloriae nomen
etiam posteris gloriosius reddet, cuius vos honorem
quaeritis et servatis in gentibus.

" Sic etenim Constantinus quondam piissimus
imperator, Romanam rempublicam a perversis idolorum cultibus revocans, omnipotenti Deo Domino
nostro Iesu Christo secum subdidit, seque cum
subiectis populis tota ad eum mente convertit.
Unde factum est ut antiquorum principum nomen
suis vir ille laudibus vinceret, et tanto in opinione
praecessores suos, quanto et in bono opere supera-
ret. Et nunc itaque vestra gloria cognitionem unius
Dei, Patris, et Filii, et Spiritus sancti, regibus ac
populis sibimet subiectis festinet infundere, ut [2] et
antiquos gentis suae reges laudibus ac meritis
transeat, et quanto in subiectis suis etiam aliena
peccata deterserit, tanto etiam de peccatis propriis
ante omnipotentis Dei terribile examen securior fiat.

" Reverentissimus frater noster Augustinus episcopus, in monasterii regula edoctus, sacrae Scripturae

---

[1] For *et*, Pl.   [2] *ut*, supplied Pl.

---

[1] The letter to Mellitus, which is later, shews that Gregory
changed his mind about this.

the people subject unto you, increase the zeal of your righteousness in their conversion, set yourself against the worshipping of idols, overthrow the buildings of their temples,[1] edify the manners of your subjects by the great purity of your life, with words of exhortation, fear, fair speech, correction and shewing example of well-doing : that you may find Him to be your rewarder in heaven, whose knowledge and name you make to be enlarged upon the earth. For He will Himself also make your name the more famous unto posterity, whose honour you seek and maintain among the nations.

" For so Constantine, being sometimes a most religious emperor, called the Roman commonwealth from the corrupt worshipping of idols and brought it with himself under the obeisance of the Almighty God our Lord Jesus Christ, turning to Him with his whole mind together with them that were subject to his rule. Whereby it was brought to pass that his name was of higher renown than any of the princes that went before him, and so much in glory excelled his ancestors, how much also he passed them in well-doing. Wherefore let your highness also hasten now to spread among the kings and countries subject to your dominion the knowledge of one God, the Father, the Son and the Holy Ghost, to the intent thereby you may pass in honourable fame the ancient kings of your nation, and how much the more you wipe out also the sins of other among your subjects, you may have also so much the less fear of your own sins before the dreadful bench of Almighty God's justice.

" Our most reverend brother Augustine, bishop, being brought up in the rule of a monastery, filled

171

scientia repletus, bonis auctore Deo operibus prae-
ditus, quaeque vos ammonet, audite, devote peragite,
studiose in memoria reservate: quia si vos eum in
eo quod pro omnipotente Domino loquitur, auditis,
isdem omnipotens Deus hunc pro vobis exorantem
celerius exaudit. Si enim, quod absit, verba eius
postponitis, quando eum omnipotens Deus poterit
audire pro vobis, quem vos negligitis audire pro
Deo? Tota igitur mente cum eo vos in fervore
fidei stringite, atque adnisum illius virtute quam
vobis Divinitas tribuit, adiuvate, ut regni sui vos
ipse faciat esse participes, cuius vos fidem in regno
vestro recipi facitis [1] et custodiri.

"Praeterea scire vestram gloriam volumus, quia,
sicut in Scriptura sacra ex verbis Domini omnipotentis agnoscimus, praesentis mundi iam terminus
iuxta est, et sanctorum regnum venturum est, quod
nullo unquam poterit fine terminari. Adpropin-
quante autem eodem mundi termino, multa imminent
quae antea non fuerunt: videlicet immutationes
aëris, terroresque de caelo, et contra ordinationem
temporum tempestates, bella, fames, pestilentiae,
terrae motus per loca; quae tamen non omnia
nostris diebus ventura sunt, sed post nostros dies
omnia subsequentur. Vos itaque, si qua ex his
evenire in terra vestra cognoscitis, nullo modo
vestrum animum perturbetis; quia idcirco haec
signa de fine saeculi praemittuntur, ut de animabus
nostris debeamus esse soliciti, de mortis hora suspecti,

---

[1] For *faciatis*, Pl.

with the knowledge of Holy Scripture, and endued
by the grace of God with good works, whatsoever
he adviseth you to do, gladly hear it, devoutly do
it, diligently remember it: for if you hear him in
that he speaketh unto you in the Almighty Lord's
behalf, the same Almighty God the sooner heareth
him entreating for you. For if (as God forbid) you
forbear to give heed to his words, when can Almighty
God hear him in your behalf, whom you despise to
hear in God's behalf? Wherefore with all your
heart join yourself closely with him in zealousness
of faith, and assist his endeavour with the excellency
that God hath given you, that He may Himself
make you partaker of His kingdom Whose faith
you in your kingdom cause to be received and
observed.

" Furthermore, we will your highness to know
that (according as we are taught in the Holy Scriptures by the words of the Almighty Lord) the end
of the present world now draweth onward, and the
kingdom of the saints shall follow, which can never
have an end. And the same end of the world
approaching, many things are at hand which have
not been heard of before: that is, to wit, changes
of the air, terrible sights from the heaven, tempests
contrary to the ordering of seasons, wars, famines,
pestilences, earthquakes in divers places; all which
yet shall not fall in our days, but all shall follow
close after our days. Wherefore if you know any
of these to be in your land, let not your mind in
any way be dismayed therewith; for therefore are
these signs of the end of the world sent before the
time, to the intent we should the more diligently
tender the health of our souls, live in expectation

et venturo iudici in bonis actibus inveniamur esse
praeparati. Haec nunc, gloriose fili, paucis locutus
sum, ut cum Christiana fides in regno vestro excre-
verit, nostra quoque apud vos locutio latior excrescat,
et tanto plus loqui libeat, quanto se in mente nostra
gaudia de gentis vestrae perfecta conversione
multiplicant.

" Parva autem exenia transmisi, quae vobis parva
non erunt, cum a vobis ex beati Petri apostoli fuerint
benedictione suscepta. Omnipotens itaque Deus in
vobis gratiam suam quam coepit, perficiat, atque
vitam vestram, et hic per multorum annorum curri-
cula extendat, et post longa tempora in caelestis vos
patriae congregatione recipiat. Incolumem excellentiam vestram gratia superna custodiat, domine
fili.

" Data die decima kalendarum Iuliarum, imperante
domino nostro Mauricio Tiberio piissimo Augusto
anno decimo nono, post consulatum eiusdem domini
anno decimo octavo, indictione quarta."

CAP. XXXIII

*Ut Augustinus ecclesiam Salvatoris instauraverit, et
monasterium beati Petri apostoli fecerit; et de
primo eius abbate Petro.*

AT Augustinus, ubi in regia civitate sedem episcopalem, ut praediximus, accepit, recuperavit in ea,
regio fultus adminiculo, ecclesiam quam inibi antiquo

---

¹ ξένια.

of the hour of death and be found ready prepared in good works for the coming of our Judge. Thus much have I now said in few words, right honourable son, intending also to speak more at large as I shall hear the Christian faith to be enlarged in your kingdom, and being so much the more ready to speak, how much the more manifold comfort I shall conceive by the conversions of your country when it is completed.

" I have sent you, moreover, small presents [1] which shall not seem small unto you, if you shall accept them as hallowed with the blessing of the blessed apostle Peter. And so Almighty God make perfect in you His grace according as He hath begun, and prolong your life, both here through the course of many years, and after long time receive you in the assembly of the heavenly country. The grace from on high keep your highness in safety, my lord son!

" Given the 22nd of June in the 19th year of the reign of our lord Maurice Tiberius, the most religious Augustus, in the 18th year after the consulate of our same Lord, in the 4th indiction."

CHAPTER XXXIII

How Augustine repaired the church of our Saviour, and builded the monastery of the blessed apostle Peter ; and concerning Peter, first abbot thereof.

BUT Augustine, after he had obtained to have a bishop's see appointed him in the king's city, as is above said, being stayed by the support of the king, he recovered there a church which he had learned

Romanorum fidelium opere factam fuisse didicerat,
et eam in nomine sancti Salvatoris Dei et Domini
nostri Iesu Christi sacravit, atque ibidem sibi habitationem statuit, et cunctis successoribus suis.   Fecit
autem et monasterium non longe ab ipsa civitate ad
orientem, in quo, eius hortatu, Aediberct ecclesiam
beatorum apostolorum Petri et Pauli a fundamentis
construxit, ac diversis donis ditavit, in qua et ipsius
Augustini, et omnium episcoporum Doruvernensium,
simul et regum Cantiae poni corpora possent.   Quam
tamen ecclesiam non ipse Augustinus, sed successor
eius Laurentius consecravit.   Primus autem eiusdem
monasterii abbas Petrus presbyter fuit, qui legatus
Galliam missus, demersus est in sinu maris qui
vocatur Amfleat, et ab incolis loci ignobili traditus
sepulturae: sed omnipotens Deus ut qualis meriti
vir fuerit demonstraret, omni nocte supra sepulcrum
eius lux caelestis apparuit, donec animadvertentes
vicini, qui videbant, sanctum fuisse virum qui ibi
esset sepultus, et investigantes unde vel quis esset,
abstulerunt corpus, et in Bononia civitate iuxta
honorem tanto viro congruum in ecclesia posuerunt.

---

[1] Christ Church, Canterbury.
[2] Better known by later name of St. Augustine's.
[3] Ambleteuse.   [4] St. Mary's Church.

to have been there built of old by the work of
Romans which believed, and did dedicate it in the
name of the Holy Saviour God and our Lord Jesus
Christ, and there made a house for him and all his
successors.[1] And not far from the city itself east-
ward he builded also a monastery [2] in the which
Ethelbert through his advice builded from the
foundations a church in the honour of the blessed
apostles Peter and Paul, and enriched it with
sundry gifts, in which both the body of Augustine
himself and of all the bishops of Canterbury as well
as also of the kings of Kent might be interred.
Which church yet not Augustine himself, but
Laurentius his successor did consecrate. Moreover,
the first abbot of the same monastery was one
Peter, a priest, which being sent legate unto Gaul
was drowned in a creek of the sea called Amfleat,[3]
and buried after a homely manner of the inhabitants
of the same place. But Almighty God intending
to have it known how worthy a man he was, made
that every night there appeared a light from heaven
upon the place where he lay buried, until the neigh-
bours about, which saw the light, gathering thereby
that he was some holy man that was buried there,
and searching out what and from whence he was,
removed his body from thence, and buried it in the
church [4] in the town of Boulogne according to the
honour convenient for so worthy a person.

CAP. XXXIV

Ut Aedilfrid rex Nordanhymbrorum Scottorum gentis praelio conterens ab Anglorum finibus expulerit.

His temporibus regno Nordanhymbrorum praefuit rex fortissimus et gloriae cupidissimus Aedilfrid, qui plus omnibus Anglorum primatibus gentem vastavit Brettonum; ita ut Sauli quondam regi Israeliticae gentis comparandus videretur, excepto dumtaxat hoc, quod divinae erat religionis ignarus. Nemo enim in tribunis, nemo in regibus plures eorum terras, exterminatis vel subiugatis indigenis, aut tributarias genti Anglorum, aut habitabiles fecit. Cui merito poterat illud quod benedicens filium patriarcha in personam Saulis dicebat aptari: " Beniamin lupus rapax, mane comedet praedam, et vespere dividet spolia."

Unde motus eius profectibus Aedan rex Scottorum qui Brittaniam inhabitant, venit contra eum cum inmenso ac forti exercitu; sed cum paucis aufugit victus. Siquidem in loco celeberrimo qui dicitur Degsastan, id est, Degsa lapis, omnis pene eius est caesus exercitus. In qua etiam pugna Theodbald frater Aedilfridi, cum omni illo quem ipse ducebat exercitu, peremptus est. Quod videlicet bellum Aedilfrid anno ab incarnatione Domini sexcentesimo tertio, regni autem sui, quod viginti et quatuor annis tenuit, anno undecimo perfecit:

---

[1] *ealdormen* in the Anglo-Saxon version.

[2] Gen. 49. 27.

[3] Aedan mac Gabrain, king of the Dalriadic colony of Scots (*i.e.* Irish) which settled in Britain about A.D. 500, cf. ch. I.

[4] Probably Dawston in Liddesdale.

CHAPTER XXXIV

How Ethelfrith king of the Northumbers did crush the tribes of the Scots in battle and drave them from the boundaries of the English.

About this time Ethelfrith, a man very valiant and much desirous of renown, was king of Northumberland, one that more wasted the people of the Britons than any of the princes of the English; so that it seemed he might be compared unto Saul, sometimes king of the Israelite people, save only that he was ignorant of God's religion. For none of all the colonels,[1] none of all the kings did conquer more of the land of the Britons (either driving the natives clean out of the country or subduing them, or making them tributary or planting the Angles in their places) than did this Ethelfrith. To whom that might be well applied that the patriarch said [2] when he gave his son his blessing in the person of Saul: "Benjamin is a ravening wolf: in the morning he shall devour the prey, and at night he shall divide the spoil."

Whereby Aedan,[3] king of the Scots which dwell in Britain, much grudging to see him go forward after this sort, assembled a main and a strong army against him; but with a few men he fled away vanquished, seeing that in that famous place of Degsastan,[4] that is Degsa's stone, well-nigh all his army was slain. In which field also Theodbald, brother to Ethelfrith, was killed, with all that part of the army whereof he was general. Which war namely Ethelfrith brought to an end in the year of the Lord's incarnation 603 and the 11th year of

porro Focatis anno, qui tum Romani regni apicem tenebat, primo. Neque ex eo tempore quisquam regum Scottorum in Brittannia adversus gentem Anglorum usque ad hanc diem in proelium venire audebat.

his own reign, which lasted 24 years: further in the
first year of Phocas who then wore the crown of
the Roman kingdom.   And from that time forward
unto this present never was there king of Scots [1] in
Britain which durst meet the English in the field.

[1] *i.e.* of the Dalriadic colony.

BOOK II

HISTORIAE ECCLESIASTICAE GENTIS ANGLORUM

LIBER SECUNDUS

CAP. I

De obitu beati papae Gregorii.

His temporibus, id est, anno Dominicae incarnationis sexcentesimo quinto, beatus papa Gregorius, postquam sedem Romanae et apostolicae ecclesiae tredecim annos, menses sex, et dies decem gloriosissime rexit, defunctus est, atque ad aeternam regni caelestis sedem translatus. De quo nos convenit, quia nostram, id est Anglorum, gentem de potestate Satanae ad fidem Christi sua industria convertit, latiorem in nostra Historia Ecclesiastica facere sermonem, quem recte nostrum appellare possumus et debemus apostolum. Quia cum primum in toto orbe pontificatum gereret, et conversis iamdudum ad fidem veritatis esset praelatus ecclesiis, nostram gentem eatenus idolis mancipatam, Christi fecit ecclesiam, ita ut apostolicum illum de eo liceat nobis proferre sermonem : quia etsi aliis non est apostolus, sed tamen nobis est; nam signaculum apostolatus eius nos sumus in Domino.

Erat autem natione Romanus, a patre Gordiano, genus a proavis non solum nobile, sed et religiosum ducens. Denique Felix eiusdem apostolicae sedis quondam episcopus, vir magnae gloriae in Christo et ecclesia, eius fuit atavus. Sed ipse nobilitatem

---

[1] 590–604 Pl.   [2] 1 Cor. 9. 2.
[3] Felix III (or II), bishop of Rome 483–492, Pl.
[4] *atavus* seems used in a general sense.

THE SECOND BOOK OF THE ECCLESI-ASTICAL HISTORY OF THE ENGLISH NATION

CHAPTER I

Of the death of the blessed pope Gregory.

AT this time, that is to say, in the 605th year of the Lord's incarnation, the blessed pope Gregory, after he had most gloriously governed the see of the Roman and apostolic Church 13 years, 6 months and 10 days,[1] departed this life and was translated to the eternal see in the Kingdom of Heaven. Of whom it becometh us in this our Ecclesiastical History to speak more largely, because by his diligence he converted our nation, that is the English, from the power of Satan to the faith of Christ, whom we may well and must call our apostle. For as soon as he was high bishop over the whole world and was made governor to the Churches long since converted to the belief of the truth, he made our nation a Church of Christ, which had been ever till that time the bond-slave of idols, so that we may lawfully pronounce of him that saying of the apostle:[2] that if he be not an apostle to others, yet is he so to us; for the seal of his apostleship are we in the Lord.

Now Gregory was a Roman born, his father's name Gordian, his lineage from far back not only noble but also religious. In fact Felix,[3] a man of great glory in Christ and in the Church, sometime bishop of that same see apostolic was his ancestor in past generations.[4] But the nobility of religion

religionis non minore quam parentes et cognati
virtute devotionis exercuit. Nobilitatem vero illam
quam ad saeculum videbatur habere, totam ad
nanciscendam supernae gloriam dignitatis divina
gratia largiente convertit. Nam mutato repente
habitu saeculari, monasterium petiit, in quo tanta
perfectionis gratia coepit conversari, ut, sicut ipse
postea flendo solebat adtestari, animo illius labentia
cuncta subteressent, ut rebus omnibus quae volvun-
tur emineret, ut nulla nisi caelestia cogitare soleret,
ut etiam retentus corpore ipsa iam carnis claustra
contemplatione transiret, ut mortem quoque, quae
pene cunctis poena est, videlicet ut ingressum vitae
et laboris sui praemium amaret. Haec[1] autem ipse
de se, non profectum iactando virtutum, sed deflendo
potius defectum quem sibi per curam pastoralem
incurrisse videbatur, referre consueverat. Denique
tempore quodam secreto, cum diacono suo Petro
conloquens, enumeratis animi sui virtutibus priscis,
mox dolendo subiunxit: "At nunc ex occasione
curae pastoralis saecularium hominum negotia patitur,
et post tam pulcram quietis suae speciem, terreni
actus pulvere foedatur. Cumque se pro condescen-
sione[2] multorum ad exteriora sparserit, etiam cum
interiora appetit, ad haec procul dubio minor redit.
Perpendo itaque quid tolero, perpendo quid amisi:
dumque intueor illud quod perdidi, fit hoc gravius
quod porto."

---

[1] for *Hoc*, Pl.   [2] for *descensione*, Pl.

he himself kept and maintained with no less virtuous
devotion than his parents and kinsmen had done
before him. That nobility, however, which he
seemed to have before the world, by the gift of God's
grace he turned altogether to the purchasing of the
glory of heavenly honour. For changing suddenly
his secular habit he went into a monastery, where he
began to live in such grace of perfection, that unto
his mind (as often after he was wont to witness with
weeping tears) all transitory things were in the
lower place, that he was lifted above all things that
are subject unto change, that he was wont to think
of nothing but heavenly things, that, even though
clogged with the body, he already by contemplation
did pass the very barriers of the flesh, and that he
loved death also (which to almost all men is a
punishment) as being certes an entrance of life to
him and reward of his labour. Now these things he
was himself wont to say of himself, not craking of his
increase in virtues but rather lamenting the failing
of them, in which he thought himself to have fallen
by reason of his pastoral charge. In short, talking
on a time secretly with Peter, his deacon, when he
had recounted the old gifts of his mind, straightway
he added sorrowfully : " But now by means of my
pastoral charge my mind is encombered with the
affairs of the men of this world, and after so beautiful a vision of its peace, it is now defiled with
the dust of earthly business. And when out of
indulgence to many it is dispersed upon outward
matters, then, even when desiring inward thoughts,
it returneth thereunto beyond doubt the weaker.
Therefore I weigh with myself what I do now endure,
I weigh with myself what I have forgone : and while

Haec quidem sanctus vir ex magnae humilitatis intentione dicebat: sed nos credere decet nihil eum monachicae perfectionis perdidisse occasione curae pastoralis, immo potiorem tunc sumpsisse profectum de labore conversionis multorum, quam de propriae quondam quiete conversationis habuerat: maxime quia et pontificali functus officio domum suam monasterium facere curavit; et dum primo de monasterio abstractus, ad ministerium altaris ordinatus, atque Constantinopolim apocrisiarius ab apostolica sede directus est, non tamen in terreno conversatio palatio propositum vitae caelestis intermisit. Nam quosdam fratrum ex monasterio suo, qui eum gratia germanae caritatis ad regiam urbem secuti sunt, in tutamentum coepit observantiae regularis habere; videlicet ut eorum semper exemplo, sicut ipse scribit, ad orationis placidum litus, quasi anchorae fune restringeretur, cum incessabili causarum saecularium impulsu fluctuaret, concussamque saeculi actibus mentem inter eos quotidie per studiosae lectionis roboraret alloquium. Horum ergo consortio non solum a terrenis est munitus incursibus, verum etiam ad caelestis vitae exercitia magis magisque succensus.

Nam hortati sunt eum, ut librum beati Iob magnis involutum obscuritatibus, mystica interpretatione discuteret; neque negare potuit opus quod sibi

---

[1] So called *quod ἀποκρίσεις seu responsa principum deferrent,* a post like that of the later nuncio, Pl.

I behold what I have lost, this that I carry waxeth more grievous."

Thus it was this holy man spake, of a great and passing humility: but we should believe that he lost none of his monastical perfection by reason of his pastoral charge, nay rather that he gained greater advantage from the labour of the conversion of many than he had had with the private peace of his former conversation: chiefly because, even in the discharge of his priestly office, he was careful to order his house like a monastery; and when first he was taken out of the monastery and ordained to the ministry of the altar, being afterwards sent as legate [1] from the see apostolic, to Constantinople he for all that, in the earthly prince's palace, lived so that he never gave up his purpose of heavenly life. For he began to have with him certain brethren of his monastery (which for the sake of brotherly love followed him to the imperial city) for the better keeping of the monastic observance; namely, that alway by their example (for so he writeth) he might be fastened as with the cable of an anchor to the peaceful shore of prayer, whensoever he were tossed by the restless rushing of worldly cares, and might strengthen his mind by the daily communing of diligent reading with them, whensoever it should be shaken with worldly affairs. By these men's company therefore he was not only defended from the assaults of earthly troubles, but also more and more stirred up to the exercises of heavenly life.

For they exhorted him that he would discuss and expound by allegorical interpretation the book of blessed Job, which was enwrapped with great obscurities; neither could he deny them his pains,

fraternus amor multis utile futurum imponebat.
Sed eumdem librum, quomodo iuxta litteram intel-
ligendus, qualiter ad Christi et ecclesiae sacramenta
referendus, quo sensu unicuique fidelium sit aptandus,
per triginta et quinque libros expositionis miranda
ratione perdocuit. Quod videlicet opus in regia
quidem urbe apocrisiarius inchoavit, Romae autem
iam pontifex factus explevit. Qui cum adhuc [1]
esset regia in urbe positus, nascentem ibi novam
haeresim de statu nostrae resurrectionis, cum ipso
ex quo orta est initio, iuvante se gratia catholicae
veritatis, attrivit. Siquidem Eutychius, eiusdem
urbis episcopus dogmatizabat corpus nostrum in illa
resurrectionis gloria impalpabile, ventis aëreque
subtilius esse futurum; quod ille audiens, et ratione
veritatis, et exemplo dominicae resurrectionis, probavit hoc dogma orthodoxae fidei omnimodis esse
contrarium. Catholica etenim fides habet, quod
corpus nostrum illa immortalitatis gloria sublimatum,
subtile quidem sit per effectum spiritalis potentiae,
sed palpabile per veritatem naturae; iuxta exemplum
Dominici corporis, de quo a mortuis suscitato dicit
ipse discipulis: "Palpate et videte, quia spiritus
carnem et ossa non habet, sicut me videtis habere." [1]
In cuius adsertione fidei venerabilis pater Gregorius
in tantum contra nascentem haeresim novam laborare
contendit, tanta hanc instantia, iuvante etiam
piissimo imperatore Tiberio Constantino, comminuit,

---

[1] *adhuc*, Pl.

---

[1] Luke xxiv. 39.

which of brotherly love laid upon him a labour to
serve for the profit of many. But he hath marvellously taught in 35 books of exposition how the same
book is to be understood according to the letter,
in what sort it may be referred to Christ and the
sacraments of the Church, and in what sense it may
be applied to every particular faithful man. And
this work, namely, he began to write while he was
legate in the imperial city, but finished it when he
had now become bishop of Rome. And when he was
still in office in the imperial city, he suppressed a
new heresy concerning the state of our resurrection
(which then there arose) in the very beginning of its
rising, with the aid of the grace of catholic truth.
For Eutychius, bishop of the said city, began to
teach the doctrine that our body in that glory of the
resurrection should be so subtle as is neither the wind
nor the air, so that it should not be able to be felt or
touched; which when Gregory heard he proved this
teaching to be quite contrary to the orthodox faith
by the reasoning of truth and also by the example
of the Lord's resurrection. For the Catholic faith
believeth that our body, being exalted in that glory
of immortality, shall indeed be subtle by the effect
of spiritual power, but able to be felt and touched by
reason of our true nature: according to the example
of the Lord's body of which, now risen from the dead,
Himself saith to his disciples:[1] " Touch ye and see,
for a spirit hath not flesh and bones, as ye see me
have." In the assertion of this faith the venerable
father Gregory did labour so earnestly against the
upstart heresy in its beginning, and crushed it with
such diligence (being helped thereto also by the most
religious emperor Tiberius Constantine), that from

ut nullus exinde sit inventus qui eius resuscitator existeret.

Alium quoque librum composuit egregium, qui vocatur *Pastoralis*, in quo manifesta luce patefecit, quales ad ecclesiae regimen adsumi, qualiter ipsi rectores vivere, qua discretione singulas quasque audientium instruere personas, et quanta consideratione propriam quotidie debeant fragilitatem pensare. Sed et omelias Evangelii numero quadraginta composuit, quas in duobus codicibus aequa sorte distinxit. Libros etiam Dialogorum quatuor fecit, in quibus rogatu Petri diaconi sui, virtutes sanctorum quos in Italia clariores nosse vel audire poterat, ad exemplum vivendi posteris collegit; ut sicut in libris expositionum suarum quibus sit virtutibus insudandum, edocuit, ita etiam descriptis sanctorum miraculis, quae virtutum earundem sit claritas ostenderet. Primam quoque et ultimam Ezechielis prophetae partem, quae videbantur obscuriores, per omelias viginti et duas, quantum lucis intus habeant, demonstravit. Excepto libello Responsionum, quem ad interrogationes sancti Augustini primi Anglorum gentis episcopi scripsit, ut et supra docuimus, totum ipsum libellum his inserentes historiis; libello quoque synodico, quem cum episcopis Italiae de necessariis ecclesiae causis utillimum composuit, et familiaribus ad quosdam litteris. Quod eo magis mirum est, tot eum ac tanta condere volumina potuisse, quod omni pene iuven-

---

[1] Cf. I. 27.

[2] Synodical epistle written by newly appointed popes to their suffragan patriarchs.

[3] *i.e.* he copied out books as a scribe, apart from those he composed.

thenceforth no man was found which durst revive it again.

He made also another excellent book which is called the *Pastoral;* wherein he declareth plainly what manner of men should be chosen to rule the Church, how the rulers thereof ought themselves to live, with what discretion they should instruct each several person of their hearers, and with how great consideration they should daily weigh their own weakness. Moreover too he wrote homilies to the number of 40 upon the Gospel, which he hath divided by equal share into two volumes. He made also four books of Dialogues in which, at the request of his deacon Peter, he hath gathered the virtuous deeds of holy men which himself could either know in Italy or hear of for their fame, to the example of good life for posterity: that, like as in his books of expositions he hath thoroughly taught in what virtues a man must labour, so also by describing of holy men's miracles he might shew what the excellency of the same virtues is. Furthermore, because the first and last parts of Ezekiel the prophet seemed somewhat obscure, he hath fully shewed by 22 homilies how much light is within them. We need not speak of his small book of Answers [1] which he wrote back to the questions of holy Augustine, the first bishop of the English people, as also we have declared before, placing the whole book itself in this history; neither too of the small circular letter [2] which with the bishops of Italy he hath written most profitably concerning the necessary affairs of the Church, nor of his familiar letters sent unto divers men. And this is the more marvellous that he was able to write so many and such great volumes,[3] being

tutis suae tempore, ut verbis ipsius loquar, crebris
viscerum doloribus cruciabatur, horis momentisque
omnibus fracta stomachi virtute lassescebat, lentis
quidem, sed tamen continuis febribus anhelabat.
Verum inter haec, dum sollicitus pensaret quia
Scriptura teste, " Omnis filius qui recipitur, flagel-
latur," quo malis praesentibus durius deprimebatur,
eo de aeterna certius praesumptione respirabat.

Haec quidem de immortali eius sint dicta ingenio,
quod nec tanto corporis potuit dolore restingui.
Nam alii quidem pontifices construendis ornandisque
auro vel argento ecclesiis operam dabant: hic autem
totus erga animarum lucra vacabat. Quidquid
pecuniae habuerat, sedulus hoc dispergere ac dare
pauperibus curabat, ut iustitia eius maneret in
saeculum saeculi, et cornu eius exaltaretur in
gloria; ita ut illud beati Iob veraciter dicere posset:
" Auris audiens beatificabat me, et oculus videns
testimonium reddebat mihi, quod liberassem pauperem vociferantem et pupillum cui non esset
adiutor. Benedictio perituri super me veniebat, et
cor viduae consolatus sum. Iustitia indutus sum,
et vestivit me sicut vestimento et diademate, iudicio
meo. Oculus fui caeco, et pes claudo. Pater eram
pauperum, et causam quam nesciebam, diligentissime
investigabam. Conterebam molas iniqui, et de
dentibus illius auferebam praedam." Et paulo post:

(to speak in his own words) almost in all his youth tortured with frequent pains in his bowels, at all hours and instants wearied with the weakness of his stomach, and his breathing made difficult by low fevers which yet never left him. But in these griefs of his, by counting carefully with himself that the Scripture saith,[1] " Every son which is received, is scourged," the harder he was kept down by the present adversities, the more certainly did the assurance of everlasting comfort revive him.

Let thus much be said in the praise of his excellent wit which could not, with so great suffering of the body, be anything quenched. For whereas other bishops of Rome bestowed their labour in building of churches and decking the same with gold and silver, this man gave himself altogether to the profit of souls. Whatsoever he had in possession, he was careful to distribute diligently and give to poor men, that his righteousness might remain world without end and his horn be exalted in glory; so that he might truly utter that saying of blessed Job:[2] " When the ear heard me, then it blessed me; and when the eye saw me it gave witness to me, because I had delivered the poor that cried, and the fatherless child that had none to help him. The blessing of him that was ready to perish came upon me, and the heart of the widow did I comfort. I have put on righteousness and it clothed me as with a garment and precious crown in my judgment. I have been an eye to the blind and a foot to the lame. I was a father of poor men, and the cause which I knew not I diligently searched out. I did break in pieces the jaws of the unjust man, and out of his teeth did I pluck the prey." And a little after:[3] " If I have

" Si negavi," inquit, " quod volebant pauperibus, et
oculos viduae exspectare feci. Si comedi buccellam
meam solus, et non comedit pupillus ex ea. Quia
ab infantia mea crevit mecum miseratio, et de utero
matris meae egressa est mecum."

Ad cuius pietatis et iustitiae opus pertinet etiam
hoc, quod nostram gentem per praedicatores quos
huc direxit, de dentibus antiqui hostis eripiens,
aeternae libertatis fecit esse participem: cuius
fidei et saluti congaudens, quamque digna laude
commendans, ipse dixit in expositione beati Iob:
" Ecce lingua Brittaniae, quae nil aliud noverat quam
barbarum frendere, iamdudum in divinis laudibus
Hebraeum coepit ' Alleluia ' sonare. Ecce quondam tumidus, iam substratus sanctorum pedibus
servit oceanus, eiusque barbaros motus quos terreni
principes edomare ferro nequiverant, hos pro divina
formidine sacerdotum ora simplicibus verbis ligant,
et qui catervas pugnantium infidelis nequaquam
metueret, iam nunc fidelis humilium linguas timet.
Quia enim perceptis caelestibus verbis, clarescentibus
quoque miraculis, virtus ei divinae cognitionis
infunditur, eiusdem divinitatis terrore refraenatur,
ut prave agere metuat, ac totis desideriis ad aeternitatis gratiam venire concupiscat." Quibus verbis
beatus Gregorius hoc quoque declarat, quia sanctus
Augustinus et socii eius, non sola praedicatione
verborum, sed etiam caelestium ostensione signorum,
gentem Anglorum ad agnitionem veritatis per-
ducebant.

denied to poor men their desire, and have made the eyes of the widow look long for her help. If I have eaten my morsel alone, and the fatherless child hath not eaten thereof with me. For from mine infancy mercy hath grown with me and out of my mother's womb it came forth with me."

To the work of this Gregory's piety and righteousness this pertaineth also, that he hath made our nation, by preachers which he sent hither, to be partakers of eternal liberty, wresting us from the teeth of our old enemy: and rejoicing with our faith and salvation, and commending the same with worthy praise, he saith thus in his exposition of blessed Job: " Behold the tongue of Britain, which once knew nothing but to gnash the teeth rudely, hath long since begun to sing the Hebrew *Alleluia* in giving praise to God. Behold the ocean sea once swelling high, now made calm, obeyeth to the feet of holy men; and the furious floods thereof which earthly princes with force could never fray, the same for fear of God the lips of priests doth bind with bare words; and though that sea had no fear at all of the unbelieving hosts of fighting men, yet doth it now tremble at the tongues of humble believers. For whereas by receiving of heavenly words and the manifest shewing forth of miracles beside, the excellency of the knowledge of God is poured into it, by the terror of that same divine nature it is so bridled that now it feareth to act frowardly and most earnestly desireth to come to the grace of eternity." By which words the blessed Gregory declareth this also, that holy Augustine and his company brought the English nation to the knowledge of truth, not by preaching to them of words only but also by shewing them heavenly signs.

Fecit inter alia beatus papa Gregorius, ut in ecclesiis sanctorum apostolorum Petri et Pauli, super corpora eorum missae celebrarentur. Sed et in ipsa missarum celebratione tria verba maximae perfectionis plena superadiecit: " Diesque nostros in tua pace disponas, atque ab aeterna damnatione nos eripi, et in electorum tuorum iubeas grege numerari."

Rexit autem ecclesiam temporibus imperatorum Mauricii et Focatis. Secundo autem eiusdem Focatis anno transiens ex hac vita migravit ad veram quae in caelis est vitam. Sepultus vero est corpore in ecclesia beati Petri apostoli, ante secretarium, die quarto iduum Martiarum, quandoque in ipso cum ceteris sanctae ecclesiae pastoribus resurrecturus in gloria: scriptumque in tumba ipsius epitaphium huiusmodi:

" Suscipe, terra, tuo corpus de corpore sumptum,
    Reddere quod valeas vivificante Deo.
Spiritus astra petit, leti nil iura nocebunt,
    Cui vitae alterius mors magis ipsa via est.
Pontificis summi hoc clauduntur membra sepulcro,
    Qui innumeris semper vivit ubique bonis.
Esuriem dapibus superavit, frigora veste,
    Atque animas monitis texit ab hoste sacris.
Implebatque actu, quicquid sermone docebat,
    Esset ut exemplum, mystica verba loquens.
Ad Christum Anglos convertit pietate magistra,
    Adquirens fidei agmina gente nova.
Hic labor, hoc studium, haec tibi cura, hoc pastor
                        agebas,
    Ut Domino offerres plurima lucra gregis.
Hisque Dei consul factus laetare triumphis:
    Nam mercedem operum iam sine fine tenes."

GREGORY'S EPITAPH

Amongst his other doings the blessed pope Gregory caused that in the churches of the holy apostles Peter and Paul masses should be said over their bodies. Moreover too in the very celebration of these masses he added three petitions full of the highest perfection: " And dispose our days in thy peace, and command us to be taken from eternal damnation, and to be numbered in the flock of thine elect."

Now he governed the Church in the days of the emperors Maurice and Focas. But in the second year of the said Focas' empire, departing out of this life he passed to the true life which is in heaven. His body was buried in deed in the church of the blessed apostle Peter before the vestry, the 12th day of March, with the which same body he shall rise again hereafter in glory with the other pastors of the holy Church: and on the tomb which he had for himself was written such an epitaph as followeth:

"Receive, O earth, this body formed of dust of thine, to keep
Until the same the Lord shall wake to life again from sleep.
His spirit to the stars is gone, no right hath Death to maim,
Which rather is the way for him that other life to claim.
Pontiff supreme, within the tomb his bones are buried here,
Which ever and in every place made his good deeds appear.
The hungry he with food sustained, the naked he arrayed,
With sacred warnings human souls from Satan's power he stayed.
He did in deed what things in word soever he did teach,
To be ensample unto them which heard his holy speech.
The English to Christ's faith he turned, his goodness being guide,
And with a new race made the ranks of Christian men more wide.
This was thy toil, thy zealous care, good shepherd, only fain
Unto thy Lord for offering a larger flock to gain.
With these thy triumphs then rejoice, God's consul captain made,
For of thy deeds a sure reward thou hast, which cannot fade."

Nec silentio praetereunda opinio quae de beato
Gregorio traditione maiorum ad nos usque perlata
est; qua videlicet ex causa admonitus, tam sedulam
erga salutem nostrae gentis curam gesserit. Dicunt,
quia die quadam cum advenientibus nuper mercator-
ibus multa venalia in forum fuissent conlata, multique ad emendum confluxissent, et ipsum Gregorium
inter alios advenisse ac vidisse inter alia pueros
venales positos, candidi corporis, ac venusti vultus,
capillorum quoque forma egregia. Quos cum aspi-
ceret, interrogavit, ut aiunt, de qua regione vel
terra essent adlati. Dictumque est quod de Brittania
insula, cuius incolae talis essent aspectus. Rursus
interrogavit, utrum iidem insulani Christiani, an
paganis adhuc erroribus essent implicati. Dictumque est quod essent pagani. At ille intimo ex corde
longa trahens suspiria: " Heu, proh dolor! " inquit,
" quod tam lucidi vultus homines tenebrarum auctor
possidet, tantaque gratia frontispicii mentem ab
interna gratia vacuam gestat! " Rursus ergo interrogavit, quod esset vocabulum gentis illius. Responsum est, quod Angli vocarentur. At ille, " Bene,"
inquit; " nam et angelicam habent faciem, et tales
angelorum in caelis decet esse coheredes. Quod
habet nomen ipsa provincia de qua isti sunt adlati? "
Responsum est, quod " Deiri " vocarentur iidem
provinciales. At ille: " Bene," inquit, " Deiri, de ira

ANGLES AND ANGELS

Nor must we here with silence pass over the report which the tradition of our elders hath brought unto our knowledge concerning the blessed Gregory: to wit, upon what occasion he was moved to bestow such diligent labour for the salvation of our people. Men say that on a certain day, when many merchants newly arriving in Rome had brought into the market-place divers wares to be sold, and many had flocked hither to buy, amongst others Gregory too came thither, and amongst other things he saw boys set out to be sold, of white skin and comely countenance and hair also of excellent beauty. And beholding them a while he demanded, as they say, out of what region or land they had been brought. And it was answered that they came from the isle of Britain, where such was the appearance of the inhabitants. Again he asked whether the people of that same island were Christian men or were yet intangled in the paynims' errors. And the answer was made that they were paynims. Then this good man, heavily sighing from the bottom of his heart: "Alas!" quoth he, "it is a piteous case, that the author of darkness possesseth such bright beautied people and that men of such a gracious outward shew do bear a mind void of inward grace." Again therefore he enquired what was the name of that people. Answer was given that they were called Angles. Whereon he said: "Well are they so called, for they have too an angel's face, and it is meet such men were inheritors with the angels in heaven. What is the name of the particular province from which those boys of yours were brought?" The merchants answered that the people of that same province were called Deirans. "Marry!" quoth he, "well are they

eruti, et ad misericordiam Christi vocati. Rex
provinciae illius quomodo appellatur? " Responsum
est, quod " Aelli " diceretur. At ille adludens ad
nomen ait: " Alleluia! Laudem Dei Creatoris illis
in partibus oportet cantari." Accedensque ad pontificem Romanae et apostolicae sedis, nondum enim
erat ipse pontifex factus, rogavit ut genti Anglorum
in Brittaniam aliquos verbi ministros, per quos ad
Christum converteretur, mitteret; seipsum paratum
esse in hoc opus Domino cooperante perficiendum,
si tamen apostolico papae, hoc ut fieret, placeret.
Quod dum perficere non posset; quia, etsi pontifex
concedere illi quod petierat voluit, non tamen
cives Romani, ut tam longe ab urbe secederet,
potuere permittere; mox ut ipse pontificatus officio
functus est, perfecit opus diu desideratum: alios
quidem praedicatores mittens, sed ipse praedicationem ut fructificaret, suis exhortationibus ac
precibus adiuvans. Haec iuxta opinionem quam ab
antiquis accepimus, Historiae nostrae ecclesiasticae
inserere opportunum duximus.

---

[1] Inhabitants of Deifyr, Deur or Deira (Latinized), the
northern district south of the Tees or the Tyne. Gregory
plays upon the name Deira as *de ira.*

.

called Deirans,[1] being plucked from the ire of God and called to the mercy of Christ. How is the king of that province called?" It was answered that his name was Aella,[2] Whereupon Gregory playing upon the name saith: "Alleluia! the praise of God the Creator must be sounded in those parts." And coming to the bishop of the Roman and apostolic see (for himself was not yet chosen bishop thereof), he besought him that he would send to the English people in Britain some ministers of the word, by whom they might be converted unto Christ; saying that he himself was ready to carry out this work with the help of the Lord, yet only if it should please the pope apostolic to permit of the same. And while he was not able to accomplish this (for though the bishop would have granted him that he had asked, yet the burghers of Rome could not have suffered him to depart so far from the city), afterward, as soon as himself entered upon the office of bishop, he brought to pass the work he had before so long desired: sending indeed other preachers, but himself helping to make their preaching fruitful by his exhortations and prayers. This much according to the report which we have heard from days of old we have thought fitting to put in the History of our Church.

[2] Said to have been recognized as king in 560.

THE VENERABLE BEDE

CAP. II

*Ut Augustinus Brettonum episcopos pro pace catholica,
etiam miraculo coelesti coram eis facto, monuerit;
quaeve illos spernentes ultio secuta sit.*

INTEREA Augustinus adiutorio usus Aedilbercti
regis, convocavit ad suum colloquium episcopos sive
doctores proximae Brettonum provinciae in loco qui
usque hodie lingua Anglorum " Augustinaes ac," id
est, robur Augustini, in confinio Huicciorum et
Occidentalium Saxonum, appellatur; coepitque eis
fraterna admonitione suadere, ut pace catholica
secum habita, communem evangelizandi gentibus
pro Domino laborem susciperent. Non enim paschae
Dominicum diem suo tempore, sed a quarta decima
usque ad vicesimam lunam observabant; quae
computatio octoginta quatuor annorum circulo
continetur. Sed et alia plurima unitati ecclesiasticae
contraria faciebant. Qui cum longa disputatione
habita, neque precibus, neque hortamentis, neque
increpationibus Augustini ac sociorum eius assensum
praebere voluissent, sed suas potius traditiones
universis, quae per orbem sibi in Christo concordant,
ecclesiis praeferrent, sanctus pater Augustinus hunc
laboriosi atque longi certaminis finem fecit, ut

---

[1] After Gregory's *Responsa* (1. 27) had been received 601.

[2] Teutonic invaders who conquered the country between
the Somerset Avon and the Forest of Arden. Aust on the
Severn may have been the place of conference.

[3] If the 14th of the moon after the Spring Equinox fell on
a Sunday the Britons would keep Easter on that day, the
Romans would defer it to the following Sunday. The Britons
also followed the Jewish cycle of 84 years for fixing the correct
time of Easter, which had been abandoned by Rome in 527

CHAPTER II

*How Augustine exhorted the bishops of the Britons in
behalf of Catholic peace, with a heavenly miracle
done before them ; and what vengeance fell upon
them after for dispising his words.*

MEANWHILE [1] Augustine by the aid and help of
king Ethelbert called together the bishops and
doctors of the province of the Britons nearest to him
to commune with them in a place which till this date
is called in the English tongue *Augustine's ac*,
that is, Augustine's oak, being in the borders
of the Hwiccas [2] and West Saxons; and began
with brotherly admonition to persuade them to
be at Catholic peace with him, and to undertake
the common labour of preaching the Gospel to
the nations for the Lord's sake. For they kept
not the Easter Sunday in due time, but from the
14th to the 20th moon; [3] which count is concluded in the compass of 84 years. They used,
moreover, many other things contrary to the unity
of the Church. And when after long discussion
these men neither for prayers nor exhortations,
neither for rebukes of Augustine and his company
had been willing to give their assent to him,
but rather preferred their own traditions before
all other Churches which throughout the whole
world agreed together in Christ, then the holy
father Augustine made an end of so long and

in favour of the cycle of 19 years. The day of the Paschal
full moon depends on certain tables, the essential points of
which are given in the early pages of the book of Common
Prayer.

diceret: " Obsecremus Deum, qui habitare facit
unanimes in domo Patris sui, ut ipse nobis insinuare
caelestibus signis dignetur, quae sequenda traditio,
quibus sit viis ad ingressum regni illius properandum.
Adducatur aliquis aeger, et per cuius preces fuerit
curatus, huius fides et operatio Deo devota atque
omnibus sequenda credatur." Quod cum adversarii
inviti licet, concederent, allatus est quidam de genere
Anglorum, oculorum luce privatus; qui cum oblatus
Brettonum sacerdotibus, nil curationis vel sanationis
horum ministerio perciperet; tandem Augustinus
iusta necessitate compulsus, flectit genua sua ad
Patrem Domini nostri Iesu Christi, deprecans ut
visum caeco, quem amiserat, restitueret, et per
illuminationem unius hominis corporalem, in plurimorum corde fidelium spiritalis gratiam lucis accen-
deret. Nec mora, illuminatur caecus, ac verus
summae lucis praeco ab omnibus praedicatur
Augustinus. Tum Brettones confitentur quidem
intellexisse se veram esse viam iustitiae quam
praedicaret Augustinus: sed non se posse absque
suorum consensu ac licentia priscis abdicare moribus.
Unde postulabant ut secundo synodus pluribus
advenientibus fieret.

Quod cum esset statutum, venerunt, ut perhibent,
septem Brettonum episcopi et plures viri doctissimi,
maxime de nobilissimo eorum monasterio, quod
vocatur lingua Anglorum Bancornaburg, cui tempore

---

[1] Ps. 68. 6.　　　[2] Bangor Iscoed in Flintshire.

troublesome strife by speaking in this wise: " Let us pray unto God, which doth make men to dwell all of one mind in their Father's house,[1] that he will vouchsafe to signify unto us by heavenly signs, which tradition is to be followed and by what ways we must speedily walk to the entrance of His kingdom. Let there be brought here some sick body, and by whose prayers he shall be healed, let his faith and working be deemed hallowed of God and to be followed of us all." To this, when his adversaries granted, though unwillingly, there was presented a certain man of English birth which had lost the sight of his eyes; who being offered to the British priests, when by their ministry he was not holpen nor could be cured, at length Augustine, compelled by just necessity, fell on his knees to the Father of our Lord Jesu Christ, beseeching him that he would restore to the blind man the sight which he had lost, and that by the bodily lighting of one man he would enkindle the grace of spiritual light in the hearts of many faithful. And forthwith the blind man's eyes were lightened, and Augustine is declared by all as a true herald of heavenly light. Then these Britons confessed indeed that they understood that to be the true way of righteousness, which Augustine preached unto them: but yet they said they could not give up their old customs without the consent and leave of their own people. They desired therefore that they might have a second synod of a greater multitude.

Which when it was appointed to be so, there came by report 7 British bishops and a greater number of learned men, specially out of their most notable monastery which is called in the English tongue Bancornaburg,[2] where at that time it is said Dinoot

207

illo Dinoot abbas praefuisse narratur, qui ad praefatum ituri concilium, venerunt primo ad quemdam
virum sanctum ac prudentem, qui apud eos anachore-
ticam ducere vitam solebat, consulentes, an ad
praedicationem Augustini suas deserere traditiones
deberent. Qui respondebat: "Si homo Dei est,
sequimini illum." Dixerunt: "Et unde hoc possumus probare?" At ille; "Dominus," inquit, "ait:
'Tollite iugum meum super vos, et discite a me
quia mitis sum et humilis corde.' Si ergo Augustinus ille mitis est et humilis corde, credibile est quia
iugum Christi et ipse portet, et vobis portandum
offerat: sin autem inmitis ac superbus est, constat,
qui non est de Deo, neque nobis eius sermo curandus."
Qui rursus aiebant: "Et unde vel hoc dinoscere
valemus?" "Procurate," inquit, "ut ipse prior cum
suis ad locum synodi adveniat, et si vobis adpro-
pinquantibus adsurrexerit, scientes quia famulus
Christi est, obtemperanter illum audite: sin autem
vos spreverit, nec coram vobis adsurgere voluerit,
cum sitis numero plures, et ipse spernatur a vobis."
Fecerunt ut dixerat. Factumque est, ut venientibus illis sederet Augustinus in sella. Quod illi
videntes, mox in iram conversi sunt, eumque notantes
superbiae, cunctis quae dicebat contradicere labora-
bant. Dicebat autem eis, quia "in multis quidem
nostrae consuetudini, immo universalis ecclesiae
contraria geritis: et tamen si in tribus his mihi
obtemperare vultis; ut pascha suo tempore cele-
bretis; ut ministerium baptizandi, quo Deo renasci-

---

[1] Matth. 11. 29.   [2] Ill-tempered.

was abbot. These men being now ready to go to the said meeting, came first to a certain holy and wise man which used to live amongst them an anchorite's life, and asked his counsel whether they ought at Augustine's preaching to leave their traditions or no. Who answered them: "If he be a man of God, follow him!" "And how can we prove this?" said they. The anchorite answered: "Our Lord saith, 'Take my yoke upon you and learn of me, for I am meek and lowly of heart.'[1] If therefore this Augustine be meek and lowly of heart, it is believable that himself too beareth the yoke of Christ and offereth you the same to bear: but if he be curst[2] and proud, it is certain that he is not of God, neither must we attend to his words." Then they said again: "And how have we power to discern this?" "Marry," quoth he, "provide ye that he with his company come first to the place of the synod, and if, when ye approach near, he ariseth courteously to you, then, knowing that he is the servant of Christ, hear ye him obediently! but if he despise you nor will vouchsafe to rise at your presence, though ye are more in number, let him likewise be despised by you!"

As the anchorite bade them, so did they. And it happened that when they came thither Augustine was already there and sat in his chair, which when they saw, straightways waxing wroth, they noted him of pride and endeavoured to gainsay all that he said. Now he said that "in many points ye do contrary to our custom, or rather to the custom of the universal Church: yet notwithstanding, if ye will in these three things obey unto me, that is, to celebrate Easter in due time; to accomplish the ministry of

mur, iuxta morem sanctae Romanae et apostolicae ecclesiae compleatis; ut genti Anglorum una nobiscum verbum Domini praedicetis; cetera quae agitis, quamvis moribus nostris contraria, aequanimiter cuncta tolerabimus." At illi nil horum se facturos, neque illum pro archiepiscopo habituros esse respondebant; conferentes ad invicem, quia " si modo nobis adsurgere noluit, quanto magis si ei subdi coeperimus, iam nos pro nihilo contemnet."

Quibus vir Domini Augustinus fertur minitans praedixisse, quia si pacem cum fratribus accipere nollent, bellum ab hostibus forent accepturi; et si nationi Anglorum noluissent viam vitae praedicare, per horum manus ultionem essent mortis passuri. Quod ita per omnia, ut praedixerat, divino agente iudicio patratum est.

Siquidem post haec ipse de quo diximus, rex Anglorum fortissimus Aedilfrid, collecto grandi exercitu, ad Civitatem Legionum, quae a gente Anglorum Legacaestir, a Brettonibus autem rectius Carlegion appellatur, maximam gentis perfidae³ stragem dedit. Cumque bellum acturus videret sacerdotes eorum, qui ad exorandum Deum pro milite bellum agente convenerant, seorsum in tutiore loco consistere, sciscitabatur qui essent hi, quidve acturi illo convenissent. Erant autem plurimi eorum de monasterio Bancor, in quo tantus fertur

---

¹ The difference between the British and Roman custom is not certain.

² Chester.

³ *perfidus* is applied to *heretics* as well as *unbelievers* (I. 7).

baptism, by which we are born again to God, according to the manner of the holy Roman and apostolic Church; [1] and to preach along with us the word of the Lord to the English nation; all the other things that ye do, though they be contrary to our customs, we shall be content to bear with." But they answered that they would do none of the things requested, neither would count him for archbishop: saying with themselves: " Nay, if he would not so much as rise to us, how much the more, if we now begin to subject ourselves to him, will he hereafter despise us and set us at nought ! "

To whom the man of God, Augustine, is said to have threatfully prophesied, that, if they would not have peace with brethren, they should have war from enemies; and if they would not preach to the English nation the way of life, they should through their hands suffer the vengeance of death. Which thing in all points was brought so to pass, as he had foresaid, by the working of God's judgment.

For it happened afterwards that the very same king of the English of whom we have spoken, the mighty Ethelfrith, gathering a large army, made at the City of Legions [2] (which the English nation call Legacaestir, but the Britons better Carlegion) a very great slaughter of this heretical [3] people. And being now ready to give battle, when he spied their priests (which had come together to pray to God for the soldiers fighting in the war) to stand apart from the rest in a safer place, he demanded what these men were and to what end they had collected there. Now the most part of these priests were of the monastery of Bangor, where there is said to have been so great a number of monks, that this monastery being

fuisse numerus monachorum, ut cum in septem
portiones esset cum praepositis sibi rectoribus
monasterium divisum, nulla harum portio minus
quam trecentos homines haberet, qui omnes de
labore manuum suarum vivere solebant. Horum
ergo plurimi ad memoratam aciem, peracto ieiunio
triduano, cum aliis orandi causa convenerant,
habentes defensorem nomine Brocmailum, qui eos
intentos precibus a barbarorum gladiis protegeret.
Quorum causam adventus cum intellexisset rex
Aedilfrid, ait: " Ergo si adversum nos ad Deum
suum clamant, profecto et ipsi quamvis arma non
ferant, contra nos pugnant qui adversis nos inpre-
cationibus persequuntur." Itaque in hos primum
arma verti iubet, et sic ceteras nefandae militae
copias non sine magno exercitus sui damno delevit.
Exstinctos in ea pugna ferunt, de his qui ad orandum
venerant, viros circiter mille ducentos, et solum
quinquaginta fuga esse lapsos. Brocmail ad primum
hostium adventum cum suis terga vertens, eos quos
defendere debuerat, inermes ac nudos ferientibus
gladiis reliquit. Sicque completum est praesagium
sancti pontificis Augustini, quamvis ipso iam multo
ante tempore ad caelestia regna[1] sublato, ut etiam
temporalis interitus ultione sentirent perfidi, quod
oblata sibi perpetuae salutis consilia spreverant.

---

[1] for *regni*, Pl.

divided into 7 companies, with each company his several assigned ruler, none of these companies had less than 300 persons, who did all ever live by the labour of their own hands. A great number therefore of them, after three days' fasting, had come with others to the aforesaid army to pray for the soldiers, having by them a defender named Brocmail who should keep them from the swords of the barbarians while they thus earnestly bent to their prayers. And when king Ethelfrith had understood the cause of their coming thither, he said: "Then if these men cry and call upon their God against us, truly though they themselves have no armour, yet they fight against us, who pursue us with curses to bring evil upon us." Accordingly he commanded his soldiers to assault these men first, and so he vanquished after the other parts of this detestable host, but yet not without a great loss of his own men. It is reported that there were slain in that battle, of them which had come to pray, about 1200 men, and that only 50 escaped by flight. Brocmail at the first coming of the enemy turned his back with his men, and whom he ought to have defended, these he left without defence and naked to the strokes of the sword. And so in this manner was fulfilled the prophecy of the holy bishop Augustine (though he himself long before had been raised to the heavenly realms), so that these heretical men learnt by the vengeance also of temporal death, that they had despised the counsels of eternal salvation offered to them.

THE VENERABLE BEDE

CAP. III

Ut idem Mellitum ac Iustum episcopos fecerit ; et de obitu eius.

Anno Dominicae incarnationis sexcentesimo quarto Augustinus Brittaniarum archiepiscopus ordinavit duos episcopos, Mellitum videlicet et Iustum: Mellitum quidem ad praedicandum provinciae Orientalium Saxonum, qui Tamense fluvio dirimuntur a Cantia et ipsi Orientali mari contigui, quorum metropolis Lundonia civitas est, super ripam praefati fluminis posita, et ipsa multorum emporium populorum terra marique venientium: in qua videlicet gente tunc temporis Saberct nepos Aedilbercti, ex sorore Ricula regnabat, quamvis sub potestate positus eiusdem Aedilbercti, qui omnibus, ut supra dictum est, usque ad terminum Humbrae fluminis, Anglorum gentibus imperabat. Ubi vero et haec provincia verbum veritatis praedicante Mellito accepit, fecit rex Aedilberct in civitate Lundonia ecclesiam sancti Pauli apostoli, in qua locum sedis episcopalis et ipse et successores eius haberent. Iustum vero in ipsa Cantia Augustinus episcopum ordinavit in civitate Dorubrevi, quam gens Anglorum a primario quondam illius qui dicebatur Hrof, Hrofaescaestrae cognominat. Distat autem a Doruverni millibus passuum ferme viginti quatuor ad occidentem, in qua rex Aedilberct ecclesiam beati Andreae apostoli fecit, qui etiam episcopis utriusque huius ecclesiae dona multa, sicut et Doruvernensis, obtulit: sed et territoria ac

NEW BISHOPS

CHAPTER III

How the same Augustine made Mellitus and Justus bishops ; and of his death.

In the 604th year of the incarnation of our Lord, Augustine archbishop of the Britains ordained two bishops, to wit Mellitus and Justus : the one, that is Mellitus, to preach to the province of the East Saxons, which are separated from Kent with the river Thames and are fast joined to the East Sea, whose chief city is London, of situation set upon the bank of the said flood, and itself a mart of many people arriving thither by land and sea : in the which country at that time reigned Sabert, Ethelbert's nephew by his sister Ricula, although set under the dominion of the same Ethelbert who was (as has been said before) lord over all the English races as far as the boundary of the flood Humber. Now when this province also by the preaching of Mellitus received the word of truth, king Ethelbert builded in the city of London the church of the apostle St. Paul, where both Mellitus himself and his successors should have their episcopal see : The other, which was Justus, Augustine ordained bishop in Kent itself in the city of Rochester which is called Hrofaescaestrae of the English nation, from the name of Hrof that was sometime principal man thereof. Now it is in distance from Canterbury town about 24 miles westward, in the which city king Ethelbert, builded the church of the blessed apostle Andrew, and also gave many gifts to the bishops of both these churches, like as he also gave to the bishops of Canterbury : moreover, he added territories and

215

possessiones in usum eorum qui erant cum episcopis,
adiecit.

Defunctus est autem Deo dilectus pater Augustinus, et positum corpus eius foras, iuxta ecclesiam
beatorum apostolorum Petri et Pauli, cuius supra
meminimus, quia ea necdum fuerat perfecta, nec
dedicata. Mox vero ut dedicata est, intro inlatum,
et in porticu illius aquilonali decenter sepultum est:
in qua etiam sequentium archiepiscoporum omnium
sunt corpora tumulata, praeter duorum tantummodo,
id est, Theodori et Berctualdi, quorum corpora in
ipsa ecclesia posita sunt, eo quod praedicta porticus
plura capere nequivit. Habet haec in medio pene
sui altare in honore beati papae Gregorii dedicatum,
in quo per omne sabbatum a[1] presbytero loci illius
agendae eorum solemniter celebrantur. Scriptum
vero est in tumba eiusdem Augustini epitaphium
huiusmodi:

" Hic requiescit domnus Augustinus Doruvernensis
archiepiscopus primus, qui olim huc a beato Gregorio
Romanae urbis pontifice directus, et a Deo operatione
miraculorum suffultus, Aedilberctum regem ac
gentem illius ab idolorum cultu ad Christi fidem
perduxit, et completis in pace diebus officii sui,
defunctus est septimo kalendas Iunias, eodem rege
regnante."

[1] a supplied, Pl.

possessions thereto for the better maintaining of them that lived with these bishops.

After this the beloved man of God, father Augustine, died, and his body was laid by the church of the blessed apostles Peter and Paul (of which church we have made mention before), without the door thereof, because it was not yet finished nor dedicated. But as soon as the church was dedicated, his body was brought in and decently buried in the north chapel of the church: where also were interred the bodies of all the archbishops following, except two only, that is Theodore and Bertwald; whose bodies were laid in the church itself, because the said chapel could receive no more. This chapel hath almost in the middle of it an altar dedicated in the honour of the blessed pope Gregory, at the which altar every Saturday masses [1] in their memory are solemnly celebrated by the priest of that place. Moreover, in the tomb of the same Augustine was written such an epitaph as followeth:

" Here lieth in rest the lord Augustine, first archbishop of Canterbury, who aforetime sent hither of the blessed Gregory, bishop of the city of Rome, and strengthened of God by working of miracles, won over Ethelbert the king and his people from the worship of idols to the faith of Christ, and so fulfilling in peace the days of his office he died the 26th of May [2] in the reign of the same king."

[1] *Agenda* is a mass for the dead.
[2] The year is uncertain.

CAP. IV

Ut Laurentius cum coepiscopis suis Scottos unitatem
sanctae ecclesiae maxime in pascha observando
sequi monuerit, et ut Mellitus Roman venerit.

SUCCESSIT Augustino in episcopatum Laurentius,
quem ipse idcirco adhuc vivens ordinaverat, ne se
defuncto status ecclesiae tam rudis, vel ad horam
pastore destitutus, vacillare inciperet. In quo et
exemplum sequebatur primi pastoris ecclesiae, hoc
est, beatissimi apostolorum principis Petri, qui
fundata Romae ecclesia Christi Clementem sibi
adiutorem evangelizandi, simul et successorem
consecrasse perhibetur. Laurentius archiepiscopi
gradu potitus strenuissime fundamenta ecclesiae,
quae nobiliter iacta vidit, augmentare, atque ad
profectum debiti culminis, et crebra voce sanctae
exhortationis, et continuis piae operationis exemplis
provehere curavit. Denique non solum novae quae
de Anglis erat collecta, ecclesiae curam gerebat, sed
et veterum Brittaniae incolarum, necnon et Scottorum qui Hiberniam insulam Brittaniae proximam
incolunt, populis pastoralem impendere sollicitudinem curabat. Siquidem ubi Scottorum in
praefata ipsorum patria, quomodo et Brettonum in
ipsa Brittania vitam ac professionem minus ecclesiasticam in multis esse cognovit, maxime quod
paschae sollemnitatem non suo tempore celebrarent,
sed, ut supra docuimus, a decima-quarta luna usque
218

CHAPTER IV

How Laurence with his fellow bishops warned the Scots to follow the unity of the holy Church, specially in keeping Easter, and how Mellitus came to Rome.

THE successor to Augustine in the bishopric was Laurence, whom Augustine himself, while he yet lived, had thereunto ordained, lest that after he was dead the state of the Church as yet so rude might begin to totter, if it should have lacked a pastor even for an hour. Wherein too he followed the example of the first pastor of the Church, that is of the most blessed prince of the apostles, Peter, who when he had laid at Rome the foundation of Christ's Church, is said to have consecrated Clement to be his helper in preaching the Gospel, as well as to be his successor. Laurence having now obtained the rank of archbishop gave heed most diligently to enlarge the foundations of the Church, which he saw had been well and strongly laid, and to lift up the building to reach the due highness, both by often words of holy exhortation and continual examples of godly working. In short he wrought heedfully not only for the new Church which was now gathered of the English, but also for the Church of the old inhabitants of Britain and of the Scots too who harboured in Ireland, the next isle to Britain, on the which folk he laboured to bestow the care of a pastor. For as soon as he knew the life and profession of the Scots in their forenamed country to be scarce ecclesiastical in many points (like as was the Britons' at that time in Britain itself), specially because they celebrated not the solemnity of Easter in due time, but (as we have

ad vicesimam Dominicae resurrectionis diem observandum esse putarent; scripsit cum coepiscopis suis
exhortatoriam ad eos epistolam: obsecrans eos, et
contestans unitatem pacis et catholicae observationis cum ea quae toto orbe diffusa est Ecclesia
Christi, tenere; cuius videlicet epistolae principium
hoc est:

" Dominis carissimis fratribus episcopis, vel abbatibus per universam Scottiam, Laurentius, Mellitus,
et Iustus episcopi, servi servorum Dei. Dum nos
sedes apostolica, more suo sicut in universo orbe
terrarum, in his occiduis partibus ad praedicandum
gentibus paganis dirigeret, atque in hanc insulam,
quae Brittania nuncupatur, contigit introisse;[1]
antequam cognosceremus,[1] credentes quod iuxta
morem universalis Ecclesiae ingrederentur, in magna
reverentia sanctitatis tam Brettones quam Scottos
venerati sumus; sed cognoscentes Brettones, Scottos
meliores putavimus. Scottos vero per Daganum
episcopum in hanc, quam superius memoravimus,
insulam, et Columbanum abbatem in Galliis venientem, nihil discrepare a Brettonibus in eorum con-
versatione didicimus. Nam Daganus episcopus ad
nos veniens, non solum cibum nobiscum, sed nec in
eodem hospitio quo vescebamur, sumere voluit."
Misit idem Laurentius cum coepiscopis suis, etiam
Brettonum sacerdotibus litteras suo gradui condignas,
quibus eos in unitate catholica confirmare satagit.

---

[1] Stops corrected, Pl.

[1] *i.e.* Ireland.
[2] Not certainly known.
[3] Apostle of Burgundy and founder of a monastic rule.
[4] The Saxons had driven out the Britons and taken their
lands, and were still under the curses pronounced by British

before shewed) thought that they must observe the
day of our Lord's resurrection from the 14th moon
to the 20th; he, I say, with his fellow bishops wrote
unto them an exhorting epistle, beseeching and
warning them to hold fast the unity of peace and
catholic observation with that Church of Christ
which was spread over all the whole world; of which
epistle namely the beginning is as follows:

" To our dearest brethren the bishops and abbots
throughout all Scotland,[1] Laurence, Mellitus and
Justus bishops, servants of the servants of God.
Whenas the see apostolic (according to the accustomed manner thereof as it doth in all parts of the
world) sent us to preach to paynim people in these
western parts, and so it happened us to enter into
this isle which is called Britain; where thinking,
before we had experience, that men walked according to the customed way of the universal Church, we
honoured with great reverence of holiness as well the
Britons as the Scots; but having experience of the
Britons we thought the Scots better. Marry now,
we have learnt by bishop Dagan[2] coming to this
before-mentioned island, and by the coming of
Columban,[3] abbot in France, that the Scots do nothing
differ from the Britons in their conversation. For
bishop Dagan coming to us would not only not eat
with us, but not so much as take his meat in the same
house where we were eating."[4] The same Laurence with his fellow bishops sent also letters meet
for his degree to the priests of the Britons wherein
he endeavoured to strengthen them in catholic

bishops against the invaders. The Celts were prone to
imprecations.

Sed quantum haec agendo profecerit, adhuc praesentia tempora declarant.

His temporibus venit Mellitus, Lundoniae episcopus, Romam, de necessariis ecclesiae Anglorum cum apostolico papa Bonifatio tractaturus. Et cum idem papa reverentissimus cogeret synodum episcoporum Italiae, de vita monachorum et quiete ordinaturus, et ipse Mellitus inter eos adsedit anno octavo imperii Focatis principis, indictione decima tertia, tertio die kalendarum Martiarum : ut quaeque erant regulariter decreta, sua quoque auctoritate subscribens confirmaret, ac Brittaniam rediens, secum Anglorum ecclesiis mandanda atque servanda deferret, una cum epistolis quas idem pontifex Deo dilecto archiepiscopo Laurentio, et clero universo, similiter et Aedilbercto regi atque genti Anglorum direxit. Hic est Bonifatius, quartus a beato Gregorio Romanae urbis episcopo, qui impetravit a Focate principe, donari ecclesiae Christi templum Romae quod Pantheon vocabatur ab antiquis, quasi simulacrum esset omnium deorum : in quo ipse eliminata omni spurcitia, fecit ecclesiam sanctae Dei genetricis, atque omnium martyrum Christi ; ut exclusa multitudine daemonum, multitudo ibi sanctorum memoriam haberet.

---

[1] The Catholic Easter was not adopted in Wales before 755–777.

[2] Boniface IV, 608–615.   [3] 610.

unity. But how much he hath availed by so doing, these present days do still declare.[1]

About this time came Mellitus, bishop of London, to Rome, there to counsel with the apostolic pope Boniface [2] for necessary causes of the English Church. And whenas the same most reverend pope called a synod of the bishops of Italy to appoint some order as concerning the life of monks and their quiet state, Mellitus also himself sat amongst them the 8th year of the reign of the emperor Focas, the 13th indiction, and the 27th day of February: [3] that what things so ever were decreed according to rule, he also by subscribing thereunto might confirm them with his authority, and returning to Britain might bring them with him to the English churches to be committed to them and observed, as also beside epistles which the same bishop of Rome wrote and sent to the archbishop Laurence beloved of God and all the clergy, and likewise also to king Ethelbert and the English nation. This is the Boniface which was the 4th bishop of Rome after blessed Gregory, who by earnest suit obtained of the emperor Focas a temple at Rome to be granted to the Church of Christ, which temple of ancient time was called Pantheon, as it were to stand for all the gods: out of which temple this Boniface casting forth all filthiness made a church therein in the honour of the holy mother of God and all the martyrs of Christ beside; that the army of devils being shut out thence, the army of martyrs might have there memorial.

THE VENERABLE BEDE

CAP. V

Ut defunctis Aedilbercto et Sabercto regibus, successores
eorum idolatriam resuscitarint, ob quod et Mellitus
ac Iustus a Brittania discesserint.

ANNO ab incarnatione Dominica sexcentesimo
decimo sexto, qui est annus vicesimus primus, ex
quo Augustinus cum sociis ad praedicandum genti
Anglorum missus est, Aedilberct rex Cantuariorum,
post regnum temporale, quod quinquaginta et sex
annis gloriosissime tenuerat, aeterna caelestis regni
gaudia subiit: qui tertius quidem in regibus gentis
Anglorum, cunctis australibus eorum provinciis quae
Humbrae fluvio et contiguis ei terminis sequestrantur
a borealibus, imperavit; sed primus omnium caeli
regna conscendit. Nam primus imperium huiusmodi
Aelli rex Australium Saxonum; secundus Caelin rex
Occidentalium Saxonum, qui lingua ipsorum [1] Ceaulin
vocabatur; tertius, ut dixi, Aedilberct rex Cantuariorum; quartus Reduald rex Orientalium Anglorum, qui etiam vivente Aedilbercto eidem suae
genti ducatum praebebat, obtinuit; quintus Aeduini
rex Nordanhymbrorum gentis, id est, eius quae ad
borealem Humbrae fluminis plagam inhabitat,
maiore potentia cunctis qui Brittaniam incolunt,
Anglorum pariter et Brettonum populis praefuit,
praeter Cantuariis tantum; necnon et Mevanias

---

[1] for *eorum*, Pl.

[1] They reached Britain in 597. The date of Ethelbert's
accession is uncertain.

[2] He was *Bretwalda*, the title given to Egbert in the Anglo-
Saxon Chronicle under the date 827, meaning probably a war
leadership, *imperium*, over the English invading tribes south
of the Humber, and not a territorial domination, *regnum*.

THE BRETWALDAS

CHAPTER V

How when the kings Ethelbert and Sabert were dead, their successors brought up again idolatry, where-upon Mellitus and Justus departed out of Britain.

IN the 616th year of the incarnation of our Lord (which was the 21st after that Augustine and his company were sent to the English nation to preach [1]), Ethelbert king of Kent, after his temporal reign which he had kept most gloriously the space of 56 years, entered into the eternal bliss of the kingdom of heaven: who was in deed the third king of the English nation, and had lordship over all their southern provinces which are separated from the northern by the flood Humber and the borders adjoining thereto; but he was the first of all the kings that ascended into the kingdom of heaven. For the first that had lordship after this sort [2] was Aella king of the South Saxons; the second Caelin king of the West Saxons, who was called in their own tongue Ceawlin; the third, as I have said, was Ethelbert king of the Kentishmen; the fourth was Redwald king of the East English, who also, while Ethelbert yet lived, was gaining the leadership for the same his own nation; the fifth was Edwin king of the Northumbrian nation, that is, king of those that dwell about the north part of the flood Humber, who, being a prince of greater power than all other that inhabited Britain, was head over both the English and the Britons too, except the people of Kent; and added moreover to the English lordship the Mevanian islands [3] of the Britons, which lie

[3] Anglesey and Man.

THE VENERABLE BEDE

Brettonum insulas, quae inter Hiberniam et Brittaniam sitae sunt, Anglorum subiecit imperio; sextus Osuald et ipse Nordanhymbrorum rex Christianissimus, hisdem finibus regnum tenuit; septimus Osuiu frater eius, aequalibus pene terminis regnum nonnullo tempore coercens, Pictorum quoque atque Scottorum gentes, quae septentrionales Brittaniae fines tenent, maxima ex parte perdomuit, ac tributarias fecit. Sed haec postmodum. Defunctus vero est rex Aedilberct die vigesima quarta mensis Februarii, post viginti et unum annos acceptae fidei, atque in porticu sancti Martini, intra ecclesiam beatorum apostolorum Petri et Pauli sepultus, ubi et Berctae regina condita est.

Qui inter cetera bona, quae genti suae consulendo conferebat, etiam decreta illi iudiciorum, iuxta exempla Romanorum, cum consilio sapientium constituit; quae conscripta Anglorum sermone hactenus habentur, et observantur ab ea: in quibus primitus posuit, qualiter id emendare deberet, qui aliquid rerum vel ecclesiae, vel episcopi, vel reliquorum ordinum furto auferret: volens scilicet tuitionem eis, quos et quorum doctrinam susceperat, praestare.

Erat autem idem Aedilberct filius Irminrici, cuius pater Octa, cuius pater Oeric, cognomento Oisc, a quo reges Cantuariorum solent Oiscingas cognominare. Cuius pater Hengist, qui cum filio suo Oisc invitatus a Vurtigerno Brittaniam primus intravit, ut supra retulimus.

At vero post mortem Aedilbercti, cum filius eius Eadbald regni gubernacula suscepisset, magno tenellis

---

[1] Witanagemôt or Witan, the assembly of the wise.
[2] Kentish code known as the *Laws of Ethelbert*, to be found in Thorpe's *Ancient Laws and Institutes of England*.
226

betwixt Ireland and Britain; the sixth was Oswald, himself also king of the Northumbrians, a most Christian prince, whose kingdom was within the same boundaries; the seventh was Oswy his brother, who governed the realm within almost equal bounds for a certain time, and after, he subdued for the most part the Pictish and Scottish races also which dwelt in the north quarters of Britain, and made them tributary. But we will speak of these things hereafter. Now king Ethelbert died the 24th day of February, 21 years being full past after he had received the faith, and was laid in St. Martin's chapel within the church of the blessed apostles Peter and Paul, where also queen Bertha is buried.

Which king, beside all other benefits that he of wise policy bestowed upon his subjects, appointed them, with his council of wise men,[1] judicial dooms [2] according to the example of the Romans; which being written in the English tongue are until this day kept of them and practised: in which dooms he for the first time ordained what amends he ought to make, which had by theft taken away anything from the churches, bishops or the other orders: wishing doubtless to provide a safeguard for them whom and whose doctrine he had received.

Now the said Ethelbert was son of Irminric, whose father was Octa, whose father was Eric called also Oisc, of whom the kings of the Kentishmen are wont to be called Oiscings. This Eric's father's name was Hengist, who with Oisc his son, being sent for of Vurtigern, first entered Britain, as we have shewed before.

But after the death of Ethelbert, when Eadbald his son had taken on him the rule of the realm, he

ibi adhuc ecclesiae crementis detrimento fuit.
Siquidem non solum fidem Christi recipere noluerat,
sed et fornicatione pollutus est tali, qualem nec inter
gentes auditam apostolus testatur, ita ut uxorem
patris haberet. Quo utroque scelere occasionem
dedit ad priorem vomitum revertendi, his qui sub
imperio sui parentis, vel favore vel timore regio,
fidei et castimoniae iura susceperant. Nec supernae
flagella districtionis perfido regi castigando et
corrigendo defuere: nam crebra mentis vesania,
et spiritus immundi invasione premebatur.

Auxit autem procellam huiusce perturbationis,
etiam mors Sabercti regis Orientalium Saxonum, qui
ubi regna perennia petens, tres suos filios, qui
pagani perduraverant, regni temporalis heredes
reliquit, coeperunt illi mox idolatriae, quam viventi
eo aliquantulum intermisisse videbantur, palam
servire, subiectisque populis idola colendi liberam
dare licentiam. Cumque viderent pontificem celebratis in ecclesia missarum sollemniis, eucharistiam
populo dare, dicebant, ut vulgo fertur, ad eum
barbara inflati stultitia: " Quare non et nobis
porrigis panem nitidum, quem et patri nostro Saba,"
sic namque eum appellare consuerant, " dabas, et
populo adhuc dare in ecclesia non desistis ? " Quibus
ille respondebat: " Si vultis ablui fonte illo salutari
quo pater vester ablutus est, potestis etiam panis

---

[1] Ethelbert's second wife. Cf. 1 Cor. v. 1.   [2] Mellitus.

[3] Early fonts were of the nature of tanks, often supplied
by a spring (*fons*), and hence font came to be the prevailing
name. Bede uses *lavacrum* (bath) as well as *fons*. The raised
form of font was introduced when infant baptism became the
rule, and aspersion took the place of immersion.

greatly damaged the growth of the Church which was yet right young and tender there. For he would not only not accept the faith of Christ, but he was also defiled with such a fornication as the apostle witnesseth not to have been heard of even amongst the Gentiles, which was that he married his father's wife.[1] With which two heinous offences he gave occasion to his subjects to return to their former vomit, which under his father's dominion, either for favour or fear of the king, had yielded to the laws of faith and chastity. But the scourges of punishment from on high wanted not to the chastisement and correction of the unbelieving king: for he was plagued with often frenzy of mind and the assault of an unclean spirit.

Moreover, the death also of Sabert king of the East Saxons increased the storm of this disturbance of the Church, who departing to the everlasting kingdoms left his three sons, which had remained yet paynims, heirs of his temporal kingdom on earth; and these began straightway and openly to follow idolatry which, while their father lived, they seemed somewhat to have relented, and gave free licence to the people subject to them to worship idols. These princes, when they saw the bishop,[2] after he had celebrated the solemnities of the mass in the church, give the people the sacrament, being puffed up with barbarous and rude folly, would say (as the common report is), " Why dost thou not offer us also the white bread which thou didst both give to our father Saba (for so they were wont to call him) and which thou dost not yet cease to give the people in the church ?" To whom he answered : " If ye will be washed in that wholesome font,[3] wherein your father was

sancti, cui ille participabat, esse participes : sin
autem lavacrum vitae contemnitis, nullatenus valetis
panem vitae percipere." At illi, " Nolumus,"
inquiunt, " fontem illum intrare, quia nec opus illo
nos habere novimus, sed tamen pane illo refici
volumus." Cumque diligenter ac saepe ab illo
essent admoniti, nequaquam ita[1] fieri posse ut absque
purgatione sacrosancta quis oblationi sacrosanctae
communicaret, ad ultimum furore commoti, aiebant :
" Si non vis adsentire nobis in tam facili causa quam
petimus, non poteris iam in nostra provincia
demorari." Et expulerunt eum, ac de suo regno
cum suis abire iusserunt.

Qui expulsus inde, venit Cantiam, tractaturus cum
Laurentio et Iusto coepiscopis, quid in his esset
agendum. Decretumque est communi consilio, quia
satius esset ut omnes patriam redeuntes, libera ibi
mente Domino deservirent, quam inter rebelles fidei
barbaros sine fructu resident. Discessere itaque
primo Mellitus ac Iustus, atque ad partes Galliae
secessere, ibi rerum finem exspectare disponentes.
Sed non multo tempore reges[2] qui praeconem a se
veritatis expulerant, daemonicis cultibus impune
serviebant. Nam egressi contra gentem Geuissorum
in praelium, omnes pariter cum sua militia corruerunt,
nec, licet auctoribus perditis, excitatum ad scelera

---

[1] *ita*, Pl.   [2] *reges*, Pl.

---

[1] Tribal name of the West Saxons.

washed, ye are also able to be partakers of the holy bread whereof he was partaker: but if ye contemn the laver of life, ye can in no wise receive the bread of life." "We will not," say they in reply, "enter that font, for we know we have no need thereof, but yet nevertheless we wish to be refreshed with that bread." And when they had been often and diligently warned of the bishop that it could by no means be, that without most holy cleansing anyone might communicate of this most holy oblation, they at last, in their fury and rage, said to the bishop: "If thou wilt not consent to us in so small a matter as we ask of thee, thou shalt not be able henceforth to abide in our province." And straightway they expelled him, commanding him and all his company to depart their realm.

Who being expelled thence went into Kent to commune there with Laurence and Justus his fellow-bishops, what were best to be done in this case. And by common consent it was concluded that it were better for them all to return to their own country and there to serve the Lord with a free mind, than to abide without profit amongst barbarous men that were rebels of the faith. And so at first Mellitus and Justus departed and withdrew to the coasts of France, purposing to attend for the issue of these matters. But these kings, which had driven from them the preacher of truth, were not long time enslaved to the worshipping of devils without punishment. For going out to battle against the tribe of the Gewissas,[1] they were all slain along with their army; but although the authors of mischief were thus destroyed, yet could not the common people once stirred to naughtiness be amended and

231

vulgus potuit recorrigi, atque ad simplicitatem fidei
et caritatis quae est in Christo, revocari.

CAP. VI

*Ut correptus ab apostolo Petro Laurentius Aeodbaldum
regem ad Christum converterit, qui mox Mellitum et
Iustum ad praedicandum revocaverit.*

CUM vero et Laurentius Mellitum Iustumque
secuturus ac Brittaniam esset relicturus, iussit ipsa
sibi nocte in ecclesia beatorum apostolorum Petri et
Pauli de qua frequenter iam diximus, stratum parari,
in quo cum post multas preces ac lacrymas ad
Dominum pro statu ecclesiae fusas, ad quiescendum
membra posuisset atque obdormisset, apparuit ei
beatissimus apostolorum princeps, et multo illum
tempore secretae noctis flagellis artioribus afficiens,
sciscitabatur apostolica districtione, quare gregem
quem sibi ipse crediderat, relinqueret, vel cui pasto-
rum oves Christi in medio luporum positas fugiens
ipse dimitteret. "An mei," inquit, "oblitus es
exempli, qui pro parvulis Christi, quos mihi in indicium suae dilectionis commendaverat, vincula, ver-
bera, carceres, adflictiones, ipsam postremo mortem,
mortem autem crucis, ab infidelibus et inimicis
Christi ipse cum Christo coronandus pertuli?"
His beati Petri flagellis simul et exhortationibus
animatus famulus Christi Laurentius, mox mane

recalled to the simplicity of faith and charity which
is in Christ.

CHAPTER VI

*How Laurence chastened by the apostle Peter converted
king Eadbald to Christ, who shortly after called
back Mellitus and Justus to preach.*

WHEN now Laurence also was ready to go after
Mellitus and Justus and forsake Britain, he commanded, the very night before he went, his bed to be
laid in the church of the blessed apostles Peter and
Paul, of which church we have oftentimes before
spoken; where, when after many his prayers and
tears poured forth to the Lord for the state of the
Church, reposing his body to rest and going to sleep,
the most blessed chief of the apostles appeared to
him, and scourging him with sharp stripes a great
while in the close and secret night, sought to know
with apostolic severity, why he should forsake the
flock which he himself had committed unto him, and
to what shepherd, running now away himself, he
would leave the sheep of Christ beset in the midst of
wolves. "Hast thou," quoth he, "forgot mine
example, who for the little ones of Christ, which he
commended to me in token of His love, did suffer
fetters, stripes, imprisonings, afflictions, and at the
last death itself, yea the death of the cross, by
infidels and the enemies of Christ, that I might
myself be crowned with Christ?" By these stripes
of the blessed Peter and these his exhortations
Laurence the servant of Jesus Christ, being stirred
up, came straightway to the king early in the morning

THE VENERABLE BEDE

facto venit ad regem, et retecto vestimento quantis
esset verberibus laceratus ostendit. Qui multum
miratus, et inquirens quis tanto viro tales ausus
esset plagas infligere: ut audivit quia suae causa
salutis episcopus ab apostolo Christi tanta esset
tormenta plagasque perpessus, extimuit multum;
atque anathematizato omni idolatriae cultu, abdi-
cato connubio non legitimo, suscepit fidem Christi,
et baptizatus, ecclesiae rebus quantum valuit, in
omnibus consulere ac favere curavit. Misit etiam
Galliam, et revocavit Mellitum ac Iustum, eosque
ad suas ecclesias libere instituendas redire praecepit:
qui post annum ex quo abierunt, reversi sunt; et
Iustus quidem ad civitatem Hrofi, cui praefuerat,
rediit, Mellitum vero Lundonienses episcopum recipere noluerunt, idolatris magis pontificibus servire
gaudentes. Non enim tanta erat ei, quanta patri
ipsius regni potestas, ut etiam nolentibus ac contra-
dicentibus paganis antistitem suae posset ecclesiae
reddere. Verumtamen ipse cum sua gente, ex quo
ad Dominum conversus est, divinis se studuit
mancipare praeceptis. Denique et in monasterio
beatissimi apostolorum principis, ecclesiam sanctae
Dei genitricis fecit, quam consecravit archiepiscopus
Mellitus.

---

[1] Augustine's monastery at Canterbury, east of the church
built by Ethelbert.

and loosing his garment shewed him how sore he was beaten and pitifully his flesh torn. The king much amazed thereat enquired who durst be so bold as to whip and scourge such a man: and when he heard that for his own salvation's sake the bishop had suffered so grievous beatings of the apostle of Christ, he feared greatly; and so having cursed all worship of idols, and renouncing his unlawful marriage, he embraced the faith of Christ, and being baptized he endeavoured to consider and befriend the cause of the Church in all points to his uttermost power. He sent also into France and called home Mellitus and Justus, commanding them to return to their churches and give instruction freely: and they returned again the year after their departure; and Justus went back to Rochester where he was bishop, but as for Mellitus the Londoners would not receive him for bishop, choosing rather to obey idolatrous high priests. For Eadbald was not a king of so great power as was his father, that he might restore the bishop to his church notwithstanding the paynim Londoners' ill-will and resistance. But yet for his own part and all his subjects, from the day that he was converted to the Lord he was earnest to submit himself to the commandments of God. At last also he built a church in honour of the holy mother of God in the monastery [1] of the most blessed chief of the apostles, which church Mellitus the archbishop consecrated.

THE VENERABLE BEDE

CAP. VII

Ut Mellitus episcopus flammas ardentis suae civitatis orando restinxerit.

Hoc enim regnante rege beatus archiepiscopus Laurentius regnum caeleste conscendit, atque in ecclesia et monasterio sancti apostoli Petri iuxta praedecessorem suum Augustinum sepultus est die quarto nonarum Februariarum: post quem Mellitus, qui erat Lundoniae episcopus, sedem Doruvernensis ecclesiae tertius ab Augustino suscepit: Iustus autem adhuc superstes Hrofensem regebat ecclesiam. Qui cum magna ecclesiam Anglorum cura ac labore gubernarent, susceperunt scripta exhortatoria a pontifice Romanae et apostolicae sedis Bonifatio, qui post Deusdedit ecclesiae praefuit, anno incarnationis Dominicae sexcentesimo decimo nono. Erat autem Mellitus corporis quidem infirmitate, id est, podagra gravatus, sed mentis gressibus sanis, alacriter terrena quaeque transiliens, atque ad caelestia semper amanda, petenda, et quaerenda pervolans. Erat carnis origine nobilis, sed culmine mentis nobilior.

Denique ut unum virtutis eius, unde cetera intelligi possint, testimonium referam; tempore quodam civitas Doruvernensis per culpam incuriae igni correpta, crebrescentibus coepit flammis consumi: quibus cum nullo aquarum iniectu posset aliquis obsistere, iamque civitatis esset pars vastata

---

[1] Boniface V.

CHAPTER VII

*How bishop Mellitus quenched with his prayer the
flames burning his city.*

For in the reign of this king Eadbald the blessed
archbishop Laurence ascended to the heavenly
kingdom and was buried the second day of February
in the church and monastery of the holy apostle
Peter fast by his predecessor Augustine, and after
him Mellitus who was bishop of London succeeded
to the see of Canterbury church, third archbishop
after Augustine: whenas Justus was still alive and
governed the church of Rochester. Which two
prelates, since they did rule the English Church with
great labour and diligence, received exhorting
epistles from Boniface,[1] bishop of the Roman and
apostolic see, who after Deusdedit governed the
Church in the year of the incarnation of our Lord 619.
Now Mellitus was troubled with infirmities of the
body, that is to say, with the gout, yet, notwithstanding, the walking of his mind was sure and
sound, and passing over speedily all earthly things
he hied him fast to heavenly things, which are ever
to be beloved, to be wished and to be sought for.
After the flesh he was noble by the birth he came of,
but more noble by the height he came to of his mind.

In a word I will rehearse one token of his good
power by which the rest may be understood; when
upon a certain time the city of Canterbury was
from fault of negligence taken with fire and began
to consume away by much increasing of the
flames, so that no man by any casting of water
was able to stay it, the greatest part of the city

THE VENERABLE BEDE

non minima, atque ad episcopium furens se flamma
dilataret, confidens episcopus in divinum, ubi
humanum deerat, auxilium, iussit se obviam saevienti-
bus, et huc illucque volantibus ignium globis efferri.
Erat autem eo loci ubi flammarum impetus maxime
incumbebat, martyrium beatorum Quatuor Corona-
torum. Ibi perlatus obsequentum manibus episcopus,
coepit orando periculum infirmus abigere, quod firma
fortium manus multum laborando nequiverat. Nec
mora, ventus qui a meridie flans, urbi incendia
sparserat, contra meridiem reflexus, primo vim sui
furoris a laesione locorum quae contra erant, abstraxit,
ac mox funditus quiescendo, flammis pariter sopitis
atque exstinctis compescuit. Et quia vir Dei igne
divinae caritatis fortiter ardebat, quia tempestates
potestatum aëriarum a sua suorumque laesione
crebris orationibus vel exhortationibus repellere
consueverat, merito ventis flammisque mundialibus
praevalere, et ne sibi suisque nocerent, obtinere
poterat.

Et hic ergo postquam annis quinque rexit ecclesiam
Aeodbaldo regnante migravit ad caelos, sepultusque
est cum patribus suis in saepedicto monasterio et
ecclesia beatissimi apostolorum principis, anno ab
incarnatione Domini sexcentesimo vicesimo quarto,
die octavo kalendarum Maiarum.

---

[1] Who had a church at Rome on the Caelian Hill. Names
are given for them, but otherwise they are unknown.
[2] Cf. Eph. ii. 2.

238

being at length near burnt and the furious flashes extending themselves to the bishop's palace, the bishop trusting in God's help, where the help of man now failed, commanded that he might be carried out of his house and set against these fierce flaws of fire flying all round about. Now in that part where the assault of the flames fell most sorely there was the tomb of the blessed Four Crowned Martyrs.[1] When the bishop by the hands of his servants was brought thither, he began with prayer, sick as he was, to drive away the peril which the stout strength of strong men with much labour could not before bring to pass. And behold, the wind that blew from the south, whereby this fire was spread abroad over the city, now suddenly being bent against the south, first drew off the blast of his fury from hurting the places right over in the other side, and straightway sinking utterly to rest stayed his blowing, while the flames in like manner were quieted and died out. And for as much as the man of God did fervently burn with the fire of divine charity, seeing he was wont with his often prayers and exhortations to drive from the hurt of himself and all his the storms of the powers of the air,[2] he might now justly prevail against the winds and flames of the present world, and obtain that they injured not him nor his.

And this man then, after he had ruled the Church 5 years, passed away to the heavens in the reign of Eadbald, and was buried with his fathers in the oft-mentioned monastery and church of the most blessed chief of the apostles, in the 624th year of the Lord's incarnation, on the 24th day of April.

239

CAP. VIII

Ut Bonifatius papa Iusto successori eius pallium et epistolam miserit.

Cui statim successit in pontificatum Iustus, qui erat Hrofensis ecclesiae episcopus. Illi autem ecclesiae Romanum pro se consecravit episcopum, data sibi ordinandi episcopos auctoritate a pontifice Bonifatio, quem successorem fuisse Deusdedit supra meminimus; cuius auctoritatis ista est forma:

" Dilectissimo fratri Justo, Bonifatius. Quam devote, quamque etiam vigilanter pro Christi Evangelio elaboraverit vestra fraternitas, non solum epistolae a vobis directae tenor, immo indulta desuper operi vestro perfectio indicavit. Nec enim omnipotens Deus, aut sui nominis sacramentum, aut vestri fructum laboris deseruit, dum ipse praedicatoribus Evangelii fideliter repromisit: ' Ecce ego vobiscum sum omnibus diebus usque ad consummationem saeculi.'[1] Quod specialiter iniuncto vobis ministerio eius clementia demonstravit, aperiens corda gentium ad suscipiendum praedicationis vestrae singulare mysterium. Magno enim praemio fastigiorum vestrorum delectabilem cursum, bonitatis suae suffragiis illustravit, dum creditorum vobis talentorum fidelissimae negotiationis officiis uberem fructum impendens ei, quod signare possetis multiplicatis generationibus, praeparavit.[2] Hocque etiam illa vobis repensatione collatum est, qua iniuncto

---

[1] Matth. xxviii. 20. [2] Luke xix. 15.

CHAPTER VIII

How pope Boniface sent Justus, Mellitus' successor, a pall and an epistle.

To whom Justus succeeded immediately in the pontificate, who was bishop of the church at Rochester, over which church he consecrated Romanus as bishop in his place, for now he had received authority to ordain bishops from Boniface the pope, successor of Deusdedit as we have said before; the form of which authority is as follows:

" To our dearly beloved brother Justus, Boniface. How godly and how earnestly also you have, dear brother, laboured for the Gospel of Christ, not only the tenor of your epistle directed to us, but rather the perfection granted unto your work from on high hath declared. For Almighty God hath not forsaken either the meaning of His name or the fruit of your travail, seeing Himself faithfully hath promised the preachers of the Gospel, saying : [1] ' Lo, I am with you always, even unto the end of the world.' Which thing especially His clemency hath shewed in this ministry appointed you, by opening the hearts of the Gentiles to receive the singular mystery of your preaching. For He hath made honourable with a great reward the acceptable course of your eminence by the approval of His goodness, seeing that Himself, by bestowing abundant fruit upon the exercise of your most faithful trading [2] with the talents entrusted to you, hath prepared for that course what you could set forth for manifold generations. And this too is given you in such recompense, for that you, persisting continually in

241

THE VENERABLE BEDE

ministerio iugiter persistentes, laudabili patientia
redemptionem gentis illius exspectastis, et vestris
ut proficerent meritis, eorum est salvatio propinata ;
dicente Domino : ' Qui perseveraverit usque in
finem, hic salvus erit.' Salvati ergo estis spe
patientiae, et tolerantiae virtute, ut infidelium corda
naturali ac superstitioso morbo purgata, sui conse-
querentur misericordiam Salvatoris. Susceptis namque apicibus filii nostri Adulualdi regis, reperimus
quanta sacri eloquii eruditione eius animum ad verae
conversionis et indubitatae fidei credulitatem fraternitas vestra perduxerit. Qua ex re de longanimitate
clementiae caelestis certam adsumentes fiduciam,
non solum suppositarum ei gentium plenissimam
salutem, immo quoque vicinarum, vestrae praedicationis ministerio credimus subsequendam : quatenus, sicut scriptum est, consummati operis vobis
merces a retributore omnium bonorum Domino
tribuatur, et vere ' Per omnem terram exisse sonum
eorum, et in fines orbis terrae verba ipsorum,'
universalis gentium confessio, suscepto Christianae
sacramento fidei, protestetur.

" Pallium praeterea per latorem praesentium
fraternitati tuae, benignitatis studiis invitati direximus, quod videlicet tantum in sacrosanctis cele-
brandis mysteriis utendi licentiam impertivimus :
concedentes etiam tibi ordinationes episcoporum,
exigente opportunitate, Domini praeveniente misericordia celebrare : ita ut Christi Evangelium pluri-

---

[1] Matth. x. 22.   [2] *I.e.* Eadbald.   [3] Ps. xix. 4.
242

the ministry appointed to you, looked with laudable patience for the redemption of that people, and their salvation was granted unto you, that they might get some good by your deserving; as the Lord saith:[1] 'He that endureth the end shall be saved.' Ye are therefore saved by the hope of patience and by the virtue of longsuffering, so that the hearts of infidels being purged from their natural and superstitious disease may attain to the mercy of their Saviour. For after receiving the letters of our son king Adulwald,[2] we have understood with what great learning of the holy word you, my brother, have brought his mind to belief in true conversion and in the undoubted faith. Whereupon we, putting sure affiance in the forbearance of the heavenly mercy, do believe that not only the full salvation of king Adulwald's subjects but rather also of the next inhabitants about him must come to follow after the ministry of your preaching: to the end that, as it is written, the payment of your perfected work may be given you from the Lord, the rewarder of all good, and that truly the universal confession of all nations receiving the mystery of the Christian faith may manifestly declare, ' Their sound hath gone forth over all the earth, and their words to the uttermost parts of the world.'[3]

" Furthermore, called thereunto heartily of our bounteousness we have sent you, my brother, by the bearer of our present letter, a pall, which namely we have given you licence to use only in the celebration of the most holy mysteries: granting you, moreover, by the aid of the Lord's mercy the ordaining of bishops when occasion requireth: so that the Gospel of Christ by the preaching of many may the

morum adnuntiatione, in omnibus gentibus quae necdum conversae sunt, dilatetur. Studeat ergo tua fraternitas, hoc quod sedis apostolicae humanitate percepit, intemerata mentis sinceritate servare, intendens cuius rei similitudine tam praecipuum indumentum humeris tuis baiulandum susceperis. Talemque te Domini implorata clementia exhibendum stude, ut indulti muneris praemia non cum reatitudine, sed cum commodis animarum, ante tribunal summi et venturi Iudicis repraesentes. Deus te incolumem custodiat, dilectissime frater."

CAP. IX

De imperio regis Aeduini, et ut veniens ad evangelizandum ei Paulinus, primo filiam eius cum aliis, fidei Christianae sacramentis imbuerit.

Quo tempore etiam gens Nordanhymbrorum, hoc est, ea natio Anglorum, quae ad aquilonalem Humbrae fluminis plagam habitabat, cum rege suo Aeduino, verbum fidei praedicante Paulino, cuius supra meminimus, suscepit. Cui videlicet regi in auspicium suscipiendae fidei et regni caelestis, potestas etiam terreni creverat imperii: ita ut, quod nemo Anglorum ante eum, omnes Brittaniae fines, qua vel ipsorum vel Brettonum provinciae habitabant,[1] sub ditione acciperet.[2] Quin et Mevanias

---

[1] for *habitant*, Pl.   [2] for *acceperit*, Pl.

---

[1] P. 157.   [2] Omen.

better be spread over all nations that be not yet converted. Be therefore, my brother, zealous to keep with pure sincerity of mind this authority which thou hast gotten by the bounty of the see apostolic, earnestly considering what it is that is figured by the vestment of such exceeding honour, which thou hast received to be worn upon thy shoulders. And calling for the mercy of the Lord, endeavour to prove thyself such a man as may shew and present the rewards of the gift we have bestowed, before the tribunal of the supreme Judge that is to come, not with the loss but with the gain of souls. God have thee in His safe keeping, most beloved brother!"

CHAPTER IX

Of the reign of king Edwin, and how Paulinus, coming to preach the Gospel to him, first instructed his daughter in the mysteries of the Christian faith and others with her.

ABOUT this time the people also of Northumberland (that is, that nation of the English which dwelt toward the north side of the flood Humber), received together with their king Edwin the word of faith by the preaching of Paulinus, of whom we have spoken before.[1] To the which king to wit in a good abodement [2] of receiving the faith and the heavenly kingdom was granted also greater power by the increase of his earthly dominion: insomuch that he brought under subjection all the coasts of Britain, where either the provinces of the English themselves or the Britons had their habitation, which thing no one of the English kings had done before him.

insulas, sicut et supra docuimus, imperio subiugavit Anglorum: quarum prior quae ad austrum est et situ amplior, et frugum proventu atque ubertate felicior, nongentarum sexaginta familiarum mensuram, iuxta aestimationem Anglorum; secunda trecentarum et ultra spatium tenet.

Huic autem genti occasio fuit percipiendae fidei, quod praefatus rex eius cognatione iunctus est regibus Cantuariorum, accepta in coniugem Aedilbergae filia Aedilbercti regis, quae alio nomine Tatae vocabatur. Huius consortium cum primo ipse missis procis a fratre eius Aeodbaldo, qui tunc regno Cantuariorum praeerat, peteret; responsum est, non esse licitum Christianam virginem pagano in coniugem dari, ne fides et sacramenta coelestis Regis consortio profanarentur regis qui veri Dei cultus esset prorsus ignarus. Quae cum Aeduino verba nuntii referrent, promisit se nil omnimodis contrarium Christianae fidei quam virgo colebat, esse facturum: quin potius permissurum ut fidem cultumque suae religionis cum omnibus qui secum venissent, viris sive feminis, sacerdotibus seu ministris, more Christiano servaret. Neque abnegavit se etiam eandem subiturum esse religionem; si tamen examinata a prudentibus sanctior ac Deo dignior posset inveniri.

Itaque promittitur virgo, atque Aeduino mittitur, et iuxta quod dispositum fuerat, ordinatur episcopus

---

[1] P. 225.   [2] Cf. p. 108.   [3] The Witan apparently.

246

Moreover, too, he joined on the Mevanian islands (as we have also shewn before [1]) to the dominion of the English: of which isles the first (that is nearest the south and is both in situation larger and more plentiful in produce of crops and more fertile) hath dwelling-room for the number of 960 families, according to the estimate of the English [2]; the second hath space of ground for 300 tenements or somewhat more.

Now the occasion to this people of receiving the faith was that the aforenamed king was joined in affinity to the kings of Kent by the marriage of Ethelberga, otherwise called Tata, daughter of king Ethelbert. Which lady when at the first king Edwin sought for wife at the hands of her brother Eadbald, then king of Kent, by the sending of wooers, answer was given that it was not lawful for a Christian maiden to be given for wife to a paynim, lest the faith and sacraments of the King of Heaven might be profaned by the company of such a king as knew not at all the worshipping of the true God. Which answer when the ambassadors brought back to Edwin, he promised that in any case he would do nothing which should be contrary to the Christian faith which the maiden professed; but rather permit that she, with all the men and women, priests and attendants which came with her, should observe after the Christian manner the faith and practice of their religion. Neither did he deny but that himself also would submit to the same religion, so that after the examination of wise men [3] it were able to be found holier and meeter for God.

And accordingly the maiden was promised and sent also unto Edwin, and according to appointment

247

vir Deo dilectus Paulinus qui cum illa veniret, eamque et comites eius, ne paganorum possent societate pollui, quotidiana exhortatione et sacramentorum caelestium celebratione confirmaret.

Ordinatus est autem Paulinus episcopus a Iusto archiepiscopo, sub die duodecima kalendarum Augustarum, anno ab incarnatione Domini sexcentesimo vicesimo quinto: et sic cum praefata virgine ad regem Aeduinum quasi comes copulae carnalis advenit. Sed ipse potius toto animo intendens, ut gentem quam adibat, ad agnitionem veritatis advocans, iuxta vocem apostoli, uni vero [1] sponso virginem castam exhiberet Christo. Cumque in provinciam venisset, laboravit multum, ut et eos qui secum venerant, ne a fide deficerent, Domino adiuvante contineret, et aliquos, si forte posset, de paganis ad fidei gratiam praedicando converteret. Sed sicut apostolus ait, quamvis multo tempore illo laborante in verbo: "Deus saeculi huius excaecavit mentes infidelium, ne eis fulgeret illuminatio evangelii gloriae Christi."

Anno autem sequente venit in provinciam quidam sicarius, vocabulo Eumer, missus a rege Occidentalium Saxonum, nomine Cuichelmo, sperans se regem Aeduinum regno simul et vita privaturum: qui habebat sicam bicipitem toxicatam; ut si ferri vulnus minus ad mortem regis sufficeret, peste iuvaretur veneni. Pervenit autem ad regem primo die paschae,

[1] for *viro*, Pl.

---

[1] Like Liudhard, p. 111. [2] 2 Cor. xi. 2.
[3] 2 Cor. xi. 4. [4] Anglo-Saxon *handseax*.

made, Paulinus the man beloved of God was ordained bishop to go with her,[1] and by daily exhortation and celebration of the heavenly sacraments to strengthen her and her company that they might not be defiled with the fellowship of paynims.

Now Paulinus was made bishop by the archbishop Justus about the 21st day of July, the 625th year of our Lord's incarnation; and in this way he came in company of the above-mentioned maiden unto king Edwin, as if he had been the companion of their carnal union. But he himself was rather bent, with all his mind to call that country to which he went, to the acknowledging of the truth, that, according to the saying of the apostle, he might present her as a chaste virgin to Christ the one true husband.[2] And when he was now come into the province, he laboured earnestly with the Lord's help to keep them which came with him from falling from their faith, and by preaching to convert, if by any means it were possible, some of those paynims to the grace of faith. But, as the apostle saith,[3] albeit he laboured long in the word: " The God of this world hath blinded the minds of them which believe not, lest the light of the glorious Gospel of Christ should shine unto them."

Now in the following year there came into this province a desperate ruffian named Eumer (sent by Cwichelm, king of the West Saxons), with the hope to dispatch king Edwin of his kingdom and life at the same time; and this man had a double-edged short sword [4] to this intent dipped in poison, that if the stroke of the sword were not forceable enough to kill the king out of hand, yet it might be helped forward with the infection of the poison. Now he

249

iuxta amnem Deruventionem, ubi tunc erat villa
regalis, intravitque quasi nuntium domini sui referens :
et cum simulatam legationem ore astuto volveret,
exsurrexit repente, et evaginata sub veste sica,
impetum fecit in regem. Quod cum videret Lilla
minister regi amicissimus, non habens scutum ad
manum quo regem a nece defenderet, mox inter-
posuit corpus suum ante ictum pungentis : sed tanta
vi hostis ferrum infixit, ut per corpus militis occisi
etiam regem vulneraret. Qui cum mox undique
gladiis impeteretur, in ipso tumultu etiam alium de
militibus, cui nomen erat Fordheri, sica nefanda
peremit.

Eadem autem nocte sacrosancta Dominici paschae
pepererat regina filiam regi, cui nomen Aeanfled.
Cumque idem rex praesente Paulino episcopo
gratias ageret diis suis pro nata sibi filia, e contra
episcopus gratias coepit agere Domino Christo,
regique adstruere, quod ipse precibus suis apud illum
obtinuerit, ut regina sospes et absque dolore gravi
sobolem procrearet. Cuius verbis delectatus rex,
promisit se abrenunciatis idolis Christo serviturum,
si vitam sibi et victoriam donaret pugnanti adversus
regem, a quo homicida ille, qui eum vulneraverat,
missus est : et in pignus promissionis implendae,

---

[1] The royal *villa* or residence established here probably
on the site of a Roman town, Derventio, as in chap. xiv. at
Cataracta and Campodunum.

came on the first day of Easter unto the king, who lay at the river Derwent where there was then a royal township,[1] and entered there as if bringing a message from his master; and when with crafty speech he was rehearsing his feigned embassy, he steppeth forth suddenly and drawing his sword from under his garment made assault upon the king. Which when Lilla the king's most loyal thane saw (having no buckler ready at hand, wherewith he might defend the king from present death), he stept straightway with his own body between the king and the stroke of the piercing sword; but the murderer struck his sword so far and fiercely, that through the body of this soldier now quite slain he even wounded the king himself. Which thing when he had thus done, being straightway beset with weapons on all sides, right in the confusion he slew also with the same bloody sword another of the thanes, whose name was Forthere.

Now it happened that on the same most holy night of the Lord's Easter the queen was delivered of a daughter to the king, whose name was Eanfled. And when the king in the presence of the bishop Paulinus gave thanks to his gods for the birth of his daughter, the bishop contrariwise began to give thanks to the Lord Christ, and to add furthermore that he hath obtained by his prayers of Christ, that the queen might bring forth her child safely and without grievous pain. With which his words the king, being much delighted, promised that he would renounce idols and serve Christ, if so be that Christ would grant him life and victory in his wars against the king by whom this man-queller who had wounded him had been sent; and in pledge of performing this

251

eandem filiam suam Christo consecrandam Paulino
episcopo adsignavit; quae baptizata est die sancto
pentecostes, prima de gente Nordanhymbrorum, cum
undecim aliis de familia eius.

Quo tempore curatus a vulnere sibi pridem inflicto,
rex collecto exercitu venit adversus gentem Occidentalium Saxonum, ac bello inito, universos quos in
necem suam conspirasse didicerat, aut occidit, aut
in deditionem recepit. Sicque victor in patriam
reversus, non statim et inconsulte sacramenta fidei
Christianae percipere voluit: quamvis nec idolis
ultra servivit, ex quo se Christo serviturum esse
promiserat. Verum primo diligentius ex tempore,
et ab ipso venerabili viro Paulino rationem fidei
ediscere, et cum suis primatibus quos sapientiores
noverat, curavit conferre, quid de his agendum
arbitrarentur. Sed et ipse cum esset vir natura
sagacissimus, saepe diu solus residens, ore quidem
tacito, sed in intimis cordis multa secum conloquens,
quid sibi esset faciendum, quae religio servanda
tractabat.

his promise he committed this his same daughter to bishop Paulinus to be consecrated to Christ; who was baptized first of the people of the Northumbrians upon the holy day of Pentecost[1] with eleven others of the king's family.

At which time the king being recovered of the wound before inflicted on him, made an army and marched against the nation of the West Saxons, and when war was begun he slew or else took prisoners all them whom he understood to have conspired to his death. And so returning home to his country in triumph, yet would he not by and by or without further counsel receive the sacraments of the Christian faith: although he served not idols any more from that day he promised he would serve Christ. But at the first he was careful more diligently at leisure, and from the mouth of the venerable man Paulinus himself, to learn thoroughly the reason of the faith, and to confer with his nobles, whom he knew to be the wiser, what were best, as they thought, to be done in these matters. Moreover (as he was by nature a man of excellent understanding), sitting oftentimes by himself alone for a great space, in much silence of outward voice, but in his inward thought communing many things with himself, he debated diversely what he should do and what religion were best to be followed.

[1] Easter and Pentecost were the regular times for baptism.

THE VENERABLE BEDE

CAP. X

Ut papa Bonifatius eumdem regem missis litteris sit hortatus ad fidem.

Quo tempore exhortatorias ad fidem litteras a pontifice sedis apostolicae Bonifatio accepit, quarum ista est forma:

Exemplar epistolae beatissimi et apostolici papae urbis Romanae ecclesiae Bonifatii, directae viro glorioso Aeduino regi Anglorum.

" Viro glorioso Aeduino regi Anglorum, Bonifatius episcopus servus servorum Dei.

" Licet summae divinitatis potentia humanae locutionis officiis explanari non valeat, quippe quae sui magnitudine ita invisibili atque investigabili aeternitate consistit, ut haec nulla ingenii sagacitas, quanta sit, comprehendere disserereque sufficiat: quia tamen eius humanitas ad insinuationem sui reseratis cordis ianuis, quae de semetipsa proferentur,[1] secreta humanis mentibus inspiratione clementer infundit; ad adnuntiandum vobis plenitudinem fidei Christianae sacerdotalem curavimus sollicitudinem prorogare, ut perinde Christi evangelium, quod Salvator noster omnibus praecepit gentibus praedicari, vestris quoque sensibus inserentes, salutis vestrae remedia propinemus.[2] Supernae igitur maiestatis clementia, quae cuncta solo verbo praeceptionis

---

[1] for *proferetur* MSS.
[2] for *propinentur* MSS., see Pl.

---

[1] Paulinus was consecrated in July 625 and Boniface V died in October 625, which leaves little time for communications between Northumbria and Rome. The letters of this

254

LETTER OF BONIFACE

CHAPTER X

How pope Boniface sent a letter and exhorted the same king to the faith.

ABOUT which time he haply received from Boniface, bishop of the see apostolic, a letter exhorting him to the faith, of which the form is such:

Copy of the letter of the most blessed and apostolic pope of the church of the city of Rome, Boniface, unto the puissant prince Edwin king of the English.[1]

" To the puissant prince Edwin king of the English, Boniface, bishop, servant of the servants of God.

" Although the power of the supreme divinity cannot be expressed by the employment of words of man (for it consisteth by the greatness thereof of so unspeakable and unsearchable eternity, that no keenness of wit is able to comprise and expound how great it is): yet for as much as the lovingkindness of God, opening the gates of the heart to the entry of itself, doth mercifully pour into men's minds by secret inspiration such things as shall be revealed concerning itself; we have thought good to extend our episcopal care in uttering unto you the rich store of the Christian faith, that bringing likewise also unto your understanding the Gospel of Christ, which our Saviour commanded to be preached to all nations, we may offer you the means of your salvation. The mercy, therefore, of the high majesty of God, who with the only word of His commandment hath founded and created all things, the heaven to

pope do not seem always conciliatory, and are in parts difficult to translate, either because the copies made were incorrect, or because the pope himself had not revised the Latin.

suae condidit et creavit, caelum videlicet et terram,
mare et omnia quae in eis sunt, dispositis ordinibus
quibus subsisterent,[1] coaeterni Verbi sui consilio, et
sancti Spiritus unitate dispensans, hominem ad
imaginem et similitudinem suam ex limo terrae
plasmatum constituit, eique tantam praemii prae-
rogativam indulsit, ut eum cunctis praeponeret,
atque servato termino praeceptionis, aeternitatis
subsistentia praemuniret.   Hunc ergo Deum Patrem,
et Filium, et Spiritum sanctum, quod est individua
Trinitas, ab ortu solis usque ad occasum, humanum
genus, quippe ut creatorem omnium atque factorem
suum, salutifera confessione fide veneratur et colit;
cui etiam summitates imperii rerumque potestates
submissae sunt, quia eius dispositione omnium
praelatio regnorum conceditur.   Eius ergo bonitatis
misericordia toti [2] creaturae suae dilatandi subsidii [3]
etiam in extremitate terrae positarum gentium corda
frigida, sancti Spiritus fervore in sui quoque agnitione
mirabiliter est dignata succendere.

" Quae enim in gloriosi filii nostri Audubaldi regis,
gentibusque ei subpositis [4] illustratione, clementia
Redemptoris fuerit operata, plenius ex vicinitate
locorum vestram gloriam conicimus cognovisse.
Eius ergo mirabile donum et in vobis certa spe caelesti
longanimitate conferri confidimus; cum profecto
gloriosam coniugem vestram, quae vestri corporis
pars esse dignoscitur, aeternitatis praemio per sacri
baptismatis regenerationem illuminatam agnovimus.

---

[1] for *subsisteret* Pl.   [2] for *totius* MSS.
[3] for *subdi* MSS.   [4] The sense requires a genitive.

wit and the earth, the sea and all that in them is, setting the degrees, in which they should abide, by the counsel of His eternal Word, and ordering them by the unity of the Holy Ghost, made man (fashioned of the mire of the earth) to His own image and likeness, and gave him such pre-eminence of reward that He set him above all things, and (so that he kept the bounds of His commandment) fenced him with the assurance of immortality. This God then, the Father and the Son and the Holy Ghost, which is the inseparable Trinity, mankind, from the rising of the sun even to the going down of the same, worshippeth and adoreth with wholesome confession of faith as the Creator of all things and their own Maker: to the which God the supreme honours of empire and the puissant powers of state are lowly subject, because by His ordinance authority over all kingdoms is granted. His merciful goodness therefore in extending His aid to all His creation hath marvellously vouchsafed to enkindle with the heat of the Holy Ghost the cold hearts of the nations set even in the uttermost parts of the earth in the acknowledgment also of Himself.

" For we reckon your highness hath come to a fuller understanding than we (the country lying so near), of what the mercy of the Redeemer hath wrought in the illumining of his highness our son king Audubald and the nations subject unto him. Therefore do we trust with certain hope that by His heavenly longsuffering the wonderful gift is being bestowed also in you; seeing indeed we have learnt the sovereign lady your wife (who is discerned to be part of your body) to be illuminated with the reward of eternity by the regeneration of holy baptism.

Unde praesenti stylo gloriosos vos adhortandos cum omni affectu intimae caritatis curavimus; quatenus abominatis idolis eorumque cultu, spretisque fanorum fatuitatibus, et auguriorum deceptabilibus blandimentis, credatis in Deum Patrem omnipotentem, eiusque Filium Jesum Christum, et Spiritum sanctum, ut credentes, a diabolicae captivitatis nexibus, sanctae et individuae Trinitatis cooperante potentia, absoluti, aeternae vitae possitis esse participes.

"Quanta autem reatitudinis culpa teneantur obstricti hi qui idolatriarum perniciosissimam superstitionem colentes amplectuntur, eorum qui [1] colunt exempla perditionis insinuant; unde de eis per Psalmistam dicitur: 'Omnes dii gentium daemonia, Dominus autem caelos fecit.' Et iterum: 'Oculos habent, et non vident; aures habent, et non audiunt: nares habent, et non odorabunt; manus habent, et non palpabunt; pedes habent, et non ambulabunt: similes ergo efficiuntur his qui spem suae confidentiae ponunt in eis.' Quomodo enim iuvandi quemlibet possunt habere virtutem hi, qui ex corruptibili materia inferiorum etiam subpositorumque tibi manibus construuntur; quibus videlicet artificium humanum adcommodans eis inanimatam membrorum similitudinem contulisti; qui nisi a te moti fuerint, ambulare non poterunt, sed tanquam lapis in uno loco positus, ita constructi nihilque intelligentiae habentes, ipsaque insensibilitate obruti, nullam neque laedendi neque iuvandi facultatem adepti sunt? Qua ergo mentis deceptione eos deos, quibus vos

[1] for *quos* MSS., see Pl.

---

[1] Ps. xcvi. 5.   [2] Ps. cxv. 4–8.

Wherefore we have thought it good to exhort your highness in this our present letter with all affection of inward charity; to the intent that loathing idols and their worship, and despising the fond foolishness of their temples and the deceitful enticements of soothsaying, ye may now believe in God the Father Almighty, and His Son Jesus Christ, and in the Holy Ghost, and that believing so ye may be loosed by the working power of the holy and inseparable Trinity from the bonds and captivity of the devil, and be enabled to be made partaker of life everlasting.

" Now in how great fault and offence they are fast held, which worship idols and embrace the deadly superstition of idolatry, the examples of their destruction that worship them can sufficiently inform you; whence it is that it is said of them through the mouth of the Psalmist: [1] ' All the gods of the Gentiles are devils but the Lord hath made the heavens.' And again: [2] ' They have eyes and see not; they have ears and hear not; they have noses and shall not smell; they have hands and shall not feel; they have feet and shall not walk: therefore are all such made like unto them as do put the hope of their confidence in them.' For how can they have power to help any man, which are made of a corruptible matter and wrought too by the hands of thy inferiors and subjects; upon which, namely, by employment of the work of craftsmen thou hast bestowed the likeness of limbs without life; which, were they not moved by thee, shall not be able to walk, but like a stone set fast in one place, so are they builded up, and having no understanding and stark with right insensibleness have gotten no ability to hurt or help? Therefore we cannot by any discretion and judgment find out

ipsi imaginem corporis tradidistis, colentes sequimini, iudicio discreto reperire non possumus.

" Unde oportet vos, suscepto signo sanctae crucis, per quod humanum genus redemptum est, execrandam diabolicae versutiae subplantationem, qui divinae bonitatis operibus invidus aemulusque consistit, a cordibus vestris abicere, iniectisque manibus hos, quos eatenus materiae compage vobis deos fabricastis, confringendos diminuendosque summopere procurate. Ipsa enim eorum dissolutio corruptioque, quae nunquam viventem spiritum habuerunt,[1] nec sensibilitatem a suis factoribus potuerunt[2] quolibet modo suscipere, vobis patenter insinuet quam nihil erat quod eatenus colebatis: dum profecto meliores vos qui spiritum viventem a Domino percepistis, eorum constructione[3] nihilominus existatis: quippe quos Deus omnipotens ex primi hominis quem plasmavit cognatione, deductis per saecula innumerabilibus propaginibus pullulare constituit. Accedite ergo ad agnitionem eius qui vos creavit, qui in vobis vitae insufflavit spiritum, qui pro vestra redemptione Filium suum unigenitum misit, ut vos ab originali peccato eriperet, et ereptos de potestate nequitiae diabolicae pravitatis coelestibus praemiis muneraret.

" Suscipite verba praedicatorum, et evangelium Dei quod vobis adnuntiant; quatenus credentes, sicut saepius dictum est, in Deum Patrem omni-

---

[1] for *habuit* MSS., see Pl.   [2] for *potuit* MSS., see Pl.
[3] for *constructioni* MSS., see Pl.

upon what blindness of mind ye worship and follow after those gods to whom your own selves have given the representation of a body.

"Wherefore it behoveth you to receive now the sign of the holy cross by which mankind was redeemed, and shake from your heart the abominable guile of the subtlety of the devil, who ever continueth in malice and envy at the works of God's goodness, and setting hands on these gods which up till now ye have fashioned as your gods by the joining together of the work of men's hands, to see that they be broken in pieces and smitten asunder utterly. For the very dissolving and ruin of them that never had breath of life in them, nor could not by any means take of their makers sense and feeling, can plainly shew you how it was nothing at all which hitherto you were worshipping; whereas assuredly you who have received the breath of life from the Lord stand forth as better than they be, that are made with hands: seeing that Almighty God hath brought you to sprout from the stock of the first man whom He formed, after innumerable shoots through many ages have sprung therefrom. Come you therefore to the acknowledging of Him that hath created you, that hath breathed into you the breath of life, that for your redemption hath sent His only begotten Son, so that He might deliver you out of original sin, and reward you after with heavenly recompence, being now delivered from the power of the corrupt wickedness of the devil.

"Receive ye the words of the preachers and the Gospel of God, of which they are the messengers to you; to the end that, believing, as has been said more than once, in God the Father Almighty and in

potentem et in Jesum Christum eius Filium, et
Spiritum sanctum, et inseparabilem Trinitatem;
fugatis daemoniorum sensibus, expulsaque a vobis
sollicitatione venenosi et deceptibilis hostis, per
aquam et Spiritum sanctum renati ei, cui credideritis,
in splendore gloriae sempiternae cohabitare, ejus
opitulante munificentia valeatis.

" Praeterea benedictionem protectoris vestri beati
Petri apostolorum principis vobis direximus, id est,
camisia [1] cum ornatura in auro una, et lena Anciriana
una: quod petimus, ut eo benignitatis animo gloria
vestra suscipiat, quo a nobis noscitur destinatum."

CAP. XI

*Ut coniugem ipsius, per epistolam, salutis illius sedulam
agere curam monuerit.*

AD coniugem quoque illius Aedilbergam huiusmodi
literas idem pontifex misit:

Exemplar epistolae beatissimi et apostolici Bonifatii
    papae urbis Romae directae Aedilbergae reginae
    Aeduini regis.

" Dominae gloriosae filiae Aedilbergae reginae,
Bonifatius episcopus servus servorum Dei.

" Redemptoris nostri benignitas humano generi
quod pretiosi sanguinis sui effusione a vinculis diabolicae captivitatis eripuit, multae providentiae quibus
salvaretur propinavit remedia; quatenus sui nominis
agnitionem diverso modo gentibus innotescens,

[1] for *camisiam*, Pl.

Jesus Christ His Son and in the Holy Ghost and the inseparable Trinity; and that abandoning the thoughts of devils and driving from you the entice- ment of the poisoned enemy that is full of deceit, ye may be born again by water and the Holy Ghost to Him in Whom ye have believed, and by the help of His bountifulness may dwell with Him in the bright- ness of everlasting glory.

" Furthermore we have sent you the blessing of your protector the blessed Peter, chief of the apostles, that is to say, by a shirt with ornament in gold, and a cloak made at Ancyra; and this gift we beseech your highness to accept with so good a heart and will as ye understand it is sent from us."

CHAPTER XI

How he exhorted the king's wife by a letter that she should diligently seek for the king's salvation.

THE same pope also sent a letter as follows to the king's wife Ethelberga:

Copy of the letter of the most blessed and apostolic Boniface, pope of the city of Rome, sent to Ethel- berga queen of king Edwin.

" To her highness the lady queen Ethelberga, our daughter, Boniface bishop, servant of the servants of God.

" The lovingkindness of our Redeemer, of His great providence hath offered mankind (whom by the shedding of His precious blood He hath delivered from the bonds of the captivity of the devil) the means by which they might be saved; that by insin- uating through divers means into the minds of the

263

Creatorem suum suscepto Christianae fidei agnoscerent sacramento. Quod equidem in vestrae gloriae sensibus caelesti conlatum munere mystica regenerationis vestrae purgatio patenter innuit. Magno ergo largitatis Dominicae beneficio mens nostra gaudio exultavit, quod scintillam orthodoxae religionis in vestra[1] dignatus est confessione succendere; ex qua re non solum gloriosi coniugis vestri, immo totius gentis subpositae vobis intelligentiam in amore sui facile inflammaret.

" Didicimus namque referentibus his, qui ad nos gloriosi filii nostri Audubaldi regis laudabilem conversionem nuntiantes pervenerunt, quod etiam vestra gloria, Christianae fidei suscepto mirabili sacramento, piis et Deo placitis iugiter operibus enitescat, ab idolorum etiam cultu seu fanorum auguriorumque inlecebris se diligenter abstineat, et ita in amore Redemptoris sui immutilata devotione persistens invigilet, ut ad dilatandam Christianam fidem incessabiliter non desistat operam commodare: cumque de glorioso coniuge vestro paterna caritas sollicite perquisisset, cognovimus, quod eatenus abominandis idolis serviens, ad suscipiendam vocem praedicatorum suam distulerit obedientiam exhibere. Qua ex re non modica nobis amaritudo congesta est, ab eo quod pars corporis vestri ab agnitione summae et individuae Trinitatis remansit extranea. Unde paternis

---

[1] for *vestri*, MSS.

nations the acknowledgment of His name, they might receive the mystery of the Christian faith and acknowledge their Creator. Which thing in deed, that it hath been by heavenly gift bestowed upon the mind of your highness, the mystical cleansing of your regeneration doth plainly confirm. Therefore our heart hath leaped for joy at this great benefit of our Lord's bountifulness to you, for that He hath vouchsafed by your confession to enkindle a spark of right religion; that thereby He might after easily make a flame in the love of Himself to rise not only in the mind of his highness your husband, but rather in the minds of all the people subject unto you.

"For we have learned by the report of them which came to us with the tidings of the laudable conversion of our son his highness king Audubald, that your highness also (after ye had received the wonderful mystery of the Christian faith) do shine and excel in good works and such as be ever pleasant in the sight of God, that ye do also diligently keep yourself from the worshipping of idols or frequenting of temples and from the allurement of fond soothsaying, and are so continually watchful in the love of your Redeemer with unchangeable devotion, that you never cease to bestow your pains unceasingly to the enlargement of the Christian faith; and whereas for our fatherly charity we had with searchings of heart inquired of the state of his highness your husband, we understood that he served so far forth to the abomination of idolatry, that he delayed to shew his obedience and give ear to the voice of the preachers. By which news no small bitterness was heaped upon us, by reason that a part of your own body hath remained in this sort alienated from the

265

officiis vestrae gloriosae Christianitati nostram commonitionem non[1] distulimus conferendam; adhortantes, quatenus divinae inspirationis imbuta subsidiis, importune et opportune agendum non differas:
ut et ipse Salvatoris nostri Domini Jesu Christi
cooperante potentia Christianorum numero copuletur;
et perinde intemerato societatis foedere iura teneas
maritalis consortii. Scriptum namque est: 'Erunt
duo in carne una.' Quomodo ergo unitas vobis
coniunctionis inesse dici poterit, si a vestrae fidei
splendore interpositis detestabilis erroris tenebris
ille remanserit alienus?

"Unde orationi continuae insistens, a longanimitate caelestis clementiae illuminationis ipsius beneficia impetrare non desinas: ut videlicet quos copulatio carnalis affectus unum quodammodo corpus
exhibuisse monstratur, hos quoque unitas fidei
etiam post huius vitae transitum in perpetua societate
conservet. Insiste ergo, gloriosa filia, et summis
conatibus duritiam cordis ipsius religiosa divinorum
praeceptorum insinuatione mollire summopere dematura: infundens sensibus eius, quantum sit praeclarum quod credendo suscepisti mysterium, quantumve sit admirabile quod renata praemium consequi meruisti. Frigiditatem cordis ipsius sancti
Spiritus adnuntiatione succende; quatenus amoto
torpore perniciosissimi cultus, divinae fidei calor

[1] for *nec*, Pl.

[1] Gen. ii. 24.

acknowledgment of the highest and inseparable
Trinity. Wherefore, as becometh a father to do, we
have not delayed to send our warning to your Christian
highness; encouraging you that, whereas ye are now
filled with the help of God's inspiration, ye delay not
to be instant in season and out of season in seeking
that he himself too by the aiding power of our Saviour
the Lord Jesus Christ may be coupled with you in
the number of Christians; and so thou mayest hold
the laws of wedlock in like manner in an unspotted
bond of union. For it is written:[1] 'They shall
be two in one flesh.' How then can it be said that
you have oneness of union if your husband, by the
darkness of detestable error set between you, shall
abide still alienated from the brightness of your
faith?

" Wherefore cease not by continuing instant in
prayer to try to obtain from the long-suffering of
the heavenly mercy the benefit of his enlightening,
that namely they, whom the knot of carnal affection
is shewn to have rendered in a certain sort one body,
may also by the unity of faith be preserved in
unending fellowship after their departure from this
life. Press on then, illustrious daughter, and with
utmost endeavour hasten speedily to soften the hard-
ness of his heart by the religious communication of
the divine commands; pouring into his mind, how
excellent a mystery it is that thou by believing hast
received, and how marvellous is the reward thou hast
deserved to attain to because thou hast been born
again. Kindle to warmth the coldness of his heart
by the message of the Holy Ghost Himself; that
when he hath set aside the numbness of the deadly
worship of idols, the heat of divine faith may enkindle

eius intelligentiam tuarum adhortationum frequentatione succendat, ut profecto sacrae Scripturae
testimonium per te expletum indubitanter perclareat: 'Salvabitur vir infidelis per mulierem
fidelem.' Ad hoc enim misericordiam Dominicae
pietatis consecuta es, ut fructum fidei creditorumque
tibi beneficiorum Redemptori tuo multiplicem resignares. Quod equidem suffragante praesidio benignitatis ipsius, ut explere valeas, assiduis non desistimus precibus postulare.

" His ergo praemissis, paternae vobis dilectionis
exhibentes officia, hortamur, ut nos reperta portitoris
occasione, de his quae per vos superna potentia
mirabiliter in conversione coniugis vestri summissaeque vobis gentis dignatus fuerit operari, prosperis
quantocius nuntiis relevetis, quatenus sollicitudo
nostra, quae de vestri vestrorumque omnium animae
salute optabilia desideranter exspectat, vobis nuntiantibus relevetur, illustrationemque divinae propitiationis in vobis diffusam opulentius agnoscentes,
hilari confessione largitori omnium bonorum Deo et
beato Petro apostolorum principi uberes merito
gratias exsolvamus.

" Praeterea benedictionem protectoris vestri beati
Petri apostolorum principis vobis direximus; id est,
speculum argenteum, et pectinem eboreum inauratum: quod petimus, ut eo benignitatis animo
gloria vestra suscipiat, quo a nobis noscitur destinatum."

---

his understanding by thy often encouragements, that so it may truly appear to be fulfilled assuredly in thee, which is testified in holy Scripture:[1] 'The unbelieving husband shall be saved by the woman that believeth.' For unto this end thou hast gained the pitifulness of the Lord's goodness, that thou shouldest render back to thy Redeemer the multiplied fruit of thy faith and the good gifts committed unto thee. And verily that thou mayest have strength to fulfil this work by the help of the protection of His lovingkindness, we cease not to ask with continual prayer.

" In these words therefore sent in advance, shewing you the duty of our fatherly love, we exhort you that having found the opportunity of a bearer ye will as quickly as possible by favourable tidings give us comfort concerning those things which the power from above shall vouchsafe to work marvellously by you in the conversion of your husband and your subjects, that we (which carefully and longingly look for the happy news of the salvation of the soul of you and all yours) by this your tidings may be comforted, and acknowledging the brightness of the divine graciousness more richly spread abroad in your midst, we may with joyful confession give deservedly abundant thanks to God the giver of all good things and the blessed Peter, the chief of the apostles.

" Furthermore, we have sent you the blessing of your protector the blessed Peter, chief of the apostles, that is to say by a looking-glass of silver and a comb of ivory gilt with gold; and we pray your highness to accept this gift in that spirit of lovingkindness in the which, as ye understand, it hath been sent by us."

CAP. XII

Ut Aeduini per visionem quondam sibi exuli ostensam sit ad credendum provocatus.

Haec quidem memoratus papa Bonifatius de salute regis Aeduini ac gentis ipsius, literis agebat. Sed et oraculum caeleste quod illi quondam exulanti apud Redualdum regem Anglorum pietas divina revelare dignata est, non minimum ad suscipienda vel intelligenda doctrinae monita salutaris sensum iuvit illius. Cum ergo videret Paulinus difficulter posse sublimitatem animi regalis, ad humilitatem viae salutaris, et suscipiendum mysterium vivificae crucis inclinari, ac pro salute illius, simul et gentis cui praeerat, et verbo exhortationis apud homines, et apud divinam pietatem verbo deprecationis ageret; tandem, ut verisimile videtur, didicit in spiritu, quod [1] vel quale esset oraculum regi quondam caelitus ostensum. Nec exinde distulit quin continuo regem ammoneret explere votum, quod in oraculo sibi exhibito se facturum promiserat, si temporis illius aerumnis exemptus, ad regni fastigia perveniret.

Erat autem oraculum huiusmodi. Cum persequente illum Aedilfrido, qui ante eum regnavit, per diversa occultus loca vel regna, multo annorum tempore profugus vagaretur; tandem venit ad

---

[1] for *ut quod*, Pl.

CHAPTER XII

How Edwin was invited to believe by a vision appearing to him aforetime in banishment.

THUS much did pope Boniface by letter, when informed concerning the salvation of king Edwin and his people. Moreover, the king's mind was very much holpen to receive and understand the precepts of wholesome doctrine by a message from heaven, which divine goodness vouchsafed to reveal to him while he lay sometime in banishment at the court of Redwald king of the Angles. When then Paulinus perceived that the king's loftiness of spirit could hardly be bowed to the lowliness of the way of salvation, and to receive the mystery of the quickening cross; and when he was labouring for the king's salvation as well as that of the people over whom Edwin was ruler, both by word of exhortation before men and the word of prayer before the divine goodness: at the length he learned in the spirit (for so it is most likest to be) what and of what nature was that message which had before been declared to the king from heaven. And thereafter he made no delay, but forthwith warned the king to fulfil the vow which at the time of the message shewn to him he had promised to do, in case he were delivered from his present miseries and attained to the dignity of a kingdom.

Now the message was such as followeth. At what time the king's predecessor Ethelfrith with grievous pursuing made him lie privy in divers places and realms, and wander as a banished man for many years' space, at the length Edwin came to Redwald,

Redualdum, obsecrans ut vitam suam a tanti perse-
cutoris insidiis tutando servaret: qui libenter eum
excipiens, promisit se quae petebatur, esse facturum.
At postquam Aedilfrid in hac eum provincia appar-
uisse, et apud regem illius familiariter cum sociis
habitare cognovit, misit nuntios, qui Redualdo
pecuniam multam pro nece eius offerrent: neque
aliquid profecit. Misit secundo, misit tertio, et
copiosiora argenti dona offerens, et bellum insuper
illi si contemneretur indicens. Qui vel minis fractus,
vel corruptus muneribus, cessit deprecanti, et sive
occidere se Aeduinum, seu legatariis tradere promisit.
Quod ubi fidissimus quidam amicus illius animad-
vertit, intravit cubiculum quo dormire disponebat,
erat enim prima hora noctis, et evocatum foras,
quid erga eum agere rex promisisset, edocuit, et
insuper adjecit: "Si ergo vis, hac ipsa hora educam
te de hac provincia, et ea in loca introducam, ubi
nunquam te vel Reduald vel Aedilfrid invenire
valeant." Qui ait: "Gratias quidem ago bene-
volentiae tuae; non tamen hoc facere possum quod
suggeris, ut pactum quod cum tanto rege inii, ipse
primus irritum faciam, cum ille mihi nil mali fecerit,
nil adhuc inimicitiarum intulerit. Quin potius, si
moriturus sum, ille me magis quam ignobilior quisquam morti tradat. Quo enim nunc fugiam, qui per
omnes Brittaniae provincias, tot annorum tempor-

---

[1] Since his boyhood, some twenty-five years.

beseeching him that he would save him by protecting his life from the trains and search of so deadly an enemy: who gladly entertained him and promised to fulfil that his request. But after that Ethelfrith heard say that Edwin was seen in that province and lived there at the king's court familiarly with all his company, he sent ambassadors to offer Redwald a great sum of money to procure Edwin's death; but it prevailed nothing. He sent a second time, he sent a third time, both offering more plentiful gifts of money and threatening him beside with war if his offer were still scorned. Which Redwald, either overcome by the threats or corrupted with the bribes, granted the things which he was asked and promised either to put Edwin to death himself or else yield him up to the ambassadors. Which thing when a certain faithful friend of Edwin's had word of, he entered to the chamber where Edwin was preparing to sleep (for it was an hour within night), and calling him forth informed him what the king had promised to do against him, saying in the end thus much: "If therefore you so please, this very hour I shall lead you out of this province and bring you into such a place that neither Redwald nor Ethelfrith be ever able to find you." To whom Edwin saith: "I thank you for this your gentleness; nevertheless I cannot follow your counsel herein, namely to be myself first to make void the covenant I have entered into with so mighty a king, seeing he hath done me no wrong, hath shewn me no enmity hitherto. Nay more, if I must of necessity die, I had rather he should yield me up for death than any man of less nobility. For whither should I fly now, who in the course of so many years and seasons [1] was a wanderer through all

umque curriculis vagabundus, hostium vitabam
insidias? " Abeunte igitur amico remansit Aeduini
solus foris, residensque moestus ante palatium,
multis coepit cogitationum aestibus affici, quid
ageret, quove pedem verteret nescius.

Cumque diu tacitis mentis angoribus et caeco
carperetur igni, vidit subito intempestae noctis
silentio adpropinquantem sibi hominem vultus
habitusque incogniti: quem videns, ut ignotum et
inopinatum, non parum expavit. At ille accedens
salutavit eum, et interrogavit, quare illa hora, ceteris
quiescentibus et alto sopore pressis, solus ipse
moestus in lapide pervigil sederet. At ille vicissim
sciscitabatur, quid ad eum pertineret, utrum ipse
intus an foris noctem transigeret. Qui respondens
ait: " Ne me aestimes tuae moestitiae et insom-
niorum, et forinsecae et solitariae sessionis causam
nescire: scio enim certissime qui es, et quare moeres,
et quae ventura tibi in proximo mala formidas. Sed
dicito mihi quid mercedis [1] dare velis ei, siqui sit,
qui his te moeroribus absolvat, et Redualdo suadeat,
ut nec ipse tibi aliquid mali faciat, nec tuis te hostibus
perimendum tradat." Qui cum se omnia quae
posset, huic tali pro mercede beneficii daturum esse
responderet, adiecit ille: " Quid si etiam regem te
futurum exstinctis hostibus in veritate promittat, ita

[1] for *mercis*, Pl.

---

[1] Cf. Verg. *Aen.* iv. 2.

the provinces of Britain, avoiding the snares of my enemies?" The friend therefore departing, Edwin remained without alone, and sitting down sadly before the palace began to be troubled with many hot vexations of thought, not witting what to do or whither to turn his feet.

And after being long harassed with privy torments of mind and close fire of secret sorrow,[1] he saw suddenly in the silence of the dead of night a man drawing toward him, which was both for visage and apparel unknown to him: whom he espying thus as one unknown and unexpected, was not a little afraid. But the stranger coming unto him greeteth him, and asketh him wherefore he sat so sorrowful on the stone, watching all alone at that hour, when other men were at rest and sunk in their deep sleep. Whereon Edwin in turn demanded of him what he had to do therewith, if he passed the night within doors or without. To whom this man answered and said: "Think ye not but that I know the cause of your heaviness and watch, and of your solitary sitting without doors: for I know quite surely who ye be and wherefore ye are sad, and what mischief you fear shortly shall befall you. But tell me, what reward would you give to him, if such there should be, who should rid you out of these sorrows and persuade Redwald that neither he himself should do you any hurt nor yield you up to your enemies that they might slay you?" And when Edwin answered that he would give all that he possibly could to such an one for reward of so good a turn, this man added moreover: "What if beside this he do truly warrant you that ye shall be a king and all your enemies destroyed, yea and that in such sort that you shall not

ut non solum omnes tuos progenitores, sed et omnes qui ante te reges in gente Anglorum fuerant, potestate transcendas?" At Aeduini constantior interrogando factus, non dubitavit promittere, quin ei qui tanta sibi beneficia donaret, dignis ipse gratiarum actionibus responderet. Tum ille tertio: " Si autem," inquit, " is qui tibi tanta taliaque dona veraciter adventura praedixerit, etiam consilium tibi tuae salutis ac vitae melius atque utilius quam aliquis de tuis parentibus aut cognatis unquam audivit, ostendere potuerit, num ei obtemperare, et monita eius salutaria suscipere consentis?" Nec distulit Aeduini quin continuo polliceretur in omnibus se secuturum doctrinam illius, qui se tot ac tantis calamitatibus ereptum, ad regni apicem proveheret. Quo accepto responso, confestim is qui loquebatur cum eo, imposuit dexteram suam capiti eius, dicens: " Cum hoc ergo tibi signum advenerit, memento huius temporis, ac loquelae nostrae, et ea quae nunc promittis adimplere ne differas." Et his dictis, ut ferunt, repente disparuit, ut intelligeret non hominem esse qui sibi apparuisset, sed spiritum.

Et cum regius iuvenis solus adhuc ibidem sederet, gavisus quidem de collata sibi consolatione, sed multum solicitus ac mente sedula cogitans quis esset ille, vel unde veniret qui haec sibi loqueretur, venit ad eum praefatus amicus illius, laetoque vultu salutans eum: " Surge," inquit, " intra, et sopitis ac relictis curarum anxietatibus, quieti membra simul et

only excel all your ancestors, but also pass in power all the kings who had reigned before you in the English nation?" Here Edwin, being made more firm by questioning, doubted not to promise that he would be answerable with worthy thanksgiving to the man that should bestow on him such great benefits. Then the man spake the third time and said: "But tell me, if the man, which hath foretold that you shall hereafter undoubtedly have such and so great benefits, can give you also better counsel and more profitable for your life and salvation than ever any of your parents or kinsfolk heard of, can you then consent to obey him and receive his wholesome sayings?" But Edwin delayed not but that he promised out of hand that he would altogether follow his teaching, who should deliver him from so many grievous miseries and exalt him after to wear a royal crown. And when this answer was received, straightway the man which talked with him laid his right hand upon Edwin's head, and said: "When this sign then shall come unto you, remember well this time and this our talk, and delay not to fulfil that you do now promise me." And this being said, according to the tale told, he suddenly vanished away, to the intent that Edwin might understand that it was no man which had appeared unto him, but a ghost.

And when this young prince was still sitting solitary in the same place, rejoicing for the comfort bestowed upon him, but yet very careful and busied in pondering in his mind who it should be or whence he should come which spake these things to him, there came to him his aforesaid friend and greeting him cheerfully said: "Rise, come in, and stilling and letting pass this your cark and care set your mind at rest and

animum compone, quia mutatum est cor regis, nec
tibi aliquid mali facere, sed fidem potius pollicitam
servare disponit: postquam enim cogitationem
suam, de qua tibi ante dixi, reginae in secreto revelavit, revocavit eum illa ab intentione, ammonens
quia nulla ratione conveniat tanto regi amicum suum
optimum in necessitate positum auro vendere, immo
fidem suam, quae omnibus ornamentis pretiosior est,
amore pecuniae perdere." Quid plura? Fecit rex
ut dictum est: nec solum exulem nuntiis hostilibus
non tradidit, sed etiam eum ut in regnum perveniret,
adiuvit. Nam mox redeuntibus domum nuntiis,
exercitum ad debellandum Aedilfridum collegit
copiosum, eumque sibi occurrentem cum exercitu
multum impari (non enim dederat illi spatium quo
totum suum congregaret atque adunaret exercitum),
occidit in finibus gentis Merciorum ad orientalem
plagam amnis qui vocatur Idlae[1]: in quo certamine
et filius Redualdi, vocabulo Raegenheri, occisus est:
ac sic Aeduini iuxta oraculum quod acceperat, non
tantum regis sibi infesti insidias vitavit, verum etiam
eidem perempto in regni gloriam successit[2].

Cum ergo praedicante verbum Dei Paulino rex
credere differret, et per aliquod tempus, ut diximus,
horis competentibus solitarius sederet, quid agendum
sibi esset, quae religio sequenda sedulus secum ipse
scrutari consuesset, ingrediens ad eum quadam die

---

[1] A tributary of the Trent.
[2] Expelling the sons of Ethelfrith.

your limbs to sleep, for the king's heart is changed, nor doth he purpose to do you any wrong, but rather to keep his promised faith; for after he had discovered to the queen in secret his thought of which I told you before, she withdrew him from that purpose, warning him that it is in no wise meet for a king of such prowess to sell his best friend, when he is now brought to straitness, for gold, nay, more, to lose his honour which is more to be esteemed than all treasures, from love of money." Why make a longer tale? The king did as hath been said; and not only not betrayed the banished man to the ambassadors of his enemy, but also helped him to come to the throne. For shortly after, when the ambassadors were returning home, he gathered a mighty army to conquer king Ethelfrith, and when Ethelfrith marched against him with an army that was much weaker (for space enough had not been given him to gather all his force together and order it into one army) Redwald slew him in the borders of the Marchland men, at the east side of the river called Idle:[1] in which battle Regenhere, king Redwald's son, was slain: and thus Edwin, according to the oracle which he had received, not only avoided the snares of the king his deadly enemy, but also succeeded the same after his death in the honour of his kingdom.[2]

When therefore Paulinus for all his preaching of the word of God found that the king slacked to believe, using yet for some space at divers fitting hours to sit solitary (as we have said before) and diligently to examine with himself what were best for him to do, what religion were best to be followed, the man of God entering the presence of the king on

279

vir Dei, imposuit dexteram capiti eius, et an hoc signum agnosceret requisivit. Qui cum tremens ad pedes eius procidere vellet, levavit eum, et quasi familiari voce affatus: " Ecce," inquit, " hostium manus quos timuisti, Domino donante, evasisti; ecce, regnum quod desiderasti, ipso largiente percepisti. Memento ut tertium quod promisisti, facere ne differas, suscipiendo fidem eius, et praecepta servando, qui te et a temporalibus adversis eripiens, temporalis regni honore sublimavit; et si deinceps voluntati eius, quam per me tibi praedicat, obsecundare volueris, etiam a perpetuis malorum tormentis te liberans, aeterni secum regni in caelis faciet esse participem."

CAP. XIII

Quale consilium idem cum primatibus suis de percipienda
fide Christi habuerit; et ut pontifex eius suas aras
profanaverit.

Quibus auditis, rex suscipere quidem se fidem quam docebat, et velle et debere respondebat. Verum adhuc cum amicis principibus, et consiliariis suis sese de hoc collaturum esse dicebat, ut si et illi eadem cum illo sentire vellent, omnes pariter in fonte vitae Christo consecrarentur. Et annuente Paulino, fecit ut dixerat. Habito enim cum sapien-

a certain day, laid his right hand on his head and asked him whether he acknowledged that sign or no. And when the king trembling thereat would have fallen down at his feet, Paulinus lifted him up and spake after a familiar sort thus unto him: " Behold, by the granting of the Lord you have escaped the hand of the enemy whom you dreaded; behold, by His bountiful gift you have obtained the kingdom for which you longed. Remember that you delay not to perform the third thing which you promised, by receiving His faith and keeping His commandments, Who both delivered you from your temporal adversities, and exalted you to the honour of a temporal king; and if you shall be willing hereafter to obey His pleasure which He declareth to you through me, He will also deliver you from the perpetual torment of evils, and make you partaker with Him of the eternal kingdom in the heavens."

CHAPTER XIII

What counsel the same Edwin had with his chief men for the receiving of the faith of Christ; and how his chief priest profaned his own altars.

WHICH words when the king heard, he answered that he both would and was bound to receive the faith which Paulinus taught. But he said that he would still confer thereof with the nobles that were his friends, and his chief counsellors, that so, if they too should be willing to think the same as he did, they might all be consecrated together to Christ in the font of life. Whereunto when Paulinus agreed, the king did as he had said. For having called a

tibus consilio, sciscitabatur singillatim ab omnibus,
qualis sibi doctrina haec eatenus inaudita, et novus
divinitatis qui praedicabatur cultus videretur.

Cui primus pontificum ipsius Coifi continuo respondit: " Tu vide, rex, quale sit hoc quod nobis modo
praedicatur: ego autem tibi verissime quod certum
didici, profiteor, quia nihil omnino virtutis habet,
nihil utilitatis religio illa quam hucusque tenuimus:
nullus enim tuorum studiosius quam ego culturae
deorum nostrorum se subdidit; et nihilominus multi
sunt qui ampliora a te beneficia quam ego, et maiores
accipiunt dignitates, magisque prosperantur in
omnibus quae agenda vel adquirenda disponunt. Si
autem dii aliquid valerent, me potius iuvare vellent,
qui illis impensius servire curavi. Unde restat, si ut
ea quae nunc nobis nova praedicantur, meliora esse
et fortiora, habita examinatione perspexeris, absque
ullo cunctamine suscipere illa festinemus."

Cuius suasioni verbisque prudentibus alius opti-
matum regis tribuens assensum, continuo subdidit:
" Talis," inquiens, " mihi videtur, rex, vita hominum
praesens in terris, ad comparationem eius quod nobis
incertum est temporis, quale cum te residente ad
coenam cum ducibus ac ministris tuis tempore bru-
mali, accenso quidem foco in medio et calido effecto
coenaculo, furentibus autem foris per omnia turbinibus
hiemalium pluviarum vel nivium, adveniensque unus

---

[1] Ealdormen and thanes, A.S. version.

meeting of his wise men, he asked severally each of
them, what manner of doctrine this seemed to them
to be, which until that day had never been heard of
before, and what they thought of the new worshipping
of divinity which was now preached.

To whom Coifi, the first of the king's priests, incontinently answered: " May it like your highness to
prove what manner of doctrine this is which is now
preached unto us; but thus much I surely avouch
unto you, which I have certainly learned, that the
religion which unto this day we have observed hath
no virtue nor advantage in it at all: for none of
your subjects hath set himself more earnestly to the
worship of our gods than I; and yet, notwithstanding,
there are many of them which receive from you more
ample benefits than I, and higher dignities than I, and
better prosper in all they take in hand to do or seek
to get than I. If now the gods could aught have
done, they would rather have holpen me, who have
been careful to serve them more zealously. Wherefore it remaineth that, if you shall find after good
examination that these things which be now newly
preached to us be better and of more power, then
without longer delay we hasten to receive them."

To whose wise persuasion and words another of
the king's nobles consenting forthwith added:
" Such seemeth to me, my Lord, the present life of
men here in earth (for the comparison of our uncertain
time to live), as if a sparrow should come to the
house and very swiftly flit through; which entereth
in at one window and straightway passeth out through
another, while you sit at dinner with your captains
and servants [1] in winter-time; the parlour being
then made warm with the fire kindled in the midst

passerum domum citissime pervolaverit qui cum per
unum ostium ingrediens, mox per aliud exierit. Ipso
quidem tempore quo intus est, hiemis tempestate
non tangitur, sed tamen parvissimo spatio serenitatis
ad momentum excurso, mox de hieme in hiemem
regrediens, tuis oculis elabitur. Ita haec vita hominum ad modicum apparet; quid autem sequatur,
quidve praecesserit, prorsus ignoramus. Unde si
haec nova doctrina certius aliquid attulit, merito
esse sequenda videtur." His similia et ceteri
maiores natu ac regis consiliarii divinitus admoniti
prosequebantur.

Adiecit autem Coifi, quia vellet ipsum Paulinum
diligentius audire de Deo quem praedicabat, verbum
facientem. Quod cum iubente rege faceret, excla-
mavit auditis eius sermonibus dicens: " Iam olim
intellexeram nihil esse quod colebamus; quia videlicet quanto studiosius in eo cultu veritatem quaere-
bam, tanto minus inveniebam. Nunc autem aperte
profiteor, quia in hac praedicatione veritas claret illa,
quae nobis vitae, salutis et beatitudinis aeternae dona
valet tribuere. Unde suggero, rex, ut templa et
altaria quae sine fructu utilitatis sacravimus, ocius
anathemati et igni contradamus." Quid plura?
praebuit palam adsensum evangelizanti beato Paulino
rex, et abrenuntiata idolatria, fidem se Christi suscipere confessus est. Cumque a praefato pontifice
sacrorum suorum quaereret, quis aras et fana idolorum cum septis quibus erant circumdata, primus

thereof, but all places abroad being troubled with raging tempests of winter rain and snow. Right for the time it be within the house, it feeleth no smart of the winter storm, but after a very short space of fair weather that lasteth but for a moment, it soon passeth again from winter to winter and escapeth your sight. So the life of man here appeareth for a little season, but what followeth or what hath gone before, that surely know we not. Wherefore if this new learning hath brought us any better surety, methink it is worthy to be followed." Thus or in like manner spake thereafter the rest of the elders and counsellors of the king, being moved of God.

But Coifi said, moreover, that he wished more diligently to hearken to Paulinus himself speaking concerning the God whom he preached. And when he did so according to the king's pleasure, Coifi, on hearing his words, with a loud voice said: " I understood long ago that it was right nought that we worshipped; for certes the more curiously I sought for the truth in that our worship, the less I found it. But now do I plainly avouch that in this preaching is manifested that truth which is able to give us the gifts of life, salvation and of bliss everlasting. Wherefore I give counsel, my lord, that out of hand we curse and give over to the flames the temples and altars which we have consecrated without fruit and profit." Why make a longer tale? The king openly gave consent to blessed Paulinus in his preaching of the Gospel, and renouncing idolatry declared that he received the faith of Christ. And demanding then of the aforesaid priest of his sacrifices, who should first profane the altars and temples with the grates

profanare deberet; ille respondit: " Ego. Quis
enim ea quae per stultitiam colui, nunc ad exemplum
omnium aptius quam ipse per sapientiam mihi a Deo
vero donatam destruam ? " Statimque abiecta super-
stitione vanitatis, rogavit sibi regem arma dare et
equum emissarium, quem ascendens ad idola de-
struenda veniret. Non enim licuerat pontificem
sacrorum vel arma ferre, vel praeter in equa equitare.
Accinctus ergo gladio accepit lanceam in manu, et
ascendens emissarium regis, pergebat ad idola.
Quod aspiciens vulgus, aestimabat eum insanire.
Nec distulit ille, mox ut adpropiabat[1] ad fanum,
profanare illud, iniecta in eo lancea quam tenebat:
multumque gavisus de agnitione veri Dei cultus,
iussit sociis destruere ac succendere fanum cum
omnibus septis suis. Ostenditur autem locus ille
quondam idolorum non longe ab Eburaco ad Orientem, ultra amnem Doruventionem, et vocatur hodie
Godmunddingaham, ubi pontifex ipse inspirante Deo
vero polluit ac destruxit eas quas ipse sacraverat aras.

[1] for *propiabat*, Pl.

wherewith they were environed: " Marry," replied
he, " I will. For who now to the good example of all
men can better than I myself, by the wisdom given
me by the true God, destroy those things which
I have myself worshipped by foolishness?" And
incontinently casting away vain superstition he besought the king to grant him harness and a stallion
war horse whereon he might mount and come to
destroy the idols. For it was not before lawful for
a priest of the sacrifices either to wear harness or to
ride on other than a mare. Girded therefore with
a sword about his loins he took a spear in his hand,
and mounting the king's war horse set forth against
the idols. Which sight when men saw they thought
he had been mad. But for all that he stayed not to
profane the temple, as soon as he approached near
unto it, casting thereupon the spear which he held
in his hand; and much rejoicing for the acknowledgment of the worship of the true God he commanded
the company, which was there with him, to set fire
to and destroy the temple together with all its courts.
Now the place where these idols sometime were is
now to be seen not far from York to the east beyond
the river Derwent, and is at the present day called
Godmunddingaham,[1] in which place the chief priest
himself by the inspiration of the true God defiled
and destroyed the altars which he himself had consecrated.[2]

[1] Goodmanham in Yorkshire.
[2] Verg. *Aen.* ii. 502.

CAP. XIV

Ut idem Aeduini cum sua gente fidelis sit factus ; et ubi
Paulinus baptizaverit.

Igitur accepit rex Aeduini cum cunctis gentis suae
nobilibus, ac plebe perplurima fidem et lavacrum
sanctae regenerationis, anno regni sui undecimo, qui
est annus Dominicae incarnationis sexcentesimus
vicesimus septimus, ab adventu vero Anglorum in
Brittaniam annus circiter centesimus octogesimus.
Baptizatus est autem Eburaci die sancto paschae,
pridie Iduum Aprilium, in ecclesia Petri apostoli,
quam ibidem ipse de ligno cum catechizaretur atque
ad percipiendum baptisma imbueretur, citato opere
construxit. In qua etiam civitate ipsi[1] doctori
atque antistiti suo Paulino sedem episcopatus donavit. Mox autem ut baptisma consecutus est, curavit,
docente eodem Paulino, maiorem ipso in loco et
augustiorem de lapide fabricare basilicam, in cuius
medio ipsum quod prius fecerat, oratorium inclu-
deretur. Praeparatis ergo fundamentis in gyro
prioris oratorii per quadrum coepit aedificare basilicam. Sed priusquam altitudo parietis esset con-
summata, rex ipse impia nece occisus opus idem successori suo Osualdo perficiendum reliquit. Paulinus
autem ex eo tempore sex annis continuis, id est, ad
finem usque imperii regis illius, verbum Dei, adnuente
ac favente ipso, in ea provincia praedicabat: crede-
bantque et baptizabantur quotquot erant praeor-
dinati ad vitam aeternam; in quibus erant Osfrid et

---

[1] for *ipse*, Pl.

---

[1] Easter Eve, Bright, p. 118.

CHAPTER XIV

How the same Edwin and all his folk were made believers, and in what place Paulinus baptized them.

So king Edwin with all the nobility of his country and most part of the commons received the faith and came to the laver of holy regeneration, the eleventh year of his reign, which is the 627th year of the Lord's incarnation, and about the 180th year after the entrance of the English into Britain. Now he was baptized at York on the holy day of Easter [1] the 12th of April, in the church of the apostle Peter, which in all speed he himself set up of wood in that same place while he was catechized and instructed against his baptism. And in this city also he granted a bishop's see for Paulinus himself, his teacher and bishop. Moreover, as soon as he was christened, at the telling of the same Paulinus, he set to building right in that place a basilica of stone greater and more magnificent, in the midst whereof he would have enclosed his own proper oratory which he had before made. Laying, therefore, the foundations in a ring about the first oratory he began to build there a basilica foursquare. But before the wall thereof could be brought to his just highness, the king himself was slain by cruel death, and left that same work to be perfected by his successor Oswald. Now Paulinus from that time, six years after, that is to the end of king Edwin's reign, preached the word of God continually by his good leave and favour in that province; and they believed and were baptized, as many as were predestined to life everlasting: amongst whom were Osfrid and Eadfrid king Edwin's

289

Eadfrid filii regis Aeduini, qui ambo ei exuli nati
sunt de Quoenburga filia Cearli regis Merciorum.

Baptizati sunt tempore sequente et alii liberi eius
de Aedilbergia regina progeniti, Aedilhun, et
Aedilthryd filia, et alter filius Vuscfrea, quorum
primi albati adhuc rapti sunt de hac vita, et Eburaci
in ecclesia sepulti. Baptizatus est et Yffi filius
Osfridi, sed et alii nobiles ac regii viri non pauci.
Tantus autem fertur tunc fuisse fervor fidei ac desiderium lavacri salutaris gente Nordanhymbrorum,
ut quodam tempore Paulinus veniens cum rege et
regina in villam regiam quae vocatur Adgefrin,
triginta sex diebus ibidem cum eis catechizandi et
baptizandi officio deditus moraretur; quibus diebus
cunctis a mane usque ad vesperam nil aliud ageret
quam confluentem eo de cunctis viculis ac locis
plebem Christi verbo salutis instruere, atque instruc-
tam in fluvio Gleni, qui proximus erat, lavacro remis-
sionis abluere. Haec villa tempore sequentium regum
deserta, et alia pro illa est facta in loco qui vocatur
Maelmin.

Haec quidem in provincia Berniciorum; sed et in
provincia Deirorum, ubi saepius manere cum rege
solebat, baptizabat in fluvio Sualua, qui vicum Cataractam praeterfluit. Nondum enim oratoria vel
baptisteria in ipso exordio nascentis ibi ecclesiae
poterant aedificari. Attamen in Campodono, ubi
tunc etiam villa regia erat, fecit basilicam, quam post-

---

1 Plummer, II. 103.
2 Yeverin in Glendale.
3 Now Bowmont Water.
4 In the north of Deira.
5 Catterick, near Richmond.
6 Slack, near Huddersfield.

sons both which he had in his banishment by dame
Quenberga, daughter to Cearl king of the Marchmen.

In time following his other children also which he
had by queen Ethelberga were baptized, as his son
Ethelhun and his daughter Ethelthryth and a second
son Wuscfrea, of the which the two first were taken
out of this life while still in their white garments of
baptism, and buried in the church at York. Yffi
son of Osfrid was christened too, with many other of
the nobility and ethelings of the royal race.[1]   And,
as is reported, then was the fervour of faith and earnest
desire of the health-giving laver so great among the
people of the Northumbrians, that on a certain time,
when Paulinus came with the king and queen to the
royal township which is called Adgefrin,[2] he stayed
in that place with them thirty-six days, only occupied
in catechizing and instructing : in each of the which
days he did nothing else from morning till evening
but instruct the commons which flocked thither out
of all places and villages thereabout in the word of
Christ's salvation, whom after he had thus instructed
he cleansed in the flood Glen,[3] for that was the next
near water, with the laver of remission.   This township of Adgefrin in the time of succeeding kings
waxed rude and desert, and another was built in
its room in a place called Maelmin.[4]

Thus much did Paulinus in the Bernicians'
province ; but also in the province of the Deirans,
where he lay most commonly with the king, he baptized in the flood Swale which runneth fast by the
village of Cataract.[5]   For as yet there could not be
builded oratories or places of baptism in the very
birth of the Church new begun there.   But yet there
was built a basilica in Campodunum,[6] where there

291

modum pagani a quibus Aeduini rex occisus est,[1]
cum tota eadem villa succenderunt: pro qua reges
posteriores fecere sibi villam in regione quae vocatur
Loidis. Evasit autem ignem altare, quia lapideum
erat; et servatur adhuc in monasterio reverentissimi
abbatis et presbyteri Thryduulfi, quod est in silva
Elmete.

CAP. XV

*Ut provincia Orientalium Anglorum fidem Christi
susceperit.*

TANTUM autem devotionis Aeduini erga cultum
veritatis habuit, ut etiam regi Orientalium Anglorum,
Earpualdo filio Redualdi, persuaderet, relictis idolorum superstitionibus, fidem et sacramenta Christi
cum sua provincia suscipere. Et quidem pater eius
Reduald iamdudum in Cantia sacramentis Christianae fidei imbutus est, sed frustra: nam rediens
domum, ab uxore sua et quibusdam perversis doctoribus seductus est, atque a sinceritate fidei depra-
vatus habuit posteriora peiora prioribus; ita ut in
morem antiquorum Samaritanorum et Christo servire
videretur, et diis quibus antea serviebat. Atque in
eodem fano et altare haberet ad sacrificium Christi,
et arulam ad victimas daemoniorum. Quod videlicet
fanum rex eiusdem provinciae Alduulf, qui nostra

---

[1] for *occisus*, Pl.

---

[1] Leeds. [2] Near Leeds.
[3] The date of Redwald's death is uncertain, Pl. II. 106.

then was a royal township, which church the paynims that slew king Edwin burned afterwards with the whole of the said town: instead of which the kings that came after made their mansion place in the country of Loidis.[1] But the altar of the said church escaped the fire, because it was made of stone: and it is kept to this day in the monastery of the right reverend abbot and priest Thrydwulf, standing in the wood Elmet.[2]

CHAPTER XV

How the province of the East English received the faith of Christ.

Now Edwin had such an earnest zeal towards the worship of the true faith that he also persuaded the king of the East English, Earpwald, the son of Redwald,[3] to leave off the superstitions of idols, and with his whole realm receive the faith and sacraments of Christ. And indeed his father Redwald had long since been instructed in Kent in the mysteries of the Christian faith, but in vain: for returning home again he was led away by his wife [4] and certain false teachers, and being in such wise corrupted from the simplicity of the faith, his end was worse than his beginning; so much so that he seemed after the manner of the old Samaritans [5] to serve both Christ and the gods he served before. And so in one temple he had both an altar for the sacrifice of Christ and another little altar for offerings made to devils. The which temple, namely, Aldwulf, king of the same province, who lived in this our time, said that it

[4] Cf. p. 279.   [5] Cf. Ezra, iv. 2.

aetate fuit, usque ad suum tempus perdurasse, et se in pueritia vidisse testabatur.

Erat autem praefatus rex Reduald natu nobilis quamlibet actu ignobilis, filius Tytili, cuius pater fuit Vuffa, a quo reges Orientalium Anglorum Vuffingas appellant. Verum Eorpuald non multo postquam fidem accepit tempore, occisus est a viro gentili, nomine Ricbercto; et exinde tribus annis provincia in errore versata est, donec accepit regnum frater eiusdem Eorpualdi Sigberct, vir per omnia Christianissimus atque doctissimus, qui vivente adhuc fratre cum exularet in Gallia, fidei sacramentis imbutus est, quorum participem, mox ubi regnare coepit, totam suam provinciam facere curavit. Cuius studiis gloriosissime favit Felix episcopus, qui de Burgundiorum partibus, ubi ortus et ordinatus est, cum venisset ad Honorium archiepiscopum, eique indicasset desiderium suum, misit eum ad praedicandum verbum vitae praefatae nationi Anglorum. Nec vota ipsius in cassum cecidere; quin potius fructum in ea multiplicem credentium populorum pius agri spiritalis cultor invenit. Siquidem totam illam provinciam iuxta sui nominis sacramentum, a longa iniquitate atque infelicitate liberatam, ad fidem et opera iustitiae, ac perpetuae felicitatis dona perduxit, accepitque sedem episcopatus in civitate Domnoc: et cum decem ac septem annos eidem provinciae pontificali regimine praeesset, ibidem in pace vitam finivit.

---

[1] On the mother's side.

dured so unto his day and witnessed that he saw it in his childhood.

Now the aforenamed king Redwald, being noble in birth although ignoble in deed, was son of Tytilus, whose father was Wuffa, from whom the kings of the East English are called Wuffings. But Earpwald not long after he had received the faith was slain by a man that was a paynim named Ricbert; and from that time three years after the province abode in error, until Sigbert, brother [1] of the same Earpwald, took the kingdom, a man in all points most Christian and learned, who, whiles his brother was yet alive, living banished in France was instructed in the mysteries of the faith; of which he went about to make all his realm partaker as soon as he began to reign. Whose good endeavour herein the bishop Felix farthered to his great glory, and when Felix came from the coasts of Burgundy (where he was born and took holy orders) to Honorius the archbishop, and had opened his longing unto him, the archbishop sent him to preach the word of life to the aforesaid nation of the East English. Where certes his desires fell not in vain; nay rather this good husbandman of the spiritual soil found in that nation manifold fruit of people that believed. For according to the good abodement of his name [2] he brought all that province, now delivered from their long iniquity and unhappiness, unto faith and works of justice, and the gifts of unending happiness; and he received the see of his bishopric in the city of Domnoc: [3] where, when he had ruled the same province seventeen years in that dignity, he ended his life in peace in the same place.

[2] *I.e.* Felix.
[3] Dunwich in Suffolk.

CAP. XVI

Ut Paulinus in provincia Lindissi praedicaverit, et de qualitate regni Aeduini.

PRAEDICABAT autem Paulinus verbum etiam provinciae Lindissi, quae est prima ad meridianam Humbrae fluminis ripam, pertingens usque ad mare, praefectumque Lindocolinae civitatis, cui nomen erat Blaecca, primum cum domo sua convertit ad Dominum. In qua videlicet civitate et ecclesiam operis egregii de lapide fecit: cuius tecto vel longa incuria, vel hostili manu deiecto, parietes hactenus stare videntur, et omnibus annis aliqua sanitatum miracula in eodem loco solent ad utilitatem eorum qui fideliter quaerunt, ostendi. In qua ecclesia Paulinus, transeunte ad Christum Iusto, Honorium pro eo consecravit episcopum, ut in sequentibus suo loco dicemus.

De huius fide provinciae narravit mihi presbyter et abbas quidam vir veracissimus de monasterio Peartaneu, vocabulo Deda, retulisse sibi quendam seniorem, baptizatum se fuisse die media a Paulino episcopo, praesente rege Aeduino, et multam populi turbam in fluvio Treenta iuxta civitatem quae lingua Anglorum Tiovulfingacaestir vocatur: qui etiam effigiem eiusdem Paulini referre esset solitus, quod esset vir longae staturae, paululum incurvus, nigro capillo, facie macilenta, naso adunco pertenui, venerabilis simul et terribilis aspectu. Habuit

---

[1] Modern *Black* or *Blake*.
[2] Partney in Lincolnshire.
[3] Not certainly identified, but may be Littleborough on the Roman road from York to Lincoln, where there is a ford over the Trent.

CHAPTER XVI

How Paulinus preached in the province of Lindsey, and of the state of Edwin's kingdom.

BUT Paulinus continued still and preached the word also in the province of Lindsey, which is the next toward the south bank of the flood Humber, reaching even unto the sea, where he first converted to the Lord the reeve of Lincoln, whose name was Blaecca,[1] with his household. In the which city he built too a well-wrought church of stone; the roof whereof either for long lack of reparation or the spoil of enemies is now cast down, but the walls thereof stand yet to be seen at this present day, and every year some or other miracles of healing are wont to be shewn in the same place for the comfort of them which seek therefor in faith. , And in this church, when Justus departed hence to Christ, Paulinus consecrated Honorius bishop in his room, as I shall shew more conveniently hereafter.

As touching the faith of this province a certain priest and abbot, a man of very good credit, whose name was Deda, of the monastery of Peartaneu,[2] told me that one of the elders of that convent (as he reported himself) had been baptized at midday by Paulinus, in the presence of king Edwin, with a mighty throng of people, in the flood Trent, near the city which is called in the English tongue Tiowulfingacaestir[3]; the which also was wont to describe Paulinus' person, saying that he was a tall man, somewhat crook-backed and black of hair, lean in face and having a hooked thin nose, of a countenance that did at once appal and strike with

297

autem secum in ministerio et Iacobum diaconum, virum utique industrium ac nobilem in Christo et ecclesia, qui ad nostra usque tempora permansit.

Tanta autem eo tempore pax in Brittania, quaquaversum imperium regis Aeduini pervenerat, fuisse perhibetur, ut, sicut usque hodie in proverbio dicitur, etiam si mulier una cum recens nato parvulo vellet totam perambulare insulam a mari ad mare, nullo se laedente valeret. Tantum rex idem utilitati suae gentis consuluit, ut plerisque in locis ubi fontes lucidos iuxta publicos viarum transitus conspexit, ibi ob refrigerium viantium, erectis stipitibus aereos caucos suspendi iuberet, neque hos quisquam, nisi ad usum necessarium, contingere prae magnitudine vel timoris eius auderet, vel amoris vellet. Tantum vero in regno excellentiae habuit, ut non solum in pugna ante illum vexilla gestarentur, sed et tempore pacis equitantem inter civitates sive villas aut provincias suas cum ministris, semper antecedere signifer consuesset; necnon et incedente illo ubilibet per plateas, illud genus vexilli, quod Romani " Tufam," Angli vero appellant " Tuuf," ante eum ferri solebat.

reverence. He had, moreover, in the ministry with him one James a deacon, a man certes of industry and great fame in Christ and the Church, who lived even unto our time.

Now in those days such is stated to have been the tranquillity throughout Britain, which way so ever the rule of king Edwin had reached, that (as it is yet to-day in a common proverb), even if a woman should have wished to walk along with her newborn babe over all the island from sea to sea, she might have done so without injury from any. The same king did so much tender the comfort of his people, that in most places where he saw clear well-springs breaking out by the side of the highways, he bade posts be set up and copper vessels hung thereon for the refreshing of wayfaring men, which vessels either for greatness of fear of the king's displeasure no men durst touch further than to his present use and need, or would wish to touch for greatness of the love they bare him. Moreover, he had such excellency of glory in the kingdom that not only in battle were banners borne before him, but in time of peace too a standard-bearer was accustomed to go before him whensoever he rode [1] about the cities, townships or shires with his thanes; yea, even when he passed through the streets to any place there was wont to be carried before him that kind of banner which the Romans call *Tufa* [2] but the English *Tuuf*.

---

[1] On a royal progress.
[2] Tuft of feathers, *ex confertis plumarum globis*, Ducange.

CAP. XVII

Ut idem ab Honorio papa exhortatorias literas acceperit,
qui etiam Paulino pallium miserit.

Quo tempore praesulatum sedis apostolicae Honorius Bonifatii successor habebat, qui ubi gentem Nordanhymbrorum cum suo rege ad fidem confessionemque Christi, Paulino evangelizante conversam esse didicit, misit eidem Paulino pallium, misit et regi Aeduino literas exhortatorias, paterna illum caritate accendens, ut in fide veritatis quam acceperant, persistere semper ac proficere curarent. Quarum videlicet literarum iste est ordo:

"Domino excellentissimo atque praecellentissimo filio Aeduino regi Anglorum, Honorius episcopus servus servorum Dei, salutem.

"Ita Christianitatis vestrae integritas circa sui conditoris cultum fidei est ardore succensa, ut longe lateque resplendeat, et in omni mundo adnuntiata vestri operis multipliciter referat fructum. Sic enim vos reges esse cognoscitis, dum Regem et Creatorem vestrum orthodoxa praedicatione ˙edocti, Deum venerando creditis, eique, quod humana valet conditio, mentis vestrae sinceram devotionem exsolvitis. Quid enim Deo nostro aliud offerre valebimus, nisi ut in bonis actibus persistentes, ipsumque auctorem humani generis confitentes, eum colere, eique vota nostra reddere festinemus? Et ideo, excellen-

---

[1] The next letter shews that the date was June 634. Edwin was slain in October 633.

LETTER OF HONORIUS

CHAPTER XVII

How the same king received a letter of exhortation from pope Honorius, who also sent a pall to Paulinus.

At that time [1] Honorius, the successor of Boniface, held the prelacy of the apostolic see, and when he learned that the people of Northumbria with their king were converted to the faith and confession of Christ by Paulinus' preaching of the Gospel, he sent the same Paulinus a pall and sent too a letter of exhortation to king Edwin, with fatherly love kindling him to see that himself and his people should always continue or rather go forward in the faith of the truth which they had received. Of which letter namely the following is the tenor:

" To the most eminent sovereign and his most excellent son Edwin, king of the English, Honorius, bishop, servant of the servants of God, sendeth greeting.

" So is the integrity of your Christianity, fired with the flame of faith towards the worship of its founder, that it shineth far and wide, and being declared through all the world bringeth back manifold fruit of your doing. For so do ye know that ye are kings, while, after ye are taught thoroughly by the right and true preaching, ye believe with worshipping of God your King and Creator, and render up to Him the sincere devotion of your mind, as far forth as man's nature can attain unto. For what other thing shall we have power to offer unto our God, than that continuing in good works and confessing Him to be the Author of mankind we hasten to worship Him and render to Him our prayers? And for that reason we exhort you, most excellent

tissime fili, paterna vos caritate qua convenit, exhor-
tamur, ut hoc quod vos divina misericordia ad suam
gratiam vocare dignata est, sollicita intentione et
adsiduis orationibus servare omnimodo festinetis;
ut qui vos in praesenti saeculo ex omni errore abso-
lutos ad agnitionem sui nominis est dignatus per-
ducere, et caelestis patriae vobis praeparet mansionem. Praedicatoris igitur vestri domini mei
apostolicae memoriae Gregorii frequenter lectione
occupati, prae oculis affectum doctrinae ipsius, quem
pro vestris animabus libenter exercuit, habetote:
quatenus eius oratio, et regnum vestrum populumque
augeat, et vos omnipotenti Deo inreprehensibiles
repraesentet. Ea vero quae a nobis pro vestris
sacerdotibus ordinanda sperastis, haec pro fidei
vestrae sinceritate, quae nobis multimoda relatione
per praesentium portitores laudabiliter insinuata est,
gratuito animo adtribuere ulla sine dilatione prae-
videmus; et duo pallia utrorumque metropolita-
norum, id est, Honorio et Paulino direximus, ut dum
quis eorum de hoc saeculo ad auctorem suum fuerit
arcessitus, in loco ipsius alter episcopum ex hac nostra
auctoritate debeat subrogare. Quod quidem tam
pro vestrae caritatis affectu, quam pro tantarum
provinciarum spatiis quae inter nos et vos esse
noscuntur, sumus invitati concedere, ut in omnibus
devotioni vestrae nostrum concursum, et iuxta vestra
desideria praeberemus.

" Incolumem excellentiam vestram gratia superna
custodiat."

son, as it is meet for a loving father to do, that ye
hasten all manner of ways ye can with earnest will
and constant supplications to keep this that the
mercy of God hath vouchsafed to grant in calling
you to His grace; that so He which hath vouchsafed
to bring you in this present world, freed from all
error, to the acknowledgment of His name, may
also prepare a mansion place for you in the heavenly
country. Be ye therefore often busied in the reading
of Gregory your preacher and my lord of apostolic
memory, having before your eyes the goodwill of
the teaching of the selfsame, which he gladly practised for the sake of your souls: that so his prayer
may both increase your kingdom and your people,
and make you to appear in the end without fault
before Almighty God. Now as concerning those
things which you hoped should be ordained by us
for your bishops, we do without any delay and with
readiness of mind make it our care to grant them, for
the sake of the unfeignedness of your faith, of which
we have been commendably informed in divers
reports by the bearers of these our presents; and
we have sent two palls belonging to the two metro-
politans, that is, for Honorius and Paulinus, in order
that when one of them is called out of this world to
the Author of his being, the other should appoint a
bishop in his place by this our authority. And this
thing truly we are moved to grant, as well for the
good will of your love, as for the situation of such
great provinces at the distance which is known to
separate us from you, to the intent we might in all
points shew our readiness to meet your devotion and
act according to your wishes.

"May the grace from above have your excellency
in safe keeping!"

CAP. XVIII

*Ut Honorius, qui Iusto in episcopatum Dorovernensis
ecclesiae successit, ab eodem papa Honorio pallium
et literas acceperit.*

Haec inter Iustus archiepiscopus ad caelestia regna
sublevatus quarto Iduum Novembrium die et
Honorius pro illo est in praesulatum electus [1]: qui
ordinandus venit ad Paulinum, et occurrente sibi illo
in Lindocolino quintus ab Augustino Doruvernensis
ecclesiae consecratus est antistes. Cui etiam praefatus
papa Honorius misit pallium et literas, in quibus
decernit hoc ipsum, quod in epistola ad Aeduinum
regem missa decreverat; scilicet ut cum Doruvernensis vel Eburacensis antistes de hac vita transierit,
is qui superest consors eiusdem gradus habeat potest-
atem alterum ordinandi, in loco eius qui transierat,
sacerdotem; ne sit necesse ad Romanam usque
civitatem per tam prolixa terrarum et maris spatia
pro ordinando archiepiscopo semper fatigari. Quarum
etiam textum literarum in nostra hac Historia ponere
commodum duximus.

" Dilectissimo fratri Honorio, Honorius.

" Inter plurima quae Redemptoris nostri misericordia suis famulis dignatur bonorum munera praero-
gare, illud etiam clementer collata suae pietatis
munificentia tribuit, quod [2] per fraternos affatus
unianimam dilectionem quadam contemplatione

---

[1] for *effectus*, Pl.
[2] for *quoties*, Pl.

---

[1] Bede does not give the year, which may have been 627.

CHAPTER XVIII

*How Honorius who succeeded Justus in the bishopric
of the church of Canterbury received from the same
pope Honorius a pall and letter.*

ABOUT this time the archbishop Justus was uplifted
to the heavenly realms—the 10th day of November [1]
—and Honorius was chosen to the prelacy in his room:
who coming to Paulinus to be ordained, met him at
Lincoln and there was consecrated bishop of the
church at Canterbury, being the fifth after Augustine.
To whom also the aforesaid pope Honorius sent a
pall and letter, in the which he appointed the very
selfsame thing that he appointed before in the epistle
sent to King Edwin; which is, that when the bishop
of Canterbury or the bishop of York hath departed
this life, then his fellow of the same degree, which
remaineth alive, shall have power to ordain a bishop
to succeed, in the room of him which is now deceased;
that it may not be needful always to travel and toil
over such long space of land and sea as far as to Rome
for the ordaining of an archbishop. Of which letter
too I have thought it not amiss to insert a copy in this
our History.

" To Honorius, our dearly beloved brother
Honorius.

" Among many other good gifts which the pitifulness of our Redeemer vouchsafeth of His grace to
give unto His servants, this also doth He mercifully
grant by bestowing of the bountifulness of His goodness, that through the brotherly greeting of letters
(as it were by a sort of looking on one another), He
may (by this our beholding each of the other's visage

alternis aspectibus repraesentat. Pro quibus maiestati eius gratias indesinenter exsolvimus, eumque votis supplicibus exoramus, ut vestram dilectionem in praedicatione Evangelii laborantem et fructificantem, sectantemque magistri et capitis sui sancti Gregorii regulam, perpeti stabilitate confirmet, et ad augmentum Ecclesiae suae potiora per vos suscitet incrementa; ut fide et opere, in timore Dei et caritate, vestra adquisitio decessorumque vestrorum quae per domini Gregorii exordia pullulat, convalescendo amplius extendatur; ut ipsa vos dominici eloquii promissa in futuro respiciant, vosque vox ista ad aeternam festivitatem evocet: 'Venite ad me omnes qui laboratis et onerati estis, et ego reficiam vos.' Et iterum: ' Euge, serve bone et fidelis; quia super pauca fuisti fidelis, super multa te constituam: intra in gaudium Domini tui.' Et nos equidem, fratres carissimi, haec vobis pro aeterna caritate exhortationis verba praemittentes, quae rursus pro ecclesiarum vestrarum privilegiis congruere posse conspicimus, non desistimus impertire. Et tam iuxta vestram petitionem, quam filiorum nostrorum regum vobis per praesentem nostram praeceptionem vice beati Petri apostolorum principis auctoritatem tribuimus, ut quando unum ex vobis divina ad se iusserit gratia vocari, is qui superstes fuerit alterum in loco defuncti debeat episcopum ordinare. Pro qua etiam re singula vestrae dilectioni pallia pro eadem ordinatione

---

[1] Matth. xi. 28.   [2] Matth. xxv. 23.
[3] Northumbria and Kent.

in turn) make manifest our mutual unity of love. For
which benefit we render thanks unceasingly unto
His majesty, and beseech Him with prayers of supplication that He may strengthen your love to endure
steadfastly in labouring and gathering fruit in the
preaching of the Gospel, and in following the rule of
your head and master, holy Gregory, and that He
may raise greater increase by you unto the growth
of the Church; that the gain which you and your
predecessors have won (which springeth out of the
first planting of our lord Gregory) may more abundantly be spread by becoming strong through faith and
work in the fear of God and in charity; that the very
promises uttered by our Lord may hereafter have
regard unto you and that that voice of His may call
you forth to eternal joyfulness[1]: 'Come unto me all
ye that labour and are heavy laden and I will refresh
you.' And again[2]: 'Well done, good and faithful
servant; because thou hast been faithful over a few
things, I will set thee over many things: enter thou
into the joy of thy Lord!' And we for our part,
beloved brethren, send forward these words of exhortation to you in behalf of the eternal charity, and defer
not to grant you the things which again we see are
able to be meet for the privileges of your churches.
And as in accordance with your request, so in
accordance with that of the kings[3] our sons, by our
express commandment in the stead of the blessed
Peter, chief of the apostles, we grant you authority,
that when the Divine Grace hath bidden one of you
to be called to Itself, he who shall be left alive must
ordain a bishop to be successor in place of the departed
one. For which thing's sake also we have sent a
pall to each of you, beloved, to be used for celebrating

celebranda direximus, ut per nostrae praeceptionis auctoritatem possitis Deo placitam ordinationem efficere; quia ut haec vobis concederemus, longa terrarum marisque intervalla, quae inter nos ac vos obsistunt, ad haec nos condescendere coegerunt, ut nulla possit ecclesiarum vestrarum iactura per cuiuslibet occasionis obtentum quoquo modo provenire; sed potius commissi vobis populi devotionem plenius propagare. Deus te incolumem custodiat, dilectissime frater.

"Data die tertio Iduum Iunii, imperantibus dominis nostris Augustis, Heraclio anno vicesimo quarto, post consulatum eiusdem anno vicesimo tertio; atque Constantino filio ipsius anno vicesimo tertio, et consulatus eius anno tertio; sed et Heraclio felicissimo Caesare id est[1] filio eius anno tertio, indictione septima, id est, anno Dominicae incarnationis sexcentesimo tricesimo quarto."

CAP. XIX

Ut primo idem Honorius et post Iohannes literas genti Scottorum pro pascha simul et pro Pelagiana haeresi miserit.

Misit idem papa Honorius literas etiam genti Scottorum, quos in observatione sancti paschae errare compererat, iuxta quod supra docuimus: sollerter exhortans, ne paucitatem suam in extremis terrae finibus constitutam sapientiorem antiquis sive moder-

---

[1] for *item*, Pl.

---

[1] Heracleonas, younger son of Heraclius.

the same ordination, that by the authority of this our commandment you be able to render the ordination acceptable to God; for that the long spaces of land and sea, which are hindrances betwixt us and you, have compelled us to condescend herein to grant this much unto you, that no loss may happen to your churches by any pretenced occasion in any manner of way; but rather it be possible to set for the farther the devotion of the people committed to your charge. God have you in his safe keeping, most beloved brother.

" Given the 11th of June, in the reign of our lords the Augusti, the 24th year of Heraclius, the 23rd year after the consulship of the same; and in the 23rd year of Constantine son of the same, and the third year of his consulship; moreover, too, in the third year of the most fortunate Caesar Heraclius,[1] that is, his son, in the 7th indiction, that is, in the 634th year of the Lord's incarnation."

CHAPTER XIX

How first the same Honorius and after him John sent letters to the Scottish nation on account of the keeping of Easter as well as on account of the Pelagian heresy.

THE same pope Honorius sent a letter also unto the Scottish nation, whom he had learned to be in error in the observation of the holy time of Easter, as we have before specified; earnestly exhorting them that they should not reckon their own small number, set as they were in the utmost ends of the earth, to be wiser than the churches of Christ, either ancient,

309

nis quae per orbem erant Christi ecclesiis aestimarent;
neve contra paschales computos, et decreta syno-
dalium totius orbis pontificum, aliud pascha celebrarent.

Sed et Iohannes qui successori eiusdem Honorii
Severino successit, cum adhuc esset electus in pontificatum, pro eodem errore corrigendo literas eis magna
auctoritate atque eruditione plenas direxit; evidenter
adstruens, quia dominicum paschae diem a quinta
decima luna usque ad vicesimam primam, quod in
Nicaena synodo probatum est, oportet inquiri.
Necnon et pro Pelagiana haeresi, quam apud eos
reviviscere didicerat, cavenda ac repellenda, in
eadem illos epistola admonere curavit; cuius
epistolae principium hoc est:

" Dilectissimis et sanctissimis Tomiano, Colum-
bano, Cromano, Dinnao, et Baithano episcopis;
Cromano, Ernianoque, Laistrano, Scellano, et Segeno
presbyteris; Sarano, ceterisque doctoribus seu
abbatibus Scottis, Hilarus archipresbyter, et servans
locum sanctae sedis apostolicae, Iohannes diaconus,
et in Dei nomine electus: item Iohannes primicerius, et servans locum sanctae sedis apostolicae,
et Iohannes servus Dei, consiliarius eiusdem apostolicae sedis. Scripta quae perlatores ad sanctae
memoriae Severinum papam adduxerunt, et eo de
hac luce migrante, reciproca responsa ad ea quae
postulata fuerant, siluerunt. Quibus reseratis, ne
diu tantae quaestionis caligo indiscussa remaneret,

---

[1] Severinus was buried August 2, 640; John IV consecrated December 25, 640, and the letter written between
August and December, Pl.

either new, which were throughout the world; nor should celebrate another Easter contrary to the commonly accounted Easters, and to the decrees of the bishops of the whole world sitting in synods.

Moreover, John, who succeeded Severinus, the successor of the same Honorius, when he was yet but elected to the chief bishopric, sent a letter [1] unto them of great authority and full of good learning for the sake of amending the same error: plainly asserting therein that the Easter Sunday ought to be sought for from the 15th moon up to the 21st, as was approved in the council of Nicaea. Further too he was careful in the same letter to warn them to beware of and eschew the Pelagian heresy which he had learned did begin to rise again amongst them; the beginning of which epistle is this:

" To the well beloved and most holy Tomene, Colman, Cronan, Dima and Baeithin, bishops; Cronan, Ernan, Laisren, Scellan and Seghine, priests; Saran and the other doctors or abbots of the Scots, Hilary, arch-presbyter and keeper of the vacant holy see apostolic, John, deacon and in the name of God chosen bishop; also John, superintendent and keeper of the vacant holy see apostolic, and John servant of God, Councillor of the same apostolic see.[2] The letters which your bearers have brought to pope Severinus of holy memory, have had no answer made in return to the matters which had been required therein, seeing the pope departed from this life. Which we have now opened, lest the darkness of so great a question might have lasted on and been unexamined,

---

[2] During a vacancy the arch-presbyter, the archdeacon, and the *primicerius notariorum* acted as vicegerents of the Roman see. *Notarius* means shorthand writer, Pl.

reperimus quosdam provinciae vestrae contra ortho-
doxam fidem, novam ex veteri haeresim renovare
conantes, pascha nostrum in quo immolatus est
Christus, nebulosa caligine refutantes, et quarta
decima luna cum Hebraeis celebrare nitentes."
Quo epistolae principio manifeste declaratur, et
nuperrime temporibus illis hanc apud eos haeresim
coortam, et non totam eorum gentem, sed quosdam
in eis hac fuisse implicitos.

Exposita autem ratione paschalis observantiae, ita
de Pelagianis in eadem epistola subdunt: " Et hoc
quoque cognovimus, quod virus Pelagianae haereseos
apud vos denuo reviviscit: quod omnino hortamur ut
a vestris mentibus huiusmodi venenatum super-
stitionis facinus auferatur. Nam qualiter ipsa quoque execranda haeresis damnata est, latere vos non
debet; quia non solum per istos ducentos annos
abolita est, sed et quotidie a nobis perpetuo anathe-
mate sepulta damnatur; et hortamur, ne quorum
arma combusta sunt, apud vos eorum cineres suscitentur.
tur. Nam quis non execretur superbum eorum
conamen et impium, dicentium posse sine peccato
hominem existere ex propria voluntate, et non ex
gratia Dei? Et primum quidem blasphemiae
stultiloquium est, dicere esse hominem sine peccato;
quod omnino non potest nisi unus Mediator Dei et
hominum homo Christus Jesus qui sine peccato est
conceptus et partus. Nam ceteri homines cum
peccato originali nascentes testimonium praevarica-

---

[1] Cf. iii. 25. The Irish were not Quarto-deciman heretics
who kept Easter on the 14th day of the moon after the Spring
Equinox, whether this fell on a Sunday or not.

and we find therein that certain of your province, contrary to the right faith, do go about to renew a new from an old heresy, rejecting through the mist of darkness our Easter in which Christ was sacrificed, and striving to celebrate the same with the Hebrews on the 14th moon." [1] And by this beginning of the latter it appeareth plainly, both that at that time this heresy was but a very little before risen in Scotland, and that not all the country but certain among them only had been entangled therein.

Now when the reckoning of the observance of Easter had been set out, they add thereto as follows concerning the Pelagians in the same letter: " And this also we understand, that the poison of the Pelagian heresy beginneth to spring again amongst you; and we exhort you to provide that the poisoned crime of this manner of superstition be utterly removed from your minds. For it ought not to be hid from you how also the selfsame abominable heresy hath been condemned; seeing that not only hath it been done away with these 200 years, but also is daily buried by us and condemned with continual cursing; and we exhort you that ye suffer not their ashes to be stirred to life amongst you, whose weapons have been burnt and consumed. For who would not abhor the proud intent and wicked words of them which affirm that a man may live without sin of his own voluntary will, and not through the grace of God? And first of all it is blasphemous folly of speech to say that man is without sin; for none can be so save the one Mediator of God and man, the man Jesus Christ who was conceived and born without sin. For as for other men they are all born with original sin, and are known to bear the witness of

313

tionis Adae, etiam sine actuali peccato existentes,
portare noscuntur; secundum prophetam dicentem:
'Ecce enim in iniquitatibus conceptus sum et in
peccatis concepit me mater mea.' "

CAP. XX

*Ut occiso Aeduino Paulinus Cantiam rediens Hrofensis
ecclesiae praesulatum susceperit.*

Aт vero Aeduini cum decem et septem annis genti
Anglorum simul et Brittonum gloriosissime praeesset,
e quibus sex etiam ipse, ut diximus, Christi regno
militavit, rebellavit adversus eum Caedualla rex
Brettonum, auxilium praebente illi Penda viro strenuissimo de regio genere Merciorum, qui et ipse ex [1] eo
tempore gentis eiusdem regno annis viginti et duobus varia sorte praefuit: et conserto gravi praelio in
campo qui vocatur Haethfelth, occisus est Aeduini die
quarta Iduum Octobris, anno Dominicae incarnationis
sexcentesimo tricesimo tertio, cum esset annorum
quadraginta et octo: eiusque totus vel interemptus
vel dispersus est exercitus. In quo etiam bello ante
illum unus filius eius Osfrid iuvenis bellicosus cecidit,
alter Eadfrid necessitate cogente ad Pendam regem
transfugit, et ab eo postmodum regnante Osualdo
contra fidem iurisiurandi peremptus est.

Quo tempore maxima est facta strages in ecclesia
vel gente Nordanhymbrorum, maxime quod unus ex

---

[1] for *eo tempore,* Pl.

---

[1] Ps. li. 5.

Adam's fall, yea, though they live without actual sin; according to the prophet, saying:[1] "Behold I was shapen in wickedness, and in sin hath my mother conceived me."

CHAPTER XX

How when Edwin was slain Paulinus returned to Kent and there took the prelacy of the church of Rochester.

But in truth when Edwin reigned most triumphantly seventeen years over the English and the Britons both, of which years for six he himself fought for the kingdom of Christ, Cadwallon[2] king of the Britons made a rebellion against him, having aid thereunto of Penda a stout man of the king's blood of the Marchmen, who also himself from that time was head over the realm of the said nation with divers' fortune two-and-twenty years; and when they had joined battle fiercely in the field which is called Heathfield,[3] Edwin was slain the 12th day of October in the 633rd year of the Lord's incarnation, when he was 48 years of age; and all his army was either destroyed or put to flight. In the which war also one son of his, the warlike young Osfrid, fell before his father; a second, Eadfrid, of urgent necessity fled over to king Penda, and was afterwards put to death against the faith of the king's oath in the reign of Oswald.

At which time there was a very great slaughter made in the church and nation of the Northumb-

[2] According to Welsh tradition, Edwin, when an exile, took refuge with Cadvan, King of Gwynedd, the father of Cadwallon, Pl.

[3] Supposed to be Hatfield Chase, near Doncaster.

ducibus a quibus acta est paganus, alter quis barbarus
erat pagano saevior. Siquidem Penda cum omni
Merciorum gente idolis deditus, et Christiani erat
nominis ignarus: at vero Caedualla, quamvis nomen
et professionem haberet Christiani, adeo tamen erat
animo ac moribus barbarus, ut ne sexui quidem
muliebri, vel innocuae parvulorum parceret aetati, quin
universos atrocitate ferina morti per tormenta contra-
deret, multo tempore totas eorum provincias debac-
chando pervagatus, ac totum genus Anglorum Brittaniae finibus erasurum se esse deliberans. Sed nec
religioni Christianae, quae apud eos exorta erat,
aliquid inpendebat honoris. Quippe cum usque hodie
moris sit Brettonum, fidem religionemque Anglorum
pro nihilo habere, neque in aliquo eis magis communi-
care quam paganis. Adlatum est autem caput
Aeduini regis Eburacum, et inlatum postea in ecclesiam
beati apostoli Petri, quam ipse coepit, sed successor
eius Osualdus perfecit, ut supra docuimus, positum
est in porticu sancti papae Gregorii, a cuius ipse
discipulis verbum vitae susceperat.

Turbatis itaque rebus Nordanhymbrorum huius
articulo cladis, cum nil alicubi praesidii nisi in fuga esse
videretur, Paulinus adsumpta secum regina Aedil-
berge quam pridem adduxerat, rediit Cantiam
navigio, atque ab Honorio archiepiscopo et rege
Eadbaldo multum honorifice susceptus est. Venit
autem illuc duce Basso, milite regis Aeduini fortissimo,

---

[1] Matth. x. 23.

rians, especially because that one of the captains, which caused it, was a paynim, the other, because he was a savage, was fiercer than the paynim. For king Penda with all the nation of the Marchmen was given over to idolatry and was ignorant of the Christian name: but indeed Cadwallon, although he had the name of a Christian and professed that life, yet was he in mind and manners so much a savage, that he spared not even the sex of women or the harmless infancy of young children, but delivered them all to death with torments according to his beastly cruelty, wasting a long time and raging over all the provinces, purposing, moreover, with himself to exterminate out of the borders of Britain the whole race of Englishmen. Nay he did not either pay any reverence to the Christian religion which had risen up amongst them. For unto this day the Briton's manner and custom is to set light by the faith and religion of the English, neither in any one point more to communicate with them than with paynims. Now king Edwin's head was brought unto York, and afterwards carried into the church of the blessed apostle Peter (which church he himself began to build, but his successor Oswald finished it, as we have before declared), and there laid in the chapel of the holy pope Gregory, from whose disciples he himself had received the word of life.

And so the state of Northumberland being much troubled with the season of this disaster, seeing that there was none other remedy but only by flight,[1] Paulinus taking with him queen Ethelberga whom long sithens he had brought to that country, took ship and returned to Kent, and was there very honourably received of Honorius the archbishop and king Eadbald. Moreover, he came with Bassus for guide, a

habens secum Eanfledam filiam, et Vuscfrean filium
Aeduini, necnon et Yffi filium Osfridi filii eius, quos
postea mater metu Eadbaldi et Osualdi regum, misit
in Galliam nutriendos regi Daegbercto qui erat
amicus illius, ibique ambo in infantia defuncti, et
iuxta honorem vel regiis pueris, vel innocentibus
Christi congruum, in ecclesia sepulti sunt. Attulit
quoque secum vasa pretiosa Aeduini regis perplura,
in quibus et crucem magnam auream, et calicem
aureum consecratum ad ministerium altaris, quae
hactenus in ecclesia Cantiae conservata monstrantur.

Quo in tempore, Hrofensis ecclesia pastorem minime
habebat, eo quod Romanus praesul illius ad Honorium
papam a Iusto archiepiscopo legatarius missus
absorptus fuerat fluctibus Italici maris: ac per hoc
curam illius praefatus Paulinus invitatione Honorii
antistitis et Eadbaldi regis suscepit ac tenuit, usque-
dum et ipse suo tempore ad caelestia regna cum
gloriosi fructu laboris ascendit. In qua ecclesia
moriens pallium quoque, quod a Romano papa
acceperat, reliquit.

Reliquerat autem in ecclesia sua Eburacensi
Iacobum diaconum, virum utique ecclesiasticum et
sanctum, qui multo exhinc tempore in ecclesia
manens magnas antiquo hosti praedas docendo et
baptizando eripuit: cuius nomine vicus in quo
maxime solebat habitare, iuxta Cataractam, usque
hodie cognominatur. Qui quoniam cantandi in
ecclesia erat peritissimus, recuperata postmodum

---

[1] Second cousin.
[2] Sailing from Provence to Italy.
[3] After he had left Northumbria.

brave thane of King Edwin's, and Paulinus had with him Eanfled the daughter and Wuscfrea the son of Edwin, as well as Yffi son of Osfrid, Edwin's son, and afterwards their mother Ethelberga, for fear of the kings Eadbald and Oswald, sent her two children into France to be brought up in the court of king Dagobert, who was her friend,[1] and there they both died in their infancy, and were buried in the church with such honour as is meet for king's children and innocent babes of Christ. Paulinus brought with him also much precious plate of King Edwin's, amongst which there was too a great golden cross and golden chalice consecrated for the ministry of the altar, which are yet preserved and to be seen in the church of Kent.

At which time the church of Rochester was without a pastor, because that Romanus the prelate thereof, being sent from the archbishop Justus as legate to pope Honorius, had been drowned in the waves of the Italian sea;[2] and so for this cause the aforesaid Paulinus, at the offer of Honorius the bishop and Eadbald the king, took the charge thereof and held it until he himself too in his due time ascended to the heavenly realms with the fruit of his glorious travail. Who at his decease left also in his church of Rochester the pall which he had received from the pope of Rome.[3]

Moreover, he had left in his church of York James his deacon, a godly man and true officer of the Church, who living long after in that church by teaching and baptizing took many preys from the old enemy; of whose name the village near Cataract, in which he for the most part abode and dwelt, hath a name to this day. Who because he was cunning in singing in church, when the country was afterwards become

pace in provincia, et crescente numero fidelium, etiam magister ecclesiasticae cantionis iuxta morem Romanorum seu Cantuariorum multis coepit existere : et ipse senex ac plenus dierum, iuxta scripturas, patrum viam secutus est.

quiet again, and the company of the faithful was increasing, also began to be a master to many of church music according to the fashion of the Romans and Kentish men;[1] and he himself when old and full of days, according to the words of Scripture,[2] followed the way which his fathers went.

[1] Gregorian plain-song introduced into Kent by Augustine.
[2] Job xlii. 17.

BOOK III

HISTORIAE ECCLESIASTICAE
GENTIS ANGLORUM

LIBER TERTIUS

CAP. I

Ut primi successores Aeduini regis et fidem suae gentis prodiderint, et regnum porro Osualdus Christianissimus rex utrumque restauravit.

At interfecto in pugna Aeduino, suscepit pro illo regnum Deirorum, de qua provincia ille generis prosapiam et primordia regni habuerat, filius patrui eius Aelfrici, vocabulo Osric, qui ad praedicationem Paulini fidei erat sacramentis imbutus. Porro regnum Berniciorum, nam in has duas provincias gens Nordanhymbrorum antiquitus divisa erat, suscepit filius Aedilfridi qui de illa provincia generis et regni originem duxerat, nomine Eanfrid. Siquidem tempore toto quo regnavit Aeduini, filii praefati regis Aedilfridi qui ante illum regnaverat, cum magna nobilium iuventute apud Scottos sive Pictos exulabant, ibique ad doctrinam Scottorum catechizati et baptismatis sunt gratia recreati. Qui ut mortuo rege inimico patriam sunt redire permissi, accepit

---

[1] Deira, from the Humber to the Tyne or Tees, and, north of Deira, Bernicia extending to the Forth.

[2] Cf. Scott, *Rob Roy*, ch. xviii: "His limbs, from the bottom of his kilt to the top of his short hose, were covered with a fell of thick, short, red hair, especially around his knees, which resembled in this respect the limbs of a red-coloured Highland bull."

THE THIRD BOOK OF THE ECCLESIASTICAL
HISTORY OF THE ENGLISH NATION

CHAPTER I

*How the first successors of king Edwin both did forsake
the faith of their nation, and further how the most
Christian king Oswald restored both kingdoms
[623-634].*

Now king Edwin being slain in battle, the son of
Elfric his uncle by his father's side, called Osric
(who after hearing Paulinus preach was instructed in
the mysteries of the faith), succeeded to the kingdom
of the Deirans in Edwin's stead, of the which province
he had had the pedigree of his parentage and the
first beginnings of his kingdom. Furthermore, the
realm of the Bernicians (for the nation of the Northumbrians had been divided of old time into these
two provinces)[1] was ruled by Ethelfrith's son, named
Eanfrid, who had of that province the beginning of
his kindred and kingdom. For in all the time of
Edwin's reign the sons of the aforenamed king
Ethelfrith, who had reigned before Edwin, were
banished with a great number of young nobles and
so lived amongst the Scots and Redshanks,[2] and there
they were instructed and renewed by the grace of
baptism according to the doctrine of the Scots. And
these princes as being suffered after the death of the
king their enemy to return to their country, the

primus eorum, quem diximus, Eanfrid regnum
Berniciorum. Qui uterque rex ut terreni regni
infulas sortitus est, sacramenta regni caelestis quibus
initiatus erat, anathematizando prodidit, ac se priscis
idolatriae sordibus polluendum perdendumque
restituit.

Nec mora, utrumque rex Brettonum Ceadualla
impia manu, sed iusta ultione peremit. Et primo
quidem proxima aestate Osricum, dum se in oppido
municipio temerarie obsedisset, erumpens subito cum
suis omnibus imparatum cum toto [1] exercitu delevit.
Dein cum anno integro provincias Nordanhymbrorum
non ut rex victor possideret sed quasi tyrannus
saeviens disperderet, ac tragica caede dilaceraret,
tandem Eanfridum inconsulte ad se cum duodecim
lectis militibus, postulandae pacis gratia venientem
simili sorte damnavit. Infaustus ille annus et
omnibus bonis exosus usque hodie permanet, tam
propter apostasiam regum Anglorum qua se fidei
sacramentis exuerant, quam propter vesanam Bret-
tonici regis tyrannidem. Unde cunctis placuit
regum tempora computantibus, ut ablata de medio
regum perfidorum memoria, idem annus sequentis
regis, id est, Osualdi, viri Deo dilecti regno adsigna-
retur: quo, post occisionem fratris Eanfridi, superveniente cum parvo exercitu, sed fide Christi munito,
infandus Brettonum dux cum immensis illis copiis

[1] for *suo*, Pl.

---

[1] Eboracum, York, the capital of the country, which
Cadwallon was then in occupation of.

eldest of them, whom we have named, Eanfrid took the kingdom of the Bernicians. Each of which kings, when the lot of the diadem of an earthly kingdom fell to him, execrated and forsook the mysteries of the heavenly kingdom in which he had been initiated, and yielded himself again to be defiled and lost with the former old filth of idolatry.

And without delay Cadwallon, the king of the Britons, slew both of them, with pitiless might but righteous vengeance. And first, the next summer ensuing, he destroyed Osric with his whole army, bursting out upon him with all his men and taking him unprepared, after Osric had pended him in the fenced town.[1] Then afterward by the space of a whole year he held the provinces of the people of Northumberland, not as a king that were a conqueror but as an outrageous cruel tyrant, destroying them and with tragical slaughter rending them to pieces; and at length by a like fate he condemned Eanfrid to death when he came unto him unadvisedly with 12 chosen thanes, minding to entreat upon peace. That year continueth also unto this day unhappy and hateful to all good men, as well for the apostasy of the English kings, whereby they had put from them the mysteries of the faith, as for the British king's furious tyranny. Wherefore all they that reckon the chronicles of the kings, have thought it best to take away from the midst the memory of the apostate kings, and assign the same year to the reign of the king that followed next, that is to say, Oswald, a man beloved of God: who, after that his brother Eanfrid was slain, coming unlooked for with a small army, but fenced with the faith of Christ, the Britons' cursed captain and that innumerable host, whereof

quibus nihil resistere posse iactabat, interemptus est in loco qui lingua Anglorum Denisesburna, id est rivus Denisi vocatur.

CAP. II

Ut de ligno crucis quod idem rex contra barbaros pug-naturus erexerat, inter innumera sanitatum miracula, quidam a dolentis brachii sit languore curatus.

OSTENDITUR autem usque hodie et in magna venera-tione habetur locus ille, ubi venturus ad hanc pugnam Osuald signum sanctae crucis erexit, ac flexis genibus Dominum deprecatus est, ut in tanta rerum necessi-tate suis cultoribus caelesti succurreret auxilio. Denique fertur quia facta citato opere cruce, ac fovea praeparata in qua statui deberet, ipse fide fervens hanc arripuerit, ac foveae imposuerit, atque utraque manu erectam tenuerit, donec adgesto a militibus pulvere terrae figeretur. Et hoc facto, elata in altum voce cuncto exercitui proclamaverit: " Flectamus omnes genua, et Deum omnipotentem vivum ac verum in commune deprecemur, ut nos ab hoste superbo ac feroce sua miseratione defendat: scit enim ipse quia iusta pro salute gentis nostrae bella suscepimus." Fecerunt omnes ut iusserat, et sic incipiente diluculo

---

[1] Now Rowley Water near Hexham.

he made his vaunt that nothing could be able to withstand it, were slain in the place which in the tongue of the English is called Denisesburna,[1] that is the river of Denise.

CHAPTER II

How of the wood of the cross which the same king had set up, when he was going to fight against the barbarians, innumerable miracles of healing were wrought, and among them a certain man was cured of the feebleness of an afflicted arm.

Now that place is shewed until this day and is had in great reverence, where Oswald, when he should come to this battle, did set up the sign of the holy cross, and beseeched the Lord on bended knees, that with His heavenly help He should succour His worshippers being in so sore a strait. In short, the report is that (the cross being made with quick speed and the hole prepared wherein it should be set), the king himself, being fervent in faith, did take it in haste and did put it in the hole, and further held it with both his hands when it was set up until it was fastened to the earth with dust which the soldiers heaped about it. And when this was done, he lifted up his voice and cried out aloud to the whole army: " Let us all bend our knees and together pray earnestly the almighty, living and true God of His mercy to defend us from the proud and cruel enemy: for He knoweth that we have enterprised warfare in a rightful quarrel for the safeguard of our nation." All did as he had commanded; and thus in the dawning of the day they marched forward against the enemy, and according

in hostem progressi, iuxta meritum suae fidei victoria
potiti sunt. In cuius loco orationis innumerae virtutes sanitatum noscuntur esse patratae, ad indicium
videlicet ac memoriam fidei regis. Nam et usque
hodie multi de ipso ligno sacrosanctae crucis astulas
excidere solent, quas cum in aquas miserint eisque
languentes homines aut pecudes potaverint sive
asperserint, mox sanitati restituuntur.

Vocatur locus ille lingua Anglorum Hefenfelth,
quod dici potest Latine Caelestis Campus, quod certo
utique praesagio futurorum antiquitus nomen accepit:
significans nimirum quod ibidem caeleste erigendum
tropaeum, caelestis inchoanda victoria, caelestia usque
hodie forent miracula celebranda. Est autem locus
iuxta murum illum, ad aquilonem, quo Romani quondam ob arcendos barbarorum impetus, totam a mari
ad mare praecinxere Brittaniam, ut supra docuimus.[1]
In quo videlicet loco consuetudinem multo iam tempore fecerant fratres Hagustaldensis ecclesiae quae
non longe abest, advenientes omni anno pridie quam
postea idem rex Osuald occisus est, vigilias pro
salute animae eius facere, plurimaque psalmorum
laude celebrata, victimam pro eo mane sacrae
oblationis offerre. Qui etiam crescente bona consuetudine, nuper ibidem ecclesia constructa, sacra-
tiorem et cunctis honorabiliorem locum omnibus
fecere. Nec immerito, quia nullum, ut comperimus,

---

[1] Cf. p. 59.

to the merit of their faith achieved the victory. In the place of which prayer manifold mighty works of healing are known to have been wrought, questionless in token and remembrance of the king's faith. For even until this present day many men do customably cut chips from the very wood of the holy cross, and when they have put them into water and given thereof to sick men or beasts to drink, or sprinkled them therewith, the sick are shortly restored to health.

That place is in the English tongue called Hefenfelth, which in the Latin can have the meaning Heaven's Field, which got its name so long before not without a sure and certain foresight of things to come, as signifying undoubtedly that in the same place a heavenly memorial was to be set up, a heavenly victory should be begun, heavenly miracles should be ever wrought even unto our days. Now the place is near to that wall which standeth towards the north, wherewith the Romans did once compass all whole Britain from sea to sea to keep off the invasions of the barbarians, as we have declared before.[1] In the which very place the brethren of Hexham church, which is not far from thence, do, of custom now long time established, come every year, the day before that upon which the same king Oswald was slain, to keep dirges there for his soul, and after many psalms of praise being said solemnly, to offer for him in the morning the sacrifice of holy oblation. And they too, as this good custom increased in fame, made the place more holy and more honoured of all men by reason of the church that was lately builded in the same place. And not without a cause, considering that (as we have learned), no sign of the

fidei Christianae signum, nulla ecclesia, nullum altare
in tota Berniciorum gente erectum est, priusquam
hoc sacrae crucis vexillum novus militiae ductor,
dictante fidei devotione, contra hostem immanissimum
pugnaturus statueret.

Nec ab re est unum e pluribus quae ad hanc crucem
patrata sunt, virtutis miraculum enarrare. Quidam
de fratribus Hagustaldensis ecclesiae nomine Bothelm,
qui nunc usque superest, ante paucos annos dum
incautius forte noctu in glacie incederet, repente
corruens brachium contrivit, ac gravissima fracturae
ipsius coepit molestia fatigari; ita ut ne ad os quidem
adducere ipsum brachium ullatenus dolore arcente
valeret. Qui cum die quadam mane audiret unum
de fratribus ad locum eiusdem sanctae crucis ascendere
disposuisse, rogavit ut aliquam sibi partem de illo
ligno venerabili rediens adferret, credere se dicens
quia per hoc, donante Domino, salutem posset consequi. Fecit ille ut rogatus est, et reversus ad vesperam, sedentibus iam ad mensam fratribus, obtulit
ei aliquid de veteri musco quo superficies ligni erat
obsita. Qui cum sedens ad mensam non haberet ad
manum ubi oblatum sibi munus reponeret, misit hoc
in sinum sibi. Et dum iret cubitum, oblitus hoc
alicubi deponere, permisit suo in sinu permanere. At
medio noctis tempore, cum evigilaret, sensit nescio
quid frigidi suo lateri adiacere, admotaque manu
requirere quid esset, ita sanum brachium manumque
reperit, ac si nihil unquam tanti languoris habuisset.

Christian faith, no church, no altar was set up in all the country of the Bernicians, before that this new captain of warfare, at the bidding of his devout faith, did set up this banner of the holy cross, as he was going to give battle to his terrible enemy.

And it is not amiss to relate fully one marvellous mighty work out of many which have been wrought at this cross. One of the brethren of Hexham church, called Bothelm, who liveth yet at this day, a few years past, when in the night he was stepping heedlessly upon ice, suddenly falling down crushed his arm, and began to be so vexed with the grievous trouble of the hurt thereof, that for vehemency of pain he was not even able to bring his arm in any way to his mouth. And this man, hearing one morning that one of the brethren had appointed to go up to the place of the same holy cross, prayed him that at his return he would bring him a piece of that venerable wood, saying that he believed that he could thereby by the gift of the Lord gain his health. The brother did as he was desired; and when he was come home again about evening, the brethren being now set at the table to eat, he gave the afflicted party some of the old moss that was grown upon the overmost part of the wood. Who sitting then at table and having at hand no better place to lay up the gift wherewith he was presented, put it into his bosom. And when he went to bed, forgetting to put this moss anywhere else he let it remain in his bosom. But at midnight he waked, and feeling a cold thing lying near to his side and moving his hand thereto to find what that should be, he found his arm and hand whole and sound, as if he had never had aught of such great feebleness.

CAP. III

*Ut idem rex postulans de gente Scottorum antistitem acce-
perit Aedanum, eidemque in insula Lindisfarnensi
sedem episcopatus donaverit.*

IDEM ergo Osuald, mox ubi regnum suscepit,
desiderans totam cui praeesse coepit gentem fidei
Christianae gratia imbui, cuius experimenta permax-
ima in expugnandis barbaris iam ceperat, misit ad
maiores natu Scottorum, inter quos exulans ipse
baptismatis sacramenta, cum his qui secum erant
militibus, consecutus erat; petens ut sibi mitteretur
antistes, cuius doctrina ac ministerio gens quam
regebat Anglorum, Dominicae fidei et dona disceret,
et susciperet sacramenta. Neque aliquanto tardius
quod petiit impetravit: accepit namque pontificem
Aedanum summae mansuetudinis et pietatis ac
moderaminis virum, habentemque zelum Dei, quamvis
non plene secundum scientiam. Namque diem
paschae Dominicum more suae gentis, cuius saepius
mentionem fecimus, a quarta decima luna usque ad
vicesimam observare solebat. Hoc etenim ordine
septentrionalis Scottorum provincia, et omnis natio
Pictorum illo adhuc tempore pascha Dominicum
celebrabat, aestimans se in hac observatione sancti ac
laude digni patris Anatolii scripta secutam. Quod
an verum sit, peritus quisque facillime cognoscit.
Porro gentes Scottorum, quae in australibus Hiberniae

---

[1] Cf. ii. 19. To Bede the Irish are Scots.

[2] North of Ireland.

[3] Bishop of Laodicea about A.D. 270. The Anatolian
Canon on which the Celts relied was really a forgery. Bright,
p. 79.

CHAPTER III

*How the same king asking for a bishop from the Scottish
nation received Aidan, and gave the same the see of
a bishopric in the isle of Lindisfarne.*

THE same Oswald therefore, as soon as he was come
to the throne, being desirous that all the people
whom he began to rule, should be filled with the grace
of the Christian faith, whereof he had now gotten very
great proofs in vanquishing the barbarians, sent to the
aldermen of the Scots, among whom he, living in
banishment and the soldiers which were with him,
had obtained the sacraments of baptism; making
request unto them that they would send him a prelate,
by whose teaching and ministry the English people
which he ruled might both learn the gifts of our
Lord's faith and receive the sacraments. And not
long after he obtained what he sought: for he received
Aidan as bishop, a man of marvellous meekness,
godliness, and sobriety, and one that had the zeal of
God, though not fully according to knowledge. For
he was wont to keep Easter Sunday from the 14th
day after the change of the moon until the 20th [1]
according to the custom of his nation, whereof we
have divers times made mention. For the north
province of the Scots [2] and all the nation of the Redshanks did at that time still solemnize Easter Sunday
by that rule, thinking that in this keeping of Easter
they had followed the advertisement written by the
holy and praiseworthy father Anatolius. [3] And
whether this be true, everyone that is skilled very
readily knoweth. Furthermore, the Scottish nations
which dwelt in the southern parts of the isle of Ireland

insulae partibus morabantur, iamdudum ad admoni-
tionem apostolicae sedis antistitis, pascha canonico
ritu observare didicerunt.

Venienti igitur ad se episcopo, rex locum sedis
episcopalis in insula Lindisfarnensi ubi ipse petebat,
tribuit. Qui videlicet locus accedente ac recedente
reumate bis quotidie instar insulae maris circumluitur
undis, bis renudato littore contiguus terrae red-
ditur; atque eius admonitionibus humiliter ac
libenter in omnibus auscultans, ecclesiam Christi
regno suo multum diligenter aedificare ac dilatare
curavit. Ubi pulcherrimo saepe spectaculo contigit,
ut evangelizante antistite qui Anglorum linguam
perfecte non noverat, ipse rex suis ducibus ac
ministris interpres verbi existeret caelestis: quia
nimirum tam longo exilii sui tempore linguam Scottorum iam plene didicerat. Exin coepere plures per
dies de Scottorum regione venire Brittaniam atque
illis Anglorum provinciis quibus regnavit rex Osuald,
magna devotione verbum fidei praedicare, et creden-
tibus gratiam baptismi, quicumque sacerdotali
erant gradu praediti, ministrare. Construebantur
ergo ecclesiae per loca, confluebant ad audiendum
verbum populi gaudentes, donabantur munere regio
possessiones, et territoria ad instituenda monasteria,
imbuebantur praeceptoribus Scottis parvuli Anglorum,

---

[1] Or Holy Island, N.W. of Farne.

had long agone learned to keep Easter by the canonical approved custom, being advised thereto by the bishop of the apostolic see.

To bishop Aidan then, upon his coming, the king appointed his episcopal see in the island of Lindisfarne,[1] where the bishop himself desired it to be. Which same place with flowing and ebbing of the tide is twice every day environed like an island with the surges, twice joined on the mainland, the shore being voided again of the sea waves; and so following humbly and readily in all things the advice of the bishop, the king set himself very diligently to build up and enlarge the Church of Christ in his realm. Wherein it often fell out that there was a gracious and pleasant sight seen, when the bishop, who was unskilful of the English tongue, was preaching the Gospel, and the king himself was interpreter of the heavenly word to his aldermen and thanes: for that by reason of his long banishment in Scotland [2] he had by now come to understand the tongue quite well. Hereupon a greater number began as the days went on to come from the country of the Scots to Britain, and with great devotion to preach the word of faith to those provinces of the English over which king Oswald reigned, and as many of them as were endowed with the degree of priesthood to minister the grace of baptism to them that believed. Therefore churches were builded throughout the districts, the people flocked joyfully to hear the word, possessions were given by the king's bountifulness and pieces of land for the foundation of religious houses, and the little children of the English along with elder folks were instructed under Scottish

[2] During the reign of Edwin.

337

una cum maioribus studiis et observatione disciplinae regularis.

Nam monachi erant maxime qui ad praedicandum venerant. Monachus ipse episcopus Aedan, utpote de insula quae vocatur Hii, destinatus : cuius monasterium in cunctis pene septentrionalium Scottorum, et omnium Pictorum monasteriis non parvo tempore arcem tenebat, regendisque eorum populis praeerat : quae videlicet insula ad ius quidem Brittaniae pertinet, non magno ab ea freto discreta, sed donatione Pictorum, qui illas Brittaniae plagas incolunt, iamdudum monachis Scottorum tradita, eo quod illis praedicantibus fidem Christi perceperint.

CAP. IV

Quando gens Pictorum fidem Christi perceperit.

Siquidem anno incarnationis Dominicae quingentesimo sexagesimo quinto, quo tempore gubernaculum Romani imperii post Iustinianum Iustinus minor accepit, venit de Hibernia presbyter et abbas habitu et vita monachi insignis, nomine Columba Brittaniam, praedicaturus verbum Dei provinciis septentrionalium Pictorum, hoc est, eis quae arduis atque horrentibus

---

[1] Iona, a misreading of the adjective *Ioua*. Also called, Hii-colum-kill (Icolmkill), *i.e.* the island of Columba of the cell.

[2] Scots of the north of Ireland; the Dalriadic Scots were settled in what is now Argyll and the Isles; the northern

teachers in the studies and observation of monastic rule.

For they were for the most part monks who had come to preach. Aidan the bishop was himself a monk, seeing that he had been sent from the island which is called Hy [1]: the monastery of which island was no small time the head house of all the monasteries almost of the northern Scots [2] and of all the Redshanks, and had the sovereignty in ruling of all their people. The which isle in very deed belongeth to the right of Britain, being severed from it with a narrowed sea, but by the free gift of the Redshanks, who inhabit those coasts of Britain, had been long ago handed over to the Scottish monks, in consideration that by the preaching of those monks they received the faith of Christ.

CHAPTER IV

When the nation of the Redshanks received the faith of Christ.

For in the 565th year of the Lord's incarnation (at which time Justin the younger, succeeding Justinian, received the governance of the Roman empire), there came to Britain from Ireland a priest and abbot notable by his dress and life of a monk, called Columba, to preach the word of God to the provinces of the northern Redshanks, that is to say, to those that by high and hideous ridges of hills [3]

Picts were north of Argyll in the west, and of the Firth of Tay in the east; the southern Picts were in Galloway; Oswald's authority extended to the Forth and Edinburgh.

[3] Maybe the hills between Fort William and Aberdeen.

montium iugis ab australibus eorum sunt regionibus
sequestratae. Namque ipsi australes Picti, qui intra
eosdem montes habent sedes, multo ante tempore ut
perhibent, relicto errore idolatriae, fidem veritatis
acceperant, praedicante eis verbum Nynia episcopo
reverentissimo et sanctissimo viro, de natione
Brettonum, qui erat Romae regulariter fidem et
mysteria veritatis edoctus; cuius sedem episcopalem
sancti Martini episcopi nomine et ecclesia insignem,
ubi ipse etiam corpore una cum pluribus sanctis
requiescit, iam nunc Anglorum gens obtinet. Qui
locus, ad provinciam Berniciorum pertinens, vulgo
vocatur Ad Candidam Casam, eo quod ibi ecclesiam
de lapide, insolito Brettonibus more fecerit.

Venit autem Brittaniam Columba, regnante Pictis
Bridio filio Meilochon, rege potentissimo, nono anno
regni eius, gentemque illam verbo et exemplo ad
fidem Christi convertit: unde et praefatam insulam
ab eis in possessionem monasterii faciendi accepit.
Neque enim magna est, sed quasi familiarum quinque,
iuxta aestimationem Anglorum; quam successores
eius usque hodie tenent, ubi et ipse sepultus est, cum
esset annorum septuaginta septem, post annos
circiter triginta et duos ex quo ipse Brittaniae praedicaturus adiit. Fecerat autem, priusquam Brittaniam veniret, monasterium nobile in Hibernia,
quod a copia roborum Dearmach lingua Scottorum,
hoc est, campus roborum, cognominatur. Ex quo
utroque monasterio plurima exinde monasteria per

---

[1] Whithern in Galloway.
[2] Cf. p. 109.
[3] Irish *Dairmagh,* now *Durrow* in King's County.

were dissevered from the southern regions inhabited by Redshanks. For these same southern Redshanks who have their dwelling-places inside of the same mountains, had as they say, long before abandoned the error of idolatry and received the true faith, at what time the word was preached unto them by the most reverend bishop and holy man Ninian, a Briton born, who had been fully taught at Rome according to rule the faith of the mysteries of the truth; whose episcopal see, made notable for the name and church of the holy bishop Martin (where Ninian himself doth rest in the body along together with many holy men), the English nation holdeth at this very time. Which place appertaining to the Bernicians' province, is commonly called At White Building,[1] for so much as there be made a church of stone, after another fashion than the Britons were wont to build.

Now Columba came to Britain when the most puissant king Bruide, Maelchon's son, reigned over the Redshanks in the 9th year of his reign, and did by word and example convert that nation to the faith of Christ: in consideration whereof too the aforesaid isle was given to him in possession to make a monastery. For the isle is not great either, but as though it were of 5 households by estimation of the English[2]; and his successors keep it until this day, and there he himself lieth buried, dying at the age of 77 years, about 32 years after that he came to Britain to preach. But before that he travelled to Britain, he had made a famous monastery in Ireland, which for the great store of oaks is in the Scottish tongue called Dearmach, that is to say, the field of oaks.[3] Of both the which monasteries very many more

discipulos eius et in Brittania et in Hibernia propagata sunt: in quibus omnibus idem monasterium insulanum, in quo ipse requiescit corpore, principatum teneret.

Habere autem solet ipsa insula rectorem semper abbatem presbyterum, cuius iuri et omnis provincia, et ipsi etiam episcopi, ordine inusitato, debeant esse subiecti, iuxta exemplum primi doctoris illius, qui non episcopus, sed presbyter extitit et monachus: de cuius vita et verbis nonnulla a discipulis eius feruntur scripta haberi. Verum qualiscumque fuerit ipse, nos hoc de illo certum tenemus, quia reliquit successores magna continentia ac divino amore regularique institutione insignes : in tempore quidem summae festivitatis dubios circulos sequentes, utpote quibus longe ultra orbem positis nemo synodalia paschalis observantiae decreta porrexerat: tantum ea quae in propheticis, evangelicis et apostolicis literis discere poterant pietatis et castitatis opera diligenter observantes. Permansit autem huiusmodi observantia paschalis apud eos tempore non pauco, hoc est, usque ad annum Dominicae incarnationis septingentesimum decimum quintum, per annos centum quinquaginta.

At tunc veniente ad eos reverentissimo et sanctissimo patre et sacerdote Ecgbercto, de natione Anglorum, qui in Hibernia diutius exulaverat pro Christo, eratque et doctissimus in Scripturis et longae vitae

---

¹ The *provincia* of the monastery. Ecclesiastical jurisdiction was in the hands of the abbots of the great monasteries, and the bishops were members of the monastic bodies and so subject to the authority of the abbots.

² Adamnan, abbot of Iona 679–704, whom Bede as a lad may

religious houses were afterwards built in addition by his scholars both in Britain and in Ireland: of all the which, the same monastery that is in the isle wherein his body lieth, is the head house.

Moreover, the same isle is always wont to have an abbot that is a priest to be the ruler, to whose law both the whole district [1] and also the bishops themselves ought, after an unaccustomed order, to be subject, according to the example of that first teacher who was no bishop, but a priest and a monk: of whose life and sayings the report is that some things remain written by his scholars.[2] But yet what manner of man so ever he was, we know this of him for a surety, that he left successors, men that excelled in continency and love of God and practice of religious life: in observing in deed the time of the high feast of Easter they followed uncertain cycles, and no marvel, considering that, being men set so far removed from the rest of the world, no man sent unto them the decrees made in synods [3] for the keeping thereof: they diligently observed only such works of devotion and chaste conversation as they could learn in the Prophets, the Gospels and in the Apostles' writings. Now this keeping of Easter remained no small time with them, that is to wit, until the 715th year of the Lord's incarnation, by the space of 150 years.

But when the most reverend and holy father and priest Egbert [4] came to them from the English nation, living in Christ's quarrel in exile long time in Ireland, and being a man very well learned in the Scriptures

have seen, wrote a life of Columba, which Bede does not seem to have known, Pl.

[3] The Councils of Arles 314 and Nicaea 325.

[4] Cf. v. 22.

perfectione eximius, correcti sunt per eum et ad
verum canonicumque paschae diem translati; quem
tamen et antea non semper in luna quarta decima
cum Iudaeis, ut quidam rebantur, sed in die quidem
Dominica, alia tamen quam decebat hebdomada
celebrabant. Sciebant enim, ut Christiani, resurrectionem Dominicam quae prima sabbati facta est prima
sabbati semper esse celebrandam: sed ut barbari
et rustici, quando eadem prima sabbati quae nunc
Dominica dies cognominatur veniret minime didicerant. Verum quia gratia caritatis fervere non
omiserunt, et huius quoque rei notitiam ad perfectum
percipere meruerunt, iuxta promissum apostoli
dicentis: "Et si quid aliter sapitis, et hoc quoque
vobis Deus revelabit." De quo plenius in sequentibus suo loco dicendum est.

CAP. V

De vita Aedani episcopi.

AB hac ergo insula, ab horum collegio monachorum, ad provinciam Anglorum instituendam in
Christo, missus est Aedan, accepto gradu episcopatus.
Quo tempore eidem monasterio Segeni abbas et
presbyter praefuit. Unde inter alia vivendi docu-
menta, saluberrimum abstinentiae vel continentiae
clericis exemplum reliquit: cuius doctrinam id

and singular for the perfect life he led for many years, they were reformed by him and brought to keep Easter on the true and lawful day; nevertheless, they did not even before that time solemnize and keep it always upon the 14th day after the change of the moon, according to the Jews' custom (as some men supposed), but on the Sunday, though yet in another week than was convenient. For they knew, as Christian men do, that the resurrection of our Lord, which was on the first day of the week, ought always to be celebrated on the first day of the week: but as ignorant and highuplandish men, they had no wise learned when the same first day of the week, which is now named Sunday, should come. Yet forasmuch as they have not ceased to be fervent in the grace of charity, they have also deserved to attain the perfect knowledge of this thing too, according as the apostle promiseth, saying: [1] "And if in anything ye be otherwise minded, God shall reveal even this also unto you." But hereof we must treat more at large hereafter in a place convenient.

CHAPTER V

Of the life of Aidan the bishop.

FROM this isle therefore, from the convent of these monks, Aidan was sent to instruct the province of the English in Christ, after he had received the order of bishop. At which time Seghine, abbot and priest, was head of the same monastery. Whereby among other lessons of living, Aidan left the clerks a most wholesome example of abstinence and continence; and this thing did chiefly commend his doctrine to all

[1] Phil. iii. 15.

maxime commendabat omnibus, quod non aliter
quam vivebat cum suis, ipse docebat. Nihil enim
huius mundi quaerere, nil amare curabat. Cuncta
quae sibi a regibus vel divitibus saeculi donabantur,
mox pauperibus qui occurrerent erogare gaudebat.
Discurrere per cuncta et urbana et rustica loca, non
equorum dorso, sed pedum incessu vectus, nisi si
maior forte necessitas compulisset, solebat: quatenus
ubicumque aliquos vel divites vel pauperes incedens
aspexisset, confestim ad hos divertens, vel ad
fidei suscipiendae sacramentum si infideles essent,
invitaret; vel si fideles, in ipsa eos fide confortaret,
atque ad eleemosynas operumque bonorum execu-
tionem, et verbis excitaret et factis.

In tantum autem vita illius a nostri temporis
segnitia distabat, ut omnes qui cum eo incedebant,
sive adtonsi, seu laici, meditari deberent; id est, aut
legendis Scripturis, aut psalmis discendis operam dare.
Hoc erat quotidianum opus illius, et omnium qui cum
eo erant, ubicumque locorum devenissent. Et si
forte evenisset, quod tamen raro evenit, ut ad regis
convivium vocaretur, intrabat cum uno clerico, aut
duobus; et ubi paululum reficiebatur, adceleravit
ocius ad legendum cum suis, sive ad orandum egredi.
Cuius exemplis informati tempore illo religiosi quique
viri ac feminae, consuetudinem fecerunt per totum
annum, excepta remissione quinquagesimae paschalis,
quarta et sexta sabbati ieiunium ad nonam usque horam
protelare. Nunquam divitibus honoris sive timoris

---

[1] This noble ensample to his sheep he yaf
That first he wroghte, and afterward he taughte.
CHAUCER, *Prologue*, 496.
[2] The ninth hour (3 p.m.) proving too severe, *noon* (*nona*)
was moved backward till it meant midday.

men, that the learning which he taught was correspondent to the life he led with his brethren.[1] For he took no thought to gain anything of this world or to be enamoured of it. His joy was forthwith to give away to the poor that might meet him all that was granted him of kings or wealthy men of the world. He was wont to travel abroad through all places both in towns and country, not riding on horseback but walking on foot, except peradventure a greater need had forced him to ride: in order that, wherever he had espied any, whether rich or poor, as he walked, incontinent turning aside to these, either he allured them to the mystery of receiving the faith, if they were out of the faith, or strengthened them in their faith, if they were in it, and exhorted them no less in deeds than in words to almsgiving and the execution of good works.

Moreover, his life was so far removed from the slackness of our time, that all they which walked with him, were they professed into religion or were they laymen, must needs study; that is, bestow their time either in reading Scripture or in learning the Psalter. This was the daily exercise of him and of all who were with him, to what place so ever they came. And if by chance it had happened (which yet happened seldom) that he were bidden to the king's banquet, he went in accompanied with one or two clerks; and after a short repast, he made speedily haste to read with his brethren or else went forth to pray. All men and women under religious rule, being at that time taught by his examples, took a custom all the year through, saving only the 50 days after Easter, to prolong their fasting the 4th and 6th days of the week until the ninth hour.[2] If rich men had

347

gratia, si qua deliquissent, reticebat; sed aspera illos invectione corrigebat. Nullam potentibus saeculi pecuniam, excepta solum esca si quos hospitio siscepisset, umquam dare solebat, sed ea potius quae sibi a divitibus donaria pecuniarum largiebantur, vel in usus pauperum, ut diximus, dispergebat, vel ad redemptionem eorum qui iniuste fuerant venditi, dispensabat. Denique multos quos pretio data redemerat, redemptos postmodum suos discipulos fecit, atque ad sacerdotalem usque gradum erudiendo atque instituendo provexit.

Ferunt autem quia cum de provincia Scottorum rex Osuald postulasset antistitem, qui sibi suaeque genti verbum fidei ministraret, missus fuerit primo alius austerioris animi vir, qui cum aliquandiu genti Anglorum praedicans nihil proficeret, nec libenter a populo audiretur, redierit patriam, atque in conventu seniorum retulerit, quia nil prodesse docendo genti ad quam missus erat, potuisset, eo quod essent homines indomabiles, et durae ac barbarae mentis. At illi, ut perhibent, tractatum magnum in concilio quid esset agendum, habere coeperunt; desiderantes quidem genti quam petebantur, saluti esse, sed de non recepto quem miserant praedicatore dolentes. Tunc ait Aedan, nam et ipse concilio intererat, ad eum de quo agebatur sacerdotem: " Videtur mihi, frater, quia durior iusto indoctis

---

[1] As slaves.

CHOICE OF AIDAN

done anything amiss, he never for hope of honour
or fear of displeasure spared to tell them of it;
but with sharp rebuking amended them. Never was
he wont to give any money to the great men of the
world (making them only good cheer, if he had received any to hospitality), but rather such gifts as in
money were liberally given him by rich men, he did
either (as we have said) give them in a dole for the
relief of the poor, or else he laid them out for the
ransoming of those that had been wrongfully sold.[1]
Finally, many of such as he had ransomed by payment
of money he made after his scholars, and by bringing
them up in learning and virtue advanced them to the
degree of priesthood.

Now the report is that when king Oswald desired
first to have a prelate out of the province of the
Scots, who might preach the word of faith to him and
his people, another man of a more austere stomach
was first sent, who (when after a while preaching to
the English people he did nothing prevail nor was
willingly heard of the people) returned to his own
country, and so in the assembly of the elders he made
relation that in teaching he had been able to do the
people no good, to whom he had been sent, forasmuch
as they were folk that might not be tamed, and of a
hard capacity and fierce nature. Then the elders (as
they say) began in council to treat at long what were
best to be done; being in deed desirous that the people
should have the salvation which they were asked to
give them, but sorry that the preacher whom they
had sent was not welcomed. Then Aidan (for he also
was himself present at the council) saith unto the
priest whose case was in question: " Methinketh,
brother, that you have been more rigorous than reason

auditoribus fuisti, et non eis iuxta apostolicam disciplinam primo lac doctrinae mollioris porrexisti,
donec paulatim enutriti verbo Dei, ad capienda per-
fectoria et ad facienda sublimiora Dei praecepta
sufficerent." Quo audito, omnium qui consedebant
ad ipsum ora et oculi conversi, diligenter quid diceret
discutiebant, et ipsum esse dignum episcopatu, ipsum
ad erudiendos incredulos et indoctos mitti debere
decernunt, qui gratia discretionis, quae virtutum mater
est, ante omnia probatur imbutus; sicque illum
ordinantes, ad praedicandum ·miserunt. Qui ubi
tempus accepit, sicut prius moderamine discretionis,
ita postmodum et ceteris virtutibus ornatus apparuit.

CAP. VI

De religione ac pietate miranda Osualdi regis.

Huius igitur antistitis doctrina rex Osuald cum ea
cui praeerat gente Anglorum institutus, non solum
incognita progenitoribus suis regna caelorum sperare
didicit; sed et regna terrarum plusquam ulli maiorum
suorum, ab eodem uno Deo qui fecit caelum et terram,
consecutus est. Denique omnes nationes et provincias
Brittaniae, quae in quatuor linguas, id est, Brettonum,
Pictorum, Scottorum et Anglorum divisae sunt, in
ditione accepit.

---

[1] 1 Cor. iii. 2.
[2] *I.e.* by bishop under direction of abbot and convent;
Bright, p. 134 ff.

would have with unlearned hearers, and that you have not, according to the apostle's instruction,[1] first given them the milk of milder doctrine, until by little and little, nourished with the word of God, they were able to receive the more perfect things and fulfil the higher commandments of God." This being heard, all that were at the assembly turned their faces, and looking at the speaker debated diligently his saying, and concluded that he was himself worthy of the bishopric, and should himself be sent to instruct the unbelieving and unlearned, who before all things was tried to be filled with the grace of discretion, the mother of all virtues; and so ordaining[2] him they sent him to preach. Who, when he had taken the opportunity given, even as before he was seen to be guided by discretion, so did he afterwards shew himself to be beautified with all other virtues.

CHAPTER VI

Of king Oswald's wonderful religion and passing piety.

KING OSWALD therefore with that part of the English nation of whom he was sovereign governor, being instructed in this prelate's doctrine, did not only learn to hope for the heavenly kingdoms unknown to his forefathers; but also won earthly kingdoms more than any of his ancestors did, by the power of the same one God who make heaven and earth. Briefly, all the nations and provinces of Britain which had four divers languages,[3] that is to say, those of the Britons, the Redshanks, the Scots and English, became subject unto him.

[3] Cf. p. 17.

THE VENERABLE BEDE

Quo regni culmine sublimatus, nihilominus, quod mirum dictu est, pauperibus et peregrinis semper humilis, benignus et largus fuit. Denique fertur quia tempore quodam cum die sancto paschae cum praefato episcopo consedisset ad prandium, positusque esset in mensa coram eo discus argenteus regalibus epulis refertus, et iamiamque essent manus ad panem benedicendum missuri, intrasse subito ministrum ipsius cui suscipiendorum inopum erat cura delegata, et indicasse regi quia multitudo pauperum undecumque adveniens maxima per plateas sederet, postulans aliquid eleemosynae a rege : qui mox dapes sibimet adpositas deferri pauperibus, sed et discum confringi, atque eisdem minutatim dividi praecepit. Quo viso pontifex qui adsidebat delectatus tali facto pietatis, adprehendit dextram eius, et ait : " Nunquam inveterascat haec manus." Quod et ita iuxta votum benedictionis eius provenit. Nam cum interfecto illo in pugna, manus cum brachio a cetero essent corpore resectae, contigit ut hactenus incorruptae perdurent. Denique in urbe regia, quae a regina quondam vocabulo Bebba cognominatur, loculo inclusae argenteo in ecclesia sancti Petri servantur, ac digno a cunctis honore venerantur.

Huius industria regis, Deirorum et Berniciorum provinciae, quae eatenus ab invicem discordabant, in unam sunt pacem, et velut unum compaginatae in populum. Erat autem nepos Aeduini regis ex sorore

---

[1] Bebbanburh, now Bamborough.

And being advanced to so royal a majesty he was ever, notwithstanding (which is marvellous to be reported), lowly, gracious and bountiful to the poor and strangers. In short it is reported that at a certain time when on the holy day of Easter the king with the foresaid bishop were set down to dinner, and a silver dish replenished with princely dainties was set on the table before him, and they were now on the point of putting forth their hands to bless the bread, suddenly there entered in his officer to whom was committed the charge to relieve the needy, and told the king that a very great number of poor people arriving from all places did sit in the public ways, desiring some alms from the king: who by and by gave commandment that the delicacies which were set before his own person should be bestowed on the poor, and moreover the dish of silver be broken and by piecemeal parted among the same. At the sight whereof the bishop set by the king, being delighted with such an act of goodness, took him by the right hand and said: "May this hand never wax old." Which thing came even so to pass according to the prayer of his blessing. For whereas, after that the king was slain in battle (his hands, with his arms being cut off from the residue of his body), it happened that his hands to this day continue uncorrupted. In fact they are preserved within a silver shrine in the church of St. Peter, and are worshipped by all men with worthy honour in the king's city,[1] which hath his name of a lady sometime queen, called Bebba.

By this king's travail the provinces of the Deirans and Bernicians, which until that time were at variance with one another, were reconciled, and as it were joined together into one people. Now Oswald was

353

Acha, dignumque fuit, ut tantus praecessor talem
haberet de sua consanguinitate et religionis heredem
et regni.

CAP. VII

*Ut provincia Occidentalium Saxonum verbum Dei,
praedicante Birino, susceperit ; et de successoribus
eius Agilbercto et Leutherio.*

Eo tempore gens Occidentalium Saxonum qui
antiquitus Gevissae vocabantur, regnante Cynegilso
fidem Christi suscepit, praedicante illis verbum Birino
episcopo, qui cum consilio papae Honorii venerat
Brittaniam, promittens quidem se illo praesente in
intimis ultra Anglorum partibus quo nullus doctor
praecessisset, sanctae fidei semina esse sparsurum.
Unde et iussu eiusdem pontificis, per Asterium
Genuensem episcopum in episcopatus consecratus est
gradum. Sed Brittaniam perveniens, ac primum
Gevissorum gentem ingrediens, cum omnes ibidem
paganissimos inveniret, utilius esse ratus est ibi
potius verbum praedicare, quam ultra progrediens,
eos quibus praedicare deberet, inquirere.

Itaque evangelizante illo in praefata provincia, cum
rex ipse catechizatus, fonte baptismi cum sua gente
ablueretur, contigit tunc temporis sanctissimum ac
victoriosissimum regem Nordanhymbrorum Osualdum

---

[1] Archbishop of Milan but resided at Genoa.

354

king Edwin's nephew by his sister Acha's side, and it was meet that so noble a predecessor should have so worthy an heir, as well of his religion as of his realm, and that of his own kindred.

CHAPTER VII

How the province of the West Saxons received the word of God by Birinus' preaching; and of Agilbert and Lothere his successors.

AT that time the people of the West Saxons (who of old time were called Gewissas) received the faith of Christ in the reign of Cynegils, Birinus the bishop preaching to them the word, who had come to Britain with the consent of pope Honorius, promising in his presence that he would sow the seeds of the holy faith in the heart of the coasts of the English beyond, whither no teacher had gone before him. In consideration whereof too at the commandment of the same pope, he was consecrated to the order of bishop by the hands of Asterius bishop of Genoa.[1] But at his arrival into Britain and first entering among the folk of the Gewissas, whereas he found all the inhabitants in the same country utterly paynim, he thought it more expedient to preach the word there,[2] rather than in travelling further to search for such as he should preach unto.

And thus at his preaching of the Gospel in the foresaid province, when the king himself, after being taught, was cleansed in the font of baptism with his people, it happened at that time that Oswald, the most holy and very victorious king of Northumberland

[2] Instead of further north inland as he first planned.

adfuisse, eumque de lavacro exeuntem suscepisse, ac pulcherrimo prorsus et Deo digno consortio, cuius erat filiam accepturus in coniugem, ipsum prius secunda generatione Deo dicatum sibi accepit in filium. Donaverunt autem ambo reges eidem episcopo civitatem quae vocatur Dorcic, ad faciendum inibi sedem episcopalem; ubi factis dedicatisque ecclesiis, multisque ad Dominum pio eius labore populis advocatis, migravit ad Dominum, sepultusque est in eadem civitate, et post annos multos, Haedde episcopatum agente, translatus inde in Ventam civitatem, atque in ecclesia beatorum apostolorum Petri et Pauli positus est.

Defuncto autem et rege, successit in regnum filius eius Coinualch, qui et fidem ac sacramenta regni caelestis suscipere renuit, et non multo post etiam regni terrestris potentiam perdidit. Repudiata enim sorore Pendan regis Merciorum quam duxerat, aliam accepit uxorem : ideoque bello petitus, ac regno privatus ab illo, secessit ad regem Orientalium Anglorum, cui nomen erat Anna : apud quem triennio exulans fidem cognovit ac suscepit veritatis. Nam et ipse apud quem exulabat rex erat vir bonus, et bona ac sancta sobole felix, ut in sequentibus docebimus.

Cum vero restitutus esset in regnum Coinualch, venit in provinciam de Hibernia pontifex quidam, nomine Agilberctus, natione quidem Gallus, sed tunc legendarum gratia Scripturarum in Hibernia non parvo

---

[1] Dorchester in Oxfordshire.

[2] *Venta Belgarum*, Winchester.

[3] iii. 8.

[4] Probably a *vacant* bishop, σχολάζων, *i.e.* without a diocese. Bright, 159 n.

was present and lifted Cynegils up as he came forth from the laver, in an alliance most lovely altogether and worthy of God, in that Oswald took for his godson the very man whose daughter he was to take to wife, after this man had been first dedicated to God by a second birth. Moreover, both kings gave the same bishop the city which is called Dorcic [1] to make there his episcopal see; where, after that he had builded and dedicated churches and by his godly pains brought much people to the Lord, he passed to the Lord and was buried in the same city, and many years after, when Heddi was bishop, he was conveyed from thence over to the city of Wenta,[2] and laid in the church of the blessed apostles Peter and Paul.

But when the king too died, his son Cenwalh succeeded him in the kingdom, who refused to receive the faith and sacraments of the kingdom of heaven, and shortly after lost the power of his earthly kingdom also. For putting away the sister of Penda, king of the Marchmen, whom he had married, he took another wife: and for that cause he was by Penda assaulted with battle and deposed from his kingdom, and departed to the king of the East English, who was called Anna: with whom living in banishment by the space of three years he learned and received the true faith. For the king with whom he lived in banishment was both himself a virtuous man and was blessed with virtuous and holy issue, as we shall declare hereafter.[3]

Now when Cenwalh had been restored to his kingdom, there came out of Ireland into his province a certain prelate,[4] named Agilbert, a Frenchman born, yet having made long abode in Ireland for the sake of reading the Scriptures; and this bishop joined

357

tempore demoratus, coniunxitque se regi, sponte
ministerium praedicandi adsumens: cuius eruditionem
atque industriam videns rex, rogavit eum, accepta
ibi sede episcopali, suae gentis [1] manere pontificem;
qui precibus eius adnuens, multis annis eidem genti
sacerdotali iure praefuit. Tandem rex, qui Saxonum
tantum linguam noverat, pertaesus barbarae loquelae,
subintroduxit in provinciam alium suae linguae episcopum vocabulo Vini, et ipsum in Gallia ordinatum;
dividensque in duas parochias provinciam, huic in
civitate Venta, quae a gente Saxonum Vintancaestir
appellatur, sedem episcopalem tribuit: unde offensus
graviter Agilberctus, quod hoc ipso inconsulto ageret
rex, rediit Galliam, et accepto episcopatu Parisiacae
civitatis, ibidem senex ac plenus dierum obiit. Non
multis autem annis post abscessum eius a Brittania
transactis, pulsus est Vini ab eodem rege de episcopatu: qui secedens ad regem Merciorum, vocabulo
Vulfheri, emit pretio ab eodem sedem Lundoniae
civitatis, eiusque episcopus usque ad vitae suae terminum mansit. Sicque provincia Occidentalium
Saxonum tempore non pauco absque praesule fuit.

Quo etiam tempore rex praefatus ipsius gentis,
gravissimis regni sui damnis saepissime ab hostibus
adflictus, tandem ad memoriam reduxit, quod eum
pridem perfidia regno pepulerit, fides agnita Christi
in regnum revocaverit: intellexitque quod etiam
tunc destituta pontifice provincia, recte pariter

[1] for *genti*, Pl.

---

[1] He was present at the Synod of Whitby, 664, ch. 25.
Bede gives no dates in this chapter.

[2] The sale of the dignities of the Church had long been
prevalent in the Gallic Church and became so amongst the
Anglo-Saxons. Bright, p. 224.

himself to the king, taking upon him of his own
accord the ministry of preaching : and the king, seeing
his learning and industry, entreated him to receive
the see of a bishopric there and remain as bishop
of his people ; which he consenting to his prayers
accepted, and ruled the same people many years with
the authority of bishop. At the length the king, who
could only speak the Saxon tongue, being weary with
Agilbert's foreign way of speech, did privily bring
into the province another bishop of his own language
named Wini, the which also was ordained in France ;
and dividing the province into two dioceses gave to
this bishop his see in the city of Wenta which is
called by the Saxon folk Wintancaestir : wherefore
Agilbert, being highly displeased because the king
did this without his counsel, returned to France,[1]
and after he had received the bishopric of the city of
Paris, died in the same place an old man and full of
days. Moreover, when not many years had past
after his departure from Britain, Wini was by the same
king driven from his bishopric : who departing to
the king of the Marchmen, called Wulfhere, bought
of the same with money the see of the city of London,[2]
and continued bishop thereof up to the end of his life.
And so the province of the West Saxons lacked no
small time a bishop.

At which time also the foresaid king of the selfsame nation, being very often distressed with grievous
losses which in his kingdom he sustained by his
enemies, called at last to his mind that the falling
away from the faith long ago drove him from his
kingdom, while the acknowledgment of Christ's
faith brought him back again : and he understood,
that also at that time the province, being forsaken of

divino fuerit destituta praesidio. Misit ergo legatarios
in Galliam ad Agilberctum, summissa illum satisfac-
tione deprecans ad episcopatum suae gentis redire.
At ille se excusans, et eo venire non posse contestans
quia episcopatu propriae civitatis ac parochiae teneretur adstrictus; ne tamen obnixe petenti nil ferret
auxilii, misit pro se illo presbyterum Leutherium,
nepotem suum, qui ei, si vellet, ordinaretur episcopus;
dicens quod ipse eum dignum esse episcopatu iudi-
caret. Quo honorifice a populo et a rege suscepto,
rogaverunt Theodorum, tunc archiepiscopum Doruvernensis ecclesiae, ipsum sibi antistitem consecrari:
qui consecratus in ipsa civitate, multis annis episcopatum Gevissorum, ex synodica sanctione, solus
sedulo moderamine gessit.

CAP. VIII

*Ut Rex Cantuariorum Earconberet idola destrui praece-
    perit; et de filia eius Ercongota, et propinqua
    Aedilbergae, sacratis Deo virginibus.*

Anno Dominicae incarnationis sexcentesimo quadragesimo, Eadbald rex Cantuariorum transiens ex
hac vita, Earconbercto filio regni gubernacula
reliquit: quae ille suscepta viginti quatuor annis et

---

[1] Consecrated 668.

a prelate, was rightfully withal forsaken of divine help. Therefore he sent ambassadors into France to Agilbert, offering to make satisfaction, and beseeching him to return and resume the bishopric of his people. But Agilbert excusing himself testified that he could not repair thither because he was fast bound to abide at his bishopric which he had in his own city and diocese; nevertheless, to the end he might somewhat help him who did most earnestly desire him, he sent thither in his stead Lothere, a priest, his own nephew, who should be ordained bishop for him, if it were the king's pleasure; affirming that he deemed him to be well worthy of the bishopric. Which Lothere was honourably received of the people and the king, and they entreated Theodore,[1] then archbishop of the church of Canterbury, that Lothere should be consecrated their bishop: who, being consecrated in that same city, by the space of many years exercised his office as sole bishop of the Gewissas with diligent direction in accordance with the decree of the synod.[2]

CHAPTER VIII

How Earconbert, King of the Kentish men, gave commandment for idols to be destroyed; and of his daughter Earcongota and kinswoman Ethelberga, virgins dedicated to God.

In the 640th year of the Lord's incarnation Eadbald, King of the men of Kent, passing out of this life left the direction of the kingdom to his son Earconbert: which, when he had undertaken, he did prosperously hold by the space of 24 years and

[2] *Synod* is here used of the West Saxon *gemot.*

aliquot mensibus nobilissime tenuit. Hic primus regum Anglorum in toto regno suo idola relinqui ac destrui, simul et ieiunium quadraginta dierum observari principali auctoritate praecepit. Quae ne facile a quopiam posset contemni, in transgressores dignas et competentes punitiones proposuit. Cuius filia Earcongotae, ut condigna parenti soboles, magnarum fuit virgo virtutum, serviens Domino in monasterio quod in regione Francorum constructum est ab abbatissa nobilissima, vocabulo Fara, in loco qui dicitur In Brige. Nam eo tempore necdum multis in regione Anglorum monasteriis constructis, multi de Brittania monachicae conversationis gratia, Francorum vel Galliarum monasteria adire solebant; sed et filias suas eisdem erudiendas, ac sponso caelesti copulandas mittebant; maxime in Brige et in Cale, et in Andilegum monasterio: inter quas erat Saethryd, filia uxoris Annae regis Orientalium Anglorum, cuius supra meminimus, et filia naturalis eiusdem regis Aedilberg: quae utraque cum esset peregrina, prae merito virtutum, eiusdem monasterii Brigensis est abbatissa constituta. Cuius regis filia maior Sexburg, uxor Earconbercti regis Cantuariorum, habuit filiam Earcongotam, de qua sumus dicturi.

Huius autem virginis Deo dicatae, multa quidem ab incolis loci illius solent opera virtutum et signa miraculorum usque hodie narrari. Verum nos de transitu tantum illius quo caelestia regna petiit,

---

[1] Before Easter, before Christmas and after Pentecost.

[2] Faremoûtier-en-Brie, also called Eboriacum.

[3] Kings and powerful men, in the A.S. version.

[4] Chelles near Paris.

[5] Andeley-sur-Seine.

[6] *I.e.* not adopted, nor illegitimate.

certain months. This was the first King of England who of his princely authority commanded that the idols in all his whole realm should be forsaken and destroyed, and at the same time that the fast of 40 days[1] should be kept. And, that this his authority might not lightly be despised by any man, he appointed meet and convenient punishments for the transgressors thereof. Earcongota, this prince's daughter, as a worthy child of such a father, was a virgin that did mighty works, serving the Lord in the monastery that was builded in the country of the Franks by an honourable abbess called Fara in the place named In Brige.[2] For in those days, when many monasteries were not yet builded in the country of the English, many were wont for the sake of religious life to go to the religious houses of the Franks or Gaul; moreover, they[3] sent their daughters to the same to be brought up and married to the heavenly bridegroom; chiefly in the monastery of Brige and of Cale[4] and of Andilegum,[5] among whom Sacthryd, daughter to the wife of Anna, King of the East English (of which king we have made mention before), and Ethelberga the said king's natural[6] daughter: who, though strangers, were both made abbesses of the same monastery of Brige by reason of their worthy virtues. And this king's elder daughter Sexberg, wife of Earconbert, King of Kent, had a daughter Earcongota, and of her we will now treat.

Now the inhabitants of that place are wont even at this day to tell of many mighty works and miraculous signs wrought by this virgin dedicated to God. But let us be contented to speak somewhat shortly only of her departure and passage to the

aliquid breviter dicere sufficiat. Imminente ergo die
suae vocationis, coepit circuire in monasterio casulas
infirmarum Christi famularum, earumque vel maxime,
quae vel aetate provectae, vel probitate erant
morum insigniores: quarum se omnium precibus
humiliter commendans, obitum proxime suum, quem
revelatione didicerat, non celavit esse futurum:
quam videlicet revelationem huiusmodi esse perhibebat: vidisse se albatorum catervam hominum idem
monsterium intrare; hosque a se interrogatos quid
quaererent, aut quid ibi vellent, respondisse quod
ob hoc illo fuerint destinati, ut aureum illud numisma
quod eo de Cantia venerat, secum adsumerent.
Ipsa autem nocte, in cuius ultima parte, id est,
incipiente aurora, praesentis mundi tenebras transiens, supernam migravit ad lucem, multi de fratribus
eiusdem monasterii, qui aliis erant in aedibus, iam
manifeste se concentus angelorum psallentium
audisse referebant, sed et sonitum quasi plurimae
multitudinis monasterium ingredientis: unde mox
egressi dignoscere quid esset, viderunt lucem caelitus
emissam fuisse permaximam, quae sanctam illam
animam carnis vinculis absolutam, ad aeterna patriae
caelestis gaudia ducebat. Addunt et alia, quae
ipsa nocte in monasterio eodem divinitus fuerint
ostensa miracula: sed haec nos ad alia tendentes
suis narrare permittimus. Sepultum est autem
corpus venerabile virginis et sponsae Christi, in

----

[1] This does not prove that gold coins were current in Kent.
[2] A double monastery both of nuns and monks.

heavenly kingdoms. The day then of her calling
being at hand, she began to visit in the monastery
the cells of the sick handmaids of Christ, and especially
of such her sisters as either for advanced age or for
virtuous conversation were more notable than other:
unto the prayers of all whom lowly commending
herself, she hid not from them that, as she had
learned by revelation, her death would very shortly
come to pass: and this revelation, certes, she related
to be of this manner: she said she had seen a company
of men apparelled in white enter into the same
monastery; and that these when asked by her what
they sought for or what they would there, answered
that they were sent thither to the end that they
might take with them that golden coin [1] which had
come from Kent to that place. And on the selfsame
night (in the last part whereof, that is to say, when
dawn was beginning, she passing over the darkness of
the present world departed to the light that is above)
many of the brethren of the same monastery [2] which
were in other houses, reported that they heard clearly
the melody of angels harping together, and, moreover, the noise as it were of a very great multitude
coming into the monastery: whereupon they, by and
by going forth to know what manner of thing it were,
saw that there was an exceeding great light sent
forth from heaven, which led that holy soul, delivered
out of the prison of the flesh, to the everlasting joys
of the heavenly country. Besides this they report
of other miracles which were shewn by the hand of
God that very night in the same monastery: but
we, passing to other things, do leave these to the
religious persons of the monastery to relate. Further,
the honourable body of Christ's virgin and spouse

365

ecclesia beati protomartyris Stephani: placuitque
post diem tertium, ut lapis quo monumentum tege-
batur, amoveretur, et altius ipso in loco reponeretur:
quod dum fieret, tantae fragrantia suavitatis ab
imis ebullivit, ut cunctis qui adstabant fratribus ac
sororibus, quasi opobalsami cellaria esse viderentur
aperta.

Sed et matertera eius, de qua diximus, Aedilberg,
et ipsa Deo dilectam perpetuae virginitatis gloriam
in magna corporis continentia servavit: quae cuius
esset virtutis, magis post mortem claruit. Cum
enim esset abbatissa, coepit facere in monasterio suo
ecclesiam in honorem omnium apostolorum, in qua
suum corpus sepeliri cupiebat. Sed cum opus idem
ad medium ferme esset perductum, illa ne hoc
perficeret, morte praerepta est, et in ipso ecclesiae
loco ubi desiderabat, condita. Post cuius mortem
fratribus alia magis curantibus, intermissum est hoc
aedificium annis septem, quibus completis, statuerunt
ob nimietatem laboris, huius structuram ecclesiae
funditus relinquere; ossa vero abbatissae illo de loco
elevata in aliam ecclesiam, quae esset perfecta ac
dedicata transferre. Et aperientes sepulcrum eius,
ita intemeratum corpus invenere, ut a corruptione
concupiscentiae carnalis erat inmune: et ita denuo
lotum, atque aliis vestibus indutum, transtulerunt
illud in ecclesiam beati Stephani martyris; cuius

was buried in the church of the blessed first martyr Stephen: and it was thought good three days after the burial that the stone wherewith the grave was covered should be laid aside and reared up higher in the very same place: at the doing whereof such a sweet-smelling savour did break forth from the bottom of the earth, that to all the brethren and sisters that stood by there seemed as though there were store chambers of balm natural opened.

Yea, furthermore, Ethelberga, aunt by the mother's side to this Earcongota of whom we have treated, even she also in great chastity of body preserved the glory beloved of God, that resteth in perpetual virginity: and how virtuous a virgin she was, it was better known after her death. For when she was abbess, she began in her monastery to build a church in honour of all the apostles, wherein she willed her body to be buried. But, the work being well near half done, she was snatched away by death, that she might not complete it, and was buried in that very place of the church where she desired. After whose death, the brethren more intending upon other things, the building of this church ceased by the space of 7 years, which being expired, they determined utterly to leave off the building of it, for the excessive labour thereof; yet appointed to convey into another church, which had been completed and dedicated, the bones of the abbess that were taken up out of that place. And opening her grave they found her body so undecayed as it was free from the corruption of carnal concupiscence: and so when they had washed it once again and clad it in other attire, they carried it over into the church of the blessed martyr Stephen; the

367

videlicet natalis ibi solet in magna gloria celebrari die Nonarum Iuliarum.

CAP. IX

*Ut in loco in quo occisus est rex Osuald, crebra sani-
tatum miracula facta ; utque ibi primo iumentum
cuiusdam viantis, ac deinde puella paralytica sit
curata.*

REGNAVIT autem Osuald Christianissimus rex
Nordanhymbrorum novem annis, adnumerato etiam
illo anno, quem et feralis impietas regis Brettonum,
et apostasia demens regum Anglorum detestabilem
fecerat. Siquidem, ut supra docuimus, unanimo
omnium consensu firmatum est, ut nomen et
memoria apostatarum de catalogo regum Christianorum prorsus aboleri deberet, neque aliquis regno
eorum annus adnotari. Quo completo annorum
curriculo occisus est commisso gravi praelio, ab
eadem pagana gente paganoque rege Merciorum, a
quo et praedecessor eius Aeduini peremptus fuerat,
in loco qui lingua Anglorum nuncupatur Maserfelth,
anno aetatis suae trigesimo octavo, die quinto mensis
Augusti.

Cuius quanta fides in Deum, quae devotio mentis
fuerit, etiam post mortem, virtutum miraculis claruit.
Namque in loco ubi pro patria dimicans a paganis
interfectus est, usque hodie sanitates infirmorum et
hominum et pecorum celebrari non desinunt. Unde

---

[1] P. 327.   [2] P. 315.
[3] Identified with Oswestry (Oswaldestre), but Oswestry is
an unlikely place for a battle between Northumbrians and
Mercians.

day of which martyr's birth is there customably kept
solemn in great glory the seventh day of July.

CHAPTER IX

*How that many miracles in doing of cures were wrought
in the place where King Oswald was slain ; and
how that first the horse of a certain traveller was
healed, and afterwards a young girl was healed of
the palsy.*

Now Oswald, the most Christian king of Northumberland, reigned 9 years, that year being also
reckoned in, which both the deadly cruelty of the
king of the Britons and the mad apostasy of the
English kings had made abominable. For (as we
have declared before [1]), it was agreed upon with one
accord by all, that the name and memory of them
that fell away should be utterly razed out of the roll
of Christian kings, neither any year be registered in
their reign. And when the course of his years was
fulfilled, Oswald was slain in the field, in a cruel
battle, by the same paynim people and paynim
king of the Marchmen by whom also his predecessor
Edwin had been killed,[2] in a place which in the
tongue of the English is called Maserfelth,[3] in the
38th year of his age, on the fifth day of the month
August.

And how great the faith of this king was in God,
what devotion of mind he had, appeared also after
his death, by the miracles due to his virtues. For
to this day cures of the sick, both men and beasts,
cease not to be continually wrought in the place
where he was slain of the heathen, fighting for his

369

contigit ut pulverem ipsum ubi corpus eius in terram
corruit, multi auferentes, et in aquam mittentes,
suis per haec infirmis multum commodi adferrent.
Qui videlicet mos adeo increbuit, ut paulatim ablata
exinde terra fossam ad mensuram staturae virilis
reddiderit. Nec mirandum in loco mortis illius
infirmos sanari, qui semper dum viveret infirmis
et pauperibus consulere, eleemosynas dare, opem
ferre non cessabat. Et multa quidem in loco illo
vel de pulvere loci illius facta virtutum miracula
narrantur: sed nos duo tantum quae a maioribus
audivimus, referre satis duximus.

Non multo post interfectionem eius exacto tempore,
contigit ut quidam equo sedens iter iuxta locum
ageret illum; cuius equus subito lassescere, consistere, caput in terram declinare, spumas ex ore de-
mittere, et augescente dolore nimio, in terram coepit
ruere. Desiluit eques, et stramine subtracto [1]
coepit exspectare horam, qua aut melioratum
reciperet iumentum, aut relinqueret mortuum. At
ipsum diu gravi dolore vexatum, cum diversas in
partes se torqueret, repente volutando devenit in
illud loci ubi rex memorabilis occubuit. Nec mora,
quiescente dolore cessabat ab insanis membrorum
motibus, et consueto equorum more, quasi post
lassitudinem in diversum latus vicissim sese volvere,
statimque exsurgens quasi sanum per omnia, virecta
herbarum avidius carpere coepit.

[1] for *substrato*, Pl.

---

[1] Chap. X contains a third miracle and may be a later
addition, Pl.

country. Whereof it came to pass that many carried away the very dust where his body fell upon the earth, and casting it into water brought much comfort to their sick thereby. Which custom indeed was so often practised that by little and little, as the earth was taken away from there, a hole was made to the measure of a man's height. And no marvel that sick people are healed in the place where he died, who always during his lifetime ceased not to consider the sick and needy, to bestow alms and to give help. And, verily, many miracles due to his virtues are related to have been done in that place or from the dust of that place; but we have thought it sufficient to rehearse only two [1] which we have heard of our elders.

Not long time having passed after this prince's death, it fortuned a man on horseback to journey near that place, whose horse began suddenly to become tired, to stand still, to hang down his head to the earth, to foam at the mouth, and with increase of excessive pain to fall to the earth. The rider lighted down, and taking off the saddle began to tarry for the hour when either he should get back the horse in better case or leave it dead. But the beast being of long time troubled with grievous pain, as it tumbled itself this way and that, wallowed in the end of a sudden to that place where the king of worthy memory fell. And incontinent the pain ceasing, the horse left the inordinate motions of his limbs, and after the customable manner of horses rolling itself, as if it had been weary, upon either side in turn and forthwith rising as if whole in all ways, it began more greedily than wont to crop the green grass of the field.

371

Quo ille viso, ut vir sagacis ingenii, intellexit aliquid
mirae sanctitatis huic loco quo equus est curatus,
inesse; et posito ibi signo, non multo post ascendit
equum, atque ad hospitium quo proposuerat, accessit:
quo dum adveniret, invenit puellam ibi, neptem
patris familias, longo paralysis morbo gravatam: et
cum familiares domus illius de acerba puellae infirmitate ipso praesente quererentur, coepit dicere
ille de loco ubi caballus suus esset curatus. Quid
multa? imponentes eam carro, duxerunt ad locum,
ibidemque deposuerunt. At illa posita in loco,
obdormivit parumper; et ubi evigilavit, sanatam se
ab illa corporis dissolutione sentiens, postulata aqua,
ipsa lavit faciem, crines composuit, caput linteo
cooperuit, et cum his qui se adduxerant, sana pedibus
incedendo reversa est.

CAP. X

Ut pulvis loci illius contra ignem valuerit.

Eodem tempore venit alius quidam de natione
Brettonum, ut ferunt, iter faciens iuxta ipsum locum
in quo praefata erat pugna completa; et vidit unius
loci spatium cetero campo viridius ac venustius:
coepitque sagaci animo conicere quod nulla esset alia
causa insolitae illo in loco viriditatis, nisi quia ibidem
sanctior cetero exercitu vir aliquis fuisset interfectus.

---

[1] The hood worn by Saxon women.

At the sight whereof the rider, as a man of quick wit, understood that some singular holiness was in that place where the horse was healed; and putting a mark there, he shortly after mounted his horse and rode to the inn whither he had purposed to travel: upon reaching which he found a damsel there, grand-daughter to the good man of the house, of a long time diseased with a grievous palsy: and whereas the household of the inn did complain in his presence of the damsel's sore sickness, he began to tell them of the place where his horse had been healed. What need many words? They set her on a cart, and brought her to the place and laid her down upon the spot. But she, when set in the place, slept for a small time; and when she waked, feeling herself cured of that her helplessness of body, she called for water and herself washed her face, dressed up her hair, covered her head with a linen cloth [1] and walking soundly on her feet returned with them who had brought her thither.

CHAPTER X

How the dust of that place prevailed against fire.

About the same time there came a certain other traveller of the British nation, journeying, as the bruit is, near the very place wherein the foresaid battle was brought to its end; and he espied one plot more green and pleasant than was the residue of the field: and began of quickness of wit to guess, that there should be no other cause of the unwonted greenness of that place, save that on that same spot some one man holier than the rest of the army had

Tulit itaque de pulvere terrae illius secum inligans in
linteo, cogitans quod futurum erat, quia ad medelam
infirmantium idem pulvis proficeret; et pergens
itinere suo pervenit ad vicum quendam vespere,
intravitque in domum in qua vicani coenantes epula-
bantur: et susceptus a dominis domus, resedit et
ipse cum eis ad convivium, adpendens linteolum cum
pulvere quem adtulerat, in una posta parietis.
Cumque diutius epulis atque ebrietati vacarent,
accenso grandi igne in medio, contigit volantibus in
altum scintillis, culmen domus, quod erat virgis
contextum ac foeno tectum, subitaneis flammis
impleri. Quod cum repente convivae terrore confusi
conspicerent, fugerunt foras, nil ardenti domui
iamiamque periturae prodesse valentes. Consumpta
ergo domo flammis, posta solummodo in qua pulvis
ille inclusus pendebat, tuta ab ignibus et intacta
remansit. Qua visa virtute, mirati sunt valde; et
perquirentes subtilius, invenerunt quia de illo loco
adsumptus erat pulvis ubi regis Osualdi sanguis
fuerat effusus. Quibus patefactis ac diffamatis
longe lateque miraculis, multi per dies locum fre-
quentare illum, et sanitatum ibi gratiam capere sibi
suisque coeperunt.

374

been slain. . Accordingly he stole away with him some of the dust of that earth, knitting it up in a linen cloth, deeming with himself, as indeed was to come to pass, that the same dust might be profitable for the remedy of sick persons ; and continuing with his journey he came in the evening to a certain village, and entered into a house in which the villagers were at feast supping ; and being received by the masters of the house, sat down himself also at their entertainment, hanging upon one of the posts of the wall the linen cloth with the dust which he had brought. And as they set themselves further to feasting and drinking, a great fire being lighted in the midst, it happened that, the sparks flying up aloft, the roof of the house, which was built of twigs and thatched, was suddenly caught on fire and filled with flames. And when the guests espied this with sudden distress of panic, they fled out of doors, having no power to save the house now on fire and on the point of being consumed. The house, therefore, being destroyed with the flames, only the post (whereon the dust hanged, enclosed in the cloth) continued safe from the fire and therewith not hurt at all. At the sight of which mighty work they marvelled much, and with diligent inquiry and examination found out that the dust had been taken from that place where king Oswald's blood had been shed. And after that these miracles had been manifestly known and bruited abroad, much people began, as the days passed, to resort to that place and obtain there the grace of cures for themselves and their kin.

THE VENERABLE BEDE

CAP. XI

*Ut super reliquias eius lux coelestis tota nocte steterit;
et ut per eas sint daemoniaci curati.*

INTER quae nequaquam silentio praetereundum
reor, quid virtutis ac miraculi caelestis fuerit ostensum,
cum ossa eius inventa, atque ad ecclesiam in
qua nunc servantur, translata sunt. Factum est
autem hoc per industriam reginae Merciorum
Osthrydae, quae erat filia fratris eius, id est Osuiu
qui post illum regni apicem tenebat ut in sequentibus
dicemus.

Est monasterium nobile in provincia Lindissi,
nomine Beardaneu, quod eadem regina cum viro suo
Aedilredo multum diligebat, venerabatur, excolebat,
in quo desiderabat honoranda patrui sui ossa recondere:
cumque venisset carrum in quo eadem ossa
ducebantur, incumbente vespera, in monasterium
praefatum, noluerunt ea qui erant in monasterio
libenter excipere: quia etsi sanctum eum noverant,
tamen quia de alia provincia ortus fuerat, et super
eos regnum acceperat, veteranis eum odiis etiam
mortuum insequebantur. Unde factum est ut ipsa
nocte reliquiae adlatae foris permanerent, tentorio
tantum maiore supra carrum in quo inerant, extenso.
Sed miraculi caelestis ostensio, quam reverenter eae

---

[1] She was murdered in 697 and her husband, Ethelred,
became a monk and later abbot of Bardney.
[2] Bardney in Lincolnshire.

CHAPTER XI

*How that a light from heaven stood all night over king
Oswald's relics ; and how that they which were
possessed with evil spirits were healed by those relics.*

AND amongst these things it must, I think, in no
wise be passed over in silence how mighty a work
and heavenly miracle was shewed when king Oswald's
bones were found and conveyed to the church wherein
they are now kept. Now this was done by the
diligence of Osthryth,[1] the queen of the Marchmen,
who was daughter of Oswald's brother, that is to say,
of Oswy who after Oswald held the headship of the
kingdom, as we shall declare in the process that
followeth.

There is a famous monastery in the province of
Lindsey named Beardaneu,[2] which the same queen
and her husband Ethelred did greatly love, honour
and reverence, wherein she desired to lay up her
uncle's honoured bones : and when the chariot was
come, wherein the same bones were brought at the
fall of the evening unto the foresaid monastery, the
men that were in the monastery would not gladly
admit them : because, although they knew him to be
a holy man, notwithstanding, forasmuch as he was
sprung from another province and took upon him to
be king over them, they pursued him also after his
death with the hatred they had of old. Whereby it
came to pass that that same night the relics that
were brought thither did remain still without, only
a pavilion larger than ordinary being stretched out
over the chariot wherein the relics were. But the
showing of a heavenly miracle did manifestly declare

suscipiendae a cunctis fidelibus essent, patefecit.
Nam tota ea nocte columna lucis a carro illo ad
caelum usque porrecta, omnibus pene eiusdem
Lindissae provinciae locis conspicua stabat. Unde
mane facto fratres monasterii illius, qui pridie ab-
nuerant, diligenter ipsi petere coeperunt, ut apud se
eaedem sanctae ac Deo dilectae reliquiae conderen-
tur. Lota igitur ossa intulerunt in thecam, quam in
hoc praeparaverant, atque in ecclesia iuxta honorem
congruum posuerunt: et ut regia viri sancti persona
memoriam haberet aeternam, vexillum eius super
tumbam auro et purpura compositum adposuerunt,
ipsamque aquam in qua laverunt ossa, in angulo
sacrarii fuderunt. Ex quo tempore factum est, ut
ipsa terra quae lavacrum venerabile suscepit, ad
abigendos ex obsessis corporibus daemones, gratiae
salutaris haberet effectum.

Denique tempore sequente, cum praefata regina
in eodem monasterio moraretur, venit ad salutandam
eam abbatissa quaedam venerabilis, quae usque
hodie superest, vocabulo Aedilhild, soror virorum
sanctorum Aediluini et Alduini, quorum prior episcopus in Lindissi provincia, secundus erat abbas in
monasterio quod vocatur Peartaneu, a quo non longe
et illa monasterium habebat. Cum ergo veniens illo
loqueretur cum regina, atque inter alia, sermone de
Osualdo exorto, diceret quod et ipsa lucem nocte illa
supra reliquias eius ad caelum usque altam vidisset,

---

[1] Partney in Lincolnshire.

with how great reverence those relics ought to be
received of all faithful people. For all that night long
a pillar of light reaching from that chariot unto
heaven stood so that it was plainly seen in all places
almost of the same province of Lindsey. Wherefore,
when the morning was come, the brethren of that
monastery, who on the day before had denied, began
of themselves earnestly to desire that the same relics,
holy and beloved of God, might be laid up in their
house. Therefore the bones were washed and after
enclosed in a shrine which they had provided for this
purpose, and placed in the church with honour
convenient: and to the end that the holy man's
princely personage might always be remembered,
they placed besides over his tomb his standard
fashioned of purple and gold, and the very water
wherein they washed his bones they poured out in a
corner of the cemetery. From which time forward
it came to pass, that the earth itself that received
the venerable washing had effect of healthgiving
grace for driving away of devils from the bodies that
were possessed.

Finally, in process of time, when the foresaid queen
abode in the same monastery, there came to greet
her a certain honourable abbess which liveth until
this day, by name Ethelhild, sister of the holy men
Ethelwin and Aldwin, the first of which was bishop
in the province of Lindsey, the second was abbot in
the monastery which is called Peartaneu,[1] not far
from which she also had her monastery. When then
the abbess coming communed with the queen, and
among other matters, after they began to fall in talk
of Oswald, said that she herself too had seen on that
night the light above his relics, which in height

adiecit regina quia de pulvere pavimenti in quo aqua lavacri illius effusa est, multi iam sanati essent infirmi. At illa petiit sibi portionem pulveris salutiferi dari; et accipiens, inligatam panno condidit in capsella, et rediit. Transacto autem tempore aliquanto, cum esset in suo monasterio, venit illic quidam hospes, qui solebat nocturnis saepius horis repente ab inmundo spiritu gravissime vexari: qui cum benigne susceptus post coenam in lecto membra posuisset, subito a diabolo arreptus, clamare, dentibus frendere, spumare, et diversis motibus coepit membra torquere. Cumque a nullo vel teneri vel ligari potuisset, cucurrit minister, et pulsans ad ostium, nuntiavit abbatissae. At illa aperiens ianuam monasterii, exivit ipsa cum una sanctimonialium feminarum ad locum virorum; et evocans presbyterum, rogavit secum venire ad patientem. Ubi cum venientes viderent multos adfuisse qui vexatum tenere et motus eius insanos comprimere conati, nequaquam valebant, dicebat presbyter exorcismos, et quaeque poterat pro sedando miseri furore agebat. Sed nec ipse, quamvis multum laborans, proficere aliquid valebat. Cumque nil salutis furenti superesse videretur, repente venit in mentem abbatissae pulvis ille praefatus, statimque iussit ire ministram, et

---

[1] " Sang and read the prayers prescribed for this sickness," according to the A.S. version, Pl.

reached up to heaven, the queen thereto added that many sick folk had already been healed with the dust of the pavement on the which the water of the washing of his bones was poured out. Then the abbess desired to have some deal of the health-giving dust bestowed on her; and as soon as she received it she knit it up in a cloth and laid it up in a little casket, and returned home. And after some time had passed, when she was in her own monastery, a certain stranger came thither, who in the night season was wont divers times to be troubled suddenly with a foul spirit and that most grievously. And this guest, when he had been liberally entertained and had laid his limbs to rest upon a bed after supper, on a sudden being seized by the devil began to cry out, to gnash with his teeth, to foam at the mouth, and twist his limbs, flinging them now one way, now another. And when no man had been able to hold or bind him, a servant ran and knocking at the gate told the abbess. Then she opening the door of the monastery came forth herself with one of the nuns to the place where the brethren lay, and calling forth a priest required him to go with her to the patient. Where, when at their coming they saw many men present who, for all their endeavour to keep down the party afflicted and to stay his inordinate movements, availed nothing, the priest pronounced exorcisms [1] and did all that he could for the appeasing of the rage that this piteous creature was in. But neither was the priest himself, for all his much travail, able to avail aught. And when it seemed that no way of amendment was left for the mad body, the abbess suddenly remembered that aforesaid dust, and forthwith commanded a handmaid to go and bring her the

capsellam in qua erat adducere. Et cum illa adferens
quae iussa est, intraret atrium domus, in cuius in-
terioribus daemoniosus torquebatur, conticuit ille
subito, et quasi in somnum laxatus deposuit caput,
membra in quietem omnia composuit.

Conticuere omnes intentique ora tenebant,

quem res exitum haberet solliciti exspectantes. Et
post aliquantum horae spatium, resedit qui vexabatur,
et graviter suspirans: "Modo," inquit, "sanum
sapio, recepi enim sensum animi mei." At illi
sedulo sciscitabantur quomodo hoc contigisset. Qui
ait: "Mox ut virgo haec cum capsella quam portabat
adpropinquavit atrio domus huius, discessere omnes
qui me premebant spiritus maligni, et me relicto
nusquam comparuerunt." Tunc dedit ei abbatissa
portiunculam de pulvere illo; et sic data oratione a
presbytero illo, noctem quietissimam duxit: neque
aliquid ex eo tempore nocturni timoris aut vexationis
ab antiquo hoste pertulit.

CAP. XII

Ut ad tumbam eius sit puerulus a febre curatus.

SEQUENTE dehinc tempore fuit in eodem monasterio
puerulus quidam longo febrium incommodo graviter
vexatus: qui cum die quodam sollicitus horam

---

[1] Verg. *Aen.* II. 1.

little casket wherein the dust was. And she bringing it as she was commanded, as she entered the court of the house (in the inward part whereof the man that was possessed with the evil spirit was tormented), the man suddenly held his peace and laid down his head as though he were fallen asleep, and settled all his limbs to rest.

Whist were they all and set their faces attentive,[1]

carefully looking to see what end the matter would have. And after some hour's space the man that was before disquieted sat up and fetching a deep sigh said: " Now I feel myself whole, for I have come to my wits again." Whereupon they inquired of him earnestly how this had happened. And he said: " Incontinent as soon as this maid, with the little casket which she was bringing, was come nigh to the court of this house, all the wicked spirits that troubled me departed and leaving me appeared no more." Then did the abbess give him a little piece of that dust; and so, when the priest there had offered prayer, he passed the night in most quiet rest: neither from that time forth did he suffer any night alarm or trouble from his old enemy.

CHAPTER XII

How a little boy sitting hard by Oswald's tomb was healed of an ague.

IN the time following after this there was a certain little boy in the same monastery, who had been a great while sorely distressed with trouble of fevers: who on a certain day looking heavily for the hour of

accessionis exspectaret, ingressus ad eum quidam de fratribus: "Vis," inquit, "mi nate, doceam te quomodo cureris ab huius molestia languoris? Surge, ingredere ecclesiam, et accedens ad sepulcrum Osualdi, ibi reside, et quietus manens adhaere tumbae. Vide ne exeas inde, nec de loco movearis, donec hora recessionis febrium transierit. Tunc ipse intrabo, et educam te inde." Fecit ut ille suaserat, sedentemque ad tumbam sancti, infirmitas tangere nequaquam praesumpsit; quin in tantum timens aufugit, ut nec secunda die, nec tertia, neque umquam exinde eum auderet contingere. Quod ita esse gestum qui referebat mihi frater inde adveniens adiecit, quod eo adhuc tempore quo mecum loquebatur, superesset in eodem monasterio iam iuvenis ille, in quo tunc puero factum erat hoc miraculum sanitatis. Nec mirandum preces regis illius iam cum Domino regnantis multum valere apud eum, qui temporalis regni quondam gubernacula tenens, magis pro aeterno regno semper laborare ac deprecari solebat.

Denique ferunt quia a tempore matutinae laudis saepius ad diem usque in orationibus perstiterit, atque ob crebrum morem orandi, sive gratias agendi Domino semper ubicumque sedens, supinas super genua sua manus habere solitus sit. Vulgatum est autem, et in consuetudinem proverbii versum, quod

---

[1] Personified, cf. Luke iv. 39.
[2] Matins, between midnight and 3 a.m.

CURE OF BOY

the attack, one of the brethren coming in to him
saith: " Wilt thou, my son, that I teach thee how
thou mayest be delivered of the grief of this sickness? Rise, go into the church, and when thou
comest to Oswald's sepulchre, sit down there and
abiding quietly cleave unto the tomb! Beware thou
go not from thence nor stir from the place until the
hour of the abatement of the fever shall be past!
Then will I come myself and bring thee forth from
thence." The child did as the religious man had
counselled him, and when he was sitting hard by the
holy man's tomb, the sickness [1] did in no wise presume
to touch him; nay, it fled away so far in fear that
neither the next day nor the third day nor ever afterward did it dare to come nigh him. And that this
was so done, the brother who came from thence
reported to me and said furthermore, that at the time
of his talk with me that young man, on whom as a
child this miracle of healing was then done, was now
still alive in the same monastery. And it is not to
be wondered at that the prayers of that king now
reigning with the Lord avail to do much with Him,
being a man who having sometime the governance
of a temporal realm accustomed himself rather to
travail always and pray earnestly for the everlasting
kingdom.

Finally, men report that he oftentimes continued
in prayer from the time of early morning praise [2]
until it were day, and by reason of his common
custom of prayer and giving thanks to the Lord he
was wont always, wheresoever he did sit, to have
his hands with the palms turned upward above his
knees. Yea, it is commonly said, and turned into
usage of a proverb, that he also ended his life as he

385

etiam inter verba orationis vitam finierit. Nam cum
armis et hostibus circumseptus, iamiamque videret se
esse perimendum, oravit pro animabus exercitus sui.
Unde dicunt in proverbio: " Deus miserere animabus,
dixit Osuald cadens in terram."

Ossa igitur illius translata et condita sunt in
monasterio quo diximus : porro caput et manus cum
brachiis a corpore praecisas, iussit rex qui occiderat,
in stipitibus suspendi. Quo post annum veniens cum
exercitu successor regni eius Osuiu, abstulit ea, et
caput quidem in coemeterio Lindisfarnensis ecclesiae
in regia vero civitate manus cum brachiis condidit.

CAP XIII

*Ut in Hibernia sit quidam per reliquias eius a mortis
articulo revocatus.*

Nec solum inclyti fama viri Brittaniae fines lus-
travit universos, sed etiam trans oceanum longe
radios salutiferae lucis spargens, Germaniae simul et
Hiberniae partes attigit. Denique reverentissimus
antistes Acca solet referre, quia cum Roman vadens,
apud sanctissimum Fresonum gentis archiepiscopum
Vilbrordum cum suo antistite Vilfrido moraretur,
crebro eum audierit, de mirandis quae ad reliquias
eiusdem reverentissimi regis in illa provincia gesta
fuerint, narrare. Sed et in Hibernia cum presbyter

---

[1] Bamborough.

was saying his devotions. For whiles he was compassed about with the weapons of his enemies and saw that he should be slain immediately, he prayed for the souls of his army. Of the which occasion came up this proverb: " God have mercy on their souls, quoth Oswald, as he fell to the ground."

Therefore his bones were conveyed away and buried in the monastery that we have said: furthermore, the king who had killed him commanded that his head and his hands with his arms cut off from the body should be hanged on poles. And thither a year after, Oswy his successor in the kingdom came with an army and took them away, burying his head in the churchyard of the church of Lindisfarne, but his hands with his arms in his royal city.[1]

CHAPTER XIII

*How in Ireland a certain man was by his relics recalled
from the point of death.*

Nor did the renown of this famous man pass only over all the borders of Britain, but also, spreading afar the beams of wholesome light beyond the ocean sea, came to the coasts of Germany and Ireland likewise. In short, the most reverend bishop Acca [2] is wont to tell that in his journey to Rome, as he abode along with his prelate Wilfrid in the house of the most holy Wilbrord, archbishop of the Frisian nation, he heard him oftentimes report of the wondrous works which were done in that province at the relics of the same most reverend king. Moreover, too, in Ireland, at what time he, being but yet

---

[2] Bishop of Hexham, a pupil of Wilfrid the famous bishop of Northumbria.

adhuc peregrinam pro aeterna patria duceret vitam, rumorem sanctitatis illius in ea quoque insula longe lateque iam percrebuisse ferebat: e quibus unum quod inter alia retulit miraculum, praesenti nostrae Historiae inserendum credidimus.

" Tempore," inquit, " mortalitatis quae Brittaniam Hiberniamque lata strage vastavit, percussus est eiusdem clade pestis inter alios scholasticus quidam de gente Scottorum, doctus quidem vir studio literarum, sed erga curam perpetuae suae salvationis nihil omnino studii et industriae gerens: qui cum se morti proximum videret, timere coepit et pavere, ne mox mortuus, ob merita scelerum ad inferni claustra raperetur: clamavitque me, cum essem in vicino positus, et inter aegra tremens suspiria, flebili voce talia mecum querebatur: ' Vides,' inquit, ' quia iamiamque crescente corporis molestia ad articulum subeundae mortis compellor: nec dubito me post mortem corporis statim ad perpetuam animae mortem rapiendum, ac infernalibus subdendum esse tormentis: qui tempore non pauco inter studia divinae lectionis, vitiorum potius implicamentis quam divinis solebam servire mandatis. Inest autem animo, si mihi pietas superna aliqua vivendi spatia donaverit, vitiosos mores corrigere, atque ad imperium divinae voluntatis totam ex integro mentem vitamque transferre. Verum novi non hoc esse meriti mei, ut inducias vivendi vel accipiam vel me accepturum esse

---

¹ Known as the " Yellow Pest."

a priest, led the life of a pilgrim for the love he had
to the everlasting country, he reported that the
bruit of the king's holiness was by that time far
abroad spread in that isle also: and one miracle of
those wrought, which he rehearsed among other,
we have thought good to put in our present History.

" In a time of mortal sickness,"[1] said he, " which
wasted Britain and Ireland with a wide havock, a
certain scholar of the Scottish nation was stricken
amongst other with the calamity of the same plague,
a man skilful certes in the study of learning, but one
that used no diligence and labour at all for the care
of his own everlasting salvation: who, when he saw
himself to be at death's door, began to fear and
quake, lest being shortly dead he should, as his lewd
life deserved, be hurried away to the dungeons of
hell: and therewith he cried to me (as I was lodged
not far off), and trembling in the midst of sorrowful
sighs, with a lamentable voice made thus his moan
in my company: ' You see,' quoth he, ' that at this
very time by the increase of my bodily grief I am
being driven to the point of meeting death: and I
doubt not that after the death of the body I must
be hurried away to the everlasting death of the soul,
and endure the torments of hell: I who no small
time occupied in study of reading Holy Writ was
accustomed to be a slave to the entanglements of
sin rather than be obedient to the commandments
of God. But, if the heavenly goodness will grant
me some leisure to live, I propose to amend my sinful
manners and turn my whole mind and life anew to
the direction of the divine will. Yet I know that it
is not in my deserving either to obtain or hope to
obtain a truce and respite to live, except peradventure

confidam, nisi forte misero mihi et indigno venia, per
auxilium eorum qui illi fideliter servierunt, propitiari
dignatus fuerit. Audivimus autem et fama est[1]
celeberrima, quia fuerit in gente vestra rex mirandae
sanctitatis, vocabulo Osuald, cuius excellentia fidei et
virtutis, etiam post mortem, virtutum frequentium
operatione claruerit: precorque, si aliquid reliquiarum
illius penes te habes, adferas mihi, si forte mihi
Dominus per eius meritum misereri voluerit.' At
ego respondi: ' Habeo quidem de ligno, in quo caput
eius occisi a paganis infixum est; et, si firmo corde
credideris, potest divina pietas per tanti meritum
viri, et huius vitae spatia longiora concedere, et
ingressu te vitae perennis dignum reddere.' Nec
moratus ille, integram se in hoc habere fidem
respondebat.

" Tunc benedixi aquam, et astulam roboris praefati
inmittens obtuli aegro potandum. Nec mora, melius
habere coepit, et convalescens ab infirmitate, multo
deinceps tempore vixit: totoque ad Deum corde
et opere conversus, omnibus ubicumque perveniebat,
clementiam pii Conditoris, et fidelis eius famuli
gloriam praedicabat."

[1] *est,* Pl.

by the help of them which have faithfully served God, He will vouchsafe to be reconciled to me that am a wretch unworthy of pardon. Now we have heard and it is very commonly reported that there hath been in your nation a king of wonderful holiness, called Oswald, the excellency of whose faith and virtue, yea, after death, hath become well known by the performance of many mighty works: and I beseech you, if you have any of his relics in your keeping, to bring it to me, in case it may be so that the Lord will be pleased to have mercy upon me through his merits.' Whereupon I made answer: ' Forsooth, I have some of the tree whereupon his head was stuck after that he was slain of the pay-nims; and if thou wilt believe steadfastly in thine heart, the merciful goodness of God by the merits of so worthy a person can both grant thee longer time to lead this life and also make thee a meet man to enter into the life everlasting.' And he answered me incontinent that he did perfectly believe so.

"Then I blessed water, and casting in a chip of the foresaid oak-wood did give to the sick man to drink. And forthwith he did begin to amend and recovering his health from that sickness lived a long time after: and being turned to God in all heart and deed, did publicly declare to all men, wherever he came, the graciousness of our merciful Maker and the glory of His faithful servant."

THE VENERABLE BEDE

CAP. XIV

Ut defuncto Paulino, Ithamar pro eo Hrofensis ecclesiae
praesulatum susceperit ; et de humilitate mirabili
regis Osuini, qui ab Osuiu crudeli caede peremptus est.

TRANSLATO ergo ad caelestia regna Osualdo, suscepit regni terrestris sedem pro eo frater eius Osuiu,
iuvenis triginta circiter annorum, et per annos viginti
octo laboriosissime tenuit, impugnatus videlicet et ab
ea quae fratrem eius occiderat pagana gente Merciorum, et a filio quoque suo Alchfrido, necnon et a
fratruo, id est, fratris sui qui ante eum regnavit filio
Oidilualdo.

Cuius anno secundo, hoc est, ab incarnatione
Dominica anno sexcentesimo quadragesimo quarto,
reverentissimus pater Paulinus, quondam quidem
Eburacensis, sed tunc Hrofensis episcopus civitatis,
transivit ad Dominum sexto Iduum Octobrium die :
qui decem et novem annos, menses duos, dies viginti
unum episcopatum tenuit ; sepultusque est in secretario beati apostoli Andreae, quod rex Aedilberct a
fundamentis in eadem Hrofi civitate construxit.
In cuius locum Honorius archiepiscopus ordinavit
Ithamar, oriundum quidem de gente Cantuariorum,
sed vita et eruditione antecessoribus suis aequandum.

Habuit autem Osuiu primis regni sui temporibus
consortem regiae dignitatis, vocabulo Osuini, de
stirpe regis Aeduini, hoc est, filium Osrici, de quo
supra retulimus, virum eximiae pietatis et religionis :

---

[1] Set up by Penda in Deira after Oswin's death, it seems.

[2] The first native bishop.

[3] First cousin once removed.

CHAPTER XIV

How that, when Paulinus was dead, Ithamar received the
prelacy of the church of Rochester in his stead;
and of the marvellous humility of king Oswin,
who by cruel murder was slain of Oswy [644–651].

OSWALD then being transported to the kingdoms of
heaven, his brother Oswy, a young man about 30
years old, took in his stead the place of the earthly
kingdom, and held it with great disquietude and
trouble the space of eight-and-twenty years, being
assailed certes both by the paynim people of the
Marchmen which had slain his brother, and also by
his own son Alchfrid, as well as by his nephew Ethelwald,[1] that is to say, the son of his brother Oswald
that reigned before him.

In the second year of which Oswy's reign, that is,
to wit, in the 644th year from the incarnation of our
Lord, the most reverend father Paulinus, sometime
bishop of York but then bishop of the city of Rochester, passed to the Lord the tenth day of October:
who held the bishopric 19 years two months and
21 days; and was buried in the sacristy of the blessed
apostle Andrew, which king Ethelbert builded up
from the foundations in the same city of Hrof. In
whose place Honorius the archbishop ordained
Ithamar,[2] a man sprung from the nation of the men
of Kent, yet comparable in life and learning to his
predecessors.

Now Oswy at the beginning of his reign had a partaker of his estate royal, named Oswin, who descended
of king Edwin's blood [3] (that is to say, he was son
of Osric of whom we have made mention before), a

qui provinciae Derorum septem annis in maxima
omnium rerum affluentia, et ipse amabilis omnibus
praefuit.   Sed nec cum eo ille qui ceteram Transhum-
branae gentis partem ab aquilone, id est. Berniciorum provinciam regebat, habere pacem potuit;
quin potius ingravescentibus causis dissensionum
miserrima hunc caede peremit.   Siquidem congre-
gato contra invicem exercitu, cum videret se Osuini
cum illo qui plures habebat auxiliarios non posse
bello confligere, ratus est utilius tunc demissa intentione bellandi, servare se ad tempora meliora.   Re-
misit ergo exercitum quem congregaverat, ac singulos domum redire praecepit, a loco qui vocatur
Vilfaraesdun, id est, Mons Vilfari, et est a vico
Cataractone decem ferme millibus passuum contra
solstitialem occasum secretus: divertitque ipse
cum uno tantum milite sibi fidelissimo, nomine
Tondheri, celandus in domo comitis Hunualdi, quem
etiam ipsum sibi amicissimum autumabat.   Sed, heu,
proh dolor! longe aliter erat: nam ab eodem comite
proditum eum Osuiu, cum praefato ipsius milite per
praefectum suum Ediluinum detestanda omnibus
morte interfecit.   Quod factum est die decima tertia
Kalendarum Septembrium, anno regni eius nono,
in loco qui dicitur Ingetlingum; ubi postmodum
castigandi huius facinoris gratia, monasterium constructum est: in quo pro utriusque regis, et occisi

---

[1] Possibly Gariston, near Catterick.   [2] A.S. *gesith*.
[3] A.S. *gerefa*.   [4] Gilling, near Richmond.
[5] By Eanfled, Oswy's wife.

marvellous devout and godly man: who by the space
of seven years ruled the province of the Deirans in
most plenty of all things and with the love of all his
subjects. But Oswy who governed the other part
of the Northumbrian nation on the north, to wit the
province of the Bernicians, could not live peaceably
with him; nay, rather forging and increasing causes
of debate he murdered him most cruelly. For, an
army being on both parts assembled opposite, Oswin,
seeing that he was not able to join battle with him
that had a greater host of men, thought it more
expedient to give over his purpose of fighting at that
time and keep himself until better occasion served.
Therefore he discharged his army which he had
gathered together, and commanded them severally
to return home again from the place which is called
Wilfaraesdun,[1] that is Wilfar's Hill, and standeth
almost ten mile from the village of Cataract, being
withdrawn over against the setting of the sun in
summer: and Oswin conveyed himself out of the way
with one only that was his most faithful thane, named
Tondher, to hide himself in the house of Hunwald, a
retainer [2] whom also he took to be of himself a very
friend to him. But alas, sad to say! he was far
otherwise: for, being by the same retainer betrayed,
Oswin, along with his aforesaid thane, was slain of
Oswy through the means of his reeve [3] Ethelwin, by
a death that was abominable in the eyes of all. And
this was done the 20th day of August in the ninth
year of his reign in the place which is called Ingetlingum; [4] where afterward for the satisfaction of this
heinous act there was a monastery builded: [5] in the
which daily prayers should be offered to the Lord
for the redemption of both the kings' souls, to wit,

videlicet, et eius qui occidere iussit, animae redemptione cotidie Domino preces offerri deberent.

Erat autem rex Osuini et aspectu venustus, et
statura sublimis, et affatu iucundus, et moribus civilis,
et manu omnibus, id est, nobilibus simul atque
ignobilibus largus: unde contigit ut ob regiam eius
et animi, et vultus, et meritorum dignitatem ab
omnibus diligeretur, et undique ad eius ministerium
de cunctis prope provinciis viri etiam nobilissimi con-
currerent. Cuius inter ceteras virtutis et modestiae,
et, ut ita dicam, specialis benedictionis glorias, etiam
maxima fuisse fertur humilitas, ut uno probare sat
erit exemplo.

Donaverat equum optimum antistiti Aidano, in
quo ille quamvis ambulare solitus, vel amnium fluenta
transire, vel si alia quaelibet necessitas insisteret,
viam peragere posset: cui cum parvo interiecto
tempore pauper quidam occurreret eleemosynam
petens, desiliens ille praecepit equum, ita ut erat
stratus regaliter, pauperi dari: erat enim multum
misericors, et cultor pauperum, ac velut pater
miserorum. Hoc cum regi esset relatum, dicebat
episcopo, cum forte ingressuri essent ad prandium:
" Quid voluisti, domine antistes, equum regium,
quem te conveniebat proprium habere, pauperi
dare? Numquid non habuimus equos viliores plurimos, vel alias species quae ad pauperum dona
sufficerent, quamvis illum eis equum non dares, quem
tibi specialiter possidendum elegi?" Cui statim
episcopus: " Quid loqueris," inquit, " rex? Num-

both the soul of him that was slain and of him that gave command to slay him.

Now king Oswin was of countenance beautiful and of stature high, and in talk pleasant and courteous in manner, and bountiful to all, that is to say to men of high as well as men of low degree: whereby it happened that for the princely worthiness of his mind and visage and deserving acts he had the love of all men, and from all the provinces on all sides near, men even of the highest degree flocked to his service. Among all whose other honourable qualities of excellence and sobriety and, that I may so speak, of peculiar blessing, his humility is said to have been the chiefest, as one example will be sufficient to prove.

He had given to bishop Aidan a very fair horse on which the bishop (though he used most to travel on foot) might pass over flowing streams, or bring his journey to the end if any other necessity constrained: but when after a short space of time a certain poor man met the bishop and craved an alms of him, he lighted off and commanded the horse, gorgeously trapped as he was, to be given to the poor man: for he was passing pitiful, a lover of the poor and as it were a father of the wretched. When this had been reported to the king, he said to the bishop, as it chanced they were about to enter in to dinner: " What meant you, my lord bishop, to give to the poor man that royal horse which it was fitting for you to keep for your own use? Had we not store of horses of less price and other kind to be sufficient for gifts to the poor, though you should not give them that horse which I chose to be your peculiar possession?" To whom the bishop at once said: " Why talketh your Grace thus? Is that son

397

quid tibi carior est ille filius equae, quam ille filius
Dei?" Quibus dictis intrabant ad prandendum.
Et episcopus quidem residebat in suo loco. Porro
rex, venerat enim de venatu, coepit consistens ad
focum calefieri cum ministris: et repente inter cale-
faciendum recordans verbum quod dixerat illi
antistes, discinxit se gladio suo, et dedit illum minis-
tro, festinusque accedens ante pedes episcopi conruit,
postulans ut sibi placatus esset, "Quia nunquam,"
inquit, "deinceps aliquid loquar de hoc, aut iudicabo
quid vel quantum de pecunia nostra filiis Dei tribuas."
Quod videns episcopus, multum pertimuit, ac statim
exsurgens levavit eum, promittens se multum illi
esse placatum, dummodo ille residens ad epulas
tristitiam deponeret. Dumque rex, iubente ac
postulante episcopo, laetitiam reciperet, coepit e
contra episcopus tristis usque ad lacrymarum pro-
fusionem effici. Quem dum presbyter suus lingua
sua patria, quam rex et domestici eius non noverant,
quare lacrymaretur interrogasset: "Scio," inquit,
"quia non multo tempore victurus est rex: nunquam enim ante haec vidi humilem regem. Unde
animadverto illum citius ex hac vita rapiendum:
non enim digna est haec gens talem habere rectorem."
Nec multo post, dira antistitis praesagia tristi regis
funere, de quo supra diximus, impleta sunt.

Sed et ipse antistes Aidan non plus quam duo-
decimo post occisionem regis quem amabat die, id
est, pridie Kalendarum Septembrium, de saeculo
ablatus, perpetua laborum suorum a Domino praemia
recepit.

of a mare dearer in your sight than that son of God?" Which being said they entered for to dine. And the bishop for his part took his place appointed. Then the king, for he had come from hunting, standing with his thanes at the hearth began to warm himself: and suddenly, as he warmed himself, recalling the word which the bishop had spoken unto him, he ungirded his sword, giving it to a thane, and came in haste to the bishop, falling down at his feet and beseeching him to be reconciled to him: "Because," said he, "I will never hereafter speak of this, or measure what or how much of our money thou bestowest upon the sons of God." At which sight the bishop was much afraid, and rising at once lifted up the king, professing that he was right well reconciled with him, provided only he should sit down to the feast and cast away heaviness. And whilst the king at the bishop's bidding and entreaty did recover cheerfulness, the bishop contrariwise began to be made heavy even to the shedding of tears. Of whom, when his chaplain, in his mother tongue which the king and his court knew not, had demanded why he wept: "I know," said he, "that the king is not to live long: for never before this time have I seen an humble king. Whereby I perceive that he must speedily be taken out of this life: for this people is not worthy to have such a governor." And shortly after, the bishop's dreadful abodement was fulfilled with the king's cruel death, of which we have spoken before.

Moreover, bishop Aidan himself also was taken out of the world and received of the Lord the everlasting reward of his labours, even not longer than the 12th day after the king whom he loved was slain, that is to wit the 31st day of August.

THE VENERABLE BEDE

CAP. XV

*Ut episcopus Aidan nautis et tempestatem futuram
praedixerit, et oleum sanctum quo hanc sedarent,
dederit.*

Qui cuius meriti fuerit, etiam miraculorum signis
internus arbiter edocuit, e quibus tria memoriae causa
ponere satis sit. Presbyter quidam nomine Utta,
multae gravitatis ac veritatis vir, et ob id omnibus,
etiam ipsis principibus saeculi honorabilis, cum
mitteretur Cantiam ob adducendam inde coniugem
regi Osuio, filiam videlicet Aeduini regis Eanfledam,
quae occiso patre illuc fuerat adducta: qui terrestri
quidem itinere illo venire, sed navigio cum virgine
redire disponebat, accessit ad episcopum Aidanum,
obsecrans eum, pro se suisque qui tantum iter erant
adgressuri, Domino supplicare. Qui benedicens
illos, ac Domino commendans, dedit etiam oleum
sanctificatum: " Scio," inquiens, " quia ubi navem
ascenderitis, tempestas vobis et ventus contrarius
superveniet: sed tu memento ut hoc oleum quod tibi
do, mittas in mare; et statim quiescentibus ventis,
serenitas maris vos laeta prosequetur, ac cupito
itinere domum remittet." Quae cuncta ut praedixerat antistes, ex ordine completa sunt: et quidem
inprimis furentibus undis pelagi, tentabant nautae
anchoris in mare missis navem retinere, neque hoc
agentes, aliquid proficiebant: cumque verrentibus

AIDAN · AND UTTA

CHAPTER XV

How that bishop Aidan both told the shipmen beforehand of a storm that was to come, and gave them holy oil wherewith to calm it [642–644].

AND how worthy a man Aidan was, the secret Judge of men's hearts hath fully declared by the signs of miracles, three of the which let it be sufficient to recite for remembrance' sake. A certain priest called Utta, a man of great gravity and truth, and for that reason much esteemed of all, even of the princes of this world themselves, at what time he was sent to Kent to fetch thence a wife to King Oswy (to wit Eanfled, daughter of King Edwin, who after the slaying of her father had been taken thither), appointing for his journey to travel thither by land but to return with the maiden by ship, went to bishop Aidan, beseeching him to make his humble prayer to the Lord to prosper him and his who were about to venture on so hazardous a journey. And the bishop, blessing them and committing them to the Lord, gave them also hallowed oil, saying: " I know that when you shall have shipping, a tempest and a contrary wind shall rise upon you suddenly : but do thou remember that thou cast into the sea this oil that I give thee; and anon the wind being laid, comfortable fair weather will attend you and send you home again by the way you have desired." All which things were fulfilled in order as the bishop had prophesied: and truly at the beginning, when the surges of the sea did rage, the shipmen assayed to hold back the ship by casting anchors into the sea, but by doing so availed nothing : and when the

undique et implere incipientibus navem fluctibus,
mortem sibi omnes imminere, iamiamque adesse
viderent, tandem presbyter reminiscens verba antistitis, adsumpta ampulla misit de oleo in pontum, et
statim, ut praedictum erat, suo quievit a fervore.
Sicque factum est, ut vir Dei et per prophetiae
spiritum tempestatem praedixerit futuram, et per
virtutem eiusdem spiritus, hanc exortam, quamvis
corporaliter absens, sopiverit. Cuius ordinem miraculi non quilibet dubius relator, sed fidelissimus mihi
nostrae ecclesiae presbyter, Cynimund vocabulo,
narravit, qui se hoc ab ipso Utta presbytero, in quo
et per quem completum est, audisse perhibebat.

CAP. XVI

*Ut idem admotum ab hostibus urbi regiae ignem orando
amoverit.*

ALIUD eiusdem patris memorabile miraculum ferunt
multi qui nosse potuerunt. Nam tempore episcopatus eius, hostilis Merciorum exercitus, Penda duce,
Nordanhymbrorum regiones impia clade longe lateque
devastans, pervenit ad urbem usque regiam, quae ex
Bebbae quondam reginae vocabulo cognominatur,
eamque quia neque armis, neque obsidione capere
poterat, flammis absumere conatus est: disciscisque
viculis quos in vicinia urbis invenit, advexit illo plurimam congeriem trabium, tignorum, parietum, vir-

---

[1] The joint monastery of Wearmouth and Jarrow.
[2] Bamborough.

402

waves swept the ship on all sides and it began to fill, and all saw that death threatened them and was at that instant upon them, at length the priest, remembering the bishop's words, took the oil pot and did cast of the oil into the sea, and forthwith, as had been prophesied, the sea abated of his violence. And so it was that the man of God both by the spirit of prophecy foreshewed the tempest to come, and by the virtue of the same spirit, though absent in the body, calmed it when it was arisen. And no common reporter of uncertain rumour but a very credible man, a priest of our church,[1] Cynimund by name, told me the process of that miracle, who said that he had heard it of Utta the priest himself in whom and through whom the miracle was wrought.

CHAPTER XVI

How the same bishop by prayer put away the fire that enemies had put to the king's city.

ANOTHER miracle worthy remembrance wrought by the same father is reported of many who were able to have knowledge thereof. For in the time of his bishopric the army of the Marchmen that were enemies, with Penda for captain, wasting the country of the Northumbrians with cruel destruction far and wide, came even to the royal city[2] which is called after the name of Bebba, one time queen, and forasmuch as he was not able neither by battle nor by siege to win it, Penda endeavoured to destroy it by fire: and pulling in pieces the hamlets which he found in the neighbourhood of the city, carried thither a very great quantity of beams, rafters, partitions, wattles

georum, et tecti fenei, et his urbem in magna altitudine circumdedit, a parte quae terrae est contigua: et dum ventum opportunum cerneret, inlato igne comburere urbem nisus est. Quo tempore reverentissimus antistes Aidan in insula Farne, quae duobus ferme millibus passuum ab urbe procul abest, morabatur. Illo enim saepius secretae orationis et silentii causa secedere consuerat. Denique usque hodie locum sedis illius solitariae in eadem insula solent ostendere. Qui cum ventis ferentibus globos ignis ac fumum supra muros urbis exaltari conspiceret, fertur elevatis ad caelum oculis manibusque, cum lacrymis dixisse: " Vide, Domine, quanta mala facit Penda." Quo dicto, statim mutati ab urbe venti, in eos qui accenderant, flammarum incendia retorserunt, ita ut aliquot laesi, omnes territi, impugnare ultra urbem cessarent quam divinitus iuvari cognoverant.

CAP. XVII

Ut apposta ecclesiae cui idem accumbens obierat, ardente cetera domo, flammis absumi nequiverit ; et de interna vita eius.

Hunc cum dies mortis egredi e corpore cogeret, completis annis episcopatus sui sexdecim, erat in villa regia, non longe ab urbe de qua praefati sumus. In hac enim habens ecclesiam et cubiculum, saepius

and thatch, and therewith he compassed the city on the side that adjoineth to the land, in a great height: and when he saw the wind to serve, he kindled the fire and sought to consume the city. At the which time the most reverend bishop Aidan was dwelling in Farne island which is almost two miles distant from the city. For thither he oftentimes was used to depart for the sake of secret prayer and silent meditation. Indeed to this day they are wont to shew in the same island the place where he would sit to be alone. Who beholding the masses of fire and the smoke raised aloft over the city (as the wind bare them along), lifting up his eyes and hands to heaven, with tears (as is reported), said: " Behold, Lord, how great mischief Penda worketh! " Which being said, the winds, being forthwith shifted from the city, turned back again the burning of the flames upon them who had kindled it, insomuch that some being hurt, all made afraid, they were fain to leave the further assault of the city which they saw to be holpen by the hand of God.

CHAPTER XVII

How a buttress of the church whereunto the same bishop leaning departed this life could not be consumed of the flames, when the rest of the house was burning ; and of his inward life.

THIS bishop at what time the day of death compelled him to depart from this life, having brought to an end 16 years of his bishopric, was in a township of the king, not far from the city of which we have before spoken. For having there a church and a

ibidem diverti ac manere, atque inde ad praedicandum circumquaque exire consueverat: quod
ipsum et in aliis villis regis facere solebat, utpote nil
propriae possessionis, excepta ecclesia sua et adia-
centibus agellis habens. Tetenderunt ergo ei aegro-
tanti tentorium ad occidentalem ecclesiae partem,
ita ut ipsum tentorium parieti haereret ecclesiae.
Unde factum est, ut adclinis destinae quae extrin-
secus ecclesiae pro munimine erat adposita, spiritum
vitae exhalaret ultimum. Obiit autem septimo
decimo episcopatus sui anno, pridie Kalendarum
Septembrium. Cuius corpus mox inde translatum
ad insulam Lindisfarnensium, atque in coemeterio
fratrum sepultum est. At interiecto tempore aliquanto, cum fabricata esset ibi basilica maior, atque
in honorem beatissimi apostolorum principis dedicata, illo ossa eius translata, atque ad dexteram altaris
iuxta venerationem tanto pontifice dignam condita
sunt.

Successit vero ei in episcopatum Finan, et ipse illo
ab Hii Scottorum insula ac monasterio destinatus,
ac tempore non pauco in episcopatu permansit.
Contigit autem post aliquot annos, ut Penda Merciorum rex cum hostili exercitu haec in loca perveniens, cum cuncta quae poterat ferro flammaque
perderet, vicus quoque ille in quo antistes obiit una
cum ecclesia memorata flammis absumeretur. Sed
mirum in modum sola illa destina cui incumbens
obiit, ab ignibus circum cuncta vorantibus absumi non

chamber he was oftentimes accustomed to betake himself there and abide, and so from thence to go forth all about to preach: which selfsame thing he was wont to do in other townships of the king also, as having no possession of his own but his church only and small pieces of land lying thereabout. Therefore, as he was sick, they pitched him a pavilion on the western side of the church, in such fashion that the pavilion was fastened hard to the church wall. Whereupon it came to pass that, leaning to a prop which was set against the outside of the church to fortify it, he breathed out the last breath of life. Now he died in the 17th year of his bishopric the last day of August. And his body was by and by from thence carried over to the island of Lindisfarne, and in the churchyard of the brethren buried. But after some space of time, a greater building being there erected and dedicated in the honour of the most blessed chief of the apostles, his bones were transposed thither, and laid at the right side of the altar with the honour that so virtuous a bishop deserved.

There succeeded him of a truth in his bishopric Finan, himself too directed thither from the island and monastery of Iona in Scotland, and he remained in the bishopric no small time. Moreover, it fortuned some years after, that Penda king of the Marchmen invading these parts with an armed host, while destroying with fire and sword all that he could, consumed with flames also that village in which the bishop Aidan died, along with the church before spoken of. But in a marvellous manner that only prop, whereunto he leaned at the moment of his departure, could not be consumed of the flames that

potuit. Quo clarescente miraculo, mox ibidem
ecclesia restaurata, et haec eadem destina in muni-
mentum est parietis, ut ante fuerat, forinsecus
adposita. Rursumque peracto tempore aliquanto,
evenit per culpam incuriae, vicum eundem, et ipsam
pariter ecclesiam ignibus consumi. Sed ne tunc
quidem eandem tangere flamma destinam valebat:
et cum magno utique miraculo ipsa eius foramina
ingrediens, quibus aedificio erat adfixa, perederet,
ipsam tamen laedere nullatenus sinebatur. Unde
tertio aedificata ibi ecclesia, destinam illam non ut
antea deforis in fulcimentum domus adposuerunt,
sed intro ipsam ecclesiam in memoriam miraculi
posuerunt, ubi intrantes genu flectere, ac miseri-
cordiae caelesti supplicare deberent. Constatque
multos ex eo tempore gratiam sanitatis in eodem
loco consecutos: quin etiam astulis ex ipsa destina
excisis et in aquam missis, plures sibi suisque lan-
guorum remedia conquisiere.

Scripsi autem haec de persona et operibus viri
praefati; nequaquam in eo laudans vel eligens hoc,
quod de observatione paschae minus perfecte sapie-
bat: immo hoc multum detestans, sicut in libro
quem de temporibus composui, manifestissime pro-
bavi; sed quasi verax historicus, simpliciter ea quae
de illo sive per illum sunt gesta, describens, et [1]
quae laude sunt digna in eius actibus laudans, atque

---

[1] for *ea*, Pl.

swallowed all things round. Which miracle becoming known abroad, the church was shortly builded up again in the selfsame place, and this same prop set against the church on the outside to fortify the wall as before. And again, after some time had passed, it came to pass, by the oversight of the inhabitants, that the same village and along with it the church itself were consumed with fire. But not even then had the flame the power to touch the same prop: and whereas by a marvel assuredly great the flame entered and eat through the very openings of that prop, whereby it was fastened to the building, yet the fire was not suffered to injure the prop itself at all. Whereupon the church being builded a third time, that prop was no more set without to bolster up the fabric as before, but for remembrance of the miracle it was had into the church itself and laid where people entering in should have to kneel and make supplication to the heavenly mercy. And it is well known that sithen that time many have in the same place obtained the grace of health: nay, also with chips cut from the selfsame prop and cast into water, more beside have gotten cures of sickness for themselves and their belongings.

Now this much have I written of the person and works of the aforesaid man; by no manner of means choosing out this for commendation in him that he had imperfect understanding of the observation of Easter: nay, rather much abhorring him in this, as I have evidently declared in the book I have written concerning times; but as a true historian setting down in singleness of heart those things which were done of him or through him, and praising those things in his acts which are deserving of praise, and com-

ad utilitatem legentium memoriae commendans:
studium videlicet pacis et caritatis, continentiae et
humilitatis; animum irae et avaritiae victorem,
superbiae simul et vanae gloriae contemptorem;
industriam faciendi simul et docendi mandata
caelestia, sollertiam lectionis et vigiliarum, auctoritatem sacerdote dignam redarguendi superbos ac
potentes, pariter et infirmos consolandi, ac pauperes
recreandi vel defendendi clementiam. Qui, ut
breviter multa comprehendam, quantum ab eis qui
illum novere didicimus, nil ex omnibus quae in
evangelicis, vel apostolicis sive propheticis literis
facienda cognoverat, praetermittere, sed cuncta pro
suis viribus operibus explere curabat. Haec in
praefato antistite multum complector et amo, quia
nimirum haec Deo placuisse non ambigo. Quod
autem pascha non suo tempore observabat, vel
canonicum eius tempus ignorans, vel suae gentis
auctoritate ne agnitum sequeretur devictus, non
adprobo, nec laudo. In quo tamen hoc adprobo,
quia in celebratione sui paschae non aliud corde
tenebat, venerabatur, et praedicabat, quam quod
nos, id est, redemptionem generis humani per pas-
sionem, resurrectionem, ascensionem in caelos
mediatoris Dei et hominum hominis Jesus Christi.
Unde et hanc non, ut quidam falso opinantur, quarta
decima luna in qualibet feria cum Iudaeis, sed die
dominica semper agebat, a luna quarta decima usque
ad vicesimam; propter fidem videlicet Dominicae

410

mending them also to be remembered of readers for their profit: to wit, his love of peace and charity, continence and lowliness; a mind that was conqueror of wrath and covetousness, as well as despiser of pride and vainglory; diligence in keeping as well as in teaching the heavenly commandments, devotion to reading and watching, his gravity worthy of the priesthood in rebuking the proud and powerful, and likewise his mild demeanour in comforting the weak and refreshing or defending the poor. Who, to bring together many things in brief, so far as we have learned from them who knew him, laboured to neglect nothing of all the things which in the Gospels or apostolical and prophetical writings he had learned should be done, but to fulfil them all by his works according to the measure of his might. These things in the aforesaid bishop I do much embrace and love, because I question not that they were undoubtedly pleasing to God. But that he observed not Easter in his due time, either as ignorant of the canonical time thereof, or overcome with the authority of his nation from following that he wot, this I approve not nor commend. In whom nevertheless this I approve, that in the solemnization of his Easter he kept in his heart, reverenced and preached no other thing than we do, that is, the redemption of mankind by the passion, resurrection and ascension to the heavens of the mediator between God and men, the man Jesus Christ. And therefore he kept this day not (as some falsely do suppose) on the 14th of the moon on any day in the week, like the Jews, but always upon the Sunday from the 14th day of the moon to the 20th; for the faith undoubtedly which he had in our Lord's resurrection, believing it to

resurrectionis quam una sabbati factam, propterque spem nostrae resurrectionis quam eadem una sabbati quae nunc Dominica dies dicitur veraciter futuram cum sancta ecclesia credebat.

CAP. XVIII

De vita vel morte religiosi regis Sigbercti.

His temporibus regno Orientalium Anglorum, post Earpualdum Redualdi successorem, Sigberct frater eius praefuit, homo bonus ac religiosus: qui dudum in Gallia, dum inimicitias Redualdi fugiens exularet, lavacrum baptismi percepit, et patriam reversus, ubi regno potitus est, mox ea quae in Galliis bene disposita vidit imitari cupiens, instituit scholam in qua pueri literis erudirentur: iuvante se episcopo Felice quem de Cantia acceperat, eisque paedagogos ac magistros iuxta morem Cantuariorum praebente.

Tantumque rex ille caelestis regni amator factus est, ut ad ultimum relictis regni negotiis, et cognato suo Ecgrice commendatis, qui et antea partem eiusdem regni tenebat, intraret monasterium quod sibi fecerat, atque accepta tonsura pro aeterno magis regno militare curaret. Quod dum multo tempore faceret, contigit gentem Merciorum duce rege Penda adversus Orientales Anglos in bellum procedere, qui dum se inferiores in bello hostibus conspicerent, rogaverunt Sigberctum ad confirmandum militem

---

¹ μία σαββάτων: Matt. xxviii. 1.

have been the first day of the week,[1] and for the
hope of our resurrection which with the holy Church
he believed would verily happen on the same first
day of the week, which is now called the Lord's
day.

CHAPTER XVIII

Of the life and death of the devout king Sigbert [631–634]

ABOUT this time after Earpwald, Redwald's successor, Sigbert his brother, a virtuous and devout
man, reigned over the East English nation: which
prince, while he lived in banishment in France, flying
the enmity of Redwald, had long since taken the
laver of baptism, and after his return to his country,
when he obtained possession of the throne, desiring
by and by to follow that goodly order which he saw
practised in France, set up a school in the which boys
should be instructed in letters, by the help of bishop
Felix whom he had gotten from Kent, and who
appointed them masters and teachers after the
manner of the men of Kent.

And so deeply was that king a lover of the heavenly
kingdom, that leaving at the last the affairs of his
realm and entrusting them to his kinsman Egric,
who also before held part of the same kingdom, he
entered to a monastery which he had made for
himself, where being shoren in he laboured rather to
make war for the everlasting kingdom. And whilst
he was so busied a long time, it happened that the
nation of the Marchmen, with their captain, king
Penda, came forth to war against the East English,
who seeing themselves to be too weak for their
enemies in fight, beseech Sigbert for the encourage-

secum venire in praelium. Illo nolente ac contra-
dicente, invitum monasterio eruentes duxerunt in
certamen, sperantes minus animos militum trepidare,
minus praesente duce quondam strenuissimo et
eximio posse fugam meditari. Sed ipse professionis
suae non immemor, dum optimo esset vallatus
exercitu, nonnisi virgam tantum habere in manu
voluit: occisusque est una cum rege Ecgrice, et
cunctus eorum, insistentibus paganis, caesus sive
dispersus exercitus.

Successor autem regni eorum factus est Anna,
filius Eni, de regio genere, vir optimus, atque optimae
genitor sobolis, de quibus in sequentibus suo tempore
dicendum est: qui et ipse postea ab eodem pagano
Merciorum duce, a quo et praedecessores[1] eius,
occisus est.

CAP. XIX

*Ut Furseus apud Orientales Anglos monasterium fecerit ;
et de visionibus vel sanctitate eius, cui etiam caro pos
mortem incorrupta testimonium perhibuerit.*

Verum dum adhuc Sigberct regni infulas teneret;
supervenit de Hibernia vir sanctus, nomine Furseus,
verbo et actibus clarus, sed egregiis insignis virtutibus, cupiens pro Domino, ubicumque sibi opportunum
nveniret, peregrinam ducere vitam. Qui cum ad

---

[1] for *praedecessor,* Pl.

ment of their soldiers to come unto the battle with them. When of his own accord he would not agree thereto, they plucked him by force out of the monastery and brought him against his will unto the field, hoping that the soldiers in the presence of their old most valiant and excellent captain might be less afraid in their hearts and think less upon flight. But he, remembering his profession, being set in the midst of the goodly host would carry only a little rod in his hand: and was slain along with king Egric, and all their army by the setting on of the heathen was killed or scattered.

Now Anna, son to Eni, of the king's blood, was their successor in the kingdom, a man of great virtue and the father of a virtuous issue, of whom we must speak in their proper time hereafter: and this king himself also was afterwards slain of the same heathen captain of the Marchmen, by whom too his predecessors were slain.

CHAPTER XIX [1]

How Fursa builded a monastery among the East English ; and of his visions and holiness, and how his flesh remaining after his death uncorrupted provided witness for him [*c*. 630–648].

But in the time that Sigbert yet held the crown of his kingdom; there came over from Ireland a holy man called Fursa, renowned for his sayings and doings and, moreover, notable for his excellent virtues, desiring to lead a pilgrim's life in the Lord's quarrel, wheresoever he might find himself occasion.

[1] The bulk of this chapter is taken from the Latin life of St. Fursa, which Bede refers to.

provinciam Orientalium pervenisset Anglorum, susceptus est honorifice a rege praefato et solitum sibi
opus evangelizandi exsequens, multos et exemplo
virtutis et incitamento sermonis, vel incredulos ad
Christum convertit, vel iam credentes amplius in
fide atque amore Christi confirmavit.

Ubi quadam infirmitate corporis arreptus, angelica
meruit visione perfrui, in qua admonitus est coepto
verbi ministerio sedulus insistere, vigiliisque con-
suetis et orationibus indefessus incumbere; eo quod
certus sibi exitus, sed incerta eiusdem exitus esset
hora futura, dicente Domino: "Vigilate itaque,
quia nescitis diem neque horam." Qua visione
confirmatus, curavit locum monasterii, quem a
praefato rege Sigbercto acceperat, velocissime con-
struere, ac regularibus instituere disciplinis. Erat
autem monasterium silvarum,[1] et maris vicinitate
amoenum, constructum in castro quodam, quod
lingua Anglorum Cnobheresburg, id est, urbs Cnob-
heri vocatur; quod deinde rex provinciae illius
Anna, ac nobiles quique augustioribus aedificiis ac
donariis adornarunt. Erat autem vir iste de nobilissimo genere Scottorum, sed longe animo quam carne
nobilior. Ab ipso tempore pueritiae suae curam non
modicam lectionibus sacris simul et monasticis exhi-
bebat disciplinis, et, quod maxime sanctos decet,
cuncta quae agenda didicerat, sollicitus agere curabat.

---

[1] for *silvanum*, Pl.

---

[1] Matt. xxv. 13.   [2] Burgh Castle near Yarmouth.

Who coming to the country of the East English was honourably received of the said king, and pursuing his accustomed work of preaching the Gospel he wrought with many, both by the example of his goodness and the urgency of his preaching, either converting unbelievers to Christ or strengthening further in the faith and love of Christ them that already believed.

And being seized there with a certain sickness of body he was counted worthy to have the joy of an angelic vision wherein he was warned to press on earnestly in the ministry of the word, which he had begun, and persevere unweariedly in his accustomed watching and praying; for that his end was certain, but the coming hour of the same end was uncertain, according to the saying of the Lord:[1] " Watch therefore, for ye know not the day nor the hour." Being strengthened with which vision he hastened with all speed to build up a monastery in the place king Sigbert had given him and to give instruction therein to regular discipline. Now the monastery was pleasantly situated for the woods and sea adjoining, being erected in a castle which in the tongue of the English is called Cnobheresburg, that is the city of Cnobhere;[2] which afterwards Anna the king of that country and all the noble men enriched with buildings of more majesty and with offerings. Moreover, this Fursa came of the noblest race of the Scots, but he was far nobler of mind than of birth of the flesh. From the very time of his childhood he gave no small pains to the reading of the Scriptures and monastical discipline, and as especially becometh holy men, all things that he had learned ought to be done, he was diligent in endeavouring to execute.

Quid multa? Procedente tempore et ipse sibi monasterium in quo liberius caelestibus studiis vacaret, construxit: ubi correptus infirmitate, sicut libellus de vita eius conscriptus sufficienter edocet, raptus est e corpore: et a vespera usque ad galli cantum corpore exutus, angelicorum agminum et aspectus intueri, et laudes beatas meruit audire. Referre autem erat solitus, quod aperte eos inter alia resonare audiret: " Ibunt sancti de virtute in virtutem." Et iterum: " Videbitur Deus deorum in Sion." Qui reductus in corpore, et die tertia rursum eductus, vidit non solum maiora beatorum gaudia, sed et maxima malignorum spirituum certamina, qui crebris accusationibus improbi, iter illi caeleste intercludere contendebant; nec tamen protegentibus eum angelis quicquam proficiebant: de quibus omnibus si quis plenius scire vult, id est, quanta fraudis sollertia daemones et actus eius et verba superflua, et ipsas etiam cogitationes, quasi in libro descriptas, replicaverint; quae ab angelis sanctis, quae a viris iustis sibi inter angelos apparentibus laeta vel tristia cognoverit, legat ipsum, de quo dixi, libellum vitae eius, et multum ex illo, ut reor, profectus spiritalis accipiet.

In quibus tamen unum est, quod et nos in hac Historia ponere multis commodum duximus. Cum ergo in altum esset elatus, iussus est ab angelis qui eum ducebant respicere in mundum. At ille oculos

---

[1] Cf. 2 Cor. xii. 2.   [2] Ps. lxxxiv. 7.

Why make a long story? In process of time he both builded himself a monastery wherein he might with more liberty attend to the study of heavenly things: and therein being stricken with sickness he was taken out of the body,[1] as the book written of his life doth sufficiently testify: and from evening until cockcrow being out of the body he was thought worthy to behold the sight of the angelical company, and to hear their blessed thanksgivings. Further, he was wont to tell that among other things he openly heard them sing: "Holy men shall go from virtue to virtue." [2] And again: "The God of gods shall be seen in Sion." And this man, being restored again to the body and within three days after taken out again, saw not only greater joys of the blessed, but also mighty conflicts of wicked spirits which without rest went about to stop him of his journey toward heaven with their often accusations, but yet by the warding of the angels availed naught against him: of all the which things if any listeth more at large to be instructed, as with what spiteful subtleties the evil spirits unfolded his doings and superfluous words as well as his very thoughts, as if they had been written in a book; what glad and heavy tidings he learned of the holy angels, and what things of righteous men appearing unto him amongst the angels, let him read the little book itself of his life, of which I have spoken, and he shall receive therefrom, as I think, much spiritual advantage.

Among the which yet one thing there is that we have thought profitable to many to set down in this History. At what time then he was carried away heavenward, he was commanded of the angels who conducted him, to look back upon the world.

in inferiora deflectens, vidit quasi vallem tenebrosam
subtus se in imo positam. Vidit et quatuor ignes in
aere, non multo ab invicem spatio distantes. Et
interrogans angelos, qui essent hi ignes, audivit hos
esse ignes qui mundum succendentes essent con-
sumpturi. Unum mendacii, cum hoc quod in bap-
tismo abrenunciare nos Satanae et omnibus operibus
eius promisimus, minime implemus: alterum cupidi-
tatis, cum mundi divitias amori caelestium praepo-
nimus: tertium dissensionis, cum animos proxi-
morum, etiam in supervacuis rebus offendere non
formidamus: quartum impietatis, cum infirmiores
spoliare, et eis fraudem facere pro nihilo ducimus.
Crescentes vero paulatim ignes usque ad invicem sese
extenderunt, atque in immensam adunati sunt
flammam. Cumque adpropinquassent, pertimescens
ille dicit angelo: " Domine, ecce ignis mihi adpro-
pinquat." At ille: " Quod non incendisti," inquit,
" non ardebit in te: nam etsi terribilis iste ac grandis
esse rogus videtur, tamen iuxta merita operum
singulos examinat; quia uniuscuiusque cupiditas in
hoc igne ardebit. Sicut enim quis ardet in corpore
per inlicitam voluptatem, ita solutus corpore ardebit
per debitam poenam." Tunc vidit unum de tribus
angelis, qui sibi in tota utraque visione ductores
adfuerunt, praecedentem ignes flammae dividere, et
duos ab utroque latere circumvolantes, ab ignium se
periculo defendere. Vidit autem et daemones per

---

[1] *i.e.* huge. *Howgy* is still used in south-country dialects.
[2] Cf. 1 Cor. iii. 13.

Whereon he, bending down his eyes to the things below him, saw as if it were a dark valley lying underneath him at the bottom. He saw too in the air four fires not far distant one from the other. And asking the angels what fires these were, he was told that these were the fires which should kindle and consume the world. One was the fire of lying, when we no way fulfil the promise which we have made in baptism to renounce Satan and all his works. The second is the fire of covetousness, when we prefer the riches of the world before the love of heavenly matters: the third is the fire of debate, when we stick not to offend the mind of our neighbour even in trifling matters: the fourth is the fire of pitilessness, when we think it a light matter to despoil them that are weaker and to do them injury. These fires truly increasing by little and little reached so far to one another that they were joined together into one howgy[1] flame. And when they had approached nigh unto him, he said to the angel in great fear: " Lord, behold! the fire draweth to me." Then the angel said: " That which thou hast not kindled shall not burn in thee: for though that furnace there seemeth dreadful and howgy, yet it trieth everyone according to the deserts of his works; because the desire that each one hath shall burn in this fire. For as a man burneth in the body by unlawful inclination, so, when freed from the body, he shall burn by deserved pain."[2] Then he saw one of the three angels (which in both his visions throughout were with him as his guides) to go before and divide the flames, and the other two to fly round on either side and ward him from the danger of the fires. Moreover, he saw the devils flying through the fire heap up

421

ignem volantes, incendia bellorum contra iustos
struere. Sequuntur adversus ipsum accusationes
malignorum, defensiones spirituum bonorum, co-
piosior caelestium agminum visio; sed et virorum de
sua natione sanctorum, quos olim sacerdotii gradu
non ignobiliter potitos, fama iam vulgante, compererat; a quibus non pauca, quae vel ipsi, vel omnibus
qui audire vellent, multum salubria essent, audivit.
Qui cum verba finissent, et cum angelicis spiritibus
ipsi quoque ad caelos redirent, remanserunt cum
beato Furseo tres angeli, de quibus diximus, qui eum
ad corpus referrent. Cumque praefato igni maximo
adpropiarent, divisit quidem angelus, sicut prius,
ignem flammae. Sed vir Dei ubi ad patefactam
usque inter flammas ianuam pervenit, arripientes
inmundi spiritus unum de eis, quos in ignibus torre-
bant, iactaverunt in eum, et contingentes humerum
maxillamque eius incenderunt: cognovitque hominem, et quia vestimentum eius morientis acceperit,
ad memoriam reduxit. Quem angelus sanctus
statim adprehendens, in ignem reiecit. Dicebatque
hostis malignus: " Nolite repellere quem ante suscepistis: nam sicut bona eius peccatoris suscepistis,
ita et de poenis eius participes esse debetis." Con-
tradicens angelus: " Non," inquit, " propter avari-
tiam, sed propter salvandam eius animam suscepit: "
cessavitque ignis. Et conversus ad eum angelus:
" Quod incendisti," inquit, " hoc arsit in te. Si
enim huius viri in peccatis suis mortui pecuniam non

the burnings of wars against the just. After, follow
the accusations of the wicked spirits against himself,
the defence of the good spirits, a more abundant
sight of the heavenly company; moreover, too, the
sight of holy men of his own nation who had formerly
held the degree of priesthood not unworthily, as he
had learned by report already being spread abroad;
of whom he heard not a few things, such as to be
very profitable either for himself or for all that should
be ready to hear. Who, after they had ended their
communication and returned to heaven themselves
also with the angelic spirits, there remained with
blessed Fursa the three angels, of whom we have
spoken, to bring him back to the body. And when
they approached the great foresaid fire, the angel in
deed parted the fire of the flame as before. But
when the man of God was come to the entrance
opened onward between the flames, the unclean
spirits snatching up one of them which they tormented in the fires, threw him at Fursa and touching
him burned his shoulder and cheek: and he knew the
person and recalled to memory that at his death he
had taken of him a garment. And the holy angel,
immediately taking hold of the tormented soul,
threw him again to the fire. And the wicked enemy
saith: "Repel him not now whom ye received
before! for as ye took the goods of that sinner, so
ought ye also to take part of his pains." Unto whom
the angel answering saith: "He took it not of
covetousness but for the sake of saving the other's
soul:" and the fire ceased. And the angel turning
to Fursa said: "This that thou hast kindled hath
burned in thee. For if thou hadst not taken the
money of this man dead in his sins, neither would

423

accepisses, nec poena eius in te arderet." Et plura
locutus, quid erga salutem eorum qui ad mortem
poeniterent, esset agendum, salubri sermone docuit.
Qui postmodum in corpore restitutus, omni vitae
suae tempore signum incendii quod in anima pertulit,
visibile cunctis in humero maxillaque portavit:
mirumque in modum quod anima in occulto passa
sit, caro palam praemonstrabat. Curabat autem
semper, sicut et antea facere consuerat, omnibus
opus virtutum et exemplis ostendere et praedicare
sermonibus. Ordinem autem visionum suarum, illis
solummodo qui propter desiderium compunctionis
interrogabant, exponere volebat. Superest adhuc
frater quidam senior monasterii nostri qui narrare
solet, dixisse sibi quendam multum veracem ac
religiosum hominem, quod ipsum Furseum viderit in
provincia Orientalium Anglorum, illasque visiones ex
ipsius ore audierit: adiiciens quia tempus hiemis
fuerit acerrimum, et glacie constrictum, cum sedens
in tenui veste vir, ita inter dicendum propter magnitu-
dinem [1] memorati timoris vel suavitatis, quasi in
media aestatis caumate sudaverit.

Cum ergo, ut ad superiora redeamus, multis annis
in Scottia verbum Dei omnibus adnuntians, tumultus
inruentium turbarum non facile ferret, relictis omnibus quae habere videbatur, ab ipsa quoque insula
patria discessit: et paucis cum fratribus per Brettones
in provinciam Anglorum devenit, ibique praedicans
verbum, ut diximus, monasterium nobile construxit.
Quibus rite gestis, cupiens se ab omnibus saeculi

---

[1] For *multitudinem*, Pl.

---

[1] *I.e.* Ireland, cf. p. 17.

his pains burn in thee." And with more words he
taught him in wholesome discourse what was to be
done concerning their salvation which did repent in
the hour of death. And he afterwards being restored
to the body bore all the time of his life the sign of
the burning which he suffered in soul, evident to all
men in his shoulder and cheek: and the flesh marvellously openly shewed that which the soul privately
suffered. But he endeavoured ever after, as he was
also wont before, both by example to shew to all men
the work of a virtuous life and to preach it in his
words. Moreover, the due course of his visions he
was willing to set forth only to them who of longing
brought of prick of conscience used to question him.
There remaineth yet a certain elder brother of our
monastery, who is wont to relate that a certain very
truthful and devout man told him, that he saw Fursa
in person in the country of the East English and
heard of his own mouth these visions: adding thereto
that it was bitter time of winter and frostbound,
when this man, sitting but in a slight garment as he
recounted the tale, through the great fear and delight
conceived by the remembrance thereof, did so sweat
as if it had been in the middle of the heat of summer.

When then, to return to former matters, Fursa,
preaching the word of God to all many years in
Scotland,[1] did not easily endure the commotion of the
crowds that pressed in upon him, he left all that he
seemed to have and departed also from the very island
that was his native country: and with a few brethren
came from thence through the Britons to the country
of the English, and there preaching the word (as we
touched before), he builded a noble monastery. All
which things duly performed, desiring to abandon

425

huius, et ipsius quoque monasterii negotiis alienare,
reliquit monasterii et animarum curam fratri suo
Fullano, et presbyteris Gobbano et Dicullo, et ipse
ab omnibus mundi rebus liber, in anchoretica con-
versatione vitam finire disposuit. Habuit alterum
fratrem, vocabulo Ultanum, qui de monasterii pro-
batione diuturna, ad heremiticam pervenerat vitam.
Hunc ergo solus petens, annum totum cum eo in
continentia et orationibus, in quotidianis manuum
vixit laboribus.

Dein turbatam incursione gentilium provinciam
videns, et monasteriis quoque periculum imminere
praevidens, dimissis ordinate omnibus, navigavit
Galliam, ibique a rege Francorum Hloduio, vel
patricio Ercunualdo honorifice susceptus, monasterium construxit in loco Latineaco nominato, ac
non multo post infirmitate correptus, diem clausit
ultimum. Cuius corpus idem Ercunualdus patricius
accipiens, servavit in porticu quodam ecclesiae,
quam in villa sua, cui nomen est Perrona, faciebat,
donec ipsa ecclesia dedicaretur. Quod dum post
dies viginti septem esset factum, et corpus ipsum de
porticu ablatum, prope altare esset recondendum,
inventum est ita inlesum, ac si eadem hora de hac
luce fuisset egressus. Sed et post annos quatuor,
constructa domuncula cultiore receptui corporis
eiusdem, ad orientem altaris adhuc sine macula
corruptionis inventum, ibidem digno cum honore

---

[1] A bishop.
[2] Afterwards abbot of the monastery of Péronne and died 686.
[3] The men of Mercia under Penda.
[4] Clovis II, 638–656.
[5] Mayor of the palace of Neustria, 640–657.

all the business of this world and also that of the
monastery itself, he left the charge of the monastery
and care of souls to his brother Foillan[1] and to Gobban
and Dicul, priests, and purposed himself, being free
from all the things of the world, to end his days in
the life of an anchorite. He had a second brother,
called Ultan,[2] who after long proof and trial of the
monastery had gone to lead the life of an eremit.
To him then Fursa went alone, living a whole year
with him in continence and prayer and working
daily with his hands.

After, seeing the country disquieted by the
invasion of the heathen [3] and forecasting danger to
threaten also the monasteries, leaving all things in
good order, he sailed to France, and there being
honourably received of Clovis,[4] the king of the
Franks, and of Ercinwald, the patrician,[5] he builded
a monastery in a place called Latineacum,[6] and not
long after being seized with sickness he brought his
last day to a close. Whose body the same Ercinwald,
the patrician, taking kept it in a side chapel of the
church which he was making in his township which
has the name of Péronne, until the church itself
should be dedicated. Which being done 27 days
after and the body itself taken from the side chapel
to be laid anew by the altar, it was found to be so
uninjured as if the man had the same hour departed from the light of day. Moreover, four years
after a shrine being erected at the east side of the
altar, where the body of the same man should more
honourably be tombed, it was found still without
blemish of corruption and transferred to the same
spot with fitting respect; in the which place it is

[6]. Lagny-sur-Marne.

translatum est; ubi merita illius multis saepe constat
Deo operante claruisse virtutibus. Haec de corporis
eius incorruptione breviter attigimus, ut quanta
esset viri sublimitas legentibus notius existeret.
Quae cuncta in libello eius sufficientius sed et de aliis
commilitonibus ipsius, quisque legerit inveniet.

CAP. XX

*Ut defuncto Honorio, pontificatu sit functus Deusdedit;
et qui in tempore illo Orientalium Anglorum, qui
Hrofensis ecclesiae fuerint antistites.*

INTEREA defuncto Felice Orientalium Anglorum
episcopo post decem et septem annos accepti episcopatus, Honorius loco eius ordinavit Thomam diaconum
eius de provincia Gyruiorum: et hoc post quinque
annos sui episcopatus de hac vita subtracto, Berct-
gilsum, cognomine Bonifatium de provincia Cantuariorum loco eius substituit. Et ipse quoque Honorius,
postquam metas sui cursus implevit, ex hac luce
migravit anno ab incarnatione Domini sexcentesimo
quinquagesimo tertio, pridie Kalendarum Octobrium: et cessante episcopatu per annum et sex
menses, electus est archiepiscopus cathedrae Doruvernensis sextus Deusdedit de gente Occidentalium
Saxonum: quem ordinaturus venit illuc Ithamar,
antistes ecclesiae Hrofensis. Ordinatus est autem
die septimo Kalendarum Aprilium, et rexit ecclesiam
annos novem, menses septem, et duos dies; et ipse,

---

[1] Living on the borders of the Fenland.
[2] The first native archbishop. His native name is said to
have been Frithonas.

well known that his merits have been often renowned with many mighty works by the power of God. Thus much of the incorruption of his body we have briefly touched, that the reader might more clearly understand the greatness of the man's excellency. All which things, and moreover of other his fellow-soldiers, whoso readeth shall find more ample mention made in the little book of his life.

CHAPTER XX

How after the death of Honorius, Deusdedit had the charge of the bishopric ; and who in that time were bishops of the East English and of the church of Rochester [654].

In the meantime Felix, the bishop of the East English, having died after 17 years holding of the bishopric, Honorius ordained in his place Thomas, the deacon of Felix, of the province of the Gyrwas: [1] and when he, after five years of his bishopric, was taken from this life, Honorius put in his room Bertgils, surnamed Boniface, a Kentish man born. And Honorius also the archbishop, after he had completed the measure of his course, passed from the light of life in the 653rd year of the Lord's incarnation, the last day of September: and Deusdedit of the nation of the West Saxons [2] was chosen the sixth archbishop of the cathedral of Canterbury, the see being vacant for a year and six months: for whose ordination Ithamar, bishop of the church of Rochester, came to Canterbury. Now he was ordained the 26th of March and governed the church 9 years, 7 months [3] and 2 days;

[3] One reading gives 4 months. Deusdedit died July 664. His election was not the same date as his consecration.

defuncto Ithamar, consecravit pro eo Damianum qui
de genere Australium Saxonum erat oriundus.

CAP. XXI

*Ut provincia Mediterraneorum Anglorum sub rege Peada
Christiana sit facta.*

His temporibus Middilangli, id est, Mediterranei
Angli, sub principe Peada filio Pendan regis, fidem
et sacramenta veritatis perceperunt: qui cum esset
iuvenis optimus, ac regis nomine ac persona dignis-
simus, praelatus est a patre regno gentis illius;
venitque ad regem Nordanhymbrorum Osuiu, postulans filiam eius Alchfledam sibi coniugem dari: neque
aliter quod petebat impetrare potuit, nisi fidem
Christi ac baptisma, cum gente cui praeerat, acciperet.
At ille audita praedicatione veritatis, et promissione
regni caelestis, speque resurrectionis ac futurae immortalitatis, libenter se Christianum fieri velle confessus est, etiamsi virginem non acciperet: persuasus
maxime ad percipiendam fidem a filio regis Osuiu,
nomine Alchfrido, qui erat cognatus et amicus eius,
habens sororem ipsius coniugem, vocabulo Cynibur-
gam, filiam Pendan regis.

Baptizatus est ergo a Finano episcopo, cum omnibus
qui secum venerant comitibus ac militibus eorumque
famulis universis, in vico regis inlustri qui vocatur
Ad Murum. Et acceptis quatuor presbyteris, qui
ad docendam baptizandamque gentem illius et
eruditione et vita videbantur idonei, multo cum

---

[1] In the East Midlands from the borders of Essex to
Leicester.
[2] *Cognatus, cognata* are used for brother-in-law, sister-in-law.

and he it was who after the death of Ithamar
consecrated in his place Damian, a Sussex man born.

CHAPTER XXI

*How the province of the Uplandish English was made
Christian under king Peada* [653].

AT this time the Middle Englishmen,[1] that is the
Uplandish English, received the faith and the
mysteries of truth under their prince Peada, the son
of king Penda: who being an excellent young man,
and worthy of the name and dignity of king, was
of his father advanced to the government of that
nation; and he came to Oswy king of the Northumbrians, requiring Alchfled his daughter to be given
him to wife: but could in no otherwise obtain his suit
unless he would receive the faith of Christ and
baptism, together with the nation over which he was
set. Thereon, having heard the preaching of the
truth, the promise of the heavenly kingdom and the
hope of resurrection and immortality to come, he
willingly avouched that he was ready to become a
Christian, even though he should not win the maiden:
being chiefly persuaded to receive the faith by king
Oswy's son, called Alchfrid, who was his brother-in-
law [2] and friend, having to wife Peada's sister, by
name Cyneburg, king Penda's daughter.

He was therefore baptized by Finan the bishop,
with all the retainers and thanes who had come
with him, and the whole of their servants, in a famous
town of the king's which is called At Wall.[3] And he
returned home with much joy, having taken four
priests who seemed fit both by learning and conduct

[3] Walton or Walbottle near Newcastle.

gaudio reversus est.   Erant autem presbyteri Cedd, et Adda, et Betti, et Diuma, quorum ultimus natione Scottus, ceteri fuere de Anglis.   Adda autem erat frater Uttan, presbyteri inlustris, et abbatis monasterii quod vocatur Ad Caprae Caput, cuius supra meminimus.   Venientes ergo in provinciam memorati sacerdotes cum principe, praedicabant verbum, et libenter auditi sunt, multique quotidie et nobilium et infirmorum, abrenunciata sorde idolatriae, fidei sunt fonte abluti.

Nec prohibuit Penda rex, quin etiam in sua, hoc est, Merciorum natione, verbum, si qui vellent audire, praedicaretur.   Quin potius odio habebat, et despiciebat eos, quos fide Christi imbutos, opera fidei non habere deprehendit, dicens contemnendos esse eos et miseros qui Deo suo in quem crederent obedire contemnerent.   Coepta sunt haec biennio ante mortem Pendan regis.   Ipso autem occiso, cum Osuiu rex Christianus regnum eius acciperet ut in sequentibus dicemus, factus est Diuma unus ex praefatis quatuor sacerdotibus episcopus Mediterraneorum Anglorum simul et Merciorum, ordinatus a Finano episcopo.   Paucitas enim sacerdotum cogebat unum antistitem duobus populis praefici. Qui cum pauco sub tempore non paucam Domino plebem adquisisset, defunctus est apud Mediterraneos Anglos, in regione quae vocatur Infeppingum: suscepitque pro illo episcopatum Ceollach, et ipse de natione Scottorum, qui non multo post, relicto episcopatu, reversus est ad insulam Hii, ubi plurimorum caput et arcem Scotti habuere coenobiorum:

---

[1] Gateshead, on the Tyne.
[2] Not identified, probably in Mercia.

to teach and baptize his nation. Now the priests were Cedd, Adda, Betti and Diuma, of whom the last was a Scotsman born, the rest were English. Now Adda was brother of Utta, the notable priest and abbot of the monastery which is called At Goat's Head,[1] of whom we have before made mention. The foresaid priests therefore entering the province with the prince preached the word and were gladly heard, and many daily, as well noble as of the base sort, renouncing the filth of idolatry were cleansed in the font of faith.

Neither did king Penda withstand the preaching of the word even in his own nation, that is to say, the Marchmen, if any would hear it. Nay, he rather hated and despised those instructed in the faith of Christ, whom he discovered to have not the works of faith, saying that such men were worthily to be spited and wretched, which regarded not to obey their God in whom they believed. These things began two years before the death of king Penda. But after Penda was slain, when Oswy, a Christian king, succeeded to his kingdom as we shall hereafter tell. Diuma, one of the four foresaid priests, was ordained by bishop Finan to be bishop of the Uplandish English as well as of the Marchmen. For the scarcity of priests made that one bishop was set over the two nations. Who, after winning to the Lord in short time no small number of folk, died among the Uplandish Englishmen in the country that is called Infeppingum:[2] and Ceollach succeeded to the bishopric in his room, himself also a Scottish man born, who, not long after, leaving the bishopric, returned to the island of Iona, where the Scots had the chief and principal of very many convents: his

433

succedente illi in episcopatum Trumheri viro religioso, et monachica vita instituto, natione quidem Anglo, sed a Scottis ordinato episcopo; quod temporibus Vulfheri regis de quo in sequentibus dicemus, factum est.

CAP. XXII

Ut Orientales Saxones fidem quam dudum abiecerant, sub rege Sigbercto, praedicante Ceddo receperint.

Eo tempore etiam Orientales Saxones fidem quam olim expulso Mellito antistite abiecerant, instantia regis Osuiu receperunt. Erat enim rex eiusdem gentis Sigberct, qui post Sigberctum cognomento Parvum regnavit, amicus eiusdem Osuiu regis, qui cum frequenter ad eum in provinciam Nordanhymbrorum veniret, solebat eum hortari ad intelligendum deos esse non posse qui hominum manibus facti essent; dei creandi materiam lignum vel lapidem esse non posse, quorum recisurae vel igni absumerentur, vel in vasa quaelibet humani usus formarentur, vel certe despectui habita foras proiicerentur, et pedibus conculcata in terram verterentur. Deum potius intelligendum maiestate incomprehensibilem, humanis oculis invisibilem, omnipotentem, aeternum, qui caelum et terram et humanum genus creasset, regeret, et iudicaturus esset orbem in aequitate; cuius sedes aeterna non in vili et caduco

---

[1] Essex.

[2] P. 229.

[3] Sigbert the Good, to be distinguished from Sigbert the Learned, king of East Anglia, p. 413.

successor in the bishopric being Trumhere, a devout
man and brought up in monastic life, an Englishman
born but ordained bishop of the Scots; which thing
took place in the days of king Wulfhere, of whom we
shall speak hereafter.

CHAPTER XXII

*How the East Saxons at the preaching of Cedd received
again under king Sigbert the faith which they had
before abandoned* [653].

At that time also the East Saxons [1] by the impor-
tunity of king Oswy received again the faith which
formerly, expelling the bishop Mellitus out of the
country, they had abandoned.[2]   For the king of
the said nation was Sigbert [3] (who reigned after the
Sigbert surnamed the Little), a friend of the same
king Oswy who, when Sigbert oftentimes came to
the country of the Northumbrians to visit him, used
eftsoons to persuade with him to understand that
such could not be gods which had been made with
men's hands; that wood or stone could not be matter
to make a god, the pieces whereof were either wasted
with fire, or served to make any kind of vessels for
the use of man, or anyway being regarded as naught
worth were cast forth abroad and trodden underfoot
and turned into earth.   God rather,[4] said he, must be
understood to be of majesty incomprehensible, to
men's eyes invisible, almighty, everlasting, who had
made heaven and earth and mankind, governed them
and should judge the world in equity; whose everlasting mansion must be believed to be, not in base

[4] This part reads like an extract from or paraphrase of a
creed.

435

metallo, sed in caelis esset credenda: meritoque
intelligendum, quia omnes qui voluntatem eius a quo
creati sunt discerent et facerent, aeterna ab illo praemia essent percepturi. Haec et huiusmodi multa
cum rex Osuiu regi Sigbercto amicali et quasi fraterno
consilio saepe inculcaret, tandem iuvante amicorum
consensu credidit, et facto cum suis consilio, cum
exhortatione, faventibus cunctis, et adnuentibus fidei,
baptizatus est cum eis a Finano episcopo in villa regia
cuius supra meminimus, quae cognominatur Ad
Murum. Est enim iuxta murum, quo olim Romani
Brittaniam insulam praecinxere, duodecim millibus
passuum a mari orientali secreta.

Igitur rex Sigberct aeterni regni iam civis effectus,
temporalis sui regni sedem repetiit, postulans ab
Osuiu rege ut aliquos sibi doctores daret, qui gentem
suam ad fidem Christi converterent ac fonte salutari
abluerent. At ille mittens ad provinciam Mediterraneorum Anglorum, clamavit ad se virum Dei Cedd,
et dato illi socio altero quodam presbytero, misit
praedicare verbum genti Orientalium Saxonum.
Ubi cum omnia perambulantes multam Domino
ecclesiam congregassent, contigit quodam tempore
eundem Cedd redire domum, ac pervenire ad ecclesiam Lindisfaronensem, propter conloquium Finani
episcopi; qui ubi prosperatum ei opus evangelii
comperit, fecit eum episcopum in gentem Orientalium

---

[1] P. 431.

[2] They must have been Scoto-Celtic, but no question is
raised of a flaw in Cedd's ordination, such as Theodore found
in the ordination of Chad, iv. 2.

and perishable metal but in the heavens: and rightly must be so understanded, because all such as learned and performed the will of Him by Whom they were created should receive of Him everlasting rewards. Such things and many of such sort being with friendly and as it were brotherly counsel from time to time pressed upon king Sigbert by king Oswy, at length (with the help of his friends agreeing thereto) he came to believe, and advice being taken with his company and having encouragement (they all approving and consenting to the faith), he was baptized along with them of Finan the bishop in the royal township, of which we have made mention above, which is named At Wall.[1] For it is nigh unto the wall wherewith the Romans formerly fenced the island of Britain to protect it, at a distance of 12 miles from the East sea.

King Sigbert then, being now made a citizen of the everlasting kingdom, returned to the seat of his earthly kingdom, requiring of king Oswy that he would give him some teachers to convert his people to the faith of Christ and cleanse them in the health-giving font. Thereat he, sending to the country of the Uplandish Englishmen, called unto him Cedd the man of God, and giving him a certain second priest to be his companion, sent them to preach the word to the nation of the East Saxons. Where, when going about all that country they had collected together a mighty Church for the Lord, it befell upon a time that the same Cedd departed home again and came to the church of Lindisfarne to talk with Finan the bishop; who, when he found that the work of preaching the Gospel had prospered with Cedd, called unto him two other bishops [2] for the

437

Saxonum, vocatis ad se in ministerium ordinationis
aliis duobus episcopis. Qui accepto gradu episcopatus rediit ad provinciam, et maiore auctoritate
coeptum [1] opus explens, fecit per loca ecclesias,
presbyteros et diaconos ordinavit, qui se in verbo
fidei et ministerio baptizandi adiuvarent, maxime
in civitate quae lingua Saxonum Ythancaestir
appellatur, sed et in illa quae Tilaburg cognominatur:
quorum prior locus est in ripa Pentae amnis, secundus
in ripa Tamensis: in quibus collecto examine famu-
lorum Christi, disciplinam vitae regularis, in quantum
rudes adhuc capere poterant, custodiri [2] docuit.

Cumque tempore non pauco in praefata provincia,
gaudente rege, congaudente universo populo, vitae
caelestis institutio quotidianum sumeret augmentum,
contigit ipsum regem instigante omnium bonorum
inimico, propinquorum suorum manu interfici. Erant
autem duo germani fratres qui hoc facinus patrarunt;
qui cum interrogarentur quare hoc facerent, nil
aliud respondere potuerunt, nisi ob hoc se iratos
fuisse et inimicos regi, quod ille nimium suis parcere
soleret inimicis, et factas ab eis iniurias mox obse-
crantibus placida mente dimitteret. Talis erat culpa
regis pro qua occideretur, quod evangelica praecepta
devoto corde servaret: in qua tamen eius morte
innoxia, iuxta praedictum viri Dei, vera est eius culpa
punita. Habuerat enim unus ex his, qui eum occi-

---

[1] For *captum*, Pl.   [2] For *custodire*, Pl.

---

[1] Called Othona by the Romans, in the tongue of land
between the Blackwater and Crouch rivers in Essex, now
St. Peter's-on-the-Wall.

[2] Tilbury.

[3] Pant or Blackwater.

ministry of ordination, and made Cedd bishop unto
the nation of the East Saxons. And he, having now
taken the degree of bishop, returned to his province,
and perfecting with more authority the work he had
begun, he made churches in divers places, ordained
priests and deacons to aid him in the word of faith
and the ministry of baptizing, especially in the city
which in the Saxon tongue is called Ythancaestir,[1]
and, moreover, in that which is named Tilaburg:[2] of
which the first is a place on the bank of the river
Penta,[3] the second on the bank of the Thames: in
which places, assembling together a multitude of
servants of Christ, he instructed them for the keeping
of the rules of monastic life, as far as their tender
capacity could then conceive.

And when in no small time the instruction of
heavenly living gat daily increase in the aforesaid
province, to the joy of the king and the joy of the
whole people with him, it fell out that, by the instinct
of the enemy of all good, the king was himself murdered by the hands of his own alliance. Now the
executors of this heinous act were two brothers
german; who, being examined upon what motion
they committed this act, were able to answer nothing
else save that they were angered with the king and
made his enemies for this cause, that he was wont to
shew overmuch clemency to his enemies and meekly
to let se offences done by them, when presently they
entreated him. Such was the fault of the king, for
which he was murdered, because with a devout heart
he observed the commandments of the Gospel: in
the which his guiltless death nevertheless, a true
fault of his was punished, according as the man of
God had foretold him. For one of these retainers

439

derunt comitibus, inlicitum coniugium, quod cum
episcopus prohibere et corrigere non posset, excom-
municavit eum, atque omnibus qui se audire vellent
praecepit ne domum eius intraret neque de cibis
illius acciperent. Contempsit autem rex praeceptum, et rogatus a comite, intravit epulaturus domum
eius : qui cum abiisset, obviavit ei antistes. At rex
intuens eum, mox tremefactus desiluit equo, ceci-
ditque ante pedes eius, veniam reatus postulans.
Nam et episcopus pariter desiluit : sederat enim et ipse
in equo. Iratus autem tetigit regem iacentem virga
quam tenebat manu, et pontificali auctoritate pro-
testatus : " Dico tibi," inquit, " quia noluisti te
continere a domo perditi et damnati illius, tu in ipsa
domo mori habes." Sed credendum est quia talis
mors viri religiosi non solum talem culpam diluerit,
sed etiam meritum eius auxerit : quia nimirum ob
causam pietatis, quia propter observantiam man-
datorum Christi contigit.

Successit autem Sigbercto in regnum Suidhelm,
filius Sexbaldi, qui baptizatus est ab ipso Cedde in
provincia Orientalium Anglorum, in vico regio qui
dicitur Rendlaesham, id est, Mansio Rendili ; suscepitque eum ascendentem de fonte sancto Aediluald
rex ipsius gentis Orientalium Anglorum, frater Anna
regis eorumdem.

who murdered him had lived in unlawful wedlock, and when the bishop was not able to let or amend it, he excommunicated him and commanded all that should be ready to hear him, not to enter that offender's house or partake of his meat. But the king set at nought the sentence of the bishop, and when invited by the retainer, entered his house to feast there: and after departing therefrom he met with the bishop. Thereon the king looking upon him, by and by being much afeared, lighted off from his horse and fell down before the bishop's feet, asking pardon for his offence. For the bishop too lighted off his horse at the same time as the king: for he was himself too on horseback. But in anger he touched the king, as he lay on the ground, with the rod he held in his hand and protested unto him with bishoply authority, saying: "I tell thee, because thou wouldest not refrain from the house of that wicked and damnable person, thou hast to die in that very house." Yet it is to be thought that such a death of a devout man not only did wipe away such a fault but also increased his merit: because he came to his death for his goodness' sake, for observing the commandments of Christ.

Now there succeeded Sigbert in the kingdom, Swidhelm, son to Sexbald, who was baptized by the selfsame Cedd in the province of the East Englishmen in a town of the king's called Rendlesham,[1] that is to say, Rendil's Steading; and Ethelwald king of the selfsame nation of the East English, brother to Anna, former king of the same, lifted him up as he was rising from the sacred font.[2]

---

[1] Rendlesham in Suffolk.   [2] Cf. p. 357.

THE VENERABLE BEDE

CAP. XXIII

*Ut idem episcopus Cedd locum monasterii construendi ab
Oidilualdo rege accipiens, orationibus ac ieiuniis
Domino consecraverit ; et de obitu ipsius.*

Solebat autem idem vir Domini, cum apud Orientales Saxones episcopatus officio fungeretur, saepius
etiam suam, id est, Nordanhymbrorum provinciam
exhortandi gratia revisere : quem cum Oidiluald
filius Osualdi regis, qui in Derorum partibus regnum
habebat, virum sanctum et sapientem, probumque
moribus videret, postulavit eum possessionem terrae
aliquam a se ad construendum monasterium accipere,
in quo ipse rex et frequentius ad deprecandum
Dominum verbumque audiendum advenire, et defunctus sepeliri deberet. Nam et se ipsum fideliter
credidit multum iuvari eorum orationibus quotidianis,
qui illo in loco Domino servirent. Habuerat autem
idem rex secum fratrem germanum eiusdem episcopi,
vocabulo Caelin, virum aeque Deo devotum, qui ipsi
ac familiae ipsius verbum et sacramenta fidei, erat
enim presbyter, ministrare solebat, per cuius notitiam
maxime ad diligendum noscendumque episcopum
pervenit. Favens ergo votis regis antistes elegit
sibi locum monasterii construendi in montibus
arduis ac remotis, in quibus latronum magis latibula
ac lustra ferarum, quam habitacula fuisse videbantur
hominum : ut iuxta prophetiam Isaiae, " in cubilibus,
in quibus prius dracones habitabant, oriretur viror
calami et iunci," id est, fructus bonorum operum ibi

---

[1] Isai. xxxv. 7.

CHAPTER XXIII

How the same bishop Cedd, obtaining a place to build a monastery of king Ethelwald, by prayer and fasting did consecrate it to the Lord ; and of his death [664].

Now the same man of the Lord, in performing the duty of his bishopric among the East Saxons, used also oftentimes to visit again his own country, that is to say, the province of the Northumbrians for the sake of exhortation : whom, when Ethelwald, son to king Oswald, who reigned in the coasts of the Derans, saw to be a holy, wise and virtuous man, he required him to take of his gift a piece of ground towards the building of a monastery wherein the king himself should have to resort to pray to the Lord and hear the word, and be buried when he died.   For he truly believed that he should be much holpen by their daily prayers, who in that place served the Lord. Now the same king had had in his house the brother german of the same bishop, by name Caelin, a man of no less devotion to God, who used to minister the word and sacraments of faith (for he was a priest), to the king and his court, by the knowledge of whom the king came to be acquainted with the bishop and learned to love him.   Agreeing, therefore, to the requests of the king, the bishop chose out a place to erect a monastery in the high desert mountains, where there seemed to be rather starting-holes for thieves and dens for wild beasts than mansion places for men : that according to the prophecy of Isaiah,[1] " in the couches, wherein afore-time dragons had their habitation, might come the green of reeds and rushes," meaning that the fruits

443

nascerentur, ubi prius vel bestiae commorari, vel
homines bestialiter vivere consueverant.

Studens autem vir Domini acceptum monasterii
locum primo precibus ac ieiuniis a pristina flagi-
tiorum sorde purgare, et sic in eo monasterii fundamenta iacere, postulavit a rege, ut sibi totum quadragesimae tempus quod instabat, facultatem ac licentiam ibidem orationis causa demorandi concederet.
Quibus diebus cunctis, excepta Dominica, ieiunium
ad vesperam usque iuxta morem protelans, ne tunc
quidem nisi panis permodicum, et unum ovum galli-
naceum cum parvo lacte aqua mixto percipiebat.
Dicebat enim hanc esse consuetudinem eorum, a
quibus normam disciplinae regularis didicerat, ut
accepta nuper loca ad faciendum monasterium vel
ecclesiam, prius orationibus ac ieiuniis Domino con-
secrent.   Cumque decem dies quadragesimae restar-
ent, venit qui clamaret eum ad regem.   At ille, ne
opus religiosum negotiorum regalium causa inter-
mitteretur, petiit presbyterum suum Cynibillum, qui
etiam frater germanus erat ipsius, pia coepta complere.   Cui cum ille libenter adquiesceret, expleto
studio ieiuniorum et orationis, fecit ibi monasterium,
quod nunc Laestingaeu vocatur, et religiosis moribus,
iuxta ritus Lindisfarnensium ubi educatus erat,
instituit.

Qui cum annis multis et in praefata provincia episcopatum administraret, et huius quoque monasterii

---

[1] The monks of Lindisfarne.
[2] Lastingham near Whitby.

of good works should there spring, where before either beasts or men beastly living had been used to make their abode.

Now the man of the Lord, desiring first by prayer and fasting to cleanse the place he had obtained for the monastery from the former filth of iniquities there committed, and so to set thereon the foundations of the monastery, required of the king that he would grant him opportunity and leave to abide in that same place to pray all the time of the 40 days of Lent that then approached. In all which days, except the Lord's day, prolonging his fast until the evening, as the manner is, not even then did he take aught but a little bread and one hen's egg with a little milk mingled with water. For, as he said, the custom of them of whom he learned the trade of monastical life [1] was that, when places had been newly obtained for making a monastery or a church, they should first consecrate them to the Lord with prayer and fasting. In this his fast, 10 days only remaining of the 40, there came one to call him to the king. But, to the intent the godly work might not be interrupted by occasion of the prince's business, he entreated his priest Cynibill, who was also his brother german, to make an end of the good work begun. And when his brother readily agreed thereto, applying himself to fasting and prayers until they were fulfilled, Cedd made there the monastery which is now called Lastingham,[2] giving it rules and orders of religion according to the practice of Lindisfarne where he was brought up in.

Thus governing many a year both his bishopric in the foresaid province,[3] and keeping the charge of this

[3] Essex.

statutis propositis curam gereret, casu contigit ut ad ipsum monasterium tempore mortalitatis adveniens, tactus ibidem infirmitate corporis, obiret : qui primo quidem foris sepultus est ; tempore autem procedente, in eodem monasterio ecclesia est in honorem beatae Dei genitricis de lapide facta, et in illa corpus ipsius ad dexteram altaris reconditum.

Dedit autem episcopus regendum post se monasterium fratri suo Ceadda, qui postea episcopus factus est, ut in sequentibus dicemus. Quatuor siquidem hi quos diximus, germani fratres, Cedd et Cynibill et Caelin et Caedda, quod raro invenitur, omnes sacerdotes Domini fuere praeclari, et duo ex eis etiam summi sacerdotii gradu functi sunt. Cum ergo episcopum defunctum ac sepultum in provincia Nordanhymbrorum audirent fratres qui in monasterio eius erant in provincia Orientalium Saxonum, venerunt illo de suo monasterio homines circiter triginta, cupientes ad corpus sui patris, aut vivere si sic Deo placeret, aut morientes ibi sepeliri : qui libenter a suis fratribus et commilitonibus suscepti, omnes ibidem superveniente praefatae pestilentiae clade defuncti sunt, excepto uno puerulo, quem orationibus patris sui a morte constat esse servatum. Nam cum multo post haec tempore viveret, et scripturis legendis operam daret, tandem didicit se aqua baptismatis non esse regeneratum, et mox fonte lavacri salutaris ablutus, etiam postmodum ad ordinem presbyterii promotus est, multisque in ecclesia utilis fuit : de quo dubitandum non crediderim, quin inter-

---

[1] Later *priors*.
[2] Plague of 664.
[3] After the Synod of Whitby.
[4] His spiritual father Cedd.

monastery too by setting provosts [1] therein, it came to pass that as he visited the selfsame monastery in the time of a mortal sickness,[2] being taken with illness of body in the same place he died: [3] and at first indeed he was buried abroad, but as time went on, a church being there builded of stone in the honour of the blessed mother of God, his body was taken up and laid therein at the right side of the altar.

Moreover, the bishop left the monastery to be governed after him of his brother Chad who after was made a bishop, as we shall anon declare. For these four brothers german whom we have spoken of, Cedd, Cynibill, Caelin and Chad, were all (which is a rare thing) notable priests of the Lord, and two of them also in the highest degree of the priesthood held the office of bishop. When it was known in the province of Northumberland that their bishop was dead and buried, about 30 brethren of the monastery, which he erected in the province of the East Saxons, came to Lastingham from their own monastery, desiring by the body of their father either to live, if it should so please God, or to die and be buried there: who, being gladly received of their brethren and fellow-soldiers, all died in that spot with the coming upon them of the destruction of the foresaid plague, except one little boy, who (as is well known), was saved from death by the prayers of his father.[4] For living long time after this and giving his time to reading Scripture, he learned at length that he had not been born again of the water of baptism, and, being shortly cleansed by the fount of the health-giving laver, was also afterwards advanced to the order of priest and was profitable to many in the Church: of whom I should not believe it to be

447

cessionibus, ut dixi, sui patris, ad cuius corpus dilectionis ipsius gratia venerat, sit ab articulo mortis retentus, ut et ipse sic mortem evaderet aeternam, et aliis quoque fratribus ministerium vitae ac salutis docendo exhiberet.

CAP. XXIV

Ut provincia Merciorum, occiso rege Penda, fidem Christi susceperit : et Osuiu pro adepta victoria possessiones et territoria ad construenda monasteria dederit.

His temporibus rex Osuiu cum acerbas atque intolerabiles pateretur irruptiones saepedicti regis Merciorum qui fratrem eius occiderat, ad ultimum necessitate cogente promisit se ei innumera et maiora quam credi potest ornamenta regia vel donaria in pretium pacis largiturum, dummodo ille domum rediret, et provincias regni eius usque ad internecionem vastare desineret. Cumque rex perfidus nullatenus precibus illius assensum praeberet, qui totam eius gentem a parvo usque ad magnum delere atque exterminare decreverat, respexit ille ad divinae auxilium pietatis, quo ab impietate barbarica posset eripi : votoque se obligans : " Si paganus," inquit, " nescit accipere nostra donaria, offeramus ei qui novit, Domino Deo nostro." Vovit ergo quia si victor existeret, filiam suam Domino sacra virginitate dicandam offerret ; simul et duodecim posses-

---

doubted but that, as I said, by the intercessions of his father, whose body out of the love he bare him he came to visit, he was held back from the point of death, that he might both himself escape everlasting death and also extend to other brethren the ministry of life and salvation by his doctrine.

CHAPTER XXIV

How the province of the Marchmen received the faith of Christ, Penda their king being slain : and how Oswy for the victory gained gave possessions and lands to the building of monasteries [655–658].

In those days king Oswy, after suffering cruel invasions and grievous to be borne of the often before named king of the Marchmen, who had slain his brother, forced at the last by necessity promised that he would bestow upon him an infinite number of the royal treasures and presents exceeding belief, to purchase peace, provided only he would return home and cease to waste the provinces of Oswy's kingdom even to destruction. And when the unbelieving king yielded nothing in any way to his petition, having determined utterly to root out and destroy the whole nation from the highest to the lowest, Oswy turned him to look for the help of divine mercy, whereby he might be delivered from the pitilessness of his barbarous enemy : and binding himself by a vow he saith : " Sith the heathen knoweth not how to take our presents, let us offer them to him that knoweth, the Lord our God." Therefore he vowed, that [1] if he had the upper hand of his enemy, he would present his daughter to be consecrated in holy

449

siones praediorum ad construenda monasteria donaret: et sic cum paucissimo exercitu se certamini
dedit. Denique fertur quia tricies maiorem pagani
habuerint exercitum; siquidem ipsi triginta legiones
ducibus nobilissimis instructas in bello habuere,
quibus Osuiu rex cum Alchfrido filio, perparvum, ut
dixi, habens exercitum, sed Christo duce confisus
occurrit. Nam alius filius eius Ecgfrid eo tempore
in provincia Merciorum apud reginam Cynuise obses
tenebatur. Filius autem Osualdi regis Oidiluald,
qui eis auxilio esse debuerat, in parte erat adversa-
riorum, eisdemque contra patriam et patruum suum
pugnaturis ductor exstiterat, quamvis ipso tempore
pugnandi sese pugnae subtraxerat, eventumque
discriminis tuto in loco exspectabat. Inito ergo
certamine fugati sunt et caesi pagani, duces regii
triginta qui ad auxilium venerant pene omnes inter-
fecti: in quibus Aedilheri frater Annae regis Orientalium Anglorum qui post eum regnavit, auctor ipse
belli, perditis militibus sive auxiliis interemptus
est:[1] et quia prope fluvium Vinuaed pugnatum est,
qui tunc prae inundantia pluviarum late alveum
suum immo omnes ripas suas transierat, contigit ut
multo plures aqua fugientes, quam bellantes perderet
ensis.

Tunc rex Osuiu, iuxta quod Domino voverat, pro

[1] *est,* Pl.

---

[1] *boclands,* the A.S. rendering, land held by a " book," *i.e.*
a charter, instead of by folk-right according to the laws of
tribal custom. Cf. Oman, p. 379.

[2] Ealdormen and dukes in the A.S. version : *reges* and *reguli*
in Irish annals, Pl.

[3] How this was is not explained by Bede.

[4] Maybe the Went near Leeds, or the Aire.

virginity to the Lord; and would grant twelve estates of bocland [1] withal to the erecting of monasteries: and this being said he prepared himself to battle with a very small army. In short, the army of the heathen is reported to have been thirty times more in number; seeing that it contained thirty legions well appointed in war and governed with most noble princes,[2] against the which king Oswy with Alchfrid his son marched, though with a very small army, as I said, yet with a sure confidence in Christ their captain. For another son of his, Egfrid, was at that time kept in hostage in the province of the Marchmen at the court of queen Cynwise. Moreover, Ethelwald, son of king Oswald, who ought to have stood with his countrymen, was on the side of their enemies and was become a captain for the same when they were to fight against his country and his uncle, although, when the field was begun, at that very time he had withdrawn himself from the fighting and getting him to a hold hard by awaited the issue of the battle. The armies thus meeting therefore and coupling together, the heathen were put to flight and slain, the thirty royal captains which had come to aid them were almost all killed: among the which was Ethelhere, brother to Anna king of the East English, then reigning after his brother, and himself the principal mover [3] of the war, who was slain with loss of his soldiers and alliance: and whereas the field was fought nigh to the river Winwaed,[4] which at that time from abundance of rain had overflowed his bed, nay all his banks to a wide space, it came about that in the flight far more were lost in the water than were slain by the sword in the fighting.

Then king Oswy rendering thanks to God for the

conlata sibi victoria gratias Deo referens, dedit filiam
suam Aelffledam quae vixdum unius anni aetatem
impleverat, perpetua ei virginitate consecrandam:
donatis insuper duodecim possessiunculis terrarum,
in quibus ablato studio militiae terrestris, ad exer-
cendam militiam caelestem, supplicandumque pro
pace gentis eius aeterna, devotioni sedulae monachorum locus facultasque suppeteret. E quibus
videlicet possessiunculis, sex in provincia Derorum,
sex in Berniciorum dedit. Singulae vero possessiones decem erant familiarum, id est, simul omnes
centum viginti. Intravit autem praefata regis
Osuiu filia Deo dedicanda monasterium quod nuncupatur Heruteu, id est, Insula Cervi, cui tunc Hild
abbatissa praefuit: quae post biennium comparata
possessione decem familiarum in loco qui dicitur
Streanaeshalch, ibi monasterium construxit; in quo
memorata regis filia, primo discipula vitae regularis,
deinde etiam magistra exstitit, donec completo un-
desexaginta annorum numero, ad complexum et
nuptias sponsi caelestis virgo beata intraret.   In quo
monasterio et ipsa, et pater eius Osuiu, et mater eius
Aeanfled, et pater matris eius Aeduini, et multi alii
nobiles in ecclesia sancti apostoli Petri sepulti sunt.
Hoc autem bellum rex Osuiu in regione Loidis,
tertio decimo regni sui anno, decimo septimo die
Kalendarum Decembrium cum magna utriusque
populi utilitate confecit.   Nam et suam gentem ab
hostili paganorum depopulatione liberavit, et ipsam
gentem Merciorum finitimarumque provinciarum,

[1] Hartlepool in the county of Durham.
[2] Whitby.
[3] As abbess.

victory bestowed upon him, according to the vow he had made to the Lord gave his daughter Elfled, which was yet scant one year old, to be consecrated to Him in perpetual virginity: granting thereto beside the 12 little boclands where, instead of the practice of earthly warfare, place and opportunity might be furnished to the devout zeal of monks for the waging of heavenly warfare and making supplication for the everlasting peace of his nation. Of the which twelve territories to wit, six he appointed in the province of the Derans, six in the province of the Bernicians. Each territory contained ten households, making, that is to say, in all together six score. Now the aforesaid daughter of king Oswy entered the monastery called Heruteu,[1] that is, the Isle of the Hart, over which at that time Hild ruled as abbess, there to be consecrated to God: which abbess two years after, purchasing a territory of ten households in the place called Streanaeshalch,[2] builded there a monastery; in the which the said king's daughter was at the first a learner, afterward also a teacher [3] of monastical life, until at the age of fully 59 years the blessed virgin passed to be united in marriage to her heavenly Spouse. And in this monastery both she herself and her father Oswy and her mother Eanfled and her mother's father Edwin and many other noble personages were buried in the church of the holy apostle Peter. Now this war king Oswy brought to an end in the country of Leeds, the 13th year of his reign, the 15th day of November, to the great commodity of both countries. For he both delivered his own people from the ravages of his heathen enemy, and the people of the Marchmen themselves and of the neighbouring

453

desecto capite perfido, ad fidei Christianae gratiam convertit.

Primus autem in provincia Merciorum, simul et Lindisfarorum ac Mediterraneorum Anglorum, factus est episcopus Diuma, ut supra diximus, qui apud Mediterraneos Anglos defunctus ac sepultus est: secundus Cellach, qui relicto episcopatus officio vivens ad Scottiam rediit, uterque de genere Scottorum: tertius Trumheri, de natione quidem Anglorum, sed edoctus et ordinatus a Scottis, qui erat abbas in monasterio quod dicitur Ingetlingum. Ipse est locus in quo occisus est rex Osuini, ut supra meminimus. Nam regina Aeanfled propinqua illius, ob castigationem necis eius iniustae, postulavit a rege Osuio, ut donaret ibi locum monasterium construendi praefato Dei famulo Trumherae, quia propinquus et ipse erat regis occisi: in quo videlicet monasterio orationes assiduae pro utriusque regis, id est, et occisi, et eius qui occidere iussit, salute aeterna fierent. Idem autem rex Osuiu tribus annis post occisionem Pendan regis, Merciorum genti, necnon et ceteris australium provinciarum populis praefuit: qui etiam gentem Pictorum maxima ex parte regno Anglorum subiecit.

Quo tempore donavit praefato Peada, filio regis Pendan, eo quod esset cognatus suus, regnum australium Merciorum, qui sunt, ut dicunt, familiarum quinque millium, discreti fluvio Treanta ab aquilo-

---

[1] Second cousin.   [2] As Bretwalda, p. 224.

454

provinces he brought over to the grace of the Christian faith, when their unbelieving head was once cut off.

Now the first bishop made in the province of the Marchmen, as well as of the Lindisfaras and of the Middle Englishmen, was (as we said before) Diuma who died and was buried in the country of the Middle Englishmen: the second was Ceollach, who, leaving the charge of his bishopric yet living, returned to Scotland. Both these were Scottish born. The third bishop was Trumhere, of English birth but fully instructed and ordained of the Scots, who was abbot of the monastery which is named Ingetlingum. This is the very place where king Oswin was slain, as we have before recorded. For queen Eanfled, being alliant to him,[1] required of king Oswy in part of satisfaction of Oswin's unjust murder, that he would grant there a place for the erecting of a monastery for the use of the aforesaid servant of God, Trumhere, because he was himself also of kin to the slain king: to the intent that in that monastery continual prayers might be had for the eternal salvation of both kings, that is to say, as well of the slain as of him who commanded to slay. Now the same king Oswy had authority [2] by the space of three years after the death of king Penda over the people of the Marchmen as well as over the other countries of the southern provinces: subduing also the nation of the Redshanks for the most part to the allegiance of the English.

At which time he granted to the aforenamed Peada, son of king Penda, because he was his brother-in-law, the kingdom of the South Marchmen, containing, as men say, 5000 households and divided by the river Trent from the North Marchmen,

nalibus Merciis, quorum terra est familiarum septem
millium. Sed idem Peada proximo vere multum
nefarie peremptus est, proditione, ut dicunt, coniugis
suae, in ipso tempore festi paschalis. Conpletis
autem tribus annis post interfectionem Pendan regis,
rebellarunt adversus regem Osuiu duces gentis
Merciorum Immin, et Eafa, et Eadberct, levato in
regem Vulfhere, filio eiusdem Pendan adolescente,
quem occultum servaverant; et eiectis principibus
regis non proprii, fines suos fortiter simul et liber-
tatem receperunt: sicque cum suo rege liberi, Christo
vero regi pro sempiterno in caelis regno servire gaudebant. Praefuit autem rex idem genti Merciorum
annis decem et septem, habuitque primum episcopum Trumheri, de quo supra diximus, secundum
Iaruman, tertium Ceaddan, quartum Vynfridum.
Omnes hi per ordinem sibimet succedentes sub rege
Vulfhere, gentis Merciorum episcopatu sunt functi.

CAP. XXV

*Ut quaestio sit mota de tempore paschae adversus eos qui
de Scottia venerant.*

Interea Aidano episcopo de hac vita sublato, Finan
pro illo gradum episcopatus a Scottis ordinatus ac
missus acceperat: qui in insula Lindisfarnensi fecit
ecclesiam episcopali sedi congruam; quam tamen
more Scottorum, non de lapide, sed de robore secto
totam composuit, atque harundine texit, quam tem-

whose land containeth 7000 households. But the
same Peada the next spring was very foully slain by
the treason (as they say) of his wife, in the very time
of the Easter festival. Moreover, three years after
the death of king Penda the nobility of the nation of
the Marchmen, Immin, Eafa, and Eadbert rebelled
against king Oswy, advancing to the throne Wulfhere, son of the same Penda, a young man whom they
had kept privy; and expelling the governors of
Oswy, who was not their natural king, they stoutly
recovered again their boundaries as well as their
freedom: and so, living free under a king of their
own, they served joyfully the true king Christ, to be
at length partakers of the everlasting kingdom in
heaven. Now the same king reigned over the nation
of the Marchmen 17 years, and had for his first
bishop Trumhere (of whom we have spoken above),
the second Jaruman, the third Chad, the fourth
Wynfrid. All these in continual succession executed
the office of bishop of the nation of the Marchmen
under king Wulfhere.

CHAPTER XXV

*How the controversy about the time of Easter was moved
against those who had come from Scotland* [664].

In the meanwhile, after the bishop Aidan was
taken from this life, Finan in his room had received
the degree of bishop, being ordained and sent of the
Scots: who in the isle of Lindisfarne made a church
meet for a bishop's see; the which nevertheless
after the manner of the Scots he builded not of stone
but all of sawed oaken timber and thatched it with

pore sequenti reverentissimus archiepiscopus Theo-
dorus in honore beati apostoli Petri dedicavit. Sed
episcopus loci ipsius Eadberct ablata harundine,
plumbi laminis eam totam, hoc est, et tectum et
ipsos quoque parietes eius cooperire curavit.

His temporibus quaestio facta est frequens et
magna de observatione paschae, confirmantibus eis
qui de Cantia, vel de Galliis advenerant, quod Scotti
Dominicum paschae diem contra universalis ecclesiae
morem celebrarent. Erat in his acerrimus veri
paschae defensor, nomine Ronan, natione quidem
Scottus, sed in Galliae vel Italiae partibus regulam
ecclesiasticae veritatis edoctus; qui cum Finano
confligens, multos quidem correxit, vel ad soller-
tiorem veritatis inquisitionem accendit: nequaquam
tamen Finanum emendare potuit; quin potius, quod
esset homo ferocis animi, acerbiorem castigando, et
apertum veritatis adversarium reddidit. Observabat
autem Jacob diaconus quondam, ut supra docuimus,
venerabilis archiepiscopi Paulini, verum et catholicum pascha, cum omnibus quos ad correctiorem
viam erudire poterat. Observabat et regina Eanfled
cum suis, iuxta quod in Cantia fieri viderat, habens
secum de Cantia presbyterum catholicae observationis, nomine Romanum: unde nonnunquam con-
tigisse fertur illis temporibus, ut bis in anno uno
pascha celebraretur, et cum rex pascha Dominicum
solutis ieiuniis faceret, tunc regina cum suis persistens
adhuc in ieiunio diem palmarum celebraret. Haec
autem dissonantia paschalis observantiae vivente

---

[1] Which of the two was hasty is not clear.

reed, and afterwards the most reverend archbishop
Theodore dedicated it in the honour of the blessed
apostle Peter. But the bishop of the selfsame place,
Eadbert, took off the reeds and set to cover it all
with plates of lead, that is to say, both the roof and
also the walls thereof themselves.

About this time there was raised a hot and constant
disputation touching the observance of Easter, they
who had come from Kent or from France affirming
that the Scots kept the Easter Lord's day contrary
to the accustomed manner of the universal Church.
Among these there was a very earnest defender of
the true Easter, one named Ronan, a Scot born but yet
instructed fully in the rule of ecclesiastical truth in
the parts of France and Italy ; who coupling and dis-
puting with Finan set many aright or inflamed them
to a more careful inquiry of the truth : yet was he
able in no way to correct Finan ; nay, rather he
exasperated him by his reproof, being a man of
hasty nature,[1] and made him an open adversary of
the truth. On the other hand James, once deacon
(as we have shewn before) of the venerable archbishop Paulinus, with all whom he was able to instruct
in the better way, observed the true and catholic
Easter. Eanfled also, the queen, with her train
observed after the same manner as she had seen it
practised in Kent, having with her a priest of catholic
observation out of Kent, by name Romanus : whereby,
as is said, it happened sometimes in those days that
in one year Easter was kept twice, and when the
king was breaking his fast and solemnizing the Lord's
Easter, then the queen and her company continued
yet the fast and kept the day of palms. Yet this
diversity of keeping Easter, as long as Aidan lived,

459

THE VENERABLE BEDE

Aidano patienter ab omnibus tolerabatur, qui patenter
intellexerant, quia etsi pascha contra morem eorum
qui ipsum miserant facere non potuit, opera tamen
fidei, pietatis, et dilectionis, iuxta morem omnibus
sanctis consuetum, diligenter exsequi curavit : unde
ab omnibus etiam his qui de pascha aliter sentiebant,
merito diligebatur : nec solum a mediocribus, verum
ab ipsis quoque episcopis, Honorio Cantuariorum, et
Felice Orientalium Anglorum, venerationi habitus est.

Defuncto autem Finano qui post illum fuit, cum
Colmanus in episcopatum succederet, et ipse missus
a Scottia, gravior de observatione paschae necnon et
de aliis ecclesiasticae vitae disciplinis controversia
nata est : unde merito [1] movit haec quaestio sensus
et corda multorum, timentium ne forte accepto
Christianitatis vocabulo, in vacuum currerent, aut
cucurrissent. Pervenit et ad ipsas principum aures,
Osuiu videlicet regis, et filii eius Alchfridi ; qui nimirum Osuiu a Scottis edoctus ac baptizatus, illorum
etiam lingua optime imbutus, nihil melius quam quod
illi docuissent autumabat. Porro Alchfrid magis-
trum habens eruditionis Christianae Vilfridum virum
doctissimum (nam et Romam prius propter doctrinam
ecclesiasticam adierat, et apud Dalfinum archiepiscopum Galliarum Lugduni multum temporis
egerat, a quo etiam tonsurae ecclesiasticae coronam
susceperat), huius doctrinam omnibus Scottorum
traditionibus iure praeferendam sciebat : unde ei
etiam donaverat monasterium quadraginta familiarum

---

[1] *merito,* Pl.

---

[1] Gal. ii. 2.
[2] In imitation of the crown of thorns, Matt. xxvii. 29. The
Celtic clergy shaved the front of the head from ear to ear.

was borne in patience of all men, who had come to know very well, that though he was not able to celebrate Easter contrary to the custom of those who had sent him, yet he set himself diligently to perform works of faith, mercy, and love according to the manner customable with all holy men: upon which consideration he was deservedly beloved of all men, even of those which varied from him about Easter: and was held in reverence not only of the common sort but also of the bishops themselves, Honorius of the men of Kent and Felix of the East English.

But after the death of Finan which came after Aidan, when Colman succeeded to the bishopric, who also himself was sent from Scotland, there arose a sharper disputation about the observance of Easter as well as upon other rules of ecclesiastical life: by occasion whereof this inquiry rightly stirred the minds and hearts of many from fear, lest, having gained the name of Christians, they did run or had run in vain.[1] The dispute reached too to the ears of the princes themselves, to wit of king Oswy and his son Alchfrid; of whom Oswy, being brought up and baptized of the Scots and right skilful also in their tongue, thought nothing better than the manner which they had taught. In his turn Alchfrid, having for his teacher in Christian instruction Wilfrid, a man of great learning (for he had both travelled to Rome on his first visit for the sake of ecclesiastical teaching and spent a long time at Lyons with Dalfinus, archbishop of France, of whom also he had taken the crown [2] of ecclesiastical tonsure), knew that Wilfrid's teaching was rightly to be chosen rather than all the traditions of the Scots: wherefore also he had granted him a monastery of 40 households

461

in loco qui dicitur Inhrypum; quem videlicet locum
paulo ante eis qui Scottos sequebantur in possessionem monasterii dederat. Sed quia illi postmodum
data sibi optione, magis loco cedere quam suam
mutare consuetudinem volebant, dedit eum illi qui
dignam loco et doctrinam haberet, et vitam. Venerat eo tempore Agilberctus, Occidentalium Saxonum episcopus, cuius supra meminimus, amicus
Alchfridi regis, et Vilfridi abbatis, ad provinciam
Nordanhymbrorum, et apud eos aliquandiu demora-
batur; qui etiam Vilfridum, rogatu Alchfridi, in
praefato suo monasterio presbyterum fecit. Habebat
autem secum ipse presbyterum nomine Agathonem.
Mota ergo ibi quaestione de pascha, vel tonsura, vel
aliis rebus ecclesiasticis, dispositum est ut in monasterio quod dicitur Strenaeshalc, quod interpretatur
Sinus Fari, cui tunc Hild abbatissa Deo devota femina
praefuit, synodus fieri et haec quaestio terminari
deberet. Veneruntque illo reges ambo, pater scilicet.
et filius; episcopi, Colman cum clericis suis de Scottia, Agilberctus cum Agathone et Vilfrido presbyteris.
Iacobus et Romanus in horum parte erant: Hild
abbatissa cum suis in parte Scottorum, in qua erat
etiam venerabilis episcopus Cedd, iamdudum ordinatus a Scottis, ut supra docuimus, qui et interpres
in eo concilio vigilantissimus utriusque partis exstitit.

---

¹ Ripon.

² P. 357.

³ The etymology of Strenaeshalc, Streanaeshalch, Whitby,
is much disputed. For *farus* cf. p. 54.

⁴ It was a gathering of all ranks in the Church system, a
Concilium mixtum, in which the king presided, introduced
the subject of discussion and pronounced the decision which

in the place which is called Inhrypum;[1] which place
indeed a little before he had given to those which
followed the Scots, to have in possession for a monastery. But because afterwards, when choice was
offered to them, they preferred to depart and yield
up the place rather than to change their accustomed
manner, it was given by the prince to him whose life
and teaching he held to be worthy thereof. About
that time Agilbert, bishop of the West Saxons, of
whom we have made mention before,[2] a friend of
king Alchfrid and of Wilfrid the abbot, had come to
the province of Northumberland and was staying
with them for a space; who also at the request of
Alchfrid made Wilfrid a priest in his monastery
aforesaid. Now Agilbert had with him a priest
named Agatho. The question therefore concerning
Easter and the tonsure and other ecclesiastical
matters being there raised, it was agreed on both
sides that in the monastery called Strenaeshalc
(which is by interpretation Lighthouse Bay,[3] over
which Hild, a woman vowed to God, was abbess), a
synod [4] should be kept for the deciding of this
question. And thither came both the kings, namely,
the father and the son; the bishops, Colman with
his clergy of Scotland, and Agilbert with Agatho
and Wilfrid, priests. On the part of these last were
James and Romanus: Hild the abbess with her
company were of the Scottish part, whereon also
was the venerable bishop Cedd long since ordained
of the Scots, as we have shewn before, who in that
assembly came forward also as a most watchful
interpreter on both sides.

was agreed to. Fuller, *Church History*, § 91 says : " In this
council, or collation (call it which you please)."

Primusque rex Osuiu praemissa praefatione, quod
oporteret eos qui una Deo servirent, unam vivendi
regulam tenere, nec discrepare in celebratione sacramentorum caelestium, qui unum omnes in caelis
regnum exspectarent; inquirendum potius quae
esset verior traditio, et hanc ab omnibus communiter
esse sequendam : iussit primo dicere episcopum suum
Colmanum, qui esset ritus, et unde originem ducens
ille quem ipse sequeretur. Tunc Colmanus:
" Pascha," inquit, " hoc quod agere soleo, a maioribus
meis accepi, qui me huc episcopum miserunt, quod
omnes patres nostri, viri Deo dilecti, eodem modo
celebrasse noscuntur. Quod ne cui contemnendum
et reprobandum esse videatur, ipsum est quod beatus
evangelista Iohannes discipulus specialiter Domino
dilectus, cum omnibus quibus praeerat ecclesiis,
celebrasse legitur." Quo haec et his similia dicente,
iussit rex et Agilberctum proferre in medium morem
suae observationis, unde initium haberet, vel qua
hunc auctoritate sequeretur. Respondit Agilberctus: " Loquatur, obsecro, vice mea discipulus meus
Vilfrid presbyter, quia unum ambo sapimus cum
ceteris qui hic adsident ecclesiasticae traditionis
cultoribus; et ille melius ac manifestius ipsa lingua
Anglorum, quam ego per interpretem, potest ex-
planare quae sentimus." Tunc Vilfrid iubente rege
ut diceret, ita exorsus est : " Pascha quod facimus,"
inquit, " vidimus Romae ubi beati apostoli Petrus

464

And first king Oswy said beforehand by way of preparation that it behoved those who were united in serving God to keep one rule of living and not to vary in celebrating the heavenly sacraments, who looked all for one kingdom in the heavens; but rather they should search out what was the truer tradition and this should be followed uniformly of everyone: and first he commanded his bishop Colman to declare what his observation was, and from whence he drew the source thereof and whom he followed therein. Then Colman saith: "The Easter which I am accustomed to observe I have received of my elders of whom I was sent hither bishop, and this all our fathers, men beloved of God, are known to have solemnized after the same manner. And this observation, that none may think it a light matter or to be rejected, is the selfsame which the blessed evangelist John, the disciple whom the Lord specially loved, kept, as we read, with all the churches over the which he was head." And when he spake these and such like words the king commanded also Agilbert to declare before them all the manner of his observation, whence it was that it had beginning and by what authority he followed it. Agilbert answered: "Let, I beseech you, my scholar, the priest Wilfrid, speak herein for me, for we both, along with all the other followers after the ecclesiastical tradition, who sit here, are of one mind; beside, he can better and more clearly express our opinion in the very tongue of the English, than I am able to do, using an interpreter." Then Wilfrid, the king commanding him to speak, thus began: "The Easter which we follow we have seen to be kept by all at Rome where the blessed apostles Peter and Paul

THE VENERABLE BEDE

et Paulus vixere, docuere, passi sunt et sepulti, ab omnibus celebrari: hoc in Italia, hoc in Gallia, quas discendi vel orandi studio pertransivimus, ab omnibus agi conspeximus: hoc Africam, Asiam, Aegyptum, Graeciam, et omnem orbem, quacumque Christi Ecclesia diffusa est, per diversas nationes et linguas, uno ac non diverso temporis ordine gerere comperimus: praeter hos tantum, et obstinationis eorum complices, Pictos dico et Brettones, cum quibus de duabus ultimis oceani insulis, et his non totis, contra totum orbem stulto labore pugnant." Cui haec dicenti respondit Colmanus: "Mirum quare stultum appellare velitis laborem nostrum, in quo tanti apostoli qui super pectus Domini recumbere dignus fuit, exempla sectamur; cum ipsum sapientissime vixisse omnis mundus noverit." At Vilfridus, "Absit," inquit, "ut Iohannem stultitiae reprehendamus, cum scita legis Mosaicae iuxta literam servaret, iudaizante adhuc in multis Ecclesia, nec subito valentibus apostolis omnem legis observantiam quae a Deo instituta est, abdicare,[1] (quomodo simulacra quae a daemonibus inventa sunt, repudiare omnes qui ad fidem veniunt, necesse est), videlicet ne scandalum facerent eis qui inter gentes erant Iudaeis. Hinc est enim quod Paulus Timotheum circumcidit, quod hostias in templo immolavit, quod cum Aquila et Priscilla caput Corinthi totondit: ad nihil videlicet utile, nisi ad scandalum vitandum Iudaeorum. Hinc

---

[1] Stops as in Pl.

---

[1] Acts xvi. 3.   [2] Acts xxi. 26
[3] Acts xviii. 18.

466

lived, taught, suffered and were buried: this manner we have noted to be practised of all in Italy, and in France, countries which we have passed through in pursuit of knowledge or desire to pray: this manner we have found to be performed in Africa, Asia, Egypt, Greece and all the world (wherever the Church of Christ hath been spread, throughout different nations and tongues), after one order of time and that without variableness: apart only from these men and them that are partakers of their obstinacy, the Redshanks I mean and the Britons, with whom, being natives of the two farthermost islands of the Ocean sea, and yet not the whole of them neither, these men with fond endeavour do contend against the whole world." To whom so speaking Colman replied: " I marvel wherefore you be ready to term our endeavour fond, wherein we follow the example of so excellent an apostle who was worthy to lean upon the Lord's breast; seeing that all the world accounteth him to have lived most wisely." Whereat Wilfrid saith: " God forbid we should charge John with fondness for keeping the decrees of the Mosaic law literally, according as the Church followed yet in many things the Jewish manner, and the apostles had not power upon the sudden to renounce all observance of the law ordained of God (in the way that all that come to the faith must of necessity abandon idols invented of devils), lest forsooth they might cause offence to those Jews which lived among the Gentiles. For in the like consideration Paul did circumcise Timothy,[1] offered sacrifices in the temple,[2] shaved his head at Corinth with Aquila and Priscilla:[3] truly to no other intent but that the Jews might not be offended. Upon this consideration

quod eidem Paulo Iacobus ait: ' Vides, frater, quot
millia sunt in Iudaeis qui crediderunt; et omnes hi
aemulatores sunt legis.' Nec tamen hodie clarescente per mundum evangelio necesse est, immo nec
licitum fidelibus vel circumcidi, vel hostias Deo
victimarum offerre carnalium. Itaque Iohannes
secundum legis consuetudinem quarta decima die
mensis primi ad vesperam incipiebat celebrationem
festi paschalis, nil curans utrum haec sabbato, an alia
qualibet feria proveniret. At vero Petrus cum
Romae praedicaret, memor quia Dominus prima
sabbati resurrexit a mortuis, ac mundo spem resurrectionis contulit, ita pascha faciendum intellexit, ut
secundum consuetudinem ac praecepta legis, quartam decimam lunam primi mensis, aeque sicut
Iohannes, orientem ad vesperam semper exspectaret:
et hac exorta, si Dominica dies, quae tunc prima
sabbati vocabatur, erat mane ventura, in ipsa vespera
pascha Dominicum celebrare incipiebat, quomodo et
nos hodie facere solemus. Sin autem Dominica non
proximo mane post lunam quartam decimam, sed
sexta decima, aut septima decima, aut alia qualibet
luna, usque ad vicesimam primam esset ventura,
exspectabat eum, et praecedente sabbato, vespere,
sacrosancta paschae sollemnia inchoabat; sicque
fiebat, ut Dominica paschae dies nonnisi a quinta
decima luna usque ad vicesimam primam servaretur.
Neque haec evangelica et apostolica traditio legem

[1] Acts xxi. 20.

[2] The Roman Paschal system had not always been the same.
Rome had altered her cycle and her Paschal limits. As to
St. Peter's observance, Wilfrid says far more than can be
verified. Bright, p. 81.

James said unto the same Paul: [1] 'Thou seest, brother, how many thousands of Jews there are which believe; and they are all zealous of the law.' Notwithstanding, the light of the Gospel now shining throughout the world, it is neither necessary, no, nor lawful for believers to be circumcised or to offer up to God sacrifices of the flesh of beasts. And so John, according to the custom of the law, in the 14th day of the first month at evening began to celebrate the Paschal Festival, not regarding whether it fell out the Sabbath day or any other day of the week. But in truth Peter preaching at Rome,[2] remembering that the Lord rose again from the dead the first day after the Sabbath and gave therewith the hope of resurrection to the world, understood that Easter must be kept in such sort that, according to the custom and commandments of the Law, he ever looked (even as John did) for the rising of the moon at evening in the 14th day of his age, in the first month: and at the rising thereof, if Sunday (which then was called the first day after the Sabbath) was to come on the morrow, he began on that very evening to observe the Lord's Pasch, as we too are wont to do to-day. But if the Sunday were not to come the next morrow after the 14th day of the change of the moon, but the 16th or 17th or any other day of the moon until the one-and-twentieth, he tarried for that Sunday, and the sabbath before, upon the evening, he began the most holy solemnity of Easter; and so it came to pass that the Easter Sunday was kept only between the 15th day of the change of the moon until the one-and-twentieth and no day else. Neither doth this tradition of the Gospel and of the apostles break the

THE VENERABLE BEDE

solvit, sed potius adimplet, in qua observandum
pascha a quarta decima luna primi mensis ad vesperam, usque ad vicesimam primam lunam eiusdem
mensis ad vesperam, praeceptum est: in quam observantiam imitandam, omnes beati Iohannis successores in Asia post obitum eius, et omnis per orbem
ecclesia conversa est. Et hoc esse verum pascha,
hoc solum fidelibus celebrandum, Nicaeno concilio
non statutum noviter, sed confirmatum est, ut ecclesiastica docet historia. Unde constat vos, Colmane,
neque Iohannis, ut autumatis, exempla sectari,
neque Petri, cuius traditioni scientes contradicitis,
neque Legi, neque Evangelio in observatione vestri
paschae congruere. Iohannes enim ad legis Mosaicae
decreta tempus paschale custodiens, nil de prima
sabbati curabat; quod vos non facitis, qui nonnisi
prima sabbati pascha celebratis. Petrus a quinta
decima luna usque ad vicesimam primam diem paschae
Dominicum celebrabat; quod vos non facitis, qui a
quarta decima usque ad vicesimam lunam diem
Dominicum paschae observatis: ita ut tertia decima luna ad vesperam saepius pascha incipiatis,
cuius neque Lex ullam fecit mentionem, neque
auctor ac dator Evangelii Dominus in ea, sed in quarta
decima vel vetus pascha manducavit ad vesperam,
vel novi testamenti sacramenta in commemorationem
suae passionis ecclesiae celebranda tradidit. Item,
lunam vicesimam primam, quam Lex maxime cele-

470

Law but rather fulfil it, for in the Law it is commanded that the Passover should be solemnized from the evening of the 14th day of the change of the moon of the first month until the one-and-twentieth day of the same moon at evening: to the following of which observation all the successors of blessed John in Asia after his death and all the Church throughout the world were converted. And it was by the Nicene Council not newly decreed but confirmed (as the ecclesiastical history witnesseth), that this is the true Easter, this only is to be celebrated by believing men. Whereby it is clear, my lord Colman, that you neither follow the example of John (as you suppose), neither of Peter, whose tradition you wittingly withstand, nor do you agree with the Law nor the Gospel in the observation of your Easter. For John observing the Paschal time according to the decrees of the Mosaic law had no regard to the first day after the Sabbath; and this you do not follow, who keep Easter only on the first day after the Sabbath. Peter celebrated the Lord's Easter day from the 15th day of the change of the moon until the one-and-twentieth day; which you follow not, which keep the Lord's Easter day from the 14th day of the moon until the 20th: so that oftentimes you begin Easter in the 13th day of the change of moon at evening, of which neither hath the Law made any mention, neither did the Lord, the maker and giver of the Gospel, on that day, but on the 14th, eat either the old Passover in the evening, or hand down the sacraments of the New Testament to be celebrated of the Church in commemoration of His passion. Likewise the one-and-twentieth day of the moon, which the Law expressly commanded

brandam commendavit, a celebratione vestri paschae
funditus eliminatis : sicque, ut dixi, in celebratione
summae festivitatis, neque Iohanni, neque Petro,
neque Legi, neque Evangelio concordatis."

His contra Colmanus : " Numquid," ait, " Anatolius vir sanctus, et in praefata historia ecclesiastica
multum laudatus, Legi vel Evangelio contraria
sapuit, qui a quarta decima usque ad vicesimam
pascha celebrandum scripsit ? Numquid reverentissimum patrem nostrum Columbam, et successores
eius viros Deo dilectos, qui eodem modo pascha
facerunt, divinis paginis contraria sapuisse, vel egisse
credendum est ? Cum plurimi fuerint in eis, quorum
sanctitati caelestia signa, et virtutum quae fecerunt
miracula, testimonium praebuerunt : quos ipse sanctos
esse non dubitans, semper eorum vitam, mores et
disciplinam sequi non desisto."

At Vilfridus : " Constat," inquit, " Anatolium
virum sanctissimum, doctissimum, ac laude esse
dignissimum ; sed quid vobis cum illo, cum nec eius
decreta servetis ? Ille enim in pascha suo regulam
utique veritatis sequens, circulum decem et novem
annorum posuit, quem vos aut ignoratis, aut agnitum
et a tota Christi ecclesia custoditum, pro nihilo contemnitis. Ille sic in pascha Dominico quartam
decimam lunam computavit, ut hanc eadem ipsa die
more Aegyptiorum quintam decimam lunam ad
vesperam esse fateretur. Sic item vicesimam die
Dominico paschae adnotavit, ut hanc declinata

---

[1] Cf. III. 3.
[2] The cycle for determining on what day the Paschal full
moon would fall. The Scots retained an old cycle of 84 years.

for celebration, you do utterly exclude from the celebrating of your Easter: and thus, as I said, in the observation of the highest festival you agree neither with John, nor Peter, nor the Law, nor the Gospel."

To this Colman replied and said: "How think ye? Did Anatolius,[1] a holy man and much commended in the ecclesiastical history before of you alleged, think contrary to the Law and the Gospel, writing that Easter ought to be celebrated from the 14th unto the 20th day of the moon? Is it to be believed that our most reverend father Columba and his successors, men beloved of God, who after the same manner kept their Easter, thought or acted contrary to the divine pages? Seeing there were very many among them, to whose holiness witness was borne by heavenly signs and miracles of mighty works wrought by them: and as I doubt not but they were holy men, so I cease not myself ever to follow their life, manners and trade of discipline."

"In good sooth," saith Wilfrid thereupon, "it is well known that Anatolius was a right holy man, very well learned and worthy of much praise; but what have ye to do with him, seeing ye keep not his rulings neither? For Anatolius in his Easter, following assuredly the rule of truth, accounted the compass of nineteen years,[2] which you are either ignorant of or if ye know it, yet though it be close kept by the whole Church of Christ, ye set light by it. He reckoned the 14th day of the moon to fall on the Lord's Easter in such a way that he allowed that same day at evening to be the 15th of the change, after the manner of the Egyptians. He also assigned the 20th day to the Lord's Easter in such a way

473

eadem die esse vicesimam primam crederet. Cuius
regulam distinctionis vos ignorasse probat, quod
aliquoties pascha manifestissime ante plenilunium.
id est, in tertia decima luna facitis. De patre autem
vestro Columba et sequacibus eius, quorum sancti-
tatem vos imitari, et regulam ac praecepta caelestibus signis confirmata sequi perhibetis, possem
respondere ; quia multis in iudicio dicentibus Domino,
quod in nomine eius prophetaverint, et daemonia
eiecerint, et virtutes multas fecerint, responsurus sit
Dominus quia nunquam eos noverit. Sed absit ut
de patribus vestris hoc dicam : quia iustius multo
est, de incognitis bonum credere, quam malum.
Unde et illos Dei famulos, ac Deo dilectos esse non
nego, qui simplicitate rustica, sed intentione pia
Deum dilexerunt. Neque illis multum obesse reor
talem paschae observantiam, quandiu nullus adve-
nerat, qui eis instituti perfectioris decreta quae
sequerentur, ostenderet : quos utique credo, si qui
tunc ad eos catholicus calculator adveniret, sic eius
monita fuisse secuturos, quomodo ea quae noverant
ac didicerant, Dei mandata probantur fuisse secuti.
Tu autem et socii tui, si audita decreta sedis apostolicae, immo universalis ecclesiae, et haec literis
sacris confirmata sequi contemnitis, absque ulla
dubitatione peccatis. Etsi enim patres tui sancti
fuerunt, numquid universali quae per orbem est

---

[1] Matt. vii. 22.

that he held it for the one-and-twentieth when the sun had set. Which his rule and distinction, that ye be ignorant of is manifest by this, that some time ye keep your Easter clean before the full of the moon, that is upon the 13th day of the change. Moreover, as touching your father Columba and those which followed him, whose holiness ye claim to copy and whose rule and commandments ye say that ye follow, as the which have been confirmed by heavenly signs, to this I could have answered, that in the day of Judgment when many say unto the Lord [1] that they have prophesied and cast out devils and done many wonderful works in His name, the Lord will answer that He never knew them. But God forbid that I should say this of your fathers: for it is much more righteous to think well of such as we know not than to think evil. Wherefore also I deny not that they were servants of God and beloved of God, as the which loved God, though in rude simplicity, yet with a godly intention. Neither do I think that the manner of their observation of Easter is much prejudicial against them, as long as none had come to shew them the decrees of more perfect practice, the which they should follow: of whom I verily believe that had any catholic reckoner then come unto them, they would have followed his admonitions in the same manner in which they are shewn to have followed those commands of God which they knew and had learned. But as for thee and thy companions, if hearing the decrees of the apostolic see, nay, rather of the universal Church and these confirmed by Holy Writ, you scorn to follow them, you sin herein undoubtedly. For though thy fathers were holy men, is yet their fewness proceeding from

475

ecclesiae Christi, eorum est paucitas uno de angulo extremae insulae praeferenda? Et si sanctus erat ac potens virtutibus ille Columba vester, immo et noster si Christi erat, numquid praeferri potuit beatissimo apostolorum principi, cui Dominus ait: ' Tu es Petrus, et super hanc petram aedificabo ecclesiam meam, et portae inferi non praevalebunt adversus eam, et tibi dabo claves regni caelorum? ' "

Haec perorante Vilfrido, dixit rex: " Verene, Colmane, haec illi Petro dicta sunt a Domino? " Qui ait: " Vere, rex." At ille, " Habetis," inquit, " vos proferre aliquid tantae potestatis vestro Columbae datum? " At ait ille: " Nihil." Rursum rex: " Si utrique vestrum," inquit, " in hoc sine ulla controversia consentiunt, quod haec principaliter Petro dicta, et ei claves regni caelorum sint datae a Domino? " Responderunt: " Etiam, utique." At ille ita conclusit: " Et ego vobis dico, quia hic est ostiarius ille cui ego contradicere nolo; sed in quantum novi vel valeo, huius cupio in omnibus obedire statutis; ne forte me adveniente ad fores regni caelorum, non sit qui reserat,[1] averso illo qui claves tenere probatur."

Haec dicente rege, faverunt adsidentes quique sive adstantes, maiores una cum mediocribus; et abdicata minus perfecta institutione, ad ea quae meliora cognoverant, sese transferre festinabant.

[1] For *reseret*, Pl.

---

[1] According to the maxim, *Securus iudicat orbis terrarum.*
[2] Matt. xvi. 18.

one corner of the uttermost island of the earth to be put above the universal Church of Christ dispersed throughout the world?[1] And if he your father Columba (yea, and our father if he was Christ's) was holy and mighty in works, can he by any means be chosen above the most blessed chief of the apostles, to whom our Lord said:[2] "Thou art Peter, and upon this rock I will build my church, and the gates of hell shall not prevail against it, and I will give unto thee the keys of the kingdom of heaven"?

When Wilfrid thus concluded the king said: "Were these things, Colman, indeed spoken to that Peter of our Lord?" And the bishop said: "They were indeed, my lord king." Whereat the king saith: "Can you bring forward any so special authority given your Columba?" Whereon the bishop said: "No." Again the king said: "Whether do ye both agree in this without any question, that these words were principally spoken unto Peter, and that unto him the keys of the kingdom of heaven were given of the Lord?" They answered: "Yea, certainly." Whereon the king thus concluded and said: "And I say unto you that I will not gainsay such a porter as this is; but as I know and have power, I covet in all points to obey his ordinances; lest it may be, when I come to the doors of the kingdom of heaven, I find none to open unto me, having his displeasure who is proved to hold the keys thereof."

When the king so spake, all that sat or stood by, the greater along with them of mean degree, gave their consent thereto; and abandoning their former imperfect usage hastened to change over to those things which they had learned to be better.

THE VENERABLE BEDE

CAP. XXVI

Ut Colman victus domum redierit; et Tuda pro illo episcopatu sit functus: qualisque illis doctoribus fuerit habitus ecclesiae.

FINITOQUE conflictu, ac soluta concione, Agilberctus domum rediit. Colman videns spretam suam doctrinam, sectamque esse despectam, adsumptis his qui se sequi voluerunt, id est, qui pascha catholicum, et tonsuram coronae (nam et de hoc quaestio non minima erat), recipere nolebant, in Scottiam regressus est, tractaturus cum suis, quid de his facere deberet. Cedd, relictis Scottorum vestigiis, ad suam sedem rediit, utpote agnita observatione catholici paschae. Facta est autem haec quaestio anno Dominicae incarnationis sexcentesimo sexagesimo quarto, qui fuit annus Osuiu regis vicesimus secundus; episcopatus autem Scottorum, quem gesserunt in provincia Anglorum, annus tricesimus. Siquidem Aidan decem et septem annis, Finan decem, Colman tribus episcopatum tenuere.

Reverso autem patriam Colmano, suscepit pro illo pontificatum Nordanhymbrorum famulus Christi Tuda, qui erat apud Scottos austrinos eruditus, atque ordinatus episcopus, habens iuxta morem provinciae illius coronam tonsurae ecclesiasticae, et catholicam temporis paschalis regulam observans: vir quidem bonus ac religiosus, sed permodico tempore ecclesiam regens. Venerat autem de Scottia, tenente adhuc pontificatum Colmano, et diligenter ea quae ad fidem

---

[1] To France.   [2] At Iona.
[3] South of Ireland.

478

COLMAN AND TUDA

CHAPTER XXVI

How Colman being overcome returned home ; and Tuda took the charge of the bishopric in his place ; and what trade of life the Church led under those teachers [664].

AND the strife being thus ended and the assembly dissolved, Agilbert returned home.[1] Colman, seeing his doctrine contemned and sect reproved, taking those which would follow him, that is, which refused to accept the catholic Easter and the bearing of a shaven crown (for of this matter also there was no small disputation), returned unto Scotland, minding to deliberate there with his countrymen,[2] what he ought to do concerning these matters. Cedd, forsaking the following of the Scots, returned to his see, inasmuch as he had embraced the observance of the catholic Easter. Now this controversy was moved in the 664th year of the Lord's incarnation, which was the 22nd year of king Oswy ; but in the 30th year after the Scots had been made bishops in the province of the English. For Aidan occupied his bishopric 17 years, Finan 10 and Colman 3.

Now after the return of Colman to his country, there succeeded to the bishopric of the Northumbrians in his place Tuda, the servant of Christ, who had been instructed and ordained bishop among the South Scots,[3] bearing after the manner of that country the round crown of ecclesiastical tonsure and observing the catholic rule of the time of Easter : he was a man of virtue and holiness, but he governed the Church a very small time. Now he had come from Scotland, while Colman yet occupied the bishopric, and dili-

et veritatem pertinent, et verbo cunctos docebat et
opere.   Porro fratribus, qui in Lindisfarnensi ecclesia,
Scottis abeuntibus, remanere maluerunt, praepositus
est abbatis iure vir reverentissimus ac mansuetissimus
Eata, qui erat abbas in monasterio quod dicitur
Mailros: quod aiunt Colmanum abiturum petiisse et
impetrasse a rege Osuiu, eo quod esset idem Eata
unus de duodecim pueris Aidani, quos primo episcopatus sui tempore de natione Anglorum erudiendos
in Christo accepit.   Multum namque eundem episcopum Colmanum rex pro insita illi prudentia diligebat.   Ipse est Eata, qui non multo post eidem
ecclesiae Lindisfarnensi episcopus factus est.   Abiens
autem domum Colman adsumpsit secum partem
ossium reverentissimi patris Aidani; partem vero in
ecclesia cui praeerat, reliquit, et in secretario eius
condi praecepit.

Quantae autem parsimoniae, cuius continentiae
fuerit, ipse cum praedecessoribus suis, testabatur
etiam locus ille quem regebant, ubi abeuntibus eis,
excepta ecclesia, paucissimae domus repertae sunt;
hoc est, illae solummodo, sine quibus conversatio
civilis esse nullatenus poterat.   Nil pecuniarum
absque pecoribus habebant.   Si quid enim pecuniae
a divitibus accipiebant, mox pauperibus dabant.
Nam neque ad susceptionem potentium saeculi, vel
pecunias colligi, vel domus praevideri necesse fuit,
qui nunquam ad ecclesiam nisi orationis tantum, et
audiendi verbi Dei causa veniebant.   Rex ipse, cum

---

gently taught all men both in word and with example the things which belong to the true faith. Furthermore, at the departure of the Scots, Eata, a most reverend and meek person, was set over the brethren which chose to remain in the church at Lindisfarne, with authority of abbot, and he before was abbot in the monastery which is named Mailros[1]: and this it is said was obtained of king Oswy by the suit of Colman at the point of his departure, because that the same Eata was one of the twelve scholars of Aidan, which at his first coming as bishop he took out of the English nation to be brought up in Christ. For the same bishop Colman was dearly loved of king Oswy for the wisdom that was natural to him. This Eata is he which not long after was made bishop of the same church at Lindisfarne. Now Colman at his departing homeward took with him a portion of the bones of the most reverend father Aidan; but part he left in the church which he ruled,[2] and commanded that they be laid in the sacristy thereof.

But how spareful persons he and his predecessors were and how greatly they abstained from all pleasures, even the place where they bare rule did witness, in the which at their departure very few houses were found beside the church; that is to say, those houses only without which the conversation of common life could nowise be maintained. They had no money, but cattle. For, if they took any money of rich men, by and by they gave it to poor people. For neither was it needful that either money should be gathered or houses provided for the entertainment of the powerful of this world, who never used to come to the church but only to pray and hear the word of God. The king himself, when

opportunitas exegisset, cum quinque tantum aut sex
ministris veniebat, et expleta in ecclesia oratione
discedebat.   Quod si forte eos ibi refici contingeret,
simplici tantum et quotidiano fratrum cibo contenti,
nil ultra quaerebant.   Tota enim fuit tunc solicitudo
doctoribus illis, Deo serviendi, non saeculo; tota
cura cordis excolendi, non ventris.   Unde et in
magna erat veneratione tempore illo religionis
habitus: ita ut ubicumque clericus aliquis aut
monachus adveniret, gaudenter ab omnibus tanquam
Dei famulus exciperetur: etiam si in itinere pergens
inveniretur, adcurrebant, et flexa cervice vel manu
signari, vel ore illius se benedici gaudebant; verbis
quoque horum exhortatoriis diligenter auditum
praebebant.   Sed et diebus Dominicis ad ecclesiam
sive ad monasteria certatim, non reficiendi corporis,
sed audiendi sermonis Dei gratia confluebant: et si
quis sacerdotum in vicum forte deveniret, mox
congregati in unum vicani, verbum vitae ab illo
expetere curabant.   Nam neque alia ipsis sacerdotibus aut clericis vicos adeundi, quam praedicandi,
baptizandi, infirmos visitandi, et, ut breviter dicam
animas curandi causa fuit: qui in tantum erant ab
omni avaritiae peste castigati, ut nemo territoria ac
possessiones ad construenda monasteria, nisi a potentibus saeculi coactus, acciperet.   Quae consuetudo

---

[1] In contrast to Bede's own time, as shewn in his letter to
Egbert, archbishop of York, 734.

occasion had required it, came accompanied with only five or six persons, and after prayer ended in the church departed. But if by chance it fortuned that they refreshed themselves there, they contented themselves only with the brethren's simple daily fare, looking for nothing farther. For then [1] all the desire with those teachers was to serve God, not the world; their whole care was to comfort the heart, not the paunch. Whereof it came to pass that in that time even the habit of religious men was had in great reverence; so that wherever any of the clergy or monks came, he was joyfully received of all men, like the servant of God: again, if any were found going on a journey, they ran unto him and making low obeisance rejoiced either to receive the sign [2] from his hand or a blessing from his mouth; also they would diligently give ear to their words of exhortation. Moreover, too, upon the Sundays ordinarily the people flocked eagerly either to the church or to the monasteries, not for belly cheer but to hear the word of God: and if any of the priests came by chance abroad into the village, the inhabitants thereof would by and by gather together about him and set themselves to desire of him the word of life. For neither had either the priests themselves or the clergy other reason to come into the villages but only to preach, to baptize, to visit the sick, and (to speak all in one word) for the cure of souls: who were so far chastened from all the infection of covetousness, that none of them would take pieces of land and possessions toward the building of monasteries but through the constraint of the powerful of this world. Which custom in all points was

[2] Signaculo dominicae crucis.

per omnia aliquanto post haec tempore in ecclesiis
Nordanhymbrorum servata est. Sed de his satis
dictum.

CAP. XXVII

*Ut Ecgberct, vir sanctus de natione Anglorum, mona-
chicam in Hibernia vitam duxerit.*

EODEM autem anno Dominicae incarnationis
sexcentesimo sexagesimo quarto, facta erat eclipsis
solis die tertio mensis Maii, hora circiter decima diei:
quo etiam anno subita pestilentiae lues, depopulatis
prius australibus Brittaniae plagis, Nordanhymbrorum
quoque provinciam corripiens; atque acerba clade
diutius longe lateque desaeviens, magnam hominum
multitudinem stravit. Qua plaga praefatus Domini
sacerdos Tuda raptus est de mundo, et in monasterio
quod dicitur Paegnalaech, honorifice sepultus. Haec
autem plaga Hiberniam quoque insulam pari clade
premebat. Erant ibidem eo tempore multi nobilium
simul et mediocrium de gente Anglorum, qui tempore
Finani et Colmani episcoporum, relicta insula patria,
vel divinae lectionis, vel continentioris vitae gratia
illo secesserant. Et quidam quidem mox se monas-
ticae conversationi fideliter mancipaverunt, alii magis
circumeundo per cellas magistrorum, lectioni operam
dare gaudebant: quos omnes Scotti libentissime
suscipientes victum eis quotidianum sine pretio,

---

[1] Should be the first of May.

[2] The most noted of the visitations of the plague in the
seventh century. It was known as the Yellow Pest.

[3] Uncertain, but perhaps Whalley on the borders of
Lancashire and Cheshire.

maintained a long time hereafter in the churches of Northumbria. But thus much of these matters.

CHAPTER XXVII

How Egbert, a holy man, English born, led a religious life in Ireland [664–729].

Now in the same 664th year of the Lord's incarnation an eclipse of the sun happened on the third[1] day of the month of May about the tenth hour of the day: in the which year a sudden destructive plague,[2] consuming first the southern regions of Britain, took hold also of the province of the Northumbrians; and raging far and wide with much continuance brought low in grievous ruin an infinite number of men. In the which affliction the foresaid priest of the Lord, Tuda, was carried off from the world and honourably buried in the monastery called Paegnalaech.[3] Moreover, this affliction pressed sore on the island of Ireland with a like destruction. There were in that same place at that time many nobles as well as common sort of English race, who in the time of the bishops Finan and Colman had left their native island and departed aside thither either to read sacred writings or to live more strictly. And certain of them forthwith bound themselves faithfully to the monastical life, while others wandering rather about the cells of such as taught[4] gladly gave good heed to reading: all of whom the Scots entertained cheerfully and were forward to give them daily sustenance

[4] The Irish monasteries had regular officers for teaching. The subjects were grammar, geometry, physics and the interpretation of Scripture, Pl.

485

libros quoque ad legendum, et magisterium gratuitum
praebere curabant.

Erant inter hos duo iuvenes magnae indolis, de
nobilibus Anglorum, Edilhun et Ecgberct, quorum
prior frater fuit Ediluini, viri aeque Deo dilecti, qui
et ipse aevo sequente Hiberniam gratia legendi adiit,
et bene instructus patriam rediit, atque episcopus in
provincia Lindissi factus, multo ecclesiam tempore
nobilissime rexit. Hi ergo cum essent in monasterio
quod lingua Scottorum Rathmelsigi appellatur, et
omnes socii ipsorum vel mortalitate de saeculo rapti,
vel per alia essent loca dispersi, correpti sunt ambo
morbo eiusdem mortalitatis, et gravissime adflicti : e
quibus Ecgberct, sicut mihi referebat quidam
veracissimus et venerandae canitiei presbyter qui se
haec ab ipso audisse perhibebat, cum se aestimasset
esse moriturum, egressus est tempore matutino de
cubiculo in quo infirmi quiescebant, et residens solus
in loco opportuno, coepit sedulus cogitare de actibus
suis, et conpunctus memoria peccatorum suorum
faciem lacrimis abluebat, atque intimo ex corde Deum
precabatur, ne adhuc mori deberet, priusquam vel
praeteritas negligentias quas in pueritia sive infantia
commiserat, perfectius ex tempore castigaret, vel
in bonis se operibus habundantius exerceret. Vovit
etiam votum, quia adeo peregrinus vivere vellet, ut
nunquam in insulam in qua natus est, id est, Brittaniam, rediret; quia praeter sollemnem canonici

---

[1] Not certainly identified.

486

free, also books for reading and teaching without payment.

Among these, two young men of the English nobility were of great towardness, Ethelhun and Egbert, of the which two the former was brother unto Ethelwin, a man no less beloved of God, who himself too in the age following went to Ireland for study's sake, and being well taught returned to his country and was made bishop in the province of Lindsey and ruled the church honourably for a long time. These youths then living in the monastery which in the Scottish tongue is called Rathmalsigi,[1] all their companions either being carried off from the world by the mortality or scattered abroad in divers places, were both of them seized of the same mortal sickness and grievously tormented: and of the two, Egbert (as I learned by the report of a most trusty and venerable gray-headed priest which told me he heard the story at Egbert's own mouth), thinking he was at the point to die, departed very early out of his chamber where the sick were wont to lie,[2] and sitting down alone in a commodious place began diligently to think upon his former life, and being pricked with the remembrance of his sins washed his face with tears and beseeched God from the bottom of his heart that he might not have yet to die, before he should either more completely, as occasion served, amend his former failings which he had committed in his boyhood and infancy, or exercise himself more fully in good works. He vowed also a vow that he would be ready to live so much a pilgrim that he would never return to the island where he was born, that is to say, to Britain; that beside the

[2] The infirmary of the monastery.

temporis psalmodiam, si non valetudo corporis
obsisteret, quotidie psalterium totum in memoriam
divinae laudis decantaret; et quia in omni septimana
diem cum nocte ieiunus transiret. Cumque finitis
lacrimis, precibus et votis, domum rediret, invenit
sodalem dormientem: et ipse quoque lectulum
conscendens, coepit in quietem membra laxare. Et
cum paululum quiesceret, expergefactus sodalis
respexit eum, et ait: " O frater Ecgbercte, o quid
fecisti? Sperabam quia pariter ad vitam aeternam
intraremus. Verumtamen scito quia quae postulasti,
accipies." Didicerat enim per visionem, et quid
ille[1] petiisset, et quia petita inpetrasset. Quid multa?
Ipse Edilhun proxima nocte defunctus est: at vero
Ecgberct decussa molestia aegritudinis convaluit,
ac multo postea tempore vivens, acceptumque
sacerdotii gradum condignis ornans actibus, post
multa virtutum bona, ut ipse desiderabat, nuper, id
est, anno Dominicae incarnationis septingentesimo
vicesimo nono, cum esset ipse annorum nonaginta,
migravit ad regna caelestia. Duxit autem vitam in
magna humilitatis, mansuetudinis, continentiae,
simplicitatis et iustitiae perfectione. Unde et genti
suae, et illis in quibus exulabat nationibus Scottorum
sive Pictorum, exemplo vivendi, et instantia docendi,
et auctoritate corripiendi, et pietate largiendi de his
quae a divitibus acceperat, multum profuit. Addidit
autem votis quae diximus, ut semper in quadragesima
non plus quam semel in die reficeret, non aliud quam
panem ac lac tenuissimum, et hoc cum mensura
gustaret: quod videlicet lac pridie novum in phiala

---

[1] *ille*, Pl.

---

[1] Frequently imposed or undertaken as a penance.

ordinary service of the canonical hours, if weakness of body letted him not, he would recite every day the whole Psalter [1] for a remembrance of the praise of God; and that in every week he would pass a day and a night fasting. And his tears, his prayers and his vows thus being ended he returned home and found his fellow asleep: and himself too getting to bed began to lay his limbs to rest. And a little after as he rested, his fellow, waking and looking upon him, said: " O brother Egbert, what have ye done? My hope was that together we should enter into life everlasting. But now understand ye, ye shall have your request." For by a vision it was revealed unto him both what the other's petition had been, and that he had obtained it. What need many words? Ethelhun himself the night following departed: but in truth Egbert casting off the trouble of his sickness recovered, and living long time after and being made bishop adorned his station with a life worthy of his vocation, and after many virtuous good deeds, as he himself desired, passed to the heavenly kingdoms of late, to wit, in the 729th year of the Lord's incarnation, when he himself was 90 years of age. Now he led his life in great perfection of lowliness, meekness, continency, innocency and righteousness. Whereby he profited much both his own people and the nations wherein he lived in banishment, the Scots and Redshanks, in example of living, in diligence of teaching, in authority of correcting and in bountifulness of bestowing of the gifts which he had received from the rich. Moreover, beside his vows mentioned before, he made other, as that in Lent he never ate more than once in the day, tasting then nothing else but bread and very thin milk, and that with a certain

ponere solebat, et post noctem ablata superficie crassiore, ipse residuum cum modico, ut diximus, pane bibebat. Cuius modum continentiae etiam quadraginta diebus ante natale Domini, totidem quoque post peracta sollemnia pentecostes, hoc est, quinquagesimae, semper observare curabat.

CAP. XXVIII

Ut defuncto Tuda, Vilfrid in Gallia, Ceadda apud Occidentales Saxones, in provinciam Nordanhymbrorum sint ordinati episcopi.

INTEREA rex Alchfrid misit Vilfridum presbyterum ad regem Galliarum, qui eum sibi suisque consecrari faceret episcopum. At ille misit eum ordinandum ad Agilberectum, de quo supra diximus, qui relicta Brittania, Parisiacae civitatis factus erat episcopus; et consecratus est magno cum honore ab ipso, convenientibus plurimis episcopis in vico regio qui vocatur In Compendio. Quo adhuc in transmarinis partibus propter ordinationem demorante, imitatus industriam filii rex Osuio, misit Cantiam virum sanctum, modestum moribus, Scripturarum lectione sufficienter instructum, et ea quae in Scripturis agenda didicerat, operibus sollerter exequentem, qui Eburacensis ecclesiae ordinaretur episcopus. Erat autem presbyter vocabulo Ceadda, frater reverentissimi antistitis Ceddi, cuius saepius meminimus, et abbas monasterii illius quod vocatur Laestingaeu.

---

[1] Clothaire III, king of Neustria, Western France.

measure: to wit, milk which the day before he was wont to set fresh in a vial and when night was past, skimming away the cream, he would drink what was left along with a small portion of bread, as we have said. And this kind of abstinence he was careful to observe 40 days before Christmas, as also for as many days after the festival of Pentecost was over, that is, 50 days after Easter.

CHAPTER XXVIII

How after the death of Tuda, Wilfrid in France, Chad among the West Saxons were ordained bishops of the province of Northumbria [665].

In the meantime king Alchfrid sent the priest Wilfrid unto the king of France [1] to have him consecrated for himself and his household. Whereupon the king of France sent him unto Agilbert to be ordained, of whom we have made mention before, and who having left Britain was made bishop of the city of Paris; and of him Wilfrid was consecrated with great honour, a number of bishops meeting together in a manor of the king's which is called Compiègne. And Wilfrid making yet some abode in parts beyond the seas by reason of his ordination, king Oswy following the example of his son's forwardness sent into Kent a holy man, of virtuous behaviour, sufficiently learned in reading of Scriptures, and a diligent performer in deed of that he had learned in the Scriptures should be done, to be ordained bishop of the church of York. Now this man was a priest named Chad, brother to the most reverend bishop Cedd of whom we have often made mention, and abbot of the monastery which is called Lastingham.

Misitque rex cum eo presbyterum suum vocabulo Eadhaedum, qui postea regnante Ecgfrido, Hrypensis ecclesiae praesul factus est. Verum illi Cantiam pervenientes, invenerunt archiepiscopum Deusdedit iam migrasse de saeculo, et necdum alium pro eo constitutum fuisse pontificem. Unde diverterunt ad provinciam Occidentalium Saxonum, ubi erat Vini episcopus : et ab illo est vir praefatus consecratus antistes, adsumtis in societatem ordinationis duobus de Brettonum gente episcopis, qui Dominicum paschae diem, ut saepius dictum est, secus morem canonicum a quarta decima usque ad vicesimam lunam celebrant. Non enim erat tunc ullus, excepto illo Vine, in tota Brittania canonice ordinatus episcopus. Consecratus ergo in episcopum Ceadda, mox coepit ecclesiasticae veritati, et castitati curam impendere ; humilitati continentiae, lectioni operam dare ; oppida, rura, casas, vicos, castella propter evangelizandum, non equitando, sed apostolorum more pedibus incedendo peragrare. Erat enim de discipulis Aidani, eisdemque actibus ac moribus iuxta exemplum eius, ac fratris sui Ceddi, suos instituere curavit auditores. Veniens quoque Brittaniam Vilfrid iam episcopus factis, et ipse perplura catholicae observationis moderamina ecclesiis Anglorum sua doctrina contulit. Unde factum est, ut crescente per dies institutione catholica, Scotti omnes qui inter Anglos morabantur, aut his manus darent, aut suam redirent ad patriam.

---

[1] *Secus* here used for *contra*. The two bishops were probably from Cornwall. Bright, p. 222.

And the king sent with him his priest, Eadhed by name, who after in the reign of king Egfrid was made prelate of the church of Ripon. But they at their arrival in Kent found that the archbishop Deusdedit had now passed from the world and no other was yet appointed bishop in his room. Whereby they stroke over to the province of the West Saxons where Wini was bishop; and of him the foresaid Chad was consecrated bishop, having with him to assist and accompany him at the ordination two bishops of the British race, who celebrate the Lord's Easter day, as hath often been said before, contrary to[1] the canonical order from the 14th to the 20th moon. For there was not at this time, beside this bishop Wini, any bishop canonically ordained in all Britain.[2] Chad then being consecrated bishop began shortly to be zealous in care for ecclesiastical truth and purity of doctrine; to apply his heart to lowliness, abstinency and study; to visit continually the towns, country places, cottages, villages, houses for the sake of preaching the Gospel, not making his journey on horseback but going on foot as the apostles used. For he was one of Aidan's scholars and laboured to instruct his hearers in the same way of life and behaviour after the example of Aidan and his own brother Cedd. Wilfrid also coming to Britain, now made a bishop, did himself too by his teaching bring into the churches of the English very many rules of catholic observance. Whereby it came to pass that the catholic practice daily continuing to increase, the whole company of the Scots which lived among the Englishmen either yielded to the same or returned back to their country.

[2] There was Boniface, bishop of Dunwich, consecrated by Honorius, cf. III. 20.

CAP. XXIX

Ut Vighard presbyter ordinandus in archiepiscopum Romam de Brittania sit missus : quem remissa mox scripta papae apostolici, ibidem obiisse narraverint.

His temporibus reges Anglorum nobilissimi, Osuiu provinciae Nordanhymbrorum, et Ecgberct Cantuariorum, habito inter se consilio, quid de statu ecclesiae Anglorum esset agendum, intellexerat enim veraciter Osuiu, quamvis educatus a Scottis, quia Romana esset catholica et apostolica ecclesia, adsumpserunt cum electione et consensu sanctae ecclesiae gentis Anglorum, virum bonum, et aptum episcopatu presbyterum nomine Vighardum, de clero Deusdedit episcopi, et hunc antistitem ordinandum Romam miserunt : quatenus accepto ipse gradu archiepiscopatus, catholicos per omnem Brittaniam ecclesiis Anglorum ordinare posset antistites.

Verum Vighard Romam perveniens, priusquam consecrari in episcopatum posset, morte praereptus est, et huiusmodi literae regi Osuiu Brittaniam remissae sunt.

" Domino excellenti filio Osuio regi Saxonum, Vitalianus episcopus, servus servorum Dei.
Desiderabiles literas excellentiae vestrae suscepimus : quas relegentes, cognovimus eius piissimam devotionem, ferventissimumque amorem, quem habet propter beatam vitam ; et quia dextera Domini protegente ad veram et apostolicam fidem sit con-

---

[1] Not a monk.
[2] Pope from 657–673,

CHAPTER XXIX

How Wighard, priest, was sent to Rome from Britain to
be ordained archbishop : and how he died in that
same place, according as by letter shortly sent back
by the apostolic pope it was specified [667].

AT this time the most renowned kings of the
English, Oswy of the province of Northumberland
and Egbert of Kent, deliberating between themselves
what was to be done concerning the condition of the
Church of the English (for Oswy had now truthfully
learned, though brought up of the Scots, that the
Church of Rome was the catholic and apostolic
Church), with the choice and consent of the holy
Church of the English nation called unto them a
priest named Wighard, a good man and worthy to be
a bishop, one of the clergy [1] under Deusdedit the
bishop, and sent him to Rome to be ordained bishop,
to the intent that he, having received the office of
archbishop, might himself be able to ordain catholic
bishops for the churches of the English throughout
all Britain.

But Wighard, reaching Rome, before he could be
consecrated to the bishopric, was snatched away of
untimely death, and a letter as followeth was sent
back to Britain to king Oswy.

" To the excellent lord, our son Oswy king of the
Saxons, [2] Vitalian, bishop, servant of the servants of
God.   We have received your excellency's wishful letter, by the perusal whereof we
perceived your most godly devotion and the fervent
zeal you have to attain everlasting life ; hoping that,
as you now reign over your own people, so in the time
to come you shall reign with Christ, forasmuch as

495

versus, sperans [1] sicut in sua gente regnat, ita et cum Christo in futuro conregnare. Benedicta igitur gens, quae talem sapientissimum, et Dei cultorem promeruit habere regem : quia non solum ipse Dei cultor extitit, sed etiam omnes subiectos suos meditatur die ac nocte ad fidem catholicam atque apostolicam pro suae animae redemptione converti. Quis enim audiens haec suavia, non laetetur? Quis non exultet et gaudeat in his piis operibus? Quia et gens vestra Christo omnipotenti Deo credidit, secundum divinorum prophetarum voces, sicut scriptum est in Isaia : ' In die illa radix Iesse, qui stat in signum populorum, ipsum gentes deprecabuntur.' Et iterum : ' Audite insulae, et adtendite populi de longe.' Et post paululum : ' Parum,' inquit, ' est ut mihi sis servus ad suscitandas tribus Iacob, et faeces Israel convertendas. Dedi te in lucem gentium, ut sis salus mea usque ad extremum terrae.' Et rursum : ' Reges videbunt, et consurgent principes, et adorabunt.' Et post pusillum : ' Dedi te in foedus populi, ut suscitares terram, et possideres haereditates dissipatas, et diceres his qui vincti sunt : Excite ; et his qui in tenebris, Revelamini.' Et rursum : ' Ego Dominus vocavi te in iustitia, et adprehendi manum tuam, et servavi ; et dedi te in foedus populi, in lucem gentium, ut aperires oculos caecorum, et educeres de conclusione vinctum, de domo carceris sedentes in tenebris.' Ecce, excel-

---

[1] For *sperans ut*, Pl.

---

[1] Isai. xi. 10 ; xlix. 1, 6, 7, 8 ; xiii. 6, 7.

under the protection of the Lord's right hand you
are now converted to the true apostolic faith.
Blessed therefore is the people which hath been
found worthy to have a prince of such wisdom and
desire of God's honour: as the which not only is
found, to honour God himself, but also studieth day
and night for the conversion of all his subjects to the
catholic and apostolic faith, purchasing thereby the
salvation of his own soul. For who hearing this
pleasant report would not rejoice thereat? Who
would not leap for joy at these godly works? Forasmuch as your nation also hath believed in Christ the
almighty God, according to the oracles of the divine
prophets, as it is written in Isaiah:[1] 'In that day
the root of Jesse which standeth for an ensign of the
people, it shall the Gentiles call upon.' And again:
' Listen, O isles, and hearken ye people, from afar.'
And a little after he saith: ' It is not enough that
thou shouldest be my servant to raise up the tribes
of Jacob and to convert the dregs of Israel. I have
given thee for a light to the Gentiles that thou mayest
be my salvation unto the end of the earth.' And
again: ' Kings shall see and princes shall arise and
worship.' And a very little after: ' I have given
thee for a covenant of the people that thou shouldest
raise up the earth and possess the scattered inheri-
tages, and say to the prisoners, Go forth; and to them
that are in darkness, Shew yourselves.' And again:
' I the Lord have called thee in righteousness and
have taken thine hand and kept thee; and I have set
thee for a covenant of the people, for a light of the
Gentiles, to open the eyes of the blind and to bring
out the prisoner from the prison and them that sit in
darkness out of the prison house.' Behold, most

lentissime fili, quam luce clarius est, non solum de
vobis, sed etiam de omnibus prophetatum gentibus,
quod sint crediturae in Christo omnium conditore.
Quamobrem oportet vestram celsitudinem, utpote
membrum existens Christi, in omnibus piam regulam
sequi perenniter principis apostolorum, sive in pascha
celebrandum, sive in omnibus quae tradiderunt sancti
apostoli Petrus et Paulus, qui ut duo luminaria caeli
illuminant mundum, sic doctrina eorum corda
hominum quotidie inlustrat credentium."

Et post nonnulla, quibus de celebrando per orbem
totum uno vero pascha loquitur;

" Hominem denique," inquit, " docibilem, et in
omnibus ornatum antistitem, secundum vestrorum
scriptorum tenorem, minime valuimus nunc reperire
pro longinquitate itineris. Profecto enim dum
huiusmodi apta repertaque persona fuerit, eum
instructum ad vestram dirigemus patriam, ut ipse
et viva voce, et per divina oracula omnem inimici
zizaniam ex omni vestra insula cum divino nutu
eradicet. Munuscula a vestra celsitudine beato
principi apostolorum directa, pro aeterna eius
memoria suscepimus, gratiasque ei agimus, ac pro
eius incolumitate iugiter Deum deprecamur cum
Christi clero. Itaque qui haec obtulit munera, de
hac subtractus est luce, situsque ad limina apostolorum, pro quo valde sumus contristati cum hic esset
defunctus. Verumtamen gerulis harum nostrarum
literarum vestris missis, beneficia sanctorum, hoc est,

---

[1] Had the kings asked the pope to consecrate Wighard or
asked the pope to find for them a fit person to consecrate, as
the pope implies in his letter ?

[2] Wighard.

excellent son, how by the verdict of the prophets it is clearer than day, not only of you but also of all nations that they shall believe in Christ, the Maker of all. Wherefore it behoveth your highness, being now a member of Christ, to follow in all things and all times the godly rule of the chief of apostles, whether for observing Easter or in all things delivered by the holy apostles Peter and Paul, whose doctrine doth so daily lighten the hearts of men that believe, as the two lights of the element give light to the world."

And after some words in which he speaketh touching the celebration of the one true Easter throughout the whole world he saith:

" Finally, as touching one apt for learning and adorned with all qualities to be bishop, according to the tenor of your letters,[1] we could by no means find any now, the journey being so long to you. For assuredly, as soon as we shall espy out a meet person of this character, we shall direct him after instruction to your country, that both by his own preaching and by the divine oracles he may thoroughly root out all the tares of the enemy from all your island with the will of God. The presents which your highness directed to the blessed chief of the apostles, for his perpetual memory we have received, and thank your highness therefor, and beseech God with the clergy of Christ incessantly for your highness' preservation. Accordingly, the bearer[2] of these presents, who hath been taken from this life, is laid at the church of the apostles, we much lamenting at his departure here. But to your messengers, the bearers of this our letter, we have caused to be given the benefits of the saints, that is to say, the relics of the blessed

499

reliquias beatorum apostolorum Petri et Pauli, et
sanctorum martyrum Laurentii, Iohannis et Pauli,
et Gregorii atque Pancratii eis fecimus dari, vestrae
excellentiae profecto omnes contradendas. Nam et
coniugi vestrae, nostrae spiritali filiae, direximus
per praefatos gerulos crucem clavem auream haben-
tem de sacratissimis vinculis beatorum apostolorum
Petri et Pauli: de cuius pio studio cognoscentes,
tantum cuncta sedes apostolica una nobiscum laeta-
tur, quantum eius pia opera coram Deo fragrant et
vernant. Festinet igitur, quaesumus, vestra celsi-
tudo, ut optamus, totam suam insulam Deo Christo
dicare. Profecto enim habet protectorem, humani
generis redemptorem Dominum nostrum Jesum
Christum, qui ei cuncta prospera impertiet, ut
novum Christi populum coacervet, catholicam ibi et
apostolicam constituens fidem. Scriptum est enim:
' Quaerite primum regnum Dei, et iustitiam eius,
et haec omnia adicientur vobis.' Nimirum enim
quaerit, et impetravit, et ei omnes suae insulae, ut
optamus, subdentur. Paterno itaque affectu salu-
tantes vestram excellentiam, divinam precamur
iugiter clementiam, quae vos vestrosque omnes in
omnibus bonis operibus auxiliari dignetur, ut cum
Christo in futuro regnetis saeculo. Incolumem
excellentiam vestram gratia superna custodiat.''

Quis sane pro Vighardo repertus ac dedicatus sit
antistes, libro sequente opportunius dicetur.

---

[1] Suffered martyrdom in the Diocletian persecution, 304.

apostles Peter and Paul, and of the holy martyrs, Laurence, John and Paul and of Gregory and Pancras,[1] all to be delivered truly to your excellency. For beside to your lady wife,[2] our spiritual daughter, we have sent by the said bearers a cross having a golden key taken from the most holy chains of the blessed apostles Peter and Paul: of whose godly zeal we understanding and along with us the whole apostolic see as far rejoice as her godly works do smell sweet and blossom in the sight of God. We beseech therefore your highness, according to our wish, to hasten to dedicate all your island to God Christ. For assuredly you lack not herein a protector, our Lord Jesus Christ, the Redeemer of mankind, who will prosper you in all things, to the heaping up the number of the new people of Christ, and establishing there the catholic apostolic faith. For it is written[3]: 'Seek ye first the kingdom of God and his righteousness, and all these things shall be added unto you.' For undoubtedly your highness seeketh and hath obtained, and all your islands (as we wish) shall be set under you. And so we salute your excellency with fatherly affection, beseeching continually the mercy of God that it vouchsafe to assist you and yours in all good works, that in the world to come ye may reign with Christ. May the grace from above have your excellency in its safe keeping!"

In the next book following we shall have better occasion to declare who it was that was found and dedicated bishop in place of Wighard.

[2] Eanfled of Kent.
[3] Matt. vi. 31.

CAP. XXX

Ut Orientales Saxones tempore mortalitatis ad idolatriam reversi, sed per instantiam Iarumanni episcopi mox sint ab errore correcti.

EODEM tempore provinciae Orientalium Saxonum post Suidhelmum, de quo supra diximus, praefuere reges Sigheri et Sebbi, quamvis ipsi regi Merciorum Vulfherae subiecti. Quae videlicet provincia cum praefatae mortalitatis clade premeretur, Sigheri cum sua parte populi, relictis Christianae fidei sacramentis, ad apostasiam conversus est. Nam et ipse rex, et plurimi de plebe sive optimatibus, diligentes hanc vitam, et futuram non quaerentes, sive etiam non esse credentes, coeperunt fana quae derelicta erant, restaurare et adorare simulacra, quasi per haec possent a mortalitate defendi. Porro socius eius, et coheres regni eiusdem Sebbi, magna fidem perceptam cum suis omnibus devotione servavit, magna, ut in sequentibus dicemus, vitam fidelem felicitate complevit. Quod ubi rex Vulfheri comperit, fidem videlicet provinciae ex parte profanatam, misit ad corrigendum errorem, revocandamque ad fidem veritatis provinciam Iaruman episcopum, qui successor erat Trumheri: qui multa agens sollertia, iuxta quod mihi presbyter qui comes itineris illi et cooperator verbi extiterat, referebat, erat enim religiosus et bonus vir, longe lateque omnia perva-

CHAPTER XXX

How the East Saxons in the time of mortal sickness returned to idolatry, but by the urgency of Jaruman their bishop were soon amended of their error [665].

ABOUT the same time Sighere and Sebbi were kings over the province of the East Saxons after Swidhelm (of whom we have spoken before), although they were themselves under the allegiance of Wulfhere king of the Marchmen. And this province to wit being visited with the disaster of the foresaid mortal sickness, Sighere with the people over whom he ruled, forsaking the sacraments of the Christian faith, fell to apostasy. For both the king himself and number of the people as well as of the nobles, loving this present life and not seeking after the life to come, or even not believing any such life at all, began to renew their temples which stood desolate and to worship idols, as though they could thereby be protected from the mortal sickness. Farthermore, Sebbi his companion and fellow-heir of the same kingdom with all under him kept the faith he had received with great devotion and ended his faithful life, as we shall hereafter declare, in great felicity. And king Wulfhere, when he understood that the faith of the province, in part that is, had been profaned, for to amend their error and call the province back to the true faith sent unto them bishop Jaruman, the successor of Trumhere: who dealing very discreetly (as was reported to me by a priest, who waited upon him in his travel and had helped him in preaching of the word, for he was a devout and virtuous man), and journeying far and wide through

gatus, et populum et regem praefatum ad viam
iustitiae reduxit: adeo ut relictis sive destructis fanis
arisque quas fecerant, aperirent ecclesias, ac nomen
Christi, cui contradixerant, confiteri gauderent, magis
cum fide resurrectionis in illo mori, quam in perfidiae
sordibus inter idola vivere cupientes. Quibus ita
gestis, et ipsi sacerdotes, doctoresque eorum domum
rediere laetantes.

all parts brought both people and the foresaid king
to the way of righteousness again : so that abandoning
and throwing down their temples and the altars they
had made, they opened the churches and confessing
gladly the name of Christ, which they had gainsayed,
they chose rather to die in Him with faith in resurrection than to live amongst idols in the filth of unbelief.
Which things being so brought to pass both the
priests themselves and their teachers returned home
with joy.

MAP OF ENGLAND AND WALES

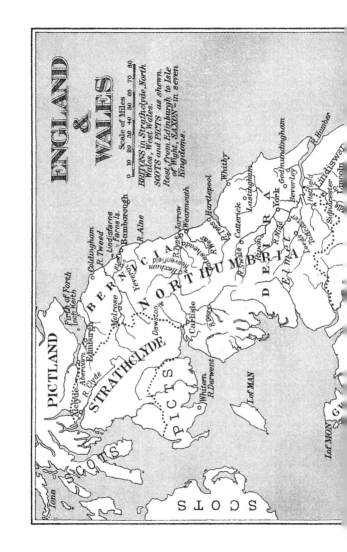

ENGLAND & WALES

Scale of Miles
0 10 20 30 40 50 60 70 80

BRITANS in Strathclyde, North
Wales, West Wales.
SCOTS and PICTS as shewn.
Rest, from Edinburgh to Isle
of Wight, SAXON²=in seven
Kingdoms.

PICTLAND

SCOTS

Iona I.

Firth of Forth
Inch Keith
Aberdorn
Edinburgh
R. Clyde
Alclyde

STRATHCLYDE

PICTS

Coldingham
R. Tweed
Melrose
Lindisfarne
Farne Is.
Bamborough
Dawston
Yeverin
BERNICIA
R. Alne

Whithern
R. Derwent
Carlisle
R. Esk
Hexham
Heavenfield
Jarrow
Wearmouth
Tyne
Gateshead

NORTHUMBRIA

I. of MAN

Whitby
Hartlepool
R. Tees
Catterick
R. Swale
Ripon
Yeastingham

DEIRA
ELMET
R. Nidd
York
Leeds
Tadcaster
Hatfield
Beverley
Godmundingham

LINDISWARA
Lincoln
Sidnacester
R. Humber

I. of MON
GWY

SCOTS

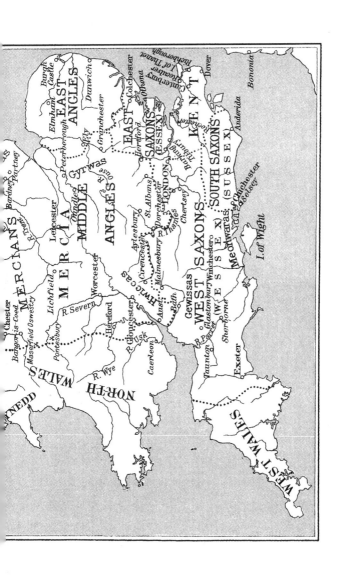